Transitions to Parenthood

Transitions to Parenthood

Rob Palkovitz
Marvin B. Sussman
Editors

The Haworth Press
New York • London

Transitions to Parenthood has also been published as *Marriage & Family Review*, Volume 12, Numbers 3/4 1988.

The Haworth Press, Inc., 12 West 32 Street, New York, NY 10001
EUROSPAN/Haworth, 3 Henrietta Street, London WC2E 8LU England

LIBRARY OF CONGRESS
Library of Congress Cataloging-in-Publication Data

Transitions to parenthood / edited by Robin J. Palkovitz and Marvin B. Sussman.
   p. cm.
   Has also been published as Marriage & family review, volume 12, number 3/4, 1988" – T.p. verso.
   Includes bibliographies.
   ISBN 0-86656-787-9
   1. Parenthood – United States. 2. Childbirth – Study and teaching – United States. 3. Parenting – United States. I. Palkovitz, Robin Joseph, 1954   . II. Sussman, Marvin B.
HQ755. 8. T74 1988
306.8'7 – dc19
88-853
CIP

Transitions to Parenthood

CONTENTS

ABOUT THE EDITORS

Rob Palkovitz, PhD, is Assistant Professor of Individual and Family Studies at the University of Delaware in Newark, as well as the director of the Delaware Parental Development Project. He is a member of the International Society for Research on Parenting, the Society for Research and Child Development, and the Christian Association for Psychological Studies. Dr. Palkovitz has published journal articles on father involvement during infancy.

Marvin B. Sussman, PhD, is UNIDEL Professor of Human Behavior at the University of Delaware College of Human Resources at Newark. He has been awarded the 1980 Ernest W. Burgess Award of the National Council on Family Relations, as well as a life-long membership for services to the Groves Conference on Marriage and the Family in 1981. In 1983, he was elected to the prestigious academy of Groves for scholarly contributions to the field. He is a member of many professional organizations, and has published widely on areas dealing with the family, community, rehabilitation organizations, sociology of medicine, and on aging. Dr. Sussman is the editor of *Marriage & Family Review.*

Acknowledgments

The editors gratefully acknowledge the professional assistance of the following persons in preparing this issue.

Guest Reviewers

Phyllis W. Berman, PhD
Health Scientist Administration, NICHD & H.D., Bethesda, MD

Sally Bould, PhD
Associate Professor of Sociology, Univ. of Delaware

David Kallen, PhD
Professor of Pediatrics and Human Development, Michigan State
 Univ.

Charles Leslie, PhD
Professor, Center for Science and Culture, Univ. of Delaware

Glen Palm, PhD
Asst. Professor, Center for Child and Family Studies, St. Cloud
 State Univ.

Alice Rossi, PhD
Professor, Dept. of Sociology, Univ. of Massachusetts

Nick Simons, MA
Counseling Psychologist, Univ. of Delaware

Proofreader

Nancy Wilson
Graduate Student, Individual and Family Studies,
   Univ. of Delaware

Secretarial Assistance

Cathy Sullivan

Pat Balthis

Trials and Triumphs
in the Transition
to Parenthood

Rob Palkovitz

It is in introductory chapters, such as this one, that editors attempt to wax eloquent, to be witty and to bring across a profound truth at the same time. My sense of duty spoke all too clearly. The demand was reminiscent of the old "Mission Impossible" series . . . "Your assignment, should you decide to accept it, is to crystallize the scientific world's collected knowledge and individual parents' experiential reality into a single, coherent, enlightening statement about the transition to parenthood . . . to be the Garrison Keillor of the empirical literature base on transition to parenthood . . . to capture simultaneously, the joys, trials, triumphs, fears, frustrations and challenges of becoming parents, to be philosophical, and above all, to strike that chord of commanding wisdom that will dazzle the readership and create an appetite for them to read this volume (as though they were reading for two) . . ." Unfortunately, in this real world episode of "Mission Impossible," the prescription for this introduction failed to self-destruct after a few seconds.

As I measured the magnitude of this charge against the shallowness of any thoughts I could collect in an attempt to meet it, I looked up from my desk and briefly escaped to the sanctuary provided by my wife's watercolor of Thompson's Meadow, where a few years ago, we had camped for a week, high in the Rockies. As

---

Rob Palkovitz, PhD, is Assistant Professor of Individual and Family Studies, University of Delaware, Newark, DE 19716.

1

captivating as the painting is, I realized that Judy's skillful rendering and our actual vacation experiences are related, but really, very different. My years of interacting with the painting have colored my memories of the actual vacation. Even while we were camping there, my image of the perfect campsite altered my experience of being there. We discussed ideas for composing this watercolor. All of the essential elements were right there in Thompson's Meadow—the wild irises, the snow-capped peaks in the background, the weathered cabin, the Big Thompson River with its rapids (and trout), and the lone hemlock standing out against the receding tree line. Yet, no single view put them into just the right juxtaposition for my ideal image of this watercolor.

Now, as I return from the brief mental vacation afforded by the painting and reconsider the charge delivered by my sense of duty, I feel less disappointment to confess that I know of no adequate way to render the experience of the transition to parenthood into a kernel of wit and wisdom so compellingly crisp, realistic, and complete as prescribed. Yet, this volume will in no way suffer from my introduction's shortcomings. The integrity and insight of each of the papers contained in this volume contributes uniquely toward the impossible charge delivered by my sense of duty.

As the diverse collection of papers in this issue indicates, the transition to parenthood is a complex topic with multiple consequences, concerns, and characteristics. (With recent advances in biotechnology, one can no longer claim that the transition to parenthood is ushered in by a single cause!)

Most clearly and universally, the transition to parenthood is characterized by change of a large proportion. As persons become parents, they assume a new role, redefine old ones, and face new challenges and questions that they had never before considered or imagined. (Even if new parents could be guided by skillful renderings with planned juxtapositions, if they had the foresight to consider and imagine the challenges of parenting, even if they could be challenged to concurrently consider the processes by realistic, impressionistic and surreal representations, the experience is *always* different than one perceives when looking at a likeness, a mere rendering. The hills tend to be steeper, the valleys more engulfing, the peaks higher and more serene, the roads etched with deeper ruts, the scenery more interesting and uniquely beautiful, and the feelings more vibrant and undeniable than one can discern from even the best of paintings. Simply stated, there are multiple realities unable to be adequately represented in the picture . . . the smells of bacon and coffee around the campfire, the morning chill, the thinness of the air at 12,000 feet, and the sound of the breeze through the meadow grass and scrub pines. In fact, there may be minimal similarity between any rendering, the set of expectations it creates, and one's personal experience when standing and breathing in the actual context.)

Although the scientific research of family scholars can help to bring about an understanding of processes in the transition to parenthood, any parent will readily tell you that parenting, nonetheless, is a uniquely demanding art. As with any art, parenting holds its share of skilled and seasoned artists, some surviving dabblers, and some downright butchers. Somehow, it is still comforting to believe that compiling data, running analyses, theorizing, and describing the process in scientific terms makes artistic expression more manageable, and the outcome more appealing.

However, scientific knowledge about parenting isn't enough. Knowing what correlates with good parenting or what parent behaviors are related to good child outcomes does not make one an artist. Even the most highly touted of the "how to parent" books falls short in this regard. Parents frequently report feelings of guilt, inadequacy and disgust as they do that which they know isn't the best for their child ("I saw myself doing this, and I knew it was wrong, and I knew what I *should* have done, but I couldn't help myself . . . I hate it when that happens").

Because the transition to parenthood is uniquely complex for each person experiencing it, there is little wonder that the fit between expectation, knowledge and experience is tentative. If one applies the Holmes and Rahe (1967) Social Readjustment Scale to the transition to parenthood, the result is instructive. A conservative estimate is that a new parent would experience 339 life-change units. A more liberal application of the scale results in an estimated accumulation of 634 life-change units. In either case, serious and far-reaching consequences would be predicted to result.

It is little wonder that the transition to parenthood is so vividly experienced by new parents. There are few single events in a person's life which create such extensive waves of change (and long-term ripples) as parenthood. No one that I know has faced parenthood casually.

The single event of the birth of a first child catapults people into an irreversible trajectory different from and experientially distinct from childlessness. It is a momentous event. In some ways the research literature falls far short of capturing the intensity, duration and pervasiveness of the transition. The rendering falls short of reality. We need to fully realize that the assumption of the role of parent thrusts one into a continual state of transition from that point on. As one faces the developmentally interdependent and continually evolving demands of the parenting role, one is faced with challenges and rewards unexperienced in any other context. This occurs continually, so long as the parent (and/or child[ren]) live(s).

It has been a full nine years since Judy and I were unexpectedly expecting our first child. Although we had dated for five years and had been married for an additional three, we still felt as though, somehow, we weren't "ready" for parenthood. My realization that my training in child development in no way prepared me (in reality) for parenting sent a series of shock waves through my system that have since dulled, with the passage of nine years and two more children, to moderate sine patterns. Still, my research, career and personal developmental paths were unalterably altered by that panicked realization. Now, I am grateful for the opportunity to bring together a collection of papers that represents the works of the discipline's noted scholars. The research and writing of these scholars has aided me considerably in my attempts to quell the storm initiated nine years ago (with recurrent squalls and numerous high and low pressure systems!). As I set about the task of digesting the scholarly literature on fathering (in quest of a job description), the writings of many of the contributors to this volume have had buffering effects on my anxieties.

This collection of papers represents an attempt to bring together the best that science has to offer, and to draw practice, policy and research implications from the data base. Yet, we have no illusions of creating new artists, or even a completely lifelike rendering of the transition to parenthood. This effort is not in vain, however. It is only through viewing different "essential" elements and peering from differing vantage points on the experience of this monumental transition that we can provide a watershed for family theorists, practitioners, and parents to discuss the necessary elements, to search for the right vantage point, to negotiate alternative juxtapositions, to dabble, to shape their renderings, and to frame the final product.

REFERENCE

Holmes, T. & Rahe, R. (1967). The social readjustment rating scale. *Journal of Psychosomatic Research, 11*, 213-218.

Another Perspective on the Trials and Triumphs in the Transition to Parenthood

Marvin B. Sussman

The usual procedure in publishing special issues which are jointly edited is for the two principals to work together in preparing an introduction or, in some instances, a reasonably lengthy chapter on the subject under purview. What you are witnessing is a break in our tradition. I was so impressed with the personal story that Rob Palkovitz presented, one of his own journey in the becoming of a parent, that I felt strongly it should stand by itself as a very human document and not be lost in the context of providing an overview on the transition to parenthood. Thus, the reader will experience two introductions. What follows are observations from a social psychological perspective which treats the larger issues and problems of parenthood. The marital dyad holds the central actors in this scenario. Still, the transition to parenthood involves larger units in the society such as groups, organizations, and institutions. There are cultural and ethnic factors to be considered if one is to obtain a complete comprehension of the coming of a child and the implications of this lifecourse transition. Further, changing patterns in the work force of the last twenty years, the consequences of the gender revolution, and the changing patterns of marriage and divorce have shattered the traditional ways of parenting.

It is a truism that the introduction of the first newborn to a marital pair modifies not only the dyadic relationship but those with other members of the immediate and extended family and relationships outside of the family. Even before the transition to parenthood, during the pregnancy, members of family and kin networks respond in

7

extraordinary ways. They give advice, plan for the birth, offer services, give gifts of money or goods, and are solicitous, kind, and
caring even in those instances where relationships previously have
been distant or strained.

The couple, while being the locus of such attention and activity,
still has to deal with new issues and potential problems effected by
the pregnancy. These include:

1. Prenatal care and dealings with professionals and functionaries
   of highly bureaucratized health care systems.
2. Exercise and diet which in some dyads may require learning
   and adoption of new and alien practices with the potential for
   evoking stress for the couple.
3. Agreement on sharing of household tasks and other activities
   related to the role patterns established before the pregnancy
   occurred.
4. Developing an understanding on responsibilities for nurturing
   and caring for the future heir.
5. Determining the method of birth to be used: traditional or non-
   traditional with father and sibs involved in the bonding process.
6. For dual work couples consider the immediate procedures and
   consequences of effecting a leave of absence from work for
   both partners as the pregnancy comes to term and in the post
   birth period. Procedures for obtaining a leave are largely effected by work organization policy and practice. Consequences are different degrees of bonding and varied patterns of
   nurturing and parenting involving the marital pair.
7. Adjustment to a new economic situation. The loss of earnings
   when a parent leaves the job or works part time; the additional
   expenses of medical care, clothing, food, furnishings, housing, child care, and other services.
8. Enter new patterns of interaction, nurturing, and socialization
   in situations where the couple has children in addition to their
   firstborn. The birth of a second or third child not only radically
   changes patterns of communication and interaction but also
   modifies the nurturing and socialization roles of the marital
   dyad. Also, with the high incidence of divorce among couples

with small children and equally high rates of remarriage the results are settings where individuals become instant parents and subsequently become putative ones. Whether parents are consistent in their rearing styles in such situations is problematic as well as the consequences for the development of the child.

9. Attention to the actual and potential negative and destructive; as well as positive and creative consequences of sibling relationships is highly recommended to couples procreating more than one child. The increasing survivability of children with some anomaly who are cared for by parents makes the issue of sibling and parent-child relationships highly salient in such families. Shifts in use of time and energy with one child usually occur with the birth of the second. Such shifts may be more pronounced when a child has abnormalities. Birth order, availability and use of family and social supports, parental values and expectations of behavior modify responses to this situation.

Transition to parenthood issues not exclusive to or relevant for the marital dyad are:

1. The decision to have a child and to become a parent, aware that it is a more demanding, socially and psychologically significant and complex role than parents and grandparents experienced, is requisite for appropriate adaptation to the demands and expected behaviors of the transition to parenthood.
2. Unmarried individuals who give birth to a child by choice or as a consequence of an unwanted pregnancy have different problems to solve than married couples in effecting a satisfactory transition to parenthood.
3. Developing a complementarity between gainful employment in the work force and family roles, especially parenting is a precursor to meeting the normative demands of the transition to parenthood.
4. Teenage pregnancy and the decision to keep the child usually involves, in addition to the mother, a number of individuals in parenting roles. For example, the rights of the putative unmar-

ried father in relation to the child are increasingly being recognized by the courts. How such fathers and members of the family and kin group, peers, and friends influence the child/parent relationship and its endemic bonding is relatively unknown.

Some of the above listed issues and problems are considered by the authors of chapters in this volume. Others beg investigation or at least discussion where the methodological problems are so formidable that meaningful research is impossible. What is possible is to recognize the amazing beauty and complexity of the birth process and the endemic responsibilities for parenting over a long time period. From my perspective, the bringing of a child into the world is a highly emotional experience for those involved and a privilege. As a privilege it presumes that individuals will assume the obligations inherent in exercising this privilege. Legal statutes attest to this view in empowering the community to exercise the "best interest of the child" doctrine to enforce appropriate parental behavior when such parents fail.

It is easy to propose a litany of what should be done by the researcher, polemicist, educator and practitioner in this area of concern. This I will not do. I feel, however, that the transition to parenthood is the most critical step in the individual and family life cycles. It is a phenomenon in need of greening and with this volume we have begun the process.

The Value of Children
and the Transition
to Parenthood

James T. Fawcett

Becoming a parent is one of life's great psychological transitions. It signifies a shift in emotional allegiances and marks entry into a new, lifetime role. It is also a transition that is eagerly sought: most people in most societies want to become parents. But why should this be so? After all, parenthood is a highly costly affair, and not just in monetary terms. Physical effort must be exerted in caring for children, and time must be spent for childrearing that might otherwise be devoted to career development or leisure. These costs, apparently, are outweighed by the pleasures expected in becoming a parent.

The delights of parenthood have long been extolled in folklore, novels, poems, religious literature, and philosophy. It is only in the past 15 years, though, that a series of scientific studies has been

James T. Fawcett is a research associate at the East-West Population Institute, East-West Center, 1777 East-West Road, Honolulu, HI 96848.

This paper draws upon findings from the Value of Children (VOC) project, a collaborative cross-national investigation involving the following researchers: Masri Singarimoun and Russell K. Darroch (Indonesia); Sung Jin Lee (Republic of Korea); Rodolfo A. Bulatao (Philippines); Peter S.J. Chen, Betty Jamie Chung, and Eddie Kuo (Singapore); Tom T.H. Sun and Tsong-Shien Wu (Taiwan); Chalio Buripakdi, Nibhon Debavalya, and Visid Prachuabmoh (Thailand); Cigdem Kagitcibasi (Turkey); and Lois W. Hoffman, Fred Arnold, and James T. Fawcett (United States). Support for these studies was provided by a number of institutions, including the East-West Population Institute, the International Development Research Centre, the Ford Foundation, the Rockefeller Foundation, the Smithsonian Institution, the Research Institute for the Study of Man, and the U.S. National Institute for Child Health and Human Development.

11

carried out around the world to ask parents and prospective parents directly about the personal satisfactions and personal costs of having children. These "value of children" studies constitute a major new approach to the understanding of human fertility and the analysis of world population problems (Fawcett, 1977, 1983; Hoffman & Hoffman, 1973). They also contribute a distinctive body of knowledge pertaining to parent-child and husband-wife relationships (Hoffman and Manis, 1978).

In this article, I first provide a brief overview of recent research on the value of children. I then discuss how perceptions of the values of children are formed, citing historical analyses as well as research conducted from a child development perspective that assesses perceptions of young people at various ages. With respect to surveys of adults, I focus on findings from the United States, Europe, and Australia, while citing selected findings from non-Western countries to show the range of differences in how people value children. I also emphasize the value of the first child, because that first birth epitomizes the transition to parenthood.

Looking beyond the factors that motivate the transition to parenthood, I present some data on how people see their lives as being changed by having children and, more specifically, what they feel they must give up in exchange for children. In a concluding section, I take note of research on the actual (as opposed to perceived) costs of children, especially recent estimates of the economic cost of raising a "high quality" child in contemporary American society.

MEASURING THE VALUE
OF CHILDREN

Based primarily on sample surveys, value of children studies have entailed interviews with tens of thousands of people in more than 20 countries (Fawcett, 1983). Most of the people interviewed were parents, so their answers reflect experience with their existing children as well as expectations about future parenting experiences. A number of studies have included childless married couples or have focused on unmarried teenagers, whose views about the value of children reflect primarily expectations about parenthood. To measure perceptions of the value of children, based on both expectations and experience, surveys have asked the following kinds of questions:

> What are some of the advantages or good things about having children, compared with not having children at all?

> And what are some of the disadvantages or bad things about having children, compared with not having children?

> Here is a list of reasons people give for wanting to have children in general, that is, why they find it satisfying to have children. Please tell me how important each one is to you, as a reason for having children.

Similar questions are asked about the satisfactions and costs of the next child, the relative advantages of having sons and daughters, what people have to give up as a result of having children, how their lives are changed by having children, and so on.

Lois and Martin Hoffman (1973) have provided a very useful scheme that categorizes the positive values of children according to the psychological needs of parents. Their eight psychological values encompass the following benefits to parents:

— Parenthood establishes a person as an adult member of a community and provides a kind of validation that a couple, as parents, are moving through the life cycle in the way that is expected of them.
— Children are a way of living beyond one's life span, of being represented in the next generation or the next century. They continue the family name and establish a link and a continuity between generations.
— Having children is the moral thing to do. It means sacrificing one's self for one's children, fulfilling one's religious obligations, and "doing the right thing."
— Children are people to love — a continuous source of affection and a permanent human relationship. In a society that is seen as impersonal, bureaucratic, and mobile, children keep parents from being lonely.
— Having a child brings change and stimulation to a life that may otherwise be dull and routine; having children around is fun.

— Producing a child and watching it grow to become a useful member of society is a source of accomplishment and achievement.

— A parent has power over a child — at least while the child is young. Parenthood provides an opportunity to guide, teach, control, and generally exert enormous influence over another human being.

— Children can give parents an edge in social comparison. Parents gain status from the accomplishments or social popularity of their children. In some cultures, parents with large families may be admired in the community.

Such conceptual analysis makes it clear that parents expect a lot of psychological benefits from having children. They may also expect economic gains, if they live in a society where children work at an early age or if they expect to rely on their children for support in their old age. In fact, in developing countries expected economic benefits from children tend to dominate the responses of parents when they are asked about the advantages of having children.

For many people, the transition to parenthood is a virtually inevitable result of the earlier transition from single to married. In answering open-ended questions about reasons for having children in one of our studies, may respondents mentioned marriage:

They [children] are the main reasons for getting married.

[Having children] makes you complete as a person and it completes your marriage too.

Without children, a married life is not a family. Children make the family.

Thus, the benefits of having children accrue to a social unit — the couple — as well as to individuals. Further, members of the extended family, especially the parents of the husband and wife, often put pressure on young couples to have children. A recent U.S. study has shown that benefits to the wife's in-laws, to her own parents, and to other kin are seen by American parents as an important reason for having a first child (Townes et al., 1976):

> Among wives without children, the single most important motivation for childbearing is the attainment of values related to significant others. Becoming a mother establishes, maintains and enhances affiliation with parents and other family members. Contrary to our expectations, parenting needs among women without children were secondary to establishing close relationships with relatives. (p. 126)

This motivation is congruent with what actually occurs — an observed increase in closeness between the generations — after a child is born.

Children are sometimes wanted to increase the size — and thus enhance the power — of an ethnic, tribal, or national group. For these reasons and because of the central role of the family in the functioning of a cultural system, customs have developed over time that give great significance to the achievement of parenthood, equating this to a large extent with becoming an adult, a "real man," or a "whole woman." Consider this description of the value of parenthood in an Indonesian village (Hull, 1975):

> For a young man the birth of the first child means the full recognition of adulthood. [He is] dramatically transformed in the eyes of his friends and neighbours into a new classification of social being who would require different attentions, and who would be expected to bear different responsibilities. (pp. 321-322)

Having a child gives an entree into some important adult social institutions — mothers' clubs, sports leagues organized by parents for children, parent-teacher associations, and the like. Parents thus become integrated into the neighborhood and the community via child-related organizations.

Ultimately, children are not only wanted for personal and social reasons but are also needed to perpetuate the species and carry on the family line. Small wonder, then, that so many of society's signals point toward the desirability of having children and that voluntary childlessness among couples is actually quite rare.

A decision about having a child is often also a decision about a standard of living and a lifestyle — including the prospect of giving

up some of those things that might be construed as alternatives to
children or alternatives to parenthood, notably the woman's job or
career aspirations (Hoffman & Hoffman, 1973). The costs or disadvantages of having children are usefully broken down into several
categories, including:

- *Direct economic costs* — food, clothing, schooling, etc.
- *Income-related opportunity costs* — mainly the wife's potential
  income foregone because of childrearing responsibilities.
- *Opportunity costs other than income* — mainly the leisure activities and free time that are lost owing to childcare.
- *Psychological costs* — restriction of freedom, loss of flexibility, increase in worry and anxiety.
- *Physical costs* — the work involved in childrearing, the physiological aspects of childbirth for the mother.

These costs of children play a critical role in controlling human
fertility, that is, in keeping childbearing well below the physiological maximum. They also interact with the benefits of children in
complex ways to influence the timing of childbearing. Analysis of
the value of children in relation to fertility has been dealt with extensively elsewhere (Arnold et al., 1975; Bulatao, 1979; Bulatao &
Lee, 1983; Fawcett, 1983) and is not addressed here, except to note
that certain patterns of the value and cost of children have been
found to characterize high and low fertility societies and the value
of children framework has proved very useful in analyzing the determinants of fertility change.

EXPECTATIONS ABOUT
THE VALUE OF CHILDREN

How are perceptions and expectations about the value of children
learned? Partly, of course, through direct experience with children.
A parent has expectations about the next child based on the actual
satisfactions and costs of rearing earlier-born children. Expectations
are also learned through the messages about children that pervade
every society in the media and through interpersonal channels, as
well as through the individual's own experience growing up within

a family setting. These messages differ across cultures and across time periods.

Each historical epoch has its own image of the child. In today's Western world, the child is seen as a precious, sentient being, to be protected, cherished, nourished, and supported by the parents with no return except the child's love and perhaps respect. It was not always so. Scholarly analyses of the image of the child through history have revealed striking differences with today's conceptions (Aries, 1962; Banks, 1954; Shorter, 1975; Zelizer, 1985).

There is ample evidence that in 18th and 19th century Europe and the United States, parents' emotional investment in young children was much less than it is today. Some scholars have attributed this to high rates of infant and child mortality, on the reasonable premise that a mother or father would withhold deep emotional attachment from a child whose chances of dying before the age of ten were really quite high. Other evidence seems to refute this, though, showing that sentimental attachment to children increased *before* child mortality rates declined. It now seems likely that several converging factors were responsible for the growing image of the child as primarily a giver and receiver of love. In addition to the mortality factor, influences cited include the decline in child labor, the increase in compulsory schooling, and the changing family structures related to urbanization. Zelizer (1985) has succinctly describes the basic changes that occurred in the United States:

> Between the 1870s and the 1930s, the value of American children was transformed. The twentieth-century economically useless but emotionally priceless child displaced the nineteenth-century useful child. To be sure, the most dramatic changes took place among the working class. . . . But the sentimentalization of childhood intensified regardless of social class. The new sacred child occupied a special and separate world, regulated by affection and education, not work or profit. (p. 209)

In contemporary Western society, the image of the child is currently being shaped by social movements that advocate alternatives to traditional lifestyles, including the option for couples of being "childfree." Further, the ideology and the fact of women's employment outside the home is forcing a new look at the costs and benefits of having children. Indeed, there have recently appeared in the U.S. marketplace "decision-making aids" for parenthood, which ask prospective parents to enumerate pros and cons of having children (Beach, Townés, & Campbell, 1978). Also available are materials to be used in schools to encourage early consciousness-raising about the value and cost of children (Clark, 1977). These educational materials assume that anticipation of benefits and costs will lead to more careful family planning and a resulting decrease in the number of unwanted children.

A few researchers have turned to studies of young people to trace the development of attitudes toward children and prospective parenthood. Research on "the value of children to children" should ideally encompass four topics (Fawcett, 1974):

1. Content—what is learned.
2. Process-how it is learned.
3. Timing—when it is learned.
4. Behavioral expression—the relationship between learning and action.

In practice, research has focused on content, with some attention to timing by studying children at different ages and some attention to process by comparing results for children and their parents. A study in the United States, for example, involved interviews with 163 mothers and two of their children between the ages of 10 and 18 (Namerow & Philliber, 1983). Using the Hoffman and Hoffman categorizing scheme discussed earlier, these researchers found strong similarities between values of children expressed by children and comparable findings from a U.S. national survey of adults. The most common positive values pertained to primary group ties—love and companionship—and to the stimulation and fun in having children. The similarity to adults was greater for children at older ages. The correspondence between mothers and their children was not very high, however, suggesting that the factors influencing the perceived value of children may come more from society at large than from the immediate family.

Quite different response patterns were shown in a study in Malaysia (Kee, 1982), in which children in four age groups (13, 15, 17, and 19) were compared with adults. The predominant values in this developing country relate to the economic value of children and the security they provide for old age. The extent to which children are viewed as a key element in old age support is strongly underlined in the findings of Kee's study, where one out of five 13-year-olds cited "security in old age" as the most important advantage of having children. It should also be noted, however, that the importance of receiving psychological gratification from children (fun, love, companionship) increased with the age of the children being surveyed, with 19-year-olds giving top ranking to the more personal emotional factors. This trend may reflect the same societal influences that cause more educated and more urbanized Third World parents to give greater prominence to the psychological dimensions of wanting children.

A comparison of children aged 14-15 in Australia and Papua New Guinea (Callan & Wilks, 1984) showed contrasting patterns quite similar to the Malaysian study. Students in Papua New Guinea gave strong emphasis to economic help and old age support from children, while very few Australian students mentioned these as an advantage of children. For example, 59% of PNG boys cited economic help, compared to 7% of Australian boys. On the psychological side, 46% of Australian girls mentioned "love and affection" as an advantage of having children, while only 20% of PNG girls gave this response. In general, the studies comparing children's responses in developed and less developed countries have shown results very similar to the "modern" and "traditional" patterns revealed in studied of adults.

THE VALUE OF HAVING CHILDREN

Figure 1 compares patterns for the most salient dimensions of the value of children for wives in the United States, Korea, and Turkey, based on national surveys that were conducted in the mid-1970s as part of the cross-national Value of Children (VOC) project. These

FIGURE 1

Percent of Wives Mentioning
Selected Advantages of Having Children

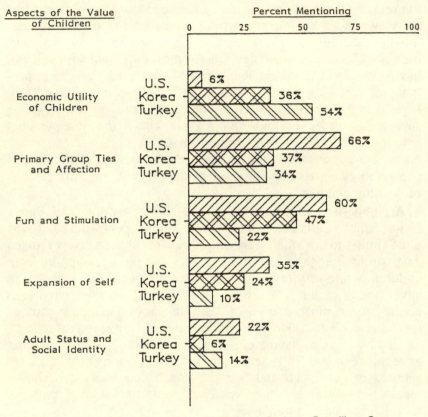

Source: National Surveys, Value of Children Project, East-West Center

findings, based on open-ended questions about the advantages of having children, show that different aspects are emphasized by parents in countries with different cultural traditions and levels of development. The categories "Primary group ties and affection" and "Fun and stimulation" are shown to be most salient to American wives. By contrast, wives in Turkey mention "Economic utility of children" more frequently than any other category, while the pattern for Korean wives falls in between the United States and Turkey on the economic utility dimension and most of the psychosocial dimensions.

The findings just discussed pertain to national populations, but there are also important differences among subgroups, such as socioeconomic classes, within countries (Fawcett, 1977):

> Urban parents (especially the more educated) emphasize the psychological and emotional benefits that derive from interacting with children and observing and guiding their growth and development. The feedback effects on the parents' own sense of maturity are also important. Rural parents, by contrast, emphasize the economic and practical benefits to be derived from children, including the long-term benefit of old-age security. (p. 100)

Another approach to understanding the value of children to parents is to examine the changes that occur over the parents' life cycle or, as Bulatao and Fawcett (1983) have labeled it, the "fertility career." This term is used to call attention to several considerations relevant to the transition to parenthood:

> That childbearing, for most people, is a normal part of the role sequence that one passes through; that childbearing is seldom happenstance behavior but involves goal-directed sequences of actions . . . ; that, despite anticipation and planning, external forces also shape fertility outcomes, as they shape occupational careers; . . . [and] that regularities exist in the process stretching from initial socialization for fertility behavior to the termination of childbearing, regularities having to do with personal development, learning, shifts in the family constellation, and changes in fertility goals and behavior. (p. 434)

Research on the fertility career is usually directed toward clarifying the sequence of events that leads to the termination of childbearing, i.e., the focus is on family limitation or, in societal terms, the transition to lower fertility. This paper, however, focuses on the initiation of childbearing—the transition to parenthood.

The First Child

Research findings that draw upon three different ways of assessing the value of the *first* child are shown in Table 1: responses of married women who have not yet had children to a question on the anticipated advantages of having children; responses of young women, married and unmarried, who do not have a child, to a question about reasons for wanting a child; and responses of married women both with and without children to a question about the advantages of having the first child. The respondents are all from modern Western societies, but represent different national/cultural backgrounds: the United States, Belgium, Australia, Greece, and Italy.

What stands out in Table 1 is the predominance of positive emotional responses and the absence of more utilitarian responses such as economic help, housework, or security in old age. Notable also is the significance of the first child for enhancing the husband-wife relationship, by providing the two parents with something in common and furthering a feeling of closeness, as well as a feeling that the first child "starts the family." While these results were all taken from female respondents, the surveys cited also included males. Perceptions of the value of the first child were very similar for both men and women.

Expectations of such powerful emotional benefits clearly exert a strong pull toward the initiation of childbearing. However, most people who have not yet had children nevertheless have a clear awareness of the expected costs. Findings on disadvantages of the first child, taken from some of the same surveys, are shown in Table 2. For these mainly urban women in modern societies, financial costs loom large. Prenatal health care, delivery costs, diapers, clothing, housing, food, medicine — presumably all these factors enter into the awareness of prospective parents, for the costs of the first child as well as later children. Also prominent for most women is the concern about loss of freedom, loss of flexibility, and in general new restrictions on the mother's life. This concern has been shown to be distinctively associated with the first and second children, although the restrictions can intensify with more children. Another, somewhat unexpected, finding about the first child is the

TABLE 1

The Value of the First Child:
Highest Ranking Responses in Three Surveys

Survey Respondents	Most Frequent Responses, in Rank Order
American women:[1] anticipated advantages of having children (responses of women with no children)	1. Stimulation, fun, activity 2. Bring love and affection 3. Benefit the husband-wife relationship
Belgian women:[2] reasons for wanting a child (response of women with no children)	1. Something in common (for husband and wife) 2. Sociability 3. Feel needed, useful
Australian women:[3] advantages of having the first child	1. Feeling of pride 2. Happiness, excitement 3. Enjoyment from growth and development
Greek immigrant women in Australia:[4] advantages of having the first child	1. Happiness, excitement 2. Feeling of pride 3. Closeness between husband and wife
Italian immigrant women in Australia:[5] advantages of having the first child	1. Happiness, excitement 2. Feeling of pride 3. Child starts the family

NOTES:

[1] Caucasian married women under age 40, no children, N = 288.
From national survey of Value of Children, 1975.

[2] Women age 25-29, no children, N = 108.
From national survey on Family Development, 1975-76.

[3] Married women under age 40 born in Australia, N = 158.
Non-representative sample.

[4] Married women under age 40 born in Greece and living in Australia;
N = 106. Non-representative sample.

[5] Married women under age 40 born in Italy and living in Australia;
N = 101. Non-representative sample.

SOURCES: Hoffman and Manis, 1979; Deven, 1983; Callan, 1980.

TABLE 2

Disadvantages of the First Child:
Highest Ranking Responses in Two Surveys

Survey Respondents	Most Frequent Responses in Rank Order
American women:[1] anticipated disadvantages of having children (responses of women with no children)	1. Financial costs 2. Loss of freedom 3. Worries about children's health and safety
Australian women:[2] disadvantages of having the first child	1. Not knowing how to care for the child 2. Financial cost 3. General restrictions, inconveniences
Greek immigrant women in Australia:[3] disadvantages of having the first child	1. No disadvantages 2. Financial cost 3. Not knowing how to care for the child 4. Worry about the health of the child
Italian immigrant women in Australia:[4] disadvantages of having the first child	1. General worries, concern about responsibility 2. General restrictions, inconveniences 3. Financial cost 4. Not knowing how to care for the child

NOTES:

1 Women under age 40 married less than six years, no children, N = 76

2 Married women under age 40 born in Australia, N = 158. Non-representative sample.

3 Married women under age 40 born in Greece and living in Australia, N = 106. Non-representative sample.

4 Married women under age 40 born in Italy and living in Australia, N = 101. Non-representative sample.

SOURCES: Hoffman and Manis, 1978; Callan, 1980

mother's concern about not knowing how to care for a child and, probably in a related vein, worry over the child's health and safety. This finding has not been prominent in developing country studies of the value of children, perhaps because in those settings new mothers have greater access to extended family and community support networks in handling initial childcare responsibilities.

Following the first birth, the context for later childbearing is substantially altered and some very influential and virtually universal factors come into play (Fawcett, 1982):

> After the first child, different motivational forces emerge. Particularly potent is the desire for a second child as a companion for the first, that is, a desire to avoid having an only child. Gender preferences also become more salient at this stage, although the nature of such preferences varies by cultural setting. Where preference for a son is strong, for example, this motivation will be heightened if the first child is a daughter. Even where preference for a particular gender is weak, however, the desire for a balance of sons and daughters in the family may result in a gender-specific motivation for the second child. Because of such factors, the motivation for another child is usually at peak strength after the first birth. (p. 670)

The motivational picture becomes somewhat less clear after the second child, with different factors becoming prominent in different societies and cultural groups. Typically, however, the perceived and actual economic burden increases with family size, as does the amount of work involved in childrearing. Analyses of the various stages of childbearing are found in Bulatao (1981), Bulatao and Fawcett (1983), and Namboodiri (1983).

Life Changes Related to Children

In the cross-national survey of the value of children, respondents were asked quite directly to describe the impact of children on their lives, by means of the following open-ended question asked at the end of the interview:

All in all, thinking about a (woman's/man's) life, how is a (woman's/man's) life changed by having children?

The responses showed interesting cross-cultural variations and some differences between men and women. I will focus here on the findings from the United States (see also Hoffman & Manis, 1978) and will cite results from just two other countries — Korea and Turkey — for contrast.

American women report a number of positive changes in their lives as a result of having children. Most prominently, over one-third of the women talked about becoming a more responsible and mature person, which includes the idea of settling down to raise a family. The second most common response, given by about one-fifth of the women, has to do with feelings of self-fulfillment and completeness as a person, or becoming a whole woman as a consequence of having children. Other responses are much less frequent. For example, about 6% cite childrearing as giving them something useful to do and another 6% mention becoming less selfish because of having children.

Even more American men (53%) than women cite increased responsibility and maturity as the positive way their lives changed (or would change) as a result of having children. One important dimension of this responsibility is a strengthening of work-related motivations owing to a concern for providing adequate income for the growing family. Other common responses (but at only 6% each) referred to self-fulfillment and becoming an adult. The results for both men and women thus point up the value of the first child for defining a new social role — the responsible, mature adult — conferred by parenthood, as well as the more psychologically-oriented gratification related to a self-image.

These specific findings about how a man's or woman's life is changed by having children were collapsed into broader coding categories to allow comparisons of women with no child, one child, and more than one child. Also, data were examined for three countries to test the universality of the results. Table 3 shows that among women interviewed in the U.S., Korea, and Turkey, the number of children does not make a consistent difference in perceptions of how one's life is changed by having children. With respect to com-

TABLE 3

How a Woman's Life is Changed by Having Children:
Responses Given by More Than 20% of Respondents,
for Three Countries, by Parity

| | PERCENTAGE MENTIONING | | | | | | | | |
| Response Category | United States No. of Children | | | Korea No. of Children | | | Turkey No. of Children | | |
	0	1	2+	0	1	2+	0	1	2+
Positive Changes									
Attain Adult Status, Meet Social Norms	7	3	4	21	25	22	11	10	6
Change Parent's Character, Assume Responsibility	45	41	42	7	10	9	9	9	8
Fulfillment of Self	14	25	27	17	27	19	6	5	6
Negative Changes									
Tied Down, Restrictions	38	44	41	49	42	34	18	21	12
More Work for Parents	3	8	7	11	2	2	28	27	21
Effects on Health, Appearance	0	1	1	20	22	27	17	6	19

SOURCE: Value of Children survey

parisons among the three countries, it appears that American women are more concerned with the personal development that comes with childbearing and childrearing, while Korean women are more attentive to the social significance of having children and their own enhanced status in the adult community. Among Turkish women, there is no strong consensus on any positive change from having children, but there is a substantial concern about the extra work that parenting entails. Women in Turkey show a fairly high level of awareness of restrictions caused by having children, but this negative change is even more salient for American and Korean women. The effect on the mother's health and physical appearance of having children is a rather strong concern in Korea and Turkey, but almost absent among American women.

These somewhat diverse findings highlight the extent to which the value of children to parents is influenced by the cultural and social setting in which the parents live. While there are common elements that appear prominently in all countries — "happiness" is a frequently-cited life change from having children — the meaning of the parent-child relationship varies greatly according to the culturally defined roles of men and women, the social and economic stratum of the family, the extent to which childcare is the mother's sole responsibility or is shared by others, and the general level of development of the society.

That parents are willing to bear substantial burdens in order to have children is apparent in responses to a Value of Children Survey question about what children interfere with or prevent the parent from doing. For American women, "being tied down" or, more specifically, having restrictions on social life or travel, were the major concerns. Interference with the wife's work or career, on the other hand, was mentioned by only 12% of American women, but was cited much more frequently by women in developing countries: 57% in Thailand, 44% in Taiwan, 35% in Korea, 28% in Turkey, 26% in Singapore, and 18% in the Philippines. The general feeling of being tied down was much less frequent in these countries (except Turkey), presumably reflecting the more limited opportunities for attractive leisure time activities in countries at lower levels of economic development.

The pattern for men is broadly similar to the pattern for women, except that men are not quite so concerned about their activities being restricted by children. Since the usual custom for men is to continue working after the birth of a child, this important aspect of the man's life may be virtually unaffected by the transition to parenthood (apart from a greater commitment to work related to a feeling of increased responsibility). However, concern among men about children interfering with the *wife's* work was quite substantial, reaching 52% among husbands in Taiwan. This would seem to indicate a recognition of the importance of women's economic contributions. An interesting sidelight on this topic is that 8% of American men were concerned that children would interfere with their involvement in sports—a worry that also showed up in a study of Australian men (Callan, 1980).

Campbell et al. (1976), in a study of American couples, found that the strongest negative motivation for those without children was related to the expectation that a child would interfere with the parents' education or career; financial costs and interference with lifestyle activities were also important.

The potential impact of children on lifestyle preferences is highlighted in studies of voluntarily childless adults. For example, Callan (1983) found that among Australian couples who had chosen not to have children, four out of five mentioned general freedom and flexibility of their lifestyle as an advantage of being childless. Other commonly cited advantages were having more money and fewer financial worries, having more time to oneself, and not having the responsibility of childrearing. In another study, Callan (1982) compared the value of children for voluntarily childless adults and a matched sample of adults with children. When asked about the disadvantages of having children, the childless were more likely than parents to cite restrictions and inconveniences. When asked about advantages of having children, the childless were more likely to mention the enjoyment that would be obtained from watching the growth and development of a child—suggesting that this is perceived as an important loss associated with the childfree lifestyle.

The Economics of Parenting and Social Policies

At the beginning of this article I asserted that the costs of children must be less than the benefits, since most people want to become parents. That assertion could be wrong on a number of grounds, however. Possibly, people underestimate costs and overestimate benefits. Or, the decision rules for having children might be other than utility maximization rules. It is also possible that the satisfactions and costs of children cannot meaningfully be balanced against each other, i.e., they are in some psychological sense incommensurable. Another viewpoint is that children may be born without systematic forethought, either as a byproduct of sexual satisfaction or as a foreordained consequence of social, cultural, and familial pressures for couples to have offspring. However, the overwhelming weight of evidence from studies of the value of children is that people do weigh the benefits and costs of childrearing, that their expectations about the positive aspects of having children are generally validated by experience, and that the various costs of children are to some degree anticipated but loom larger in reality than they did in expectation.

The focus of this article has been on survey research that measures attitudes and perceptions related to children. A parallel body of research has looked at the actual economic contributions of children and the financial costs to parents of rearing children (Espenshade, 1977). These studies show, for example, that in developing countries children as young as six often contribute useful work in the household, and that boys in particular may be doing work equivalent to a man in a rural setting by age 12-14. By some calculations, a child in a rural household in a poor country is likely to become a "net producer" for the family by about age 15, i.e., to have contributed economically to the household more than the costs of raising the child to that age.

In countries such as the United States, however, the picture is very different. As Lois and Martin Hoffman (1973) put it, "There is no evidence in the United States that children are raised for profit" (p. 60). Apart from a relatively small number of children on farms, it is rare for American children to contribute to the household economically. Rather, children are an economic drain on the family for many years. What does it actually cost to raise a child in the United States?

This simple question has spawned some very complex studies in the past 15 years (Cramer, 1979; Espenshade, 1976; Lindert, 1978; Reed & McIntosh, 1971; Turchi, 1975). The cost of a child differs greatly according to the socioeconomic status of the family and, in particular, the mother's work status. (If a mother gives up paid employment for childrearing, her potential income foregone must be figured into the cost of a child.) A recent estimate for a typical middle-income American family with two children and a mother who works part-time puts the cost of raising a child to age 18 at $82,400 in 1981 prices. If four years at a public college are added, the price of the high-quality child rises to $98,000 (Espenshade,

1984). As much as 50% of the average American family's budget will go toward raising two to three children. And, according to Espenshade, Kamenske, and Turchi (1983), "Overall, as the number of children grows, families spend a larger share of their income on current consumption, and per capita income declines."

Such economic cost estimates serve to highlight the central importance of psychological and social benefits of children, discussed earlier. Although it can be argued that most parents have children without fully appreciating the future costs, it must also be the case that the expected satisfactions are very powerful motivational forces. Indeed, the conceptual scheme provided by Hoffman and Hoffman (1973) demonstrates the wide scope of needs fulfilled by having children: adult status, social identity, love and affection, group affiliation, novelty, creativity, competence, power, morality, social comparison, and expansion of the self. One might add to this list "security," especially the provision of emotional and practical support in emergencies or in the parents' old age. In this respect, children do have potential economic value in the United States, even if parents do not usually anticipate relying on their children for basic old-age financial support.

There is no reason to expect the psychological benefits of children to diminish in the future. Indeed, the increasing urbanization, secularization, and depersonalization of society suggests a growing importance of the nuclear family with children as a source of emotional satisfaction. At the same time, though, the opportunity costs of having children are becoming higher, owing to better job prospects for women and expansion of alternatives for leisure time activities. This high satisfaction/high cost situation is a recipe for ambivalence, the behavioral evidence for which is a recent tendency for women in the United States and some other countries to postpone childbearing. In several European countries, there has also been a strong shift toward the one-child family as a compromise solution to the dilemma of a strong desire for children in the face of increasing costs. The options of non-marriage or marriage without children have also become more socially acceptable and slightly more common in recent times.

Studies of the value of children provide insight into why these shifts are occurring and raise questions relevant to social policy in the future. Does the decline in economic valuations of children suggest a greater future reliance on public social security programs? Do childrearing patterns differ for children who are wanted for different reasons and, if so, what are the consequences for child development? Are the increasing economic and opportunity costs of children a significant factor in child abuse? How can prospective parents be helped to resolve the ambivalence involved in wanting children and having to give up other lifestyle goals to rear children? How do prevailing patterns of the perceived value of children change as social and economic conditions affect the actual benefits and costs and the availability of alternatives? Continuing studies of the value of children are needed, in the United States and elsewhere, to provide new analytic insights into these important perspectives on family dynamics and family policy.

REFERENCES

Aries, Philippe (1962). *Centuries of Childhood*. New York: Alfred A. Knopf.

Arnold, Fred. Bulatao, Rodolfo A., Buripakdi, Chalio, Chung, Betty Jamie, Fawcett, James T., Iritani, Toshio, Lee, Sung Jin, and Wu, Tsong-Shien (1975). *The Value of Children: Introduction and Comparative Analysis*. Vol. 1, The Value of Children: A Cross-National Study: Honolulu: East-West Center.

Banks, J. A. (1954). *Prosperity and Parenthood*. London: Routledge and Kegan Paul.

Beach, Lee Roy, Townes, Brenda D., and Campbell, Frederick L. (1978). *The Optional Parenthood Questionnaire: A Guide to Decision Making About Parenthood*. Baltimore: National Organization for Non-Parents.

Bulatao, R. A. (1979). *On the Nature of the Transition in the Value of Children*. Papers of the East-West Population Institute, No. 60-A, March.

Bulatao, Rodolfo A. (1981). Values and disvalues of children in successive childbearing decisions. *Demography* 18, 1:1-25.

Bulatao, R. A. and Lee, R. D. (eds.) (1983). *Determinants of Fertility in Developing Countries*. New York: Academic Press.

Bulatao, Rodolfo A. and Fawcett, James T. (1983). *Influences on Childbearing Intentions Across the Fertility Career: Demographic and Socioeconomic Factors and the Value of Children*. Papers of the East-West Population Institute, No. 60-F, June.

Callan, Victor J. (1980). *The Value of Children to Australian, Greek, and Italian Parents in Sydney*. Papers of the East-West Population Institute, No. 60-C.

Callan, Victor (1982). How do Australians value children? A review and research update using the perception of parents and voluntarily childless adults. *The Australian and New Zealand Journal of Sociology* 18, 3:384:398.

Callan, Victor (1983). The voluntarily childless and their perceptions of parenthood and childlessness. *Journal of Comparative Family Studies* 14, 1:87-96.

Callan, Victor J. and Wilkes, Jeffrey (1984). Perceptions about the value and cost of children: Australian and Papuan New Guinean High School Youth. *Journal of Biosocial Science* 16, 1:35-44.

Campbell, Frederick L., Townes, Brenda D., Beach, Lee Roy, and Martin, Donald C. (1976). Shifts in values associated with fertility decisions following childbearing. Paper presented at the Workshop on Psychosocial Aspects of Fertility, Montreal, April.

Clark, Leon E. (1977). *The Cost and Value of American Children: A Teaching Module*. Washington, D.C.: Population Reference Bureau.

Cramer, James C. (1979). Employment trends of young mothers and the opportunity costs of babies in the U.S. *Demography* 16, 2:177-197.

Deven, F. (1983). Parity-specific costs and benefits of childbearing: Longitudinal data on decision-making by couples. In Netherlands Interuniversity Demographic Institute, *Population and Family in the Low Countries III*. Brussels: NIDI.

Espenshade, Thomas J. (1976). *The Cost of Children in Urban United States*. Westport, Conn.: Greenwood Press.

Espenshade, Thomas J. (1977). The value and cost of children. *Population Bulletin*, 32.

Espenshade, Thomas J. (1984). *Investing in Children*. Washington, D.C.: The Urban Institute.

Espenshade, Thomas J., Kamenske, Gloria, and Turchi, Boone A. (1983). Family size and economic welfare. *Family Planning Perspectives*, 15, 6:289-294.

Fawcett, James T. (1974). On learning to value children. Paper presented at the Conference on Population Socialization, East-West Center, Honolulu, December.

Fawcett, James T. (1977). The value and cost of children: Converging theory and research. In L. T. Ruzicka (ed.), *The Economic and Social Supports of High Fertility*. Canberra: Australian National University. 91-114.

Fawcett, James T. (1982). Value of children. In J. Ross (ed.), *International Encyclopedia of Population*, Vol. 2. New York: Free Press. 665-671.

Fawcett, James T. (1983). Perceptions of the value of children: Satisfactions and costs. In R. A. Bulatao and R. D. Lee (eds.), *Determinants of Fertility in Developing Countries*, Vol. 1. New York: Academic Press. 429-457.

Hoffman, Lois W. and Hoffman, Martin (1973). The value of children to parents. In J.T. Fawcett (ed.), *Psychological Perspectives on Population*. New York: Basic Books.

Hoffman, Lois and Manis, Jean (1978). Influences of children on marital interaction and parental satisfactions and dissatisfactions. In R. M. Lerner and G. B. Spanier (eds.), *Child Influences on Marital and Family Interaction*. New York: Academic Press. 165-213.

Hull, Terence H. (1975). *Each Child Brings its own Fortune: An Inquiry into the Value of Children in a Javanese Village*. Ph.D. dissertation, Australian National University, Canberra.

Kagitcibasi, Cigdem (1982). *The Changing Value of Children in Turkey*. Papers of the East-West Population Institute, No. 60-E.

Lee, Poo-Kong (1982). Motivation for childbearing among Malaysians. *Journal of Biosocial Science* 14, 2:157-166.

Lindert, Peter (1978). *Fertility and Scarcity in America*. Princeton: Princeton University Press.

Namboodiri, N. Krishnan (1983). Sequential fertility decision making and the life course. In R.A. Bulatao and R.D. Lee (eds.), *Determinants of Fertility in Developing Countries*, Vol. 2. New York: Academic Press. 444-472.

Namerow, Perila B. and Philliber, Susan G. (1983). The value of children to children. *Adolescence* 18, 72:775-786.

Reed, Ritchie H. and McIntosh, Susan (1971). Costs of children. In E.R. Morss and R.H. Reed (eds.), *Economic Aspects of Population Change*. Washington, D.C.: U.S. Government Printing Office. 333-350.

Shorter, Edward (1975). *The Making of the Modern Family*. New York: Basic Books.

Townes, Brenda D., Beach, Lee Roy, Campbell, Frederick L., and Martin, Donald C. (1976). Birth-planning values and decisions: Preliminary findings. In S.H. Newman and V.D. Thompson (eds.), *Population Psychology: Research and Educational Issues*. Washington, D.C.: U.S. Government Printing Office. 113-130.

Turchi, Boone A. (1975). *The Demand for Children: The Economics of Fertility in the United States*. Cambridge: Ballinger.

Zelizer, Vivian (1985). *Pricing the Priceless Child: The Changing Social Value of Children*. New York: Basic Books.

Childbirth in Cross-Cultural Perspective

Betsy Lozoff
Brigitte Jordan
Stephen Malone

In the United States in recent years disenchantment with standard maternity care has been growing: on occasion, the appropriateness of the medical model for our entire conception of birth has been challenged. Yet there has been little information available concerning the range of alternatives to current obstetric practices and, because each culture tends to consider its way of managing childbirth superior to any other, little opportunity to generate and evaluate such alternatives. A cross-cultural comparison of childbirth systems can yield the information necessary for an understanding of the process of childbirth that is unavailable from within any particular system. Cross-cultural study of childbirth is also important for another, somewhat more complex reason. Traditional birthing systems are beginning to change under the influence of Western medicine. Ironically, however, since Western obstetric practices are themselves under pressure to accommodate to changing views of childbirth,

Betsy Lozoff, MD, is Associate Professor of Pediatrics and adjunct Assistant Professor of Anthropology, Rainbow Babies & Children's Hospital and Case Western Reserve University School of Medicine, Cleveland, OH 44160.

Brigitte Jordan, PhD, is Associate Professor of Anthropology and Adjunct Professor of Pediatrics and Human Development, Michigan State University, East Lansing, MI, 48824.

Stephen Malone, MA, Minneapolis, MN.

Grant Support: This work was supported in part by a National Institutes of Health Research Career Development Award (K04 HD00509) to Dr. Lozoff and by research grant #HD M4 11575 from the National Institute of Child Health and Human Development to Dr. Jordan.

some of the very practices currently exported to developing countries are being questioned at home. Furthermore, since only women give birth, studying the many ways in which childbirth is managed in different cultures can broaden our appreciation of female networks, interests and strategies. There has been a growing recognition that our views of social organization have consistently ignored the place of women in society, a deficiency that has resulted in distorted theory and impoverished ethnography (Rosaldo & Lamphere, 1974).

The research we will be describing in this paper represents two complementary approaches to the cross-cultural study of birth. One (Jordan, 1983) consists of intensive study of childbirth in different cultures through immersion in the phenomenon, direct observation and, whenever possible, actual participation in births. This type of approach permits a detailed description of the ways in which childbirth is managed in widely differing cultures.

Anthropological participation in childbirth, we believe, is a particularly useful approach in that it encourages the investigator to see the birth process from the point of view of the people she studies, thus helping her to avoid gratuitously imposing own-society, especially medical, categories for the collection of data about birth. Nevertheless, such approaches have been notably few. Our aim in these investigations has been to broaden the scope of description and analysis by characterizing childbirth practices in relatively general terms, such as how decisions are typically made in different cultures. The second approach (Lozoff, 1982, 1983) consists of analyzing the existing ethnographic record to examine specific hypotheses. Although such analyses depend on the quality and completeness of available reports and are, by nature, somewhat crude and global, they permit one to address specific issues for which anthropological arguments have been made. For instance, criticisms of many standard hospital practices in our culture often contain implicit assumptions about childbirth practices in nonindustrial cultures, such as that mother and infant are typically in skin-to-skin contact immediately after birth. We analyzed anthropological data from a large sample of nonindustrial cultures (Murdock & White, 1969) to determine to what extent such assumptions are supported by the available data. In this paper we will treat both approaches in turn, beginning with the more general participant-observational approach.

CROSS-CULTURAL COMPARISON OF BIRTHING SYSTEMS: TOWARDS A BIOSOCIAL ANALYSIS OF CHILDBIRTH

Childbirth is an intimate and complex transaction whose topic is physiological and whose language is cultural. Neither element is available without the other. Childbirth practices are produced jointly by universal biology and particular society; the physiology of birth and its social-interactional context are mutually informing. We have proposed previously (Jordan, 1983) that a biosocial framework, which considers both the universal biological function of birth and the specific sociocultural matrix within which it is embedded, is needed in analyses of the process of parturition. Indeed, the natural childbirth movement in contemporary American obstetrics reflects a growing recognition of the intimate relationship between the physiological aspects of parturition and its social and organizational management.

In most societies birth and the immediate postpartum period are considered a time of vulnerability for mother and child; in fact, this is frequently considered a time of at least ritual danger to the entire family or community. To deal with this danger and with the existential uncertainty associated with childbirth, societies tend to produce a set of internally consistent practices and beliefs about the management of both physiological and social aspects of childbirth. Birth practices tend to be highly uniform and ritualized (and may even be invested with a sense of moral requiredness) *within* any given system. Whatever the nature of a particular birthing system may be, its practitioners will tend to see it as the best way, and perhaps the only way, to bring a child into the world. We implicitly acknowledge such recognizable and culturally specific configurations of practices and beliefs when we speak, for example, of "American obstetrics" or "Yucatecan ethno-obstetrics."

While the range of variation *within* a given culture is restricted, the range of variation *across* different cultures will depend on local history, social structure, ecology, technological development, and the like, and is therefore likely to be quite high. For instance, while in all known societies access to births is restricted to a more or less rigidly specified group of people (Ford, 1964), the identity of those allowed to attend varies across cultures (see below).

It is as yet not at all clear what the appropriate categories for cross-cultural comparison of childbirth systems should be. We would argue, however, that such a comparison will be most fruitful if it includes both the medical-physiological and social-ecological aspects of childbirth. Such a biosocial framework will provide a means of integrating the collection and analysis of data. Toward this end, we have studied four very different birthing systems through intensive fieldwork in the United States, the Netherlands, Sweden, and among the Maya Indians of Yucatan (Jordan, 1983).

The four cultures we studied present interesting contrasts. In the United States the great majority of births take place in hospitals and are attended by physicians. (Although childbirth practices in this country are changing, for the purpose of analysis we are concerned here only with those practices associated with standard hospital obstetrics.) Sweden and Holland are both industrial nations with socialized medical care and infant mortality rates that are among the lowest in the world: 7.2 infant deaths per 1,000 live births in Sweden in 1983 and 8.4 deaths per 1,000 live births in the Netherlands in 1983. In comparison, there were 11.5 infant deaths per 1,000 live births in the U.S. in 1983. (All mortality figures are from the *World Health Statistics Annual 1985*. Although the use of infant mortality rates is limited by variations in how live births are defined and other factors, such figures provide a convenient means of judging the relative safety of childbirth in different countries.) In both European countries all women receive systematic prenatal care, and abortions are available on demand. Births in Sweden occur in hospitals and are managed by highly trained midwives; in Holland about 40% of all births are home births, and delivery by a midwife is common both in the home and in the hospital. Yucatecan culture is technologically less sophisticated than that of the U.S. or the two European countries. Childbirth among Maya Indians is managed by the family, occurs in the home, and is accommodated into the routines of daily life. Women are aided by a traditional midwife, their husbands, and other family members and friends. Infant mortality figures are not available for Yucatan; in Mexico as a whole the mortality rate was 38.5 deaths per 1,000 live births in 1980. (For a detailed account of childbirth in Yucatan, see Jordan, 1983.)

Through extensive involvement in the birth process in these four cultures, we have identified features of these various birthing systems that might be appropriate for a more holistic analysis. The seven dimensions presented here — the local definition of the event; preparation for birth; attendants and support systems; the ecology of birth; the use of medication; the technology of birth; and the locus of decision-making — represent a preliminary step towards a more complete framework for cross-cultural comparison.

Definition of the Event

A society's definition of birth is fundamental; it allows those belonging to the culture to develop a set of internally consistent and mutually dependent birth practices. In the United States birth is predominantly viewed as a medical event and a pregnant woman is accordingly treated as a patient. As such she is expected to fulfill the role of "sick person" (Parsons, 1951): she is considered relatively helpless and exempt to some extent from her normal responsibilities for herself, and she is required to seek technically competent help from medical personnel for treatment of her "condition." In Sweden birth is considered an intensely fulfilling personal experience. The Dutch regard birth as a natural event. The Maya Indians similarly view birth as a difficult but normal part of family life.

The local conception of the birth event determines in large part how the problem of pain will be managed. Pain appears to be a recognized and expected part of birth in all societies. What differs among various cultures is the manner in which pain is treated — whether, for example, it is emphasized or discounted. In the United States, where pain relief is available only at the discretion of the medical attendant, attendants are constrained by medical considerations to withhold medication as long as possible. Consequently, laboring women who desire medication for pain must convince the attendants, whether through outward displays of pain or through other means, that their pain is sufficient to warrant medication. The system thus has a built-in bias for orienting both the woman and her attendants to pain. In Sweden women are informed about what kinds of medication are available, the conditions under which they are not advisable, and any known and possible side effects. Decisions about what medication to take, if anything, and when to take it are theirs. This is consistent with the Swedish treatment of birth as a personal experience. Because the Dutch view birth as a natural event, women neither expect nor receive any sort of medication for pain. It is believed that, given time, nature will take its course. Among Maya Indian women, some pain is also an expected part of birth; indeed, it is an expected part of life processes in general. Pain appears in the stories women tell about their birth experiences; such stories represent a way of indicating that distress in labor is normal and a sign of progress, and that it will eventually pass.

Preparation for Birth

All systems have both formal and informal means of disseminating information about childbirth to pregnant women, although little is known about informal educational processes. In Yucatan instruction occurs while labor is in progress. Maya Indians maintain that neither the woman nor her husband should know about the birth process before their first child is born. Nevertheless, since births take place within the family compound, only minimally separated from the rest of family life, the couple is not completely naive. The other three cultures rely heavily on prenatal care. In the United States prenatal care is variable: the proportion of women receiving prenatal care and education is highest among well-educated women in higher socioeconomic brackets and lowest among indigent women delivering in large urban hospitals. In the Netherlands and in Sweden prenatal care is free. comprehensive and universal. Routine prenatal care is the domain of midwives, and is designed in part to distinguish between normal pregnancies and those which will be potentially complicated. The Dutch and Swedish systems locate responsibility for the course of pregnancy and birth within each individual woman.

Attendants and Support Systems

The identity of birth attendants largely determines the nature of interactions between the woman giving birth and others present, and thereby influences to a significant degree the way in which she experiences the birth event. In particular, nonspecialist participants provide a source of emotional support, and their inclusion permits an interpretation of the event as a normal, albeit difficult, part of life.

For many women in the United States, only medical personnel are present during their labor and delivery. Medical attendants are typically viewed as the physician's assistants rather than as the mother's helpers, and transactions between the woman and attendants are accordingly viewed as medical transactions. Uncertainty, stress, pain, and physiological difficulties are handled by means of medical routines, such as medication, sedation, drugs to regulate contractions, and, often, instruments or surgery to deliver the baby. Yucatecan culture, by contrast, emphasizes patience and noninterference; the attitude of birth participants tends to be that the baby will be born when it is ready. Family and friends constitute a pool of nonspecialist attendants who provide emotional and physical support for the woman. In Sweden the birth team consists of the mother, a midwife and her assistant, and a nonspecialist attendant of the woman's choosing, such as her husband, friend, or relative. Swedish midwives are highly trained in performing technical procedures. While obstetric technology is readily available, midwives also tend to respect a woman's wish for privacy: a woman can be alone with her nonspecialist attendant for much of her labor if she wishes. In the Netherlands the composition of the birth team is similar. Since no medication is used during labor and delivery, all discomfort is handled through breathing and relaxation techniques, with the birth team providing the necessary encouragement and support. In these countries, much more so than in the U.S., birth is a collaborative affair in which all present participate.

The Ecology of Birth

By virtue of the mere fact that it is located somewhere, birth unavoidably occurs on someone's territory. A woman may give birth in her normal environment, such as in her home or other familiar surroundings, or in a special-purpose facility, such as a hospital or clinic. Of the birthing systems we have studied, the Yucatecan is clearly the most unspecialized with regard to birth location. A Maya woman gives birth at home, where a blanket used as a screen provides a measure of privacy, but does not separate her from familiar household activities. Although hospital deliveries are becoming increasingly common in the Netherlands, Dutch women prefer to give birth at home and will do so unless complications are expected. In Sweden all babies are delivered in hospitals. The hospital ambience, however, offers some of the comforts of home: a woman in the early hours of labor, for example, can pass the time in an early labor lounge, where she can read, watch television, eat a snack, talk to her husband or friend, and otherwise do some of the things she might do at home. In contrast to the European orientation toward minimal disturbance even in a hospital or clinic environment, American obstetric wards have traditionally been designed with a view toward organizational efficiency and the availability of technological resources. In spite of some variations in the standard hospital delivery pattern, particularly in birthing rooms, women are often confined to a hospital bed, an intravenous glucose drip is started, and a fetal monitor attached. Subsequently, laboring women are transferred to a delivery room to give birth on a delivery table. After birth, mothers and infants have customarily been separated, an arrangement required by a hospital organization that treats the mother-child unit as separate patients.

The Use of Medication in Childbirth

For present purposes we regard as medication any substance introduced into the woman's body to affect the course of labor or to provide relief from pain. The use of medication provides a convenient means of gauging the degree to which particular systems justify interference in the birth process. The Dutch system provides no medication during normal births. Even when stimulation of labor is medically indicated, such as for postmaturity, or if rapid delivery is necessary due to a pathological condition, the criteria for what is considered normal are still quite broad. For instance, while in the U.S. ruptured membranes are considered an indication for inducing labor due to the risk of infection, the predominant view in the Netherlands is that ruptured membranes do not warrant any unusual action as long as fetal heart tones are normal and the woman's temperature does not rise. Furthermore, Dutch birth personnel prefer mechanical means, such as digital stripping of the membranes, over pharmacological or surgical means for inducing labor.

The Yucatecan system similarly emphasizes noninterference in normal births. A slow labor is not inherently considered cause for concern. Maya women tend to continue with household activities until contractions become too strong. In the event that contractions should subsequently slow down, they stimulate labor by giving the woman a raw egg to swallow, which causes retching and usually stimulates contractions. In Sweden stimulation of labor, sedation, and pain relief through pharmacological methods are fairly common, although drugs are used moderately. Women have a great degree of control over the kinds and quantities of drug they receive. In contrast, reliance on pharmacological agents is pronounced in the United States, where induction and stimulation of labor and the use of analgesics and anesthetics are widespread.

The Technology of Birth

The instruments and equipment required for culturally proper management of labor and delivery constitute a significant element in a society's birthing system. The collection of objects we group together in this category include all items deemed important in a proper birth and not just "obstetric tools"; the cross of palms used in Yucatan to ward off evil spirits is just as important to the Maya Indians as the birthing stool women use or as the delivery table is in the United States.

The technology of birth offers important clues to the local definition of the birth event. In societies where tools are simple, easily replaceable, general purpose household objects, birth is more likely to remain within the realm of normal family life than it is in societies where the collection of instruments is extensive and highly specialized (Jordan, in press). The degree of technological sophistication of birth tools is also related to the extent of specialization of birth attendants, and the artifacts associated with birth help to define the nature of the relationships among birth participants through the claims to professional expertise they support.

The Yucatecan tool kit is the most unspecialized of those we studied. The majority of Maya birth equipment consists of common household objects: the woman's hammock, the wooden stool on which she sits to give birth, the bowl for washing the baby and the clean rags for swaddling the baby are all everyday items. In contrast, the technology of the American birth system—which comprises the instruments and machinery of the labor and delivery rooms, X-ray and laboratory facilities, operating rooms for Caesarean sections, newborn resuscitation equipment, and so on—is clearly quite sophisticated.

As the technology of birth increases in complexity and sophistication, there thus appear to be concomitant changes in several important aspects of the birth process: its location, the identity of birth attendants, and the distribution of knowledge about birth (Jordan, in press).

The Locus of Decision-Making

The nature of the decision-making process during labor and delivery is intimately tied to the degree of self-management allowed the woman and, ultimately, to the question of who "owns" the birth. In Yucatan decisions about whether the woman should eat, which position she should assume, when she should begin to push, whether she is pushing hard enough, and what should be considered unsatisfactory progress are made jointly by the laboring woman, her helpers and the midwife. This collaborative process implicitly acknowledges the competence of all involved. Although the midwife's opinion carries considerable weight, even such "professional" decisions as whether to call in a doctor are negotiated. Dutch midwives typically work with the assumption that a woman is able to read her own body's cues; in normal births, the woman is treated as someone who is competent to manage what is seen as a natural process. In general, however, there are relatively few decisions to be made, since the Dutch conception of birth is that it is best aided by letting nature take its course. Of those decisions that must be made, moreover, many are institutionally managed: whether birth will occur at home or in the hospital, for instance, is decided on the basis of medical and social indicators; the question of who will accompany the woman is one which, although her decision, is restricted by the policy of allowing only one companion; and decisions about medication for pain are irrelevant, since none is typically used.

Births in Sweden occur in hospitals, but it is clearly the woman who, in an uncomplicated labor, makes what decisions the system allows, such as whether she will receive medication for pain. Although medical decisions are made by the physician on call, midwives are highly trained, and the range of situations considered normal, and therefore manageable by the laboring woman and the midwife staff, is quite broad. In contrast, women giving birth in the U.S. traditionally have almost no part in the decision-making process. The assimilation of childbirth into the medical realm subjects the birth event to medical decision-making criteria: since parturition is defined as a medical event, the woman is considered a patient who is, by definition, incompetent to influence the management of her birth.

Summary and Discussion

A biosocial analysis of childbirth indicates that the U.S. birthing system differs in several respects from that of the Dutch, the Swedish, and the Maya Indians of Yucatan. The Dutch and Maya Indians regard birth as a natural process, in which very little interference is necessary. Although in Sweden births occur in hospitals, medication for pain relief is available and artificial stimulation of labor is sometimes used: Laboring women have a strong voice in the birth process. Birth is defined as a medical/pathological event only in the United States, and, as we have indicated, the medical model of birth has many important ramifications. In recent years, the appropriateness of the medical model of childbirth has come into question in many circles. Critics of the medical model sometimes argue in favor of alternative obstetric practices on anthropological grounds. In the following section we will describe research designed to address such arguments.

CHILDBIRTH IN NONINDUSTRIAL SOCIETIES

Criticisms of standard hospital routines sometimes imply that they are "unnatural" and that we in this country have lost something important and meaningful that may still exist in other cultures. There is often a tendency to romanticize birthing in traditional cultures, to assume that women slip off into the bush to drop their babies with little effort and pain before returning to their work (Ford, 1964). Discontent with the hospital practice of separating mother and infant immediately after birth has given rise to the notions that this practice is unique to industrial societies and that women in traditional cultures experience close, skin-to-skin contact with their infants immediately after birth and nurse them right away.

To determine whether or not these implicit beliefs are accurate, we (Lozoff, 1982, 1983) analyzed existing ethnographic records, available for a sample of 186 nonindustrial societies, in which the subsistence economy is based on agriculture, herding, hunting and gathering, and fishing (Murdock & White, 1969). These societies comprise a geographically, historically, and linguistically diverse sample that is representative of nonindustrial cultures as a whole. We analyzed ethnographic descriptions of childbirth and the immediate postpartum period in these various cultures to answer such questions as: Who usually attends birth? Is the father of the baby typically present? Are mother and newborn in skin-to-skin contact immediately after birth, as is implied in criticism of standard maternity care in this country, or are they typically separated for some period of time? Do women in nonindustrial cultures breastfeed their infants immediately after birth or do they wait for some period of time? It should be noted that the quality of the ethnographic material is variable and sometimes based on second-hand reports. Nonetheless, the representative nature of the sample makes its analysis a potentially valuable complement to in-depth studies of individual cultures. The data related to labor and delivery will be presented first: data related to the period immediately following birth, and in particular to the extent of contact between parents and infant, will be presented afterward.

Labor and Delivery

We found that virtually all cultures had special methods to avoid painful, difficult births, which implies that even in nonindustrial societies there is some anxiety about the pain and danger associated with childbirth. In the colonial era in this country the Puritans exhorted women to prepare for death as they approached childbirth

(Wertz & Wertz, 1979). Pain and potential mortality are recognized and expected as a part of birth in almost all societies. Perhaps as a result, we found that women giving birth had assistance and companionship in almost all societies. Women routinely gave birth alone in only 2% of the societies in Murdock and White's sample; they were permitted to give birth alone in only an additional 2%. In the remaining 96% of the societies in Murdock and White's sample women were expected to have companionship. Birth assistants were almost always women, especially women who had themselves given birth; indeed, men were often categorically excluded, with the possible exception of the father of the baby. The women present during birth were more than simply companions, however. In the 71 societies for which such information was available, the woman's assistants actively tried to influence labor by massage, herbal remedies, manipulation, and even bouncing on the abdomen. In some groups the birth assistant actually dilated the cervix manually to facilitate the birth process in difficult cases. In others, attendants functioned mostly as *doulas*, or supportive companions (Sosa, Klaus, Kennell, & Urrutia, 1976). The husband of the woman giving birth was allowed at the birth in 27% of the 120 societies for which this information was available. We found evidence that men were actually instrumental in assisting in childbirth in only two cultures. That childbirth in U.S. hospitals is typically dominated by men is thus a situation quite unlike that in nonindustrial societies.

Data concerning the presence or absence of children during childbirth were very scanty. Siblings were allowed to attend birth in only 11% of the cultures in this sample, and were specifically excluded in 25%. Sibling presence was not recorded for the remaining cultures.

In 70% of the cultures in Murdock and White's sample, the most common birth position was with the torso upright; in half, the women squatted or kneeled; in the other 20%, they sat or stood. Women delivered using the hands-and-knees position in only four cultures in the sample. Although women delivered recumbent or semi-recumbent in a third of all cultures, there was no society in this sample in which having the mother's feet in the air is the position of choice. Thus there was no analogue in this sample of the lithotomy position used in standard hospital births in this country.

Women in nearly all cultures prefer to give birth in a familiar location (Jordan, 1983). The Kung San Bushmen, for instance, seek out a favorite spot in the bush (Shostak, 1981), while in some parts of New Guinea women give birth in a special women's hut (Schiefenhovel, 1983), and a woman living in colonial America would usually have given birth in her mother's house (Scholten, 1977). Most commonly, women give birth in their own houses or huts.

It is almost universally expected that women will rest after childbirth. This was reported for in 97% of the 186 cultures in Murdock and White's sample. The average period of seclusion in these cultures was one week. In our own colonial past, women from the community took turns helping the mother for three to four weeks, so she could stay in bed and take care of her baby (Wertz & Wertz, 1979). Among the Maya Indians of Yucatan, the mother and baby are thought to be extremely vulnerable to the influence of spirits from the bush immediately after birth. All doors to the house therefore are closed during childbirth and any cracks in the house stuffed with rags to keep such spirits out (Jordan, 1983). In many other cultures, however, it is the mother and baby who are considered dangerous to the rest of society, and it is for this reason that they are secluded. The English word *quarantine* (from the French *quarante*, meaning forty) comes from the tradition of isolating a mother and her new baby for 40 days.

Early Parent-Infant Contact and Breastfeeding

Early Contact

In 1972, Klaus and Kennell reported that allowing mothers and their newborn infants to be together in the early hours after birth resulted in significant increases in the mothers' affection toward their infants. For example, mothers who experienced early contact with their infants maintained more eye contact with them when they were older, vocalized and sang to them more, and kissed them and smiled at them more than mothers who had not experienced early contact. Subsequent studies noted that early contact also had a beneficial effect on later breastfeeding. Klaus and Kennell referred to this phenomenon as mother-infant bonding, and hypothesized that there was a sensitive period for this process; that is, they argued that there was a period of time immediately after birth, when infants tend to be relatively alert, that represents an optimum time for bonding to begin. Klaus and Kennell's pioneering research stimulated additional work in this area, and the concept of bonding has been extended to include fathers (e.g., Greenberg & Morris, 1974).

Despite its controversial nature, research on early parent-infant bonding has motivated changes in the routines of many hospital maternity wards. In addition, early contact studies have fostered a belief that the practices of separating mother and infant and delaying the first nursing represent aberrations of our hospital policies and are absent in traditional cultures. We analyzed the anthropological data to determine if early parent-infant contact would indeed be emphasized in Murdock and White's sample and if such contact might be associated with any differences in later infant care.

There was no special effort to foster *immediate* body contact between mother and infant in 94% of nonindustrial cultures because both mother and newborn were bathed or rubbed. The duration of delay in contact due to bathing was not generally specified but was probably brief. The bathed newborn was given to the mother in approximately half of all societies; the infant was placed in a cradle or basket in the other half. Although the infant commonly remained in his or her mother's sight, *skin-to- skin contact* was quite rare; the infant was given nude to the mother in only 19% of the societies in this sample. Nevertheless, as we noted above, in virtually all societies mother and baby were secluded together in the period following birth and were not a part of the usual daily activities of the community.

General societal ratings of parental involvement and affection, which have been demonstrated to be reasonably reliable and valid, are available for the same 186 societies in Murdock and White's sample (Barry & Paxson, 1971). We dichotomized the following ratings relevant to the effects of postpartum contact: mother's role as caregiver; response to crying; overall quality of infant care; paternal involvement in infancy and early childhood; duration of breastfeeding; and infant's age at introduction of solid food. We compared those societies in which the baby was given to the mother with those societies in which the baby was placed in a cradle or basket. There was no difference between the two groups on any of the following measures: the percent of societies in which the mother was the primary caregiver, in which crying infants received a nurturant response, or in which infants received generally affectionate care. Thus, immediate postpartum contact was not associated with differences in maternal affection and involvement on these global rating scales. It cannot be determined whether differences might have been found if more detailed or sensitive measures had been available.

We performed a similar analysis to determine whether fathers were more involved with their children in societies which allowed them to be present at birth. Societies in which fathers were permitted to attend birth were compared with those in which fathers were prohibited from being at birth on dichotomized ratings of paternal involvement. There was no significant difference between the two groups in the percentage of societies in which fathers were closely involved with their children in infancy or early childhood, although there was a trend toward increased paternal involvement in infancy.

Early Breastfeeding

It has been found in several studies of hospital births that women who breastfeed in the first hour are more likely to be breastfeeding when their infants are two months old than women who breastfeed according to standard hospital routine—i.e., at 4-6 hours or even at 12 hours. This result has been obtained in studies conducted in Brazil (Sousa et al., 1974), Canada (Thomson, Hartsock & Larson, 1979), England (Salariya, Easton & Cater, 1978), Guatemala (Sosa et al., 1976), Jamaica (Ali & Lowry, 1981), Sweden (de Chateau, 1967), and the United States (Hally et al., 1984; Johnson, 1976; Paylor, Maloni, & Brown, 1986; Paylor, Maloni, Taylor, & Campbell, 1985; Wright & Walker, 1983).

Several different mechanisms have been proposed to explain the finding that breastfeeding in the first hour after birth has a significant effect on later breastfeeding. This research originally came under the umbrella of the "early contact" research: it was proposed that there is a sensitive period for breastfeeding as well as for early bonding. An alternative explanation is that babies are in a quiet, alert state more often in the first hour than later on, so they suck more effectively, which in turn stimulates the mother's brain to release the hormones that govern lactation. It may also be that simply by putting babies to their mother's breast, health care professionals convey a message about the importance of breastfeeding, which leads to greater success. Regardless of the mechanism involved, early breastfeeding seems to be a consistently effective intervention, and has in many cases been incorporated into hospital routines.

The research on breastfeeding in the first postpartum hour might suggest that early nursing is crucial for successful breastfeeding in humans. One might reasonably assume, therefore, that virtually all nonindustrial societies would insure that immediate suckling occurs. Our analysis of the data in Murdock and White's sample indicated that this is not in fact the case. Of the 81 societies for which the time of initial breastfeeding could be recorded from ethnographies, infants nursed within the first hour or two in 48%; nursing was delayed more than 24 hours in the majority (52%) and delayed more than 48 hours in 41%. The substantial delay in initial breastfeeding occurs in most cases because these cultures consider colostrum, the milk high in protein and immune body content that is secreted for the first few days after parturition, of no nutritional value or even harmful.

In our own culture women who delay nursing for over 24 hours often have difficulty establishing their milk supply. We analyzed Murdock and White's data to determine if lactation failure was a problem in nonindustrial cultures that delayed the first nursing. There was no difference between those cultures that adhere to a practice of early breastfeeding and those that delay breastfeeding either in the duration of breastfeeding or the age at which solid foods are introduced. Indeed, contrary to common assumptions about primitive cultures, solids were introduced before one month of age in one-third of all cultures, regardless of when infants were first breastfed. Similarly, nursing lasted two years or longer in 81% of the nonindustrial cultures, whether women nursed in the first hour or delayed the first breastfeeding.

Discussion

These anthropological results present something of a puzzle. Few human cultures emphasize skin-to-skin body contact and suckling in the immediate postpartum period, practices associated with longer breastfeeding and increased maternal involvement for individuals in industrial societies. Yet in most nonindustrial groups, mothers are affectionately involved with their infants and breastfeed successfully for two or more years. It may be easier to understand these contradictions if we consider the effect of the early period after birth in the context of the subsequent days and months.

The standard maternity hospital routine in industrial societies of separating mothers and babies is followed by an infant care pattern that commonly comprises frequent separations of mother and infant in the home, minimal body contact, and spaced feeding. In the context of this pattern of infant care, body contact immediately after birth may assume disproportionate significance in enhancing maternal affection. In contrast, in nonindustrial societies separation in the first hour may have less effect on the mother's later involvement with her infant because such separations are not repeated. The brief initial separation of mother and infant is universally followed by postpartum confinement of mother and baby together — a rooming-in period — which is itself followed by extensive mother-infant contact and prolonged and frequent breastfeeding during the baby's early months. In addition, it is likely that many factors — little girls' exposure to breastfeeding throughout their lives, assumptions that breastfeeding will be successful, a supportive environment, frequent nursing, and extensive mother-infant contact — combine to diminish the importance of nursing in the first hour. Thus, the apparent sensitivity of parents in industrial societies to immediate postpartum contact may reflect disruptive influences of our pattern of infant care and our hospital routines rather than a brief sensitive period for parenting, or for developing parental feelings, in the human species.

An appreciation of the embeddedness of perinatal customs in the broader context of infant care patterns and cultural meaning systems provides further insight into the apparent paradox presented by these anthropological data. The task universally faced in all cultures is adequate involvement of caregiver and child, primarily mother and child (Jordan, 1982). This involvement can be conceptualized as a progressive mutual engagement of the senses, which begins with the mother's first sensory contact with the baby and continues with her hearing the infant's first cry, her first sight of the baby, and first holding it and smelling it, and so on, until there is mutual sensory involvement. The culmination of this process is that the mother "owns" the child; the mother feels that this is really *her* baby for which she is prepared to care. The relationship deepens with the mother and baby "talking" to each other, mutual gazing, nipple searching and nipple giving, and so on. It may well be that there is a sensitive period for this process of mutual engagement. Regardless of whether or not a system of this sort is biologically preprogrammed, the anthropological data suggest that culture is stronger than nature. Different cultures facilitate caregiver-infant attachment in different ways: some with immediate contact, some with later contact; some with skin-to-skin contact, some without. Whatever specific means are used, all societies accomplish the task somehow, or babies would not survive.

CHILDBIRTH IN THE UNITED STATES: DISCONTENT, CHANGE AND POTENTIAL CONFLICT

Judging from the available anthropological data, it would appear that the practices of separating mother and infant immediately after birth, delaying breastfeeding and excluding fathers from childbirth are not unique to standard maternity care in the United States, common assumptions notwithstanding. Nevertheless, both of the comparative approaches to childbirth that we have described indicate that birthing practices in the U.S. do differ in important respects from those in other cultures. The pathological model of childbirth that pervades our childbirth practices is atypical of the other cultures we studied, even those that are technologically quite sophisticated. Our analysis of the anthropological data from Murdock and White's sample of nonindustrial cultures revealed that, while there is considerable behavioral variability even in so universal a process as childbirth, there are also several birthing practices that are very nearly universal. These near-universal tendencies are predominantly social in nature. In general, all cultures have *rules* governing the process of parturition, although the actual content of such rules may differ among cultures. There are also more specific practices characteristic of virtually all societies: women giving birth almost always receive assistance, usually from other women; women usually prefer to give birth in a familiar setting, most commonly their own home; and virtually all societies prescribe a period of rest and seclusion for mother and infant after birth, a "rooming-in period," during which the pair is separated from community activities and the mother is exempt from her usual responsibilities. In these respects, standard maternity care in the U.S. may not fit the pattern of childbirth practices that seems to characterize nonindustrial cultures.

We have argued that childbirth practices are best understood in the context of the sociocultural matrix in which they are embedded, including the patterns of infant care typical of the culture. One implication of this position is that the relationship between birthing practices and the various phenomena that researchers might examine as outcome variables is likely to be complex. For example, the influence of fathers' birth attendance on their subsequent involvement with their children is liable to depend on many factors, such as cultural notions about the father-child relationship, economic pressures, the division of labor within a family, and the attitudes of fathers and their partners about paternal involvement in infant care (cf. Palkovitz, 1985). As our analysis of the anthropological data from Murdock and White's sample of nonindustrial cultures indicated, whether or not fathers in nonindustrial cultures are allowed to be present at the birth of their babies had no apparent effect on the degree of fathers' later involvement with their children. Indeed, it may well be that whether an expectant father participates in birth has more to do with cultural attitudes about his relationship with his wife than about his relationship with his children. The Maya Indians, for instance, believe that the father must participate in an active capacity at birth so that he can see how his wife suffers; this is expected to prevent him from making sexual demands during the postpartum period (Jordan, 1983).

An additional implication of the view that each culture's system of childbirth is intimately linked to the culture as a whole is that, as changes occur in the larger social and cultural systems with which childbirth systems articulate, there will be corresponding changes in birthing practices. This has quite clearly been the case in the United States in recent years. Those in the feminist health movement have been pressing for the right of women to self-determination in matters regarding their bodies (cf. Jordan, 1977). One outcome of this movement has been the position that women's individual complaints about their birth experiences are not the result of rare circumstances, but are the systematic outcome of standard medical practice. The collectivization of previously individual dissatisfaction has produced powerful pressures on the American obstetric system. At the same time, major segments of the consumer movement as it relates to health care have been engaged in a comprehensive reevaluation of the expanding monopoly of professional medicine. Too, many men have been questioning practices that routinely excluded them from the delivery room and the birth of their own babies, and an increased emphasis on prepared childbirth has resulted in a greater degree of inclusion of fathers in the process of birth. As a result of these and other pressures, childbirth practices in this country are undergoing major changes. This is reflected in the growing visibility of various forms of natural childbirth, in the increasingly common efforts to restructure the physical design of obstetric wards, and in the development of family-centered perinatal care programs.

Such changes would appear to indicate that we as a culture are engaged in a reformulation of the medical definition of birth. It should be noted, however, that hospital birthing rooms make sense only within a system that places the highest premium on medical safety, since the woman's own home would be preferable by most any other criterion. The home birth movement also speaks the language of outcome statistics. At least in the public arena, all of the advantages of home births that one could cite, such as the woman's comfort, financial considerations, the humanization of birth, benefits from taking responsibility for one's life rather than delegating it to professionals and institutions, and the strengthening of the couple's and family relationships that can be obtained from the shared experience, are subordinated to discussions of medical safety. The strongest argument that the home birth movement can, and does, advance is the statistical argument that the outcome of home births is in no way inferior to that of hospital births. That such alternatives to standard hospital births do not represent fundamental changes in the prevailing view of childbirth, then, is apparent.

Regardless of whether the definition of birth in this country has changed in any fundamental respect, obstetric practices in the U.S. nevertheless are clearly changing. Furthermore, it seems quite likely that changes in obstetric practice will produce a significant increase in maternal satisfaction and perhaps infant outcome statistics, too, by reducing the dissonance between women's conceptions of themselves and the treatment they receive in maternity wards (Jordan. 1983). Yet if maternity hospital reform is in fact successful in altering parent-infant relationships' as proponents of early contact have argued, then perhaps families in the U.S. should anticipate new conflicts as this postpartum experience does not fit with the patterns of care during the rest of infancy.

For example, after frequent feeding on demand in the first few days in the hospital, many infants may well be eager to eat every 1-2 hours. There is evidence that this feeding pattern was the norm during much of human history and thus may be particularly suited to human physiology (Lozoff & Brittenham, 1979; Lozoff, 1980). Such frequent breastfeeding is in fact found in most societies, yet in the United States many women find it difficult to sustain and enjoy a "continuous" feeding pattern. In addition, breastfeeding still conflicts with societal norms and expectations. The mother in the U.S. who integrates breastfeeding with her usual activities may still encounter offended righteousness in public situations.

Maternity hospital routines which encourage early body contact between mother and baby also seem congruent with the pattern of care to which humans may be adapted. In the United States many babies, given the opportunity, seem thoroughly delighted to be in constant body contact in their early months, a desire which may stress some mothers. Women in the U.S. generally must provide such contact entirely by themselves without the help of extended family members who in other societies often hold babies while the mother works or rests. In fact, the presence of more than one adult caretaker in a household is, in cross-cultural studies, associated with increased acceptance and indulgence of infants (Rohner, 1975). If the close involvement encouraged in a family-centered childbirth experience is continued into infancy, both mother and father may also experience conflicts about work. Women's work was previously compatible with infant care; women have worked in most human societies, contributing more than 50% of the food for the group during 99% of human history. In contrast, work is generally incompatible with infant care in our culture; conflicts between work and parenthood seem to be created by the structure of work in this society.

Thus, while family-centered changes in maternal hospital practices are certainly needed, such reforms may introduce new dilemmas for parents and infants if not accompanied by transformations in the pattern of subsequent infant care. Cross-cultural study of childbirth provides an important context in which to evaluate and understand changes in hospital routines, including potential conflicts with other infant care practices.

DIRECTION FOR FURTHER RESEARCH

The above review suggests a number of areas in which further cross-cultural research is needed. We need, for example, more ethnographic studies of different birthing systems in order to add to what is known about the range of variability in human behaviors around childbirth. The recent legitimization of "women's topics" in anthropology and related disciplines has already led to the initiation of a number of such studies (Laderman, 1984; MacCormack, 1982; Sargent, 1982), and further results should become available in the next few years. We also need to examine, in more detail, the variation in function of birth attendants in other cultures. Most recent research on traditional midwives has been narrowly confined to assessments of their knowledge and skills (WHO, 1985), with a view to incorporate them in primary health care teams, particularly as village-level dispensers of contraceptive information. Studies of this type all too often do not pay sufficient attention to the cultural meaning of birth and to the social relationships it creates (Jordan, 1986). Little is thus known about continuing family-like ties between birth attendants and the child, nor about the extent to which it is common that grandmothers and other family members lend birth assistance.

Another topic that cross-cultural studies have not yet addressed adequately is the question of father involvement in pregnancy, birth, and the postpartum period. We know that there are many societies where the father of the child is expected to play a significant role during pregnancy and where he has important functions during the postpartum period. For example, a common cross-cultural belief is that the parents together have to "grow" the baby by contributing physical substances: the mother her menstrual blood (which makes the baby's muscle and blood) and the father his semen (which turns into the white parts, such as skin and bone). Fathers, like mothers, may be subject to food taboos and other restrictions on their behavior throughout the pregnancy and into the postpartum period, but information on such practices and what they may mean for the relationship between father and child are only sporadic at this time. Perhaps with the burgeoning of research on fathers in industrial societies, some in-depth studies of fathering in nonindustrial societies will become available.

Cross-cultural studies of birthing have added many valuable insights which can contribute to our understanding of parenthood. Nevertheless, there is still much work to be done.

REFERENCES

Ali, Z., & Lowry, M. (1981). Early maternal-child contact: Effects on later behavior. *Developmental Medicine and Child Neurology, 23*, 337-345.

Barry, H., & Paxson, L. M. (1971). Infancy and early childhood: Cross-cultural codes 2. *Ethnology, 10*, 466-508.

de Chateau, P. (1967). *Neonatal care routines: Influences on maternal and infant behavior and on breastfeeding*. Umea: Umea University Medical Dissertations, New Series No. 20.

Ford, C. S. (1964). *A comparative study of human reproduction* (Reprinted from the 1945 edition). Human Relations Area Files, Inc. New Haven: HRAF Press.

Greenberg, M., & Morris, N. (1974). Engrossment: The newborn's impact upon the father. *American Journal of Orthopsychiatry, 44*, 520-531.

Hally, M. R., Bond, J., Crawley, J., Gregson, B., Philips, P., & Russell, I. (1984). Factors influencing the feeding of first-born infants. *Acta Paediatrica Scandinavica, 73*, 33-39.

Johnson, N. W. (1976). Breastfeeding at one hour of age. *American Journal of Maternal Child Nursing, 1*, 12-16.

Jordan, B. (1977). The self-diagnosis of early pregnancy: An investigation of lay competence. *Medical Anthropology, 1*, 1-38.

Jordan, B. (1982). Commentary. In M. H. Klaus & M. O. Robertson (Eds.), *Birth, interaction and attachment* (pp. 7-9). Pediatric Round Table Series, no. 6. Johnson & Johnson Baby Products Company.

Jordan, B. (1983). *Birth in four cultures: A cross-cultural investigation of childbirth in Yucatan, Holland, Sweden and the United States* (3rd ed.). Montreal: Eden Press.

Jordan, B. (1986). Technology transfer in obstetrics: Theory and practice in developing countries. *Women in International Development Working Papers*, #126. East Lansing, MI: WID/MSU.

Jordan, B. (in press). The hut and the hospital: Information, power and symbolism in the artifacts of birth. *Birth: Issues in Perinatal Care and Education.*

Ladermann, Carol D. (1984). *Wives and midwives: Childbirth and nutrition in rural Malaysia*. Berkeley: University of California Press.

Lozoff, B. (1980). Reply to Jelliffe, E. F. P. "Infant care: Cache or carry." *Journal of Pediatrics, 96*, 1122-1123.

Lozoff, B. (1982). Birth in non-industrial societies. In M. H. Klaus & M. O. Robertson (Eds.), *Birth, interaction and attachment* (pp. 1-6). Pediatric Round Table Series, no. 6. Johnson & Johnson Baby Products Company.

Lozoff, B. (1983). Birth and "bonding" in non-industrial societies. *Developmental Medicine and Child Neurology, 25*, 595-600.

Lozoff, B., & Brittenham, G. M. (1979). Infant care: Cache or carry. *Journal of Pediatrics, 95*, 478-483.

MacCormack, Carol P. (1982). *Ethnography of fertility and birth*. London: Academic Press.

Murdock, G. P., & White, D. R. (1969). Standard cross-cultural sample. *Ethnology, 8*, 329-369.

Palkovitz, R. (1985). Fathers' birth attendance, early contact, and extended contact with their newborns: A critical review. *Child Development, 56*, 392-406.

Parsons, T. (1951). *The social system*. Glencoe, Illinois: Free Press.

Paylor, P. M., Maloni, J. A., & Brown, D. R. (1986). Early suckling and prolonged breastfeeding. *American Journal of Diseases in Children, 140*, 151-154.

Paylor, P. M., Maloni, J. A., Taylor, F. H., & Campbell, S. B. (1985). II. Extra early mother-infant contact and duration of breast-feeding. *Acta Paediatrica Scandinavica* (Suppl. 316), 15-22.

Rohner, R. P. (1975). *They love me, they love me not*. Human Relations Area Files, Inc., New Haven: HRAF Press.

Rosaldo, M. Z., & Lamphere, L. (1974). *Woman, culture and society*. Palo Alto, California: Stanford University Press.

Salariya, E. M., Easton, P. M., & Cater, J. E. (1978). Duration of breastfeeding after early initiation and frequent feeding. *Lancet, 2*, 1141-1143.

Sargent, Carolyn F. (1982). *The cultural context of therapeutic choice: Obstetrical care decisions among the Bariba of Benin*. Hingham, MA: D. Reidel.

Schiefenhovel, W. (1983). Geburten bei den Eipo [Birth among the Eipo]. In W. Schiefenhovel & D. Sich (Eds.), *Die Geburt aus ethnomedizinischer Sicht*. Braunschweig, West Germany: Vierweg Verlag.

Scholten, C. (1977). On the importance of the Obstetrick Art. *The William and Mary Quarterly*, 3rd series, *34*, 426-455.

Shostak, M. (1981). *Nisa: The life and words of a Kung woman*. Cambridge, MA: Harvard University Press.

Sosa, R., Klaus, M., Kennell, J. H., & Urrutia, J. J. (1976). The effect of early mother-infant contact on breastfeeding, infection and growth. Ciba Foundation

Symposium 45, *Breastfeeding and the mother* (pp. 179-193). Amsterdam, The Netherlands: Elsevier Publishing Co.

Sousa, P. L. R., Barros, F. C., Gazalle, R. V., Bergers, R. M., Pinheiro, G. N., Menezes, S. T., & Arruda, L. A. (1974). Attachment and lactation. Paper presented at XIV Congreso Internacional de Pediatria. Buenos Aires, Argentina.

Thomson, M. E., Hartsock, T., & Larson, C. (1979). The importance of immediate postnatal contact: Its effect on breastfeeding. *Canadian Family Physician, 25*, 1374-1378.

Wertz, R. W., & Wertz, D. C. (1979). *Lying-in: A history of childbirth in America*. New York: Schocken Books.

Wright, H. J., & Walker, P. C. (1983). Prediction of duration of breastfeeding in primaparas. *Journal of Epidemiology and Community Health, 37*, 89-94.

WHO (1985). *Traditional birth practices: An annotated bibliography*. Prepared by Lindsay Edouard and Cecile Li Hoi Foo-Gregory for the Maternal and Child Health Unit, Division of Family Health, WHO, Geneva. (WHO/MC/85.11).

World Health Statistics Annual 1985. Geneva, Switzerland: World Health Organization.

Dietary Habits in Transition to Parenthood: Dietary Habits Before Pregnancy, During Pregnancy and in Young Families

Leta P. Aljadir

SUMMARY. Trends in dietary patterns in transition to parenthood were inferentially derived from the literature, in the absence of research in this area. It appears from the material reviewed that dietary habits improve nutritionally from childhood to young adulthood hence most pregnant women probably enter pregnancy with acceptable dietary habits. Exceptions to this generalization may be individuals from the lower socioeconomic groups, and ethnic groups such as blacks and Hispanics, and adolescents. These population groups have been found to have a high incidence of undernutrition from various surveys.

Dietary cravings and aversions during pregnancy abound, almost universally. These are limited to the pregnant state and are therefore transitory changes in dietary habits. Generally, these do not diminish dietary quality, unless accompanied by exaggerated nausea and vomiting or the practice of pica.

What transpires with the parents' dietary habits after the birth of the child and as the child grows older is subject to speculation. Evidence suggests that food habits of young children and their parents are similar, characterized by preference for sweets. It is possible that dietary habits of young parents deteriorate until their children are grown.

Pregnancy and prospective parenthood are major events that could initiate conscious or subconscious changes in the diet. Some

---

Leta P. Aljadir, MS, is Associate Professor of Human Nutrition, Department of Nutrition and Dietetics, University of Delaware, Newark, DE 19716.

questions arise: Do pregnant women think about their food habits vis-á-vis prospective parenthood? What changes, if any, occur in dietary patterns of pregnant women? Do these changes persist after childbirth? What factors contribute to these changes?

Transition to parenthood is only one of several phases in the life-span. However, it evokes special attention from varied disciplines, perhaps because it epitomizes continuance of life itself. The transfer of culture to the offspring begins a new cycle. Man derives some security and sense of immortality from such extension of self.

As with other aspects of any culture, food habits are passed on, consciously or subconsciously, to the next generation. "Ethnic" food patterns prevail in a cultural melting pot such as the United States (Jerome, 1969; Snow & Johnson, 1978). This suggests that although dietary habits evolve over a lifetime, the modifications in dietary patterns that accrue are minor. That is, dietary habits in a healthy population are fairly resistant to major changes.

From a purely academic perspective, it would be interesting to see how transition to parenthood impacts dietary habits, and explore the factors influencing any changes.

A literature search came up negative with respect to publications on the particular topic of transition to parenthood and dietary habits. What emerged, however, were peripherally related studies on dietary habits and food consumption patterns of the population at large, with delineations by age range, sex, ethnic background, socioeconomic level and other demographic factors; dietary habits, attitudes and beliefs of pregnant and/or lactating women; and food preferences and consumption patterns of preschoolers and older children and their parents.

It is the purpose of this paper to inferentially derive trends in dietary habits during transition to parenthood. This is based on the assumption that there is such a concept as "fairly well-developed dietary habits," e.g., those of adults. In addition, these dietary habits are subject to slight but measurable modifications brought about by lifestyle changes such as marriage, pregnancy, and childrearing.

This paper will review the literature on food habits in general, with emphasis on food habits of young adults, since it is this sub-population that is most likely to yield prospective parents; dietary changes with pregnancy and lactation; their relationship, if any, to an acknowledgement by the women of transition to parenthood; and dietary habits of young families. It is hoped that this might stimulate research on the evolution of dietary habits during the transition to parenthood. At the very least, such research might elucidate factors that provoke enduring changes in dietary habits. Implications of this include development of strategies to induce dietary changes when dietary habits are deemed a liability to health. Alternately, beneficial dietary habits might be reinforced.

DIETARY/FOOD HABITS, PREFERENCES AND CONSUMPTION PATTERNS

Dietary habits, food habits and eating habits are terms that will be used interchangeably in this paper. These terms describe the general pattern of food consumption of individuals or groups based on a complex set of interactive factors including: cultural background; preferences; knowledge, beliefs and attitudes; socioeconomic factors; and food availability and advertising (Mead, 1943; Fathauer, 1960; Pilgrim, 1961; McKenzie, 1974; Wolff, 1973; Adrian & Daniel, 1976; Sims, 1978; Foley, Hertzler & Anderson, 1979; Reaburn, Krondl & Lau, 1979; Hertzler, Wenkam & Standell, 1982; Zajonc & Markus, 1982).

Dietary habits are of interest to nutritionists and other health professionals because overall nutrient intake is a function of food intake. Whereas food intake is largely a function of physiological needs in primitive organisms and lower forms of animals, food intake by humans is related to a complex system of variables (Hochbaum, 1981). The simplistic view that knowledge and motivation are all that are required for rational health and dietary behavior is, therefore, no longer accepted.

Knowledge, nonetheless, is often measured in dietary habits research, perhaps because it lends itself to quantification (Phillips, Bass & Yetley, 1978; Snow & Johnson, 1978; Kirks, Hendricks & Wyse, 1982; Smith, Levenson & Morrow, 1985). In each of these studies, knowledge was positively associated with beneficial dietary practices, although several other influential factors were also delineated, such as socioeconomic status, education and attitudes.

Brown and colleagues (1977) surveyed the dietary practices of members of the British Nutrition Society related to hypotheses on diet and health. They found that a high proportion of the membership accepted several hypotheses (e.g., the relationship between increased saturated fat, dietary cholesterol and decreased dietary fiber and "diseases of Western civilization"; increased refined carbohydrates and dental caries). Of those who accepted the hypotheses, 70-80% modified their diet and/or health practices. To the extent that the members of the Nutrition Society are knowledgeable in diet and health, this study illustrates that knowledge appears to be a fairly significant determinant of dietary practice. It must be borne in mind, however, that this group is highly specialized and that their nutrition knowledge is certainly more profound than that of the average individual. The motivational force of superficial nutrition knowledge may not necessarily translate equally.

On the other end of the scale, Wolff (1973) describes the "health foodists," who generally distrust the scientific knowledge of nutritionists. The nutritionists allegedly promote the food industry, which, in turn, has flooded the market with purified products of questionable nutritional value. These "health foodists" are highly motivated to select foods for health reasons, although their knowledge may be uncertain.

By and large, it appears that people generally choose and eat foods based on palatability and presentation rather than on nutritive value (Yudkin, 1963; McNeil & McNeil, 1984). McKenzie (1974) asserts that people choose *foods*, not *nutrients*. Johnson and Johnson (1985) appropriately suggest that nutrition and health education should focus less on fact-giving and more on strategies for changing behavior.

What do studies on dietary habits tend to explore? Since "dietary habit" is a multidimensional construct (Sims, 1978; Foley, Hertzler & Anderson, 1979; Dennis & Shifflett, 1985), studies are usually focused on measurable indicators of dietary habits. These include food preferences, food consumption patterns, food shopping practices, dietary histories and food frequency measurements (e.g., which foods are typically eaten and how frequently they occur in the diet daily, weekly or monthly). Although some methodological problems remain, the tools used have been generally demonstrated to be valid and reliable (Gersovitz, Madden & Smiciklas-Wright, 1978).

Food preferences are an integral part of dietary habits, and appear to be formulated early in life (Pilgrim, 1961; Birch, 1979b). Some research based on studies of newborns indicates that preference for the sweet taste and rejection of the bitter taste are innate (Beauchamp & Maller, 1977). Through advertent or inadvertent reinforcement, preference for sweets persists through childhood (Eppwright, et al., 1969; Ritchey & Olson, 1983).

Some of the important factors determining food preferences are age and childhood region (Pilgrim, 1961); food prestige (Reaburn, Krondl & Lau, 1979; Bass, Owsley & McNutt, 1985); familiarity (Birch, 1979a; Pliner, 1983); and conditioning and advertisement (Gussow, 1972; Zimmerman & Munro, 1972; Harper & Sanders, 1975; Birch, Zimmerman & Hind, 1980; Galst, 1980; Musaiger, 1983).

Dietary Habits of Young Adults

The National Center for Health Statistics (NCHS, 1979) in the U.S., and the British Ministry of Agriculture, Fisheries and Food (Barber & Bull, 1985) are important sources of data on food consumption and nutrient intake of various segments of the population in the Western World. There are some similarities between U.S. and British food consumption patterns. For example, energy intakes are decreasing; there is some preoccupation with body image, especially among the young adults, which has resulted in diminished intake of some nutrients such as calcium, iron, and some B vitamins, due to food restriction.

Analysis of the NCHS data for whites 15-74 years old (Randall & Lorimor, 1984), yielded an interesting finding, i.e., that dietary diversity increased with age. This was statistically significant for females, but not for males. Dietary diversity is a measure of the number of food types used, and is an indication of variety of foods consumed. It has been previously demonstrated that the greater the variety of foods in a diet, the greater is the diet's nutritional quality (Sanjur & Scoma, 1971; Schorr, Sanjur & Erichson, 1972).

Greger, Divilbiss and Aschenbeck (1979) surveyed the dietary

habits of 178 adolescent females during fall and spring. Using the
basic four food groups as a dietary evaluation tool, they found that
the average student obtained less than the recommended intake for
each of the food groups. Those who purchased the Type A school
lunch generally had more servings than those who brought bag
lunches or purchased their meals à la carte from the school cafeteria. In general, there was poor consumption of fruits, vegetables
and milk. A fair percentage of the students admitted to skipping
breakfast.

In contrast, college students tend to fare better with respect to
nutritional quality of diets (Guthrie & Scheer, 1981). The factors
contributing to an improvement in dietary habits are subject to speculation. Some of these reasons include maturation and other psychological developmental traits.

Food preferences of college students in Canada, and their parents
were assessed by means of a seven point Likert scale for 47 foods
(Pliner, 1983). Offspring resembled their parents in food scales.
There was a tendency for college students to more closely resemble
the same-sex parent. Pliner proposes that imitation of food behavior
and familiarity to food may be mechanisms through which this similarity between child and parent is manifested.

It should be noted, however, that many of these studies have
been conducted with white middle-income populations. From surveys such as the Ten-State Nutrition Survey (1972), it has been
demonstrated that regardless of ethnic group, socioeconomic status
varies inversely with nutritional status. Moreover, adolescents 10-
16 years old were found to have the highest incidence of malnutrition.

From this limited review, it appears that there are some differences between dietary habits of adolescents and young adults, with
adolescents generally having poorer nutrient intakes. There is a resemblance of food preferences between young adults and their parents. To the extent that food preferences are an indication of food
consumption, and that adult dietary habits generally result in adequate nutrient intake, it would seem that the young adult (who may
be a prospective parent) has dietary habits that would contribute to
adequate nutrition.

The adolescent female from the lower socioeconomic group, on the other hand, may be at risk for malnutrition. This population group deserves special attention in order to avoid vicious cycles of deprivation.

Dietary Habits During Pregnancy

The literature is replete with studies on dietary practices during pregnancy and lactation, and Seifrit (1961) gives an excellent global historical perspective on the topic.

Food Aversions and Cravings

Dietary cravings and aversions abound during this period, and are believed to result from physiological changes, psychological factors and/or folklore (Edwards, McSwain & Haire, 1954; Bartholomew & Poston, 1970; Hook, 1978; Snow & Johnson, 1978; Manderson & Mathews, 1981; Landman & Hall, 1983; Schwab & Axelson, 1984; Tierson, Olsen & Hook, 1985). A food craving is generally regarded as an unusual desire for a particular food; an aversion is the exaggerated dislike for a food.

Studies on deviant food practices during pregnancy, such as pica, i.e., the ingestion of nonfood items like clay, laundry starch, burnt matches, tissue paper, etc. are also widely reported (O'Rourke, et al., 1967; Roselle, 1970; Frankel, 1977; Vermeer & Frate, 1979).

Nausea and vomiting during pregnancy are also described in varying severity. Studies on the psychological/mental adjustment of pregnant women who experience these suggest physiological and psychological bases of these phenomena (Harvey & Sherfey, 1954; Guttmacher, 1960; Taylor, 1962; Fairweather, 1968; Dickens & Trethowan, 1971; Uddenberg, Nilsson & Almgren, 1971). The presence of these symptoms certainly affects food intake, hence dietary patterns.

The onset of food aversions and cravings during pregnancy is universal and has been described in ancient medical literature (Seifrit, 1961). More recently, Dickens and Trethowan (1971), Hook (1978), Schwab and Axelson (1984), Tierson, Olsen and Hook (1985) have demonstrated a high prevalence of aversions and cravings, with as many as 85% of their subjects demonstrating aversions and/or cravings. Certain trends arise from these studies: Aversions occur earlier during the first trimester than do cravings; cravings persist over longer periods of the pregnancy; cravings cause an increase in consumption of the foods craved while aversions result in diminished intake of foods to which aversions have developed; aversions are more common than cravings; aversions to coffee, tea and alcoholic beverages are common; cravings for milk, dairy products, sweets, chocolate, ice cream, fruits and juices are demonstrated repeatedly.

Research on the physiological bases of aversions and cravings (e.g., hormonal changes during pregnancy and their effect on taste perception) is ongoing. Hook (1978) hypothesizes that these changes in food preference may be a manifestation of an evolutionary development to protect the fetus from potentially embryotoxic materials. The foods for which aversions most commonly develop are coffee and alcohol, and these aversions generally start early in pregnancy, during the most vulnerable period of embryonic and fetal development. While the toxic potential of caffeine has been adequately demonstrated in animals (Tucci & Skalko, 1978), its effect in human pregnancies remains controversial (Jacobson, Goldman & Syme, 1981; Linn, et al., 1982). In contrast, the evidence for alcohol's embryotoxic activity in both animals and humans is fairly well-established (Shaywitz, Cohen & Shaywitz, 1980; West, Hodges & Black, 1981). Hook (1978) goes on to suggest that the cravings are generally for beneficial foods, and contribute to the overall nutrient intake of the pregnant woman.

Some of the dietary changes during pregnancy are dictated by folklore, hence are less universal than aversions and cravings (Edwards, McSwain & Haire, 1954; Bartholomew & Poston, 1970; Snow & Johnson, 1978; Manderson & Mathews, 1981; Landman & Hall, 1983). Few, if any, of these dietary practices have known benefits to the outcome of pregnancy. Some practices in cultures that subscribe to the "Hot/Cold" theory of physiologic states (Snow & Johnson, 1978; Manderson & Mathews, 1981; Landman & Hall, 1983), are, in fact, presently known to be deleterious to the unborn child. For instance, the Vietnamese believe that the first trimester of pregnancy is a "cold" state, requiring the use of such "hot" foods as alcohol to balance the cold state. As alluded to earlier, fetal alcohol exposure has been positively associated with the "Fetal Alcohol Syndrome," causing malformation and mental retardation in animals and humans (Shaywitz, Cohen & Shaywitz, 1980; West, Hodges & Black, 1981).

Traditional customs and folk beliefs regarding diet during pregnancy generally relate to food avoidance or enchanced intake of a particular food. Reasons cited for these practices often include the prevention of malformation, birthmarks, fetal death, or the facilitation of delivery (Landman & Hall, 1983), none of which have scientific support. Bartholomew and Poston (1970) found that the presence of a grandmother in the household encouraged superstition among pregnant women in a Southern U.S. population. Presumably, the grandmother is the bearer of folktales. Ebrahim (1980) concedes that such practices are deeply rooted in tradition; failure to recognize this in health care planning dooms any strategy to failure. One positive note on folklore-based food practices may be that these provide some comfort and satisfaction to the pregnant woman through a "cultural bridge during a period of psychological stress" (Manderson & Mathews, 1981).

Pica

This unusual craving for nonfood items has been reported to be prevalent among some ethnic groups, e.g., Black women and children and Hispanic women and children in the Eastern United States (O'Rourke, et al., 1967; Roselle, 1970; Frankel, 1977; Vermeer & Frate, 1979) with prevalence estimated anywhere from 25-75%. Its physiological basis during pregnancy is disputed, and most of the data support a cultural/traditional base for such a practice. The most common practices described in the literature include intake of large quantities of clay and dirt, intake of a few pounds of raw laundry starch, ice, paper, ashes, soot, and burnt matches.

Among the nutritional concerns are: the intake of parasitic eggs with clay and dirt; complexing of nutrients in the intestinal tract by elements in clay and dirt; intake of toxic elements in clay, dirt, paper, ashes, soot; and displacement of nutrient intake by laundry starch and ice. Presently, there are no known physiological benefits of pica.

Nausea and Vomiting During Pregnancy

Some nausea and vomiting occur in most pregnancies, and are generally attributed to hormonal changes. Moderate nausea and vomiting are regarded as physiological adjustments to the pregnant state. In contrast, the two ends of the continuum, i.e., absence of nausea, and severe nausea such as is manifested in hyperemesis gravidarum, have been associated with psychological maladjustments (Harvey & Sherfey, 1954; Guttmacher, 1960; Taylor, 1962; Fairweather, 1968; Uddenberg, Nilsson & Almgren, 1971). Harvey and Sherfey found that sexual disturbances occurred with greater frequency among pregnant women with severe nausea and vomiting. Fairweather demonstrated more ambivalence and uncertainty toward the pregnancy among pregnant women with hyperemesis than among those with moderate nausea. Uddenberg, Nilsson and Almgren investigated the psychological bases of nausea and vomiting during pregnancy. Exploring 152 cases, they were able to divide the sample into three groups, i.e., those with exaggerated or serious nausea; moderate nausea; and absence of nausea. The group with moderate nausea exhibited significantly less adjustment difficulties than either of the remaining two groups.

The psychogenic nature of these symptoms is interestingly illustrated by a large percentage of expectant British fathers (45%) who manifest the Couvade Syndrome, e.g., sympathetic symptoms including abdominal pain, nausea, cravings (Dickens & Trethowan, 1971).

How do all these impact the dietary behavior of pregnant women? Regardless of the origin of these dietary changes, that is, whether or not they are physiologically, psychologically, or culturally based, it appears that the modifications are transitory and apply only to the pregnant state. From the nutritionist's perspective, dietary practices that are potentially hazardous to the fetus or the mother should be modified. Recognition of the bases of such practices would be the first step in developing strategies to overcome deeply ingrained beliefs.

On the other hand, dietary practices without demonstrable deleterious effects, and certainly those with known beneficial effects, should be encouraged or reinforced. For instance, cravings for dairy products and fruits substantially increase the quality of the diet, and should be encouraged.

Dietary Patterns During Lactation

Lactation, like pregnancy, is a phase in a woman's life that is vulnerable to major changes in dietary patterns. The concern about dietary substances being passed on to the suckling infant, with possible adverse effects, has been a predominant reason for these dietary changes.

Whether or not such dietary changes have scientific basis and are therefore warranted remains debatable (Evans et al., 1981; Gerrard, 1978; Jakobsson & Lindberg, 1978; Jenkins, 1981). In a study of 19 breastfeeding women with colicky babies, Jakobsson and Lindberg (1978) found that removal of milk from the mother's diet diminished colic in their infants, with exacerbation of the condition on reintroduction of milk into the maternal diet. A number of anecdotal reports of similar cases were subsequently published (Gerrard, 1978; Jenkins, 1981).

Evans and colleagues (1981), however, conducted a double-blind, placebo-controlled study with 20 women who exclusively breastfed infants with persistent colic. In contrast to the findings of Jakobsson and Lindberg, Evans and colleagues did not find any effect of maternal milk intake on colic. Intake of chocolate and fruit, however, was statistically related to a higher rate of colic in the infants. The rate of colic also increased as the diversity of the mother's diet increased. The authors speculate that colic in exclusively breastfed infants may be influenced by factors in the maternal diet, although not necessarily by a single food item.

The fact that substances do pass from the maternal circulation into the breastmilk has been established through studies on drug disposition in various secretions and excretions (Lawrence, 1980; Wilson, 1984). Several factors are known to affect transfer of substances, including size of the molecule, solubility in water and in lipids, and binding to plasma proteins versus milk proteins. It is evident that there are particular drugs and contaminants that may be secreted in breastmilk in significant amounts. There is no comparable data base, however, on food substances, with the exception of caffeine (Berlin et al., 1984; Tyrala & Dodson, 1979). Intake of as few as two to four cups of coffee per day by lactating women has been related to wakefulness and irritability in the infant.

What does all this mean for the lactating woman and her family? Should she be vigilant about her diet and avoid foods that tend to elicit adverse symptoms in her infant? If she did change her dietary practices, for how long would she have to adhere to these special food choices? How would these new food practices impact the family diet?

Although there are several reports of food practices during lactation among cultures in developing countries (Bolton, 1972; Darwish, Amine & Abdalla, 1982; Rao, 1985), the literature is sparse on Western practices (Walter, 1975). Lactating women in some non-Western cultures reportedly avoid such foods as yogurt, milk, spices, onions, leeks, radishes, melons and fish.

Eaton-Evans and Dugdale (1986) investigated food avoidance in a Western culture (Australia) and found that among 123 lactating mothers, 73% restricted their diets to prevent or treat particular symptoms in their infants. Some of the foods most commonly avoided, because of associated adverse effects in infants, included cabbage, chocolate, spicy foods like curries and pizza, peas, onions, cauliflower, oranges, broccoli and brussels sprouts. The authors suggest that food avoidance during lactation is not limited to cultures in developing countries. The practice is probably prevalent in Western cultures, although not widely reported.

Regardless of the culture in which these food avoidances are practiced, their scientific bases remain to be demonstrated. Nonetheless, the probably universal practice has widespread implications, including nutritional adequacy of the mother's diet and impact of the mother's diet on the family diet, e.g., is the family diet limited to the mother's new food choices, or must there be two sets of menus if the rest of the family decides they cannot accommodate to the mother's dietary changes? In either case, additional stress is introduced into the family dynamics, over and above the stresses generally associated with the birth of the infant.

In consideration of the stress that results from these dietary changes, the questions that arise are: (1) Can these new food practices be avoided or minimized? (2) If not, for how long do these practices generally last?

The paucity of controlled studies on the effects of the maternal diet on the infant precludes an adequate answer to the first question. The anecdotal reports of the maternal diet eliciting adverse symptoms in the infant, together with scientifically established data on secretion of particular substances through breastmilk, however, indicate that there are certain foods that are more likely than others to cause the infant's discomfort. For instance, milk, chocolate, spicy foods, strongly flavored vegetables, and citrus fruits and juices appear frequently in anecdotal reports as offending foods and may have a basis for avoidance by a lactating woman. Careful and ongoing dietary observation could guide her in minimizing the list of food avoidances. The fact that drug/contaminant disposition in breastmilk is dose related may also translate to smaller size servings of suspect foods, rather than total avoidance.

Given these dietary changes, the second question is: How long do they generally last? The prevalence and duration of breastfeeding continues to increase in Western societies, after having experienced a low in the early 1970s (Martinez & Dodd, 1983; Persson & Samuelson, 1984), although these patterns may not be reflected in certain ethnic groups and in the lower socioeconomic levels (Rassin et al., 1984; Smith et al., 1982). This means that there are more families whose dietary patterns are impacted by the lactating mother's diet. The duration of breastfeeding very often lasts for six months, and occasionally 9-12 months. The infant's overall development continues steadily during this period. Sensitivity to substances in breastmilk and to various foods diminish. By the age of 12 months, most infants are eating table foods directly. Given these observations, it is likely that the most stressful period for the family (diet-wise) occurs during the first two to three months, and lasts less than one year. Unfortunately, this coincides with all the other stresses associated with childbirth. The best one can hope for is minimization of any stress, including diet-induced stress. Finally, the knowledge that this diet-induced stress lasts only for a limited time may help the family cope with this problem effectively.

Dietary Habits of Preschoolers and Their Parents

In the transition from pregnancy to childrearing, what changes take place in the mother's eating habits? In the father's eating habits? What interactions will ultimately determine the eating habits of this new, young family as the new generation begins?

There were no articles dealing directly with these questions uncovered through the literature search. There are, however, a number of studies that describe food preferences of preschoolers and older children, some including their parents. Drawing from these, one might then describe changes that are likely to occur in dietary patterns from pregnancy through young parenthood. Nonetheless, the more fundamental issue of the dynamics of parent-infant, parent-child, parent-parent interaction from which food habits emerge remains a researchable question.

Exploration of this topic may elucidate facets of food habits which could lead to a better understanding of how they form and evolve; why culturally acquired habits are difficult to change; and what strategies might be developed to either reinforce beneficial habits or modify harmful habits.

A recurrent finding with respect to food preferences of preschoolers is their preference for sweet foods. In addition to a demonstrated inborn preference for the sweet taste (Beauchamp & Maller, 1977), adult practices of rewarding, reinforcing and/or conditioning young children's behaviors with sweets (Eppwright et al., 1969; Birch, Zimmerman & Hind, 1980), and television advertisements of sweets aired during children's programs (Gussow, 1972; Galst, 1980) further encourage this preference.

Feeney, Dodds and Lowenberg (1966) found that this preference for sweets persists into later childhood and is associated with parents' preferences. Ritchey and Olson (1983) investigated family variables and children's preference for and consumption of sweets, with 122 preschool children and their parents. Although no statistically significant relationships were found among family variables and children's consumption of sweets, there was a strong association between children's and parents' consumption of sweets and T.V. watching. This persistent preference for sweets is of particular concern to nutritionists and other health professionals because a number of chronic diseases have been linked to the high intake of refined sugars in the United States (Healthy People, 1979).

Factors that modify food preferences of young children may be derived from studies by Harper and Sanders (1975) and Birch, Zimmerman and Hind (1980). Harper and Sanders demonstrated that children tended to taste new, unfamiliar foods more so when the adults offering the foods also ate the food, than when the food was merely offered to them. They also found that preschool-age children were more likely to accept these foods with repeated offerings than were older children. This suggests that receptiveness to environmental stimuli may diminish with age, and reinforces the idea of a sensitive period for molding food habits. Alternatively, there may be different kinds of stimuli which elicit food preference responses at different age groups. For instance, Kirks, Hendricks and Wyse (1982) suggest that peer pressure may be more influential in older children than it is in younger children, although Birch (1980b) demonstrated that peer pressure is effective with preschoolers.

Birch and colleagues (1980) in a study with 64 preschool children explored the social-affective context in which snack foods were presented to the children. The preschool teachers (i.e., friendly, familiar adults) were instructed to present the snacks to the children under one of three conditions, twice a day: *Reward* condition, during which the snack was given for a "potentially rewardable" behavior at the teacher's discretion; *noncontingent attention* condition, during which the snack was given in a friendly manner but not related to any particular behavior; or a *nonsocial* condition in which the snack was placed, impersonally in the child's locker. Food preference was measured at the onset of the study, at four weeks and at its completion at six weeks. Food preference was also measured six weeks after the completion of the snack study program to assess endurance of these preferences.

Food preference was enhanced when given under the *reward* and *noncontingency attention* conditions, and persisted for six weeks after the program. Moreover, the food preference was not related to sweetness of the snack. This is remarkable in view of the finding that sweetness of a food and familiarity with a food are two of the most influential factors affecting food preference in preschoolers (Birch, 1979a). It appears therefore, that food preferences are subject to conditioning at the preschool age, and that strategies may be developed to reinforce certain food preferences. For instance, the authors suggest that the use of nutrient-dense foods, rather than sweets, for rewards would enhance a preference for these foods. In addition, repeated offering of a given food in a positive social context might also enhance preference for it.

It is worth noting that food preference is a strong determinant of children's food consumption, and that it is a stronger determinant for children than it is for adults (Birch, 1979b). Birch proposes that children are unshackled by factors compounding adult food consumption. These might include such factors as socioeconomic, e.g., cost, availability; psychological, e.g., prestige; physiological, e.g., nutritional value (Dwyer & Alston, 1976; Bassler & Newell, 1982; Bass, Owsley & McNutt, 1985).

What can we glean about young parents' eating habits and attitudes from studies on young children and their parents? The trend that becomes apparent is that there is a slight similarity between young child-mother food preferences, which is less discernible between the young child and father (Bryan & Lowenberg, 1958; Birch, 1980b). Among young adults (e.g., college-age), however, there appears to be significant resemblance of food preferences with those of parents (Pliner, 1983), particularly with the same sex parent. The educational level of mothers positively correlates with dietary complexity score of children in grades K-3 (Yperman & Vermeersch, 1979). Involvement of parents in a nutrition education program for elementary school children resulted in increased quality of the children's diets, as assessed by dietary complexity (Kirks, Hendricks & Wyse, 1982).

These findings suggest several possibilities. As pointed out earlier, complexity or diversity of diet, which is positively related to nutritional quality of the diet (Sanjur & Scoma, 1971; Schorr, Sanjur & Erichson, 1972) increases with age (Greger, Divilbiss & Aschenbeck, 1979; Randall & Lorimor, 1984). Young adults generally have nutritionally acceptable dietary habits. If young parents' food preferences resemble those of their young children, it may mean that their dietary habits regress nutritionally during the period of childrearing. The fact that college age students' food preferences resemble those of their parents, whose food habits are presumably of acceptable nutritional quality, would support this speculation.

In an informal survey conducted with eight mothers of children under 12 years regarding comparison of diets prior to and following birth of children, by recall, 100% admitted to a change in dietary habits (Aljadir, unpublished data). The type of dietary change, basically included increased intake of what the subjects referred to as "junk food" such as sweets, salty snack foods, and pre-sweetened cereal. These foods are generally regarded by nutritionists as calorie-dense, in contrast to nutrient-dense. The most common reason cited for the change was accommodation to the children's food preferences.

How long these changes persist is subject to speculation. The dietary shifts are probably dependent on a number of factors such as family dynamics, number of children, ages and sex of children, and several socioeconomic variables. Recent research demonstrates that young children accept formerly rejected foods on repeated offerings. This suggests that parents of young children may have to learn to stand their ground and repeatedly offer foods until the young child accepts them. This would obviate the need to accommodate to the young child's food choices, which generally compromises the nutritional quality of the family diet.

CONCLUSION

Transition to parenthood is a momentous event capable of initiating changes in habitual patterns, including dietary habits. I have attempted to derive and integrate trends in the evolution of dietary habits with transition to parenthood, utilizing the research literature on independent but related topics: dietary habits of prospective parents; dietary habits during pregnancy; and dietary habits of young children and their parents.

There is some evidence to support that the dietary habits of young adults are generally nutritionally acceptable. Dietary cravings and aversions during pregnancy, whether psychologically or physiologically based, result in temporary changes in eating patterns. Unless these occur with severe symptoms of nausea and vomiting or with pica, which is the craving for and ingestion of nonfood items, dietary cravings and aversions of pregnancy do not generally impair the nutritional quality of a woman's diet.

In contrast, there may be reason to believe that the woman's dietary habits deteriorate with childrearing, as the vulnerable growing child's eating habits are molded by an increasing array of external influences, including the barrage of television commercials for non-nutritious products. The well-meaning young mother (and/or father) may be fighting a losing battle in trying to uphold what she/he believes to be healthful eating habits in view of these enticements.

Young parents may yield to pressures that come to bear with disciplining of children, and accommodate to the food preferences of their young children. Interestingly, Eppwright et al., (1969) noted that although parents lament the high intake of sweets by their children, 62% of the 2000 families surveyed responded positively to the use of sweets as rewards.

After reviewing the available literature, this paper raises several researchable questions: Are there, in fact, measurable dietary changes that occur with transition to parenthood? If so, what are these and how do they affect the nutritional quality of the diet? What factors affect the formation and evolution of young children's food habits? What factors operate at the various age groups? What happens to cultural food patterns in cross-cultural families? How much influence do parents' food habits exert on children's food habits at various ages? How much influence do children's food habits exert on each parent's food habits?

In addition to the purely academic benefits of researching these questions, practical applications of the information gained include development of strategies to help mold and maintain healthful lifetime eating habits.

It is hoped that the material reviewed here would stimulate research in this field.

REFERENCES

Adrian, J. and Daniel, R. (1976). Impact of socioeconomic factors on consumption of selected food nutrients in the United States. *American Journal of Agricultural Economics, 58*:31-38.

Barber, S.A. and Bull, N.L. (1985). Food and nutrient intakes by British women aged 15-25 years, with particular reference to dietary habits and iron intakes. *Ecology of Food and Nutrition, 16*:161-169.

Bartholomew, M.J. and Poston, F.E. (1970). Effect of food taboos on prenatal nutrition. *Journal of Nutrition Education, 2*:15-17.

Bass, M.A., Owsley, D.W. and McNutt, V.T. (1985). Food preferences and food prestige ratings by black women in East Tennessee. *Ecology of Food and Nutrition, 16*:75-83.

Bassler, E. and Newell, G.K. (1982). Food shopping behavior and food use by well-educated young parents. *Journal of Nutrition Education, 14*:146-149.

Beauchamp, G.K. and Maller, O. (1977). The development of flavor preferences in humans: A review. In M.R. Karl and O. Maller (Eds.), *The Chemical Senses and Nutrition* (pp. 291-310). New York: Academic Press.

Berlin, C.M., Jr., Denson, H.M., Daniel, C.H. and Ward, R.M. (1984). Disposition of dietary caffeine in milk, saliva and plasma of lactating women. *Pediatrics, 73*:59-63.

Birch, L.L. (1979a). Dimensions of preschool children's food preferences. *Journal of Nutrition Education, 11*:77-80.

Birch, L.L. (1979b). Preschool children's food preferences and consumption patterns. *Journal of Nutrition Education, 11*:189-192.

Birch, L.L. (1980a). Effects of peer model's food choices and eating behavior on preschoolers' food preferences. *Child Development, 51*:480-496.

Birch, L.L. (1980b). The relationship between children's food preferences and those of their parents. *Journal of Nutrition Education, 12*:14-18.

Birch, L.L., Zimmerman, S.I. and Hind, H. (1980). The influence of social-affective context on the formation of children's food preferences. *Child Development, 51*:856-861.

Bolton, J.M. (1972). Food taboos among the Orang Asli in West Malaysia: A potential nutritional hazard. *American Journal of Clinical Nutrition. 25*:789-799.

Brown, C.L., Brown, A.M. and Naismith, D.J. (1977). A survey of the attitudes of members of the Nutrition Society to current hypotheses relating diet and health. *Proceedings of the Nutrition Society, 36*:96A.

Bryan, M.S. and Lowenberg, M.E. (1958). The father's influence on young children's food preferences. *Journal of the American Dietetic Association, 34*: 30-35.

Darwish, O.A., Amine, E.K. and Abdalla, S.M. (1982). Food habits during pregnancy and lactation in Iraq. *Food and Nutrition Bulletin. 4(3)*:14-16.

Dennis, B. and Shifflett, P.A. (1985). A conceptual and methodological model for studying dietary habits in the community. *Ecology of Food and Nutrition, 17*:253-262.

Dickens, G. and Trethowan, W.H. (1971). Cravings and aversions during pregnancy. *Journal of Psychosomatic Research, 15*:259-268.

Dwyer, J. and Alston, E. (1976). Nutrition in family life. *Food Product Development, 10*:49-50.

Eaton-Evans, J.M. and Dugdale, A.E. (1986). Food avoidance by breastfeeding mothers in South East Queensland. *Ecology of Food and Nutrition, 19*:123-129.

Ebrahim, G.J. (1980). Cross-cultural aspects of pregnancy and breast feeding. *Proceedings of the Nutrition Society, 39*:13-15.

Edwards, C.H., McSwain, H. and Haire, S. (1954). Odd dietary practices of women. *Journal of the American Dietetic Association, 30*:976-981.

Eppwright, E.S., Fox, H.M., Fryer, B.A., Lamkin, G.H., and Vivian, V.M. (1969). Eating behavior of preschool children. *Journal of Nutrition Education, 1*:16-19.

Evans, R.W., Allardyce, R.A., Ferguson, D.M. and Taylor, B. (1981). Maternal diet and infantile colic in breast-fed infants. *Lancet i:*1340-1342.

Fairweather, D.V.I. (1968). Nausea and vomiting in pregnancy. *American Journal of Obstetrics and Gynecology, 102*:135-175.

Fathauer, G.H. (1960). Food habits—an anthropologists view. *Journal of the American Dietetic Association, 37*:335-338.

Feeney, M.C., Dodds, M.L. and Lowenberg, M.E. (1966). The sense of taste of preschool children and their parents. *Journal of the American Dietetic Association, 48*:399-403.

Foley, C., Hertzler, A.A. and Anderson, H.L. (1979). Attitudes and food habits—A review. *Journal of the American Dietetic Association, 75*:13-18.

Frankel, B. (1977). *Childbirth in the Ghetto*. San Francisco: R & E Research Associates, Inc.

Galst, J.P. (1980). Television food commercials and pronutritional public service announcements as determinants of young children's snack choices. *Child Development, 51*:935-939.

Gerrard, J. (1978). Cow's milk as a cause of colic in breastfed infants (letter). *Lancet ii:*734.

Gersovitz, M., Madden, J.P. and Smiciklas-Wright, H. (1978). Validity of the 24-hour recall and seven-day record for group comparison. *Journal of the American Dietetic Association, 73;*48-55.

Greger, J.L., Divilbiss, L. and Aschenbeck, S.K. (1979). Dietary habits of adolescent females. *Ecology of Food and Nutrition, 7*:213-218.

Gussow, J. (1972). Counternutritional messages of TV ads aimed at children. *Journal of Nutrition Education, 4*:48-52.

Guthrie, H.A. and Scheer, J.A. (1981). Nutritional adequacy of self-selected diets that satisfy the four food groups guide. *Journal of Nutrition Education, 13*:46-49.

Guttmacher, A.F. (1960). Hyperemesis. In A.F. Guttmacher and J.J. Rovinsky (eds.), *Medical, Surgical and Gynecological Complications of Pregnancy*, (pp. 178-181) Baltimore: Williams and Wilkins.

Harper, L.V. and Sanders, K.M. (1975). The effects of adults' eating on young children's acceptance of unfamiliar foods. *Journal of Experimental Child Psychology, 20*:206-214.

Harvey, W.A. and Sherfey, M.J. (1954). Vomiting in pregnancy. *Psychosomatic Medicine, 16*:1-9.

Healthy People: The Surgeon General's Report on Health Promotion and Disease Prevention. (1979). U.S. Department of Health, Education and Welfare Publication No. 79-55071, Washington, D.C.

Hertzler, A.A., Wenkam, N. and Standell, B. (1982). Classifying cultural food habits and meanings. *Journal of the American Dietetic Association, 80*:421-425.

Hochbaum, G.M. (1981). Strategies and their rationale for changing people's eating habits. *Journal of Nutrition Education, 13* (Supplement):S59-S65.

Hook, E.B. (1978). Dietary cravings and aversions during pregnancy. *American Journal of Clinical Nutrition, 31*:1355-1362.

Jacobson, M.F., Goldman, A.S. and Syme, R.H. (1981). Coffee and birth defects (letter). *Lancet, 1*:1415-1416.

Jakobsson, I. and Lindberg, T. (1978). Cow's milk as a cause of infantile colic in breastfed infants. *Lancet ii*:437-439.

Jenkins, G.H.C. (1981). Milk-drinking mothers with colicky babies. *Lancet, ii*:261.

Jerome, N.W. (1969). Northern urbanization and food consumption patterns of southern-born negroes. *American Journal of Clinical Nutrition, 22*:1667-1669.

Johnson, D.W. and Johnson, R.T. (1985). Nutrition education: A model for effectiveness, a synthesis of research. *Journal of Nutrition Education, 17(Supplement)*:S20-S24.

Kirks, B.A., Hendricks, D.G. and Wyse, B.W. (1982). Parent involvement in nutrition education for primary grade students. *Journal of Nutrition Education, 14*:137-140.

Landman, J. and Hall, J. St. E. (1983). The dietary habits and knowledge of folklore of pregnant Jamaican women. *Ecology of Food and Nutrition, 12*:203-210.

Lawrence, R.A. (1980). *Breast-Feeding. A Guide for the Medical Profession.* C.V. Mosby Co., St. Louis, pp. 157-171.

Linn, S., Schoenbaum, S.C., Monson, R.R., Rosner, B., Stubblefield, P.G., and Ryan, K.J. (1982). No association between coffee consumption and adverse outcomes of pregnancy. *New England Journal of Medicine, 306*:141-145.

Manderson, L. and Mathews, M. (1981). Vietnamese behavioral and dietary precautions during pregnancy. *Ecology of Food and Nutrition, 11*:1-8.

Martinez, G.A. and Dodd, D. (1983). 1981 Milk feeding patterns in the United States during the first 12 months of life. *Pediatrics, 71*:166-170.

McKenzie, J. (1974). The impact of economic and social status on food choice. *Proceedings of the Nutrition Society, 33*:67-73.

McNeil, N.I. and McNeil, R. (1984). How people judge the healthiness of foods. *Proceedings of the Nutrition Society, 44*:12A.

Mead, M. (1943). The factor of food habits. *American Academy of Political Science and Sociology Annals, 225*:136-141.

Musaiger, A.I. (1983). The impact of television food advertisements on dietary behaviour of Bahraini housewives. *Ecology of Food and Nutrition, 13*;109-114.

National Center for Health Statistics (1979). *Food Consumption Profiles of White and Black Persons Aged 1-74 Years: United States 1971-1974*, Hyattsville, MD:DHEW Publication No. 79-1658.

O'Rourke, D.E., Quinn, J.G., Nicholson, J.O., and Gibson, H.H. (1967). Geophagia during pregnancy. *Obstetrics and Gynecology, 29*:581-584.

Persson, L.A. and Samuelson, G. (1984). From breastmilk to family food. *Acta Paediatrica Scandinavica, 73*:685-692.

Phillips, D.E., Bass, M.E., and Yetley, E. (1978). Use of food and nutrition knowledge by mothers of preschool children. *Journal of Nutrition Education, 10*:73-75.

Pilgrim, F.J. (1961). What foods do people accept or reject? *Journal of the American Dietetic Association, 38*:439-443.

Pliner, P. (1983). Family resemblance in food preferences. *Journal of Nutrition Education, 15*:137-140.

Randall, E. and Lorimor, R. (1984). Variability in food consumption patterns of adults in the U.S. population. *Ecology of Food and Nutrition, 15*:215-224.

Rao, M. (1985). Food beliefs of rural women during the reproductive years in Dharwad, India. *Ecology of Food and Nutrition, 16*:93-103.

Rassin, D.K., Richardson, C.J., Baranowski, T., Nader, P.R., Guenther, N., Bee, D.E., and Brown, J.P. (1984). Incidence of breast feeding in a low socio-economic group of mothers in the United States: Ethnic patterns. *Pediatrics, 73*:132-137.

Reaburn, J.A., Krondl, M. and Lau, D. (1979). Social determinants of food selection. *Journal of the American Dietetic Association, 74*:637-641.

Ritchey, N. and Olson, C. (1983). Relationship between family variables and children's preference for and consumption of sweet foods. *Ecology of Food and Nutrition, 13*:257-266.

Roselle, H.A. (1970). Association of laundry starch and clay ingestion with anemia in New York City. *Archives of Internal Medicine, 125*:57-61.

Sanjur, D. and Scoma, D. (1971). Food habits of low-income children in Northern New York. *Journal of Nutrition Education, 2*:85-95.

Schorr, B.C., Sanjur, D. and Erichson, E. (1972). Teenage food habits. *Journal of the American Dietetic Association, 61*:415-420.

Schwab, E.B. and Axelson, M.L. (1984). Dietary changes of pregnant women: compulsions and modifications. *Ecology of Food and Nutrition, 14*:143-153.

Seifrit, E. (1961). Changes in beliefs and food practices in pregnancy. *Journal of the American Dietetic Association, 39*:455-466.

Shaywitz, S.E., Cohen, D.J., and Shaywitz, B.A. (1980). Behavior and learning deficits in children of normal intelligence born to alcoholic mothers. *Journal of Pediatrics, 96*:978-982.

Sims, L.S. (1978). Food-related value-orientations, attitudes and beliefs of vegetarians. *Ecology of Food and Nutrition. 7*:23-35.

Smith, J.C., Mhango, C.G., Warren, C.W., Rochat, R.W. and Huffman, S.L. (1982). Trends in the incidence of breastfeeding for Hispanics of Mexican origin and Anglos on the US-Mexico border. *American Journal of Public Health, 72*:59-61.

Smith, P.B., Levenson, P.M. and Morrow, J.R. (1985). Prenatal knowledge and informational priorities of pregnancy adolescents. *Health Values, 9* (5):33-39.

Snow, L.F. and Johnson, S.M. (1978). Folklore, food, female reproductive cycle, *Ecology of Food and Nutrition, 7*:41-49.

Taylor, H.P. (1962). Nausea and vomiting of pregnancy: Hyperemesis gravidarum. In W.S. Kroger (Ed.), *Psychosomatic Obstetrics, Gynecology and Endocrinology*, (pp. 117-130). Springfield: Charles C Thomas.

Ten-State Nutrition Survey, 1968-1970. (1972). DHEW Publication no. (HSM) 72-8130-72-8133. Atlanta.

Tierson, F.D., Olsen, C.L. and Hook, E.B. (1985). Influence of cravings and aversions on diet in pregnancy. *Ecology of Food and Nutrition, 17*:117-129.

Tucci, S.M., and Skalko, R.G. (1978). The teratogenic effects of theophylline in mice. *Toxicology Letters, 1*:337-341.

Tyrala, E.E. and Dodson, W.E. (1979). Caffeine secretion into breastmilk. *Archives of Disease in Childhood, 54*:787-800.

Uddenberg, N., Nilsson, A. and Almgren, P.E. (1971). Nausea in pregnancy: Psychological and psychosomatic aspects. *Journal of Psychosomatic Research, 15*:269-276.

Vermeer, D. and Frate, D.A. (1979). Geophagia in rural Mississippi: Environmental and cultural contents and nutritional implications. *American Journal of Clinical Nutrition, 32*:2129-2135.

Walter, M. (1975). The folklore of breastfeeding. *Bulletin of the New York Academy of Medicine, 51*:870-876.

West, J., Hodges, C., and Black, A. (1981). Prenatal exposure to ethanol alters the organization of hippocampal mossy fibers in rats. *Science, 211*:957-959.

Wilson, J.T. (1984). Human milk. In Freed, D.L.J. (ed), *Health Hazards of Milk*. Baillier Tindall, Eastbourne, England. pp. 12-26.

Wolff, R.J. (1973). Who eats for health? *American Journal of Clinical Nutrition, 26*:438-445.

Yperman, A.M. and Vermeersch, J.A. (1979). Factors associated with children's food habits. *Journal of Nutrition Education, 11*:72-76.

Yudkin, J. (1963). Changing food habits. *Lancet, ii*:728-729.

Zajonc, R.B. and Markus, H. (1982). Affective and cognitive factors in preferences. *Journal of Consumer Research, 9*:123-131.

Zimmerman, R.R. and Munro, N. (1972). Changing Head Start mothers' food attitudes and practices. *Journal of Nutrition Education, 4*:66-68.

Strain in the Transition to Parenthood

Frances K. Grossman

The concept of strain as an important factor in the transition to parenthood is a recent one. This paper defines strain as it has been used in the literature, and describes the studies that have predicted strain during this period of transition. Then interventions that have been shown to ameliorate strain in new parents are described.

Although there are a few earlier articles that studied dimensions related to strain (discussed below), until recently, most researchers focused on other aspects of the transition to parenthood: severe psychopathological reactions (e.g., Lacoursiere, 1972), and then more recently, marital and parental problems as outcomes of difficulties with this transition (e.g., Belsky, Spanier & Rovine, 1983; Grossman, Eichler, & Winickoff et al., 1980). Strain refers to the *experienced* discomfort of individuals in the transition to parenthood. It is reflected in a negative mood, often accompanied by a sense of being overwhelmed and inadequate to the demands of the situation (Feldman, in press). Thus it does not include inferred distress, as might be reflected in lower self-esteem, the development of psychophysiological symptoms, or marital tensions, which reside in the relationship between a couple.

The concept of strain implies a relatively short-lived, potentially benign reaction, and hence excludes more severe and pathological reactions such as postpartum depression or psychosis. Researchers interested in strain suggest that women and men may have uncomfortable, dysphoric reactions that are greatly influenced by the context—i.e., being in the beginning stages of family development,

Frances K. Grossman, PhD, is Professor in the Department of Psychology, Boston University, Boston, MA 02215.

and that these reactions are important, in part because if not dealt
with, they may have problematic consequences for one or more
members of the family. Strains are normal, part of life, not diseases. Finally, the concept of strain suggests a mutability. One contributing factor or another might be moved around, to relieve or
transform the strain.

Although a focus on strain requires a somewhat artificial separation of experiential, inferential, and observational measures, there
is value in looking particularly at these data, as reflecting one important dimension of men's and women's adaptations to early parenthood. Reactions of each spouse to the transition to parenthood
are viewed here as occurring within a couple's system, and as
greatly influenced by each other's reactions, as well as by other
characteristics of the family system. Thus, this paper centers on
studies that have examined these feelings and experiences in both
wives and husbands. The studies discussed gathered information on
parental experiences within the first year of the firstborn child's
life, very much within what has been considered the crisis of the
transition to parenthood. While the earlier (pre-1970s) literature is
mentioned briefly, more recent studies are given greater emphasis.

The first relevant studies were the early, and by now classical,
studies of the transition to parenthood as crisis. LeMasters (1957)
and Dyer (1963) interviewed couples and described a significant
number as having been in crisis around the transition to parenthood,
although the fact that the ratings were collected well beyond the
first year and hence were largely retrospective reduces the validity
of the findings (discussed in Grossman et al., 1980).

Hobbs (1963) was unable to replicate LeMaster's and Dyer's
findings, using a different measurement technique. In his study of
53 white, urban, first time parents, assessed when the infants were
3 to 18 weeks, few couples indicated great trauma or distress when
asked to describe their experience on a 23-item checklist. He also
found no correlation between husbands' and wives' scores. Well
over half of the men checked off that they were "somewhat" or
"very much" "bothered by" interruption of routine habits (75%)
and increased money problems (60%). For the mothers, they were
"somewhat" or "very much" "bothered by" interruption of their
routine habits (74%), tiredness and fatigue (68%), increased money

problems (66%) and feeling "edgy" or emotionally upset (60%). He found several predictors of parental distress including that the presence of extra help to care for the baby related to higher frequency of difficulty!

In another study of 32 white couples whose first child was between 6 and 32 weeks of age, Hobbs (1968) again did not replicate Dyer's or LeMaster's findings of high levels of experienced crisis. He did find, on his checklist ratings, that mothers tended to describe more experienced difficulties than fathers. He found no relationship between degree of difficulty and infant's age. The scores reflecting degree of difficulty rated from the checklist correlated with Locke-Wallace Marital Adjustment Inventory Scores (Locke & Wallace, 1959), but interview ratings of difficulty did not correlate with the marital adjustment score.

Hobbs and Cole (1976), in a replication of Hobbs' 1965 study, found significantly greater ratings of difficulty in mothers than fathers. They again found few subjects describing more than "moderate" difficulty on their checklist. They reported a significant correlation ($r = .49$, $p < .01$) between men's and women's scores, unlike Hobbs' earlier (1965) finding of no relationship.

Hobbs and Wimbish (1977) replicated the earlier Hobbs' studies using a sample" of 52 black, first time parents, heterogeneous for social class, all recruited from family planning or prenatal care clinics. Data were collected at a home visit made some time during the child's first year. As was found in the previous studies, the mean difficulty score on the checklist was significantly higher for new mothers than for new fathers. These black parents reported significantly greater difficulty than their white counterparts in previous studies.

More than 15% of the women reported being "bothered very much" about personal appearance, fatigue, excess work, and having to change plans made before the baby was born. The only item more than 15% of the men described as "bothered very much" was decreased sexual responsiveness of spouse. Husbands' and wives' scores correlated significantly ($r = .38$, $p < .05$), although not very strongly. Men describing greater difficulty were younger and had less education. No variables significantly predicted the degree of difficulty for the women.

Hobbs and Wimbish conclude that the difference between the experienced stress of men and women seems to have increased over the years of this program of research. The single most problematic change reported by black and white men and women is the interruption of life-style.

One other of this series of studies was carried out by Russell (1974), who used Hobbs' checklist (Hobbs, 1968) to study 271 couples, all of whom had a first child no older than one. From her questionnaire data collected by mail, she found a small percentage of men or women describing extensive or severe degree of difficulty, and described her sample overall as experiencing a slight or moderate degree of crisis. As in the other studies, wives described more distress than husbands. Good marital adjustment and a planned pregnancy predicted lower levels of crisis for men and women.

In addition, women who were married longer experienced less discomfort. For men, less discomfort was associated with being younger and wanting more children. Their own perceptions of their baby's temperament related to the degree of crisis in both women and men, with parents of "quiet" babies (defined in this study as babies who were more often described as eating well, adapting easily to routines, sleeping through the night and being healthy) describing less stress than parents of "active" babies (defined as babies who were described more often as crying, on the move, noisy, having feeding problems, sleeping less than most their age, and having been seriously ill). While the descriptions of the quiet and active baby seem to include considerably more than the traditional temperament items, the findings do make clear that characteristics of the infant influence parents' experiences of the transition to parenthood.

In evaluating the studies in this series, Russell makes two important points. One is that the studies using interviews tended to elicit descriptions of higher levels of distress than studies using mailed questionnaires. The second is that studies with exclusively middle class respondents reported higher degrees of stress than those including blue-collar couples as well.

These studies make clear that what constitutes a crisis is partly a matter of definition. Whether researchers find crises depends upon what type of measures they use and possibly when they ask. It is probably true, as Cox (1985) argues, that it is more fruitful to conceptualize and study aspects of the complex transition to parenthood than it is to attempt to decide whether the transition constitutes a crisis.

Further, these studies underline the weakness of retrospective reports about an experience as complicated, intense and fatiguing as early parenting. Only prospective studies give any confidence about teasing out predictors of strain, although even with those there are serious problems describing causal links.

However, despite these methodological hazards, several conclusions seem likely from these data. Men and women experience some strain in the transition to parenthood, and women generally experience more than men. Black families and White families appear to struggle with similar issues. Some particularly difficult aspects of the early postpartum period include disruption of routine habits, increased financial problems, and for women particularly, fatigue.

The next studies presented are prospective, longitudinal studies of the transition to parenthood. In what can be considered the progenitor of these recent studies, Shereshefsky and Yarrow (1973) followed 64 middle- and upper-middle-class women and their husbands from early in their first pregnancy to 6 months postpartum. Because their emphasis was primarily on the women, and they did not report any variable reflecting parents' experiences in isolation from their clinical judgments of how the parents were doing, the results are not directly pertinent. (Another longitudinal study, by Entwisle and Doering, 1981, had data only to 3 weeks postpartum, with the exception of a brief telephone interview at 6 months postpartum. Their one experiential measure was depression, but because of their focus on the very early postpartum period, the depression they studied was the early postpartum "blues," which seems qualitatively different from the distress experienced later in that first year.)

The next longitudinal study described here is a project that has added importantly to our knowledge about strain, as well as about many other aspects of the transition to parenthood. The Becoming a Family Project (Cowan & Cowan, in press a, b, c; Cowan &

Cowan, 1983; Cowan, Cowan, Coie & Coie, 1978; Cowan, Cowan, Homing, Garrett, Coysh, Curtis-Boles & Boles, 1985) is a prospective longitudinal study that began following 72 couples late in their expectancy with their first child. The most recent follow-up comes from a contact when the child was 3-1/2 (Cowan & Cowan, 1985). In addition to these 72 families, they followed 24 couples from before they made the decision to have a baby, and a number of these remained childless and in the study. A particularly attractive aspect of this project is the wide range of socioeconomic statuses of couples represented. Twenty-three couples attended a 6 month couples' group, beginning in late pregnancy. At the expectancy and 6 month postpartum visits, which are the ones considered here, the women and men filled out questionnaires and were interviewed.

The measure of strain they used was Abiden and Burke's Parenting Stress Index (Abiden, 1981; Burke & Abiden, 1980). This scale, designed to focus particularly on the stresses experienced by parents in relation to their children, is made up of 150 items, grouped into a number of subscales describing parental and child characteristics, as well as aspects of the interaction between them, and to various life circumstances that could influence stress.

In one paper (Cowan & Cowan, 1983), for both men and women, self-esteem and marital satisfaction measured concurrently were significant correlates of parenting strain. For men, low self-esteem and high life stress late in their wives' expectancy predicted higher parental stress at 6 months postpartum. For the women, marital satisfaction and self-esteem were significant longitudinal predictors of parenting stress at 6 months postpartum. The Cowans interpret these findings, in the context of other data going beyond the one year transition, as reflecting men's individually-focused instrumental outlook, and women's emphasis on the quality of the expressive network they inhabit. It is clear from their findings at later data points that men's and women's parenting stress is influenced by both individual and couple dimensions, although the apparent pathways of these lines of influence, and their relative centrality, are often different.

In a more detailed examination of antecedents in men's lives of their parenting stress at 6 months (Cowan et al., 1985), they found several significant predictors in addition to low self-esteem. In particular, a description of less cohesion in their family of origin, and the men's own predictions late in the expectancy that they would not be very involved in caring for the child, predicted higher parenting stress at 6 months.

Beyond these specific findings, the Cowans present a convincing argument that the family has to be understood as an interconnected, interdependent system, with individual psychological characteristics of each parent, couple characteristics, historical factors from each parent's family of origin, current social supports and work dimensions all playing a role in how families traverse the transition to parenthood. They also believe, on the basis of their own data as well as those of others, that the centerpost or key to the transition is the quality of the marriage, and a couple's capacity to keep it satisfying and involving in the face of all the inevitable changes it must undergo in the process of this transition.

The Boston University Pregnancy and Parenthood Project (Grossman et al., 1980) is also a longitudinal study that has examined many of the same issues. This paper discusses data from couples expecting their first child, who were first seen early in their expectancy. The pertinent follow-up visits were at 2 months and one year postpartum, although the study has data from two and five years, as well (Fedele, Golding, Grossman & Pollack, in press; Grossman, in press; Pollack & Grossman, 1985). At each visit, each parent was interviewed individually and given a variety of self-administered scales to complete. While there was no direct measure of strain, parents' experienced discomfort was reflected in their responses to tests of anxiety and depression assessed by standardized tests.

For the women, their anxiety and depression at 2 months postpartum was strongly predicted by their anxiety and depression early in pregnancy. Women who had been more satisfied with their marriages during the pregnancy were significantly less anxious and depressed at 2 months. Women who had better overall life adaptation when assessed early in the pregnancy were less depressed at 2 months. Women who were more affiliative in early pregnancy were significantly less anxious, and women who had been more autonomous and affiliative were significantly less depressed (Grossman, in press; Fedele et al., 1985).

Anxiety and depression in pregnancy continued to predict their anxiety at one year postpartum, and their adaptation to pregnancy predicted both their anxiety and depression. Women who had been functioning better in their lives in pregnancy were less anxious at one year. Women's affiliativeness was not significantly predictive of their experienced discomfort at one year, but more autonomous women were significantly less anxious at one year ($r = -.58$, $p < .001$). Women were significantly more anxious at this point if their husbands had been rated as less autonomous and affiliative in the expectancy; and men's affiliation predicted women's depression as well.

For the men, higher anxiety at 2 months and 1 year was related to their own lower life adaptation and higher anxiety in the expectancy. (Men's depression was not measured at these visits.) Men were significantly more anxious at 2 months and 1 year if their wives had been less affiliative in pregnancy.

Grossman, et al., as the Cowans, emphasize the centrality, as well as the interconnectedness, of the couple system, with personality characteristics of each influencing the experiences and adaptations of the other, in what must be circular, interactive loops.

Both studies, then, were able to predict some aspects of strain in early parenthood from the expectancy. Although the studies underline the fact that the outcomes depend upon what variables and measures are used, nonetheless, personality factors, experiences from the family of origin, and marital dimensions all seem to play some role. Predictors of men's strain appear similar to, but not identical with, predictors of women's strain, with suggestive evidence that men's own personal adaptation is a particular strong predictor for them, compared with the centrality of the marriage for their wives.

The next three described are short term longitudinal studies. In one, Kach and McGhee (1982) looked at the discrepancies between expectations of parenthood versus actual experience in 12 middle class couples seen 4 to 6 weeks before the birth and then 2 months postpartum. There was a control group of 7 couples only seen at the postpartum visit and a third group of 7 couples seen 4 to 6 weeks after the birth of their second child and then again at 2 months. All were recruited from childbirth education classes. Kach and McGhee found that for mothers, but not fathers, greater discrepancy of expectations from experience predicted more problems with such issues as energy, confidence as a parent, sexual responsiveness, and upset schedules and routines. Mothers who felt they had had less preparation for parenting, who were older (in a study in which the mean ages of the participants ranged from 28 to 30, depending on the group), and who had been married longer, had larger discrepancies between expectations and experience.

Looking at the specific areas where expectations were violated, mothers and fathers indicated they went out less than expected, and mothers spent more time diapering and washing the baby's clothes than they had anticipated. On an open-ended questionnaire about their unexpected experiences as a parent, a large proportion of mothers mentioned their surprise at their degree of attachment and love for the baby. Negative statements made by more than one-third of the mothers and a smaller though still significant proportion of the fathers included lack of sleep and energy, and the time and responsibility involved caring for the baby. More than half of the fathers and mothers noted lack of sleep as one of the five most difficult problems since the birth of the baby. More than one-third of the mothers also listed extra work required by the baby, not knowing what to do when the baby cried or was sick, and lack of social life or time for oneself. Besides lack of sleep or energy, the only other item listed by at least one-third of the fathers was lack of social life or time for oneself.

There were no differences in the posttest scores between couples who had had the pretest questionnaire and those who did not, and no differences between experienced couples prebirth expectancies and first time couples postpartum experiences: the couples who had been through it before already knew!

It is important to note that while first time parenthood turned out to be a less positive experience than couples had expected, viewed from the vantage point of two months postpartum, it nonetheless still was positive.

Finally, expectations significantly influenced mothers' experiences, while fathers did not experience a dramatic change, and the degree of change was not predicted by their discrepancy scores.

In another short-term longitudinal study of the role of infant temperament on the reactions of parents, Sirignano and Lachman

(1985) assessed 22 primiparous couples in late pregnancy and again 8 to 12 weeks postpartum, and compared them with 13 childless couples over the same time span. They focused on four aspects of adult adaptation: self-efficacy expectations, sense of personal control, anxiety, and depression, all of which meet the operative criteria for strain.

Their results are complex, with some areas of what they call adult personality showing change, sometimes simply in response to the transition to parenthood and sometimes related to specific dimensions of perceived infant temperament. New parents described themselves as more efficacious at the postpartum visit, whereas nonparents did not, when examined across the same time period. Fathers showed more change overall then mothers. Parents who perceived their infants as having characteristics of an easy temperament generally experienced more positive changes then parents who perceived more difficult temperamental characteristics in their infants, and this relationship between perceived infant temperament and positive parent change was more true for men than for women. Neither anxiety level nor depression changed for mothers between late pregnancy and 8 to 12 weeks postpartum. Fathers' trait anxiety was lower at the second visit if they described their infants as easily adaptable and predominantly positive. Overall, then, perceived infant temperament did relate to change in the subjective life and comfort of new parents.

The only study that I am aware of that has focused explicitly on strain during this transition is that of Feldman (in press; Feldman & Nash, 1984; Feldman, Nash & Aschenbrenner). She and her colleagues studied 31 highly educated couples recruited in prenatal exercise classes during the last trimester in their expectancy and again when their first born was 6 to 8 months old. Both visits were in the researchers' laboratory. Each member of the couple filled out a variety of self-report scales and completed a lengthy interview. During the postpartum visit, each was also observed interacting with the baby.

An overall good mood score improved from the expectancy to 6 months postpartum, and significantly more for women than for men. For the women, the negative items (self-ratings of feeling hurt, sad, tense and overwhelmed) declined, while positive items (feeling content, fulfilled, calm) stayed the same. The women's overall good mood was strongly predicted by that same score late in pregnancy, while that was not true for the men. Feldman and Nash (1974) suggest that these findings, so discrepant from the earlier reports of crisis, are in part related to the time of the follow-ups, i.e., 6 months postpartum. This is a period when many infants have become enjoyable to many parents, and much easier than the earlier postpartum period. In fact, these data are consistent with the generally positive view expressed by parents in the Kach and McGhee (1982) study. In the transition to parenthood, as in marriage (e.g., Breskin, 1986) and in life (Campbell, 1981), people's overall evaluation of their experience is not simply the sum of their complaints. New parents often experience considerable discomfort and stress and nonetheless view the time as positive and special.

In the second study (Feldman, in press), strain was the primary outcome variable. This was operationally defined as the individual's score on 5 items of a self-report mood scale, including feeling overwhelmed, tense or keyed up, inadequate, sad for no reason and discouraged. The selection of these items was based initially on an a priori basis, and then supported by factor analyses for men and women separately, and for the groups combined.

Women's strain in early parenthood was predicted from their own expectancy scores by a less satisfying marriage, a low score on instrumentality (derived from the Bem Sex Role Inventory, Bem, 1974), and being responsible for the masculine household tasks during pregnancy (based on 4 items from an 8-item Household Responsibilities Checklist). The men's expectancy scores predicted little of the variance of the women's postpartum strain, when other variables were partialed out. The men's marital tension was the strongest predictor from the men's scores of women's strain. When men's and women's scores were all entered into the regression equation, women's being low on instrumentality and men's being high on instrumentality, and both partners describing marital problems were strong predictors of women's strain. It is important to emphasize that marital dimensions, evaluated by the woman or her husband, were the best predictors of women's strain.

For men, using only their own scores from the expectancy, strain was predicted by their level of stress (a single score based on reports of stressful life events), if the pregnancy were unplanned, being younger in age, and having a negative experience of the expectancy. Men also experienced more strain if their wives had described in the pregnancy a changing self-concept towards feeling more motherly, and a low assumption of responsibility for feminine household tasks. Finally, combining women's and men's scores to predict to the men's strain at 6 to 8 months, significant predictors were husband's stress and having a negative expectancy experience and if the pregnancy was unplanned, and younger wives and wives whose self concept had changed to being more motherly. It is important to note that marital factors were not important predictors for the men.

It is noteworthy that approximately 50% of the variance of strain in early parenthood was predicted by using predictors from late in the expectancy alone. Even without looking at the very real and salient concurrent stressors, such as infant characteristics, parental health and socioeconomic factors, a significant proportion of parents' distress can be accounted for. Beyond this point, Feldman draws several conclusions from her findings. One is that predictors of strain are significantly different for men and for women. Secondly, it is possible to make a more accurate prediction of a parent's degree of strain in the transition to parenthood if characteristics of their spouse as well as of themselves from the expectancy are known.

The results of the studies presented so far are similar in some respects, despite obvious differences in design, measures and conceptualization. They emphasize the centrality of the marriage for women's sense of comfort and confidence in the transition to parenthood. Most show strong indirect effects, that is, effects of one spouse's experiences and characteristics on the other. Lastly, they agree that predictors of men's and women's strain are different, although there are different views of what the nature of the sex differences is.

The next group of studies have either capitalized on an experiment in nature, or experimentally manipulated the experience of parents, in an effort to improve parents' experiences of the postpartum period. Because such studies focusing on *both* men and women can be counted on the fingers of both hands, and such studies focusing on *experiential* aspects of parents' lives are equally rare, several particularly relevant and important studies looking just at women are included.

This next study seems to form a bridge between the primarily descriptive studies and those attempting to influence the transition. Sostek, Scanlon and Abramson (1982) looked at the amount of naturally occurring postpartum contact between mother and newborn, in a sample of 34 primiparous women, representing a wide range of socioeconomic status, and their normal, full-term babies. A sizable minority of mothers — 6, representing 18% of the sample — were separated from the infants for at least 24 hours because of elevations in the women's own temperatures, with no other symptoms. In addition, women without fever varied in the amount of time they chose to spend with their babies. Both of these dimensions were used as independent variables. The measure relevant to strain was a forced-choice confidence questionnaire (Leiderman, Leifer, Barnett & Grobstein, 1973), indicating whether the mother thought she or specific others (her husband, her mother, a pediatrician, etc.) would be more competent at a variety of infant care tasks and an anxiety scale. The confidence measure was given at 3 days after the birth and then again 4-6 weeks postpartum, and was mailed to mothers at 6 months postpartum. The anxiety scale was given only at the 4-6 week follow-up. Reduced contact, whether through separation due to fever or to mother's choice, significantly predicted reduced confidence in mothering during the newborn period, but these differences had disappeared by 4 to 6 weeks postpartum. Separated mothers tended to express more overt anxiety at 4-6 weeks. The authors conclude that there are clear although transient improvements in maternal affect — anxiety and confidence — from increased postpartum contact. Further, they suggest that this is consistent with the literature, which supports the view that maternal affect is the response system most influenced by postpartum contact (e.g., Carlsson et al., 1978, 1979; deChateau & Wiberg, 1977a & b).

A number of other intervention studies have controlled the amount of contact between newborn and parents, in an effort to increase parental skill and/or attachment (e.g., Klaus & Kennell, 1976; Belsky, 1985; reviewed in Belsky, 1985, in Belsky & Benn, 1982, and in Sostek, Scanlon & Abramson, 1982). Many focus on preterm infants. Most attempt to influence mother-infant interactions only. Finally, as was mentioned, few consider experiential components of the parents' feelings about themselves as an outcome measure. Thus, little of this literature is directly pertinent. Three studies that did focus on full term, healthy infants, and measured some aspects of strain are described here.

Seashore, Leifer, Barnett and Leiderman (1973) found that maternal self-confidence was enhanced by extended mother-infant contact, especially for first time mothers. Durand (1960) and Greenberg, Rosenberg and Lind (1973) reported that rooming in, with the greater contact involved, related to greater feelings of confidence and competence. These and other results of early and/or extended contacts are controversial, with some recent failures to replicate (e.g., Carlsson et al., 1978, 1979). The safest conclusion is that it is not yet clear whether early and/or extended contact with the infant in the newborn period has any substantial effect on the mother's experience of strain, and particularly whether any effects last beyond the newborn period. How extended contact, either with the mother or father, influences the father's experiences of early parenthood has hardly been considered.

Another popular form of intervention has used the Brazelton Neonatal Behavioral Assessment (Brazelton, 1973) to sensitize parents to neonatal capacities, increase their own confidence, and the like (reviewed in Belsky, 1985; Belsky & Benn, 1982). In one of the few of these studies attempting to influence mothers and fathers experiences of early parenthood, Myers (1982) studied 42 middle-class first time parents. For the two experimental groups, either the mother or the father was taught to administer the Brazelton to their healthy, full-term infants. Outcome data relevant to this paper was collected in the hospital at least 6 hours after the treatment. They had two measures of comfort, one a single question asking whether the parents felt being in the study made them "more sure," or "less sure" of themselves as parents, or resulted in "no change." Another measure involved their ratings of 3 items on 5-point Likert-like scales. She found no effect in the self-described confidence of middle-class parents on the in-hospital measure from the intervention. From the single item statement of confidence, she found treatment effects for mothers only at 4 weeks postpartum. These findings provide little solid support for the role of the intervention in reducing parental strain.

One naturally occurring intervention that has been considered to have an effect on individual's experience of the transition to parenthood is childbirth education. Doering, Entwisle and Quinlan (1980) carried out a longitudinal study focused on preparation for childbirth as an important variable influencing women's enjoyment of the birth experience. They found some evidence that father's involvement in childbirth education classes increases both their own and their wives feeling of confidence and satisfaction during the postpartum period.

Cowan and Cowan (in press, b) reviewed the literature on parent groups designed to help couples make the transition to parenthood. Riebstein (in M. Lieberman, 1981) reported no improvement in maternal adjustment related to participation in a support group. In fact, Riebstein indicated that discussing their distress in a leaderless group tended to increase their feeling of role strain and dissatisfaction.

Cowan and Cowan (in press, b) also described their own couple's groups, which began in late pregnancy and continued for 6 months. Twenty-three of the couples in their Becoming a Family Project were in one of the groups, and were compared with data from 24 couples not in a group. Outcomes were assessed at 6 and 18 months. Here we are concerned with the former. While it was clear that the intervention had a positive influence on aspects of the marriage, they did not collect data reflecting directly on strain. They suggest that possibly the groups helped normalize the strains of the transition to first time parenthood, giving couples and individuals a sense that they could both understand and possibly even influence what they were experiencing. They also found stronger effects of the intervention at 18 months then they had at 6, and emphasize that new adaptations take some period to become stabilized.

In sum, when the intervention literature is selected on the basis of studies of both men and women, and on their self-perceived experiences during the first year of parenting, little of substance remains. There is some evidence that increased contact between mothers and

infants enhances mother's comfort and confidence, and thus, reduces strain, but there have been few studies, and sufficient problems replicating these few to raise serious questions about the effects. Further, nothing is known about the effects on fathers of
mothers' increased contact with the infant. Having parents observe,
or administer, the Brazelton exam to their newborn has not yet been
demonstrated to have a strong or lasting effect. Childbirth education
classes might well make a difference, but the studies necessary to
demonstrate that have by and large not yet been done. Couple's
groups may help, although their effect on strain has not been demonstrated, but it is also possible that they could increase experienced discomfort. The conclusion to date has to be that while it is
easy to imagine interventions that seem as though they should reduce strain in couples during the transition to parenthood, no satisfactory demonstration of that effect has been made.

This examination of the literature on the transition to parenthood
highlights a transition being made by researchers of early family
development. Increasingly, it has become clear that a convincing
study of a parent or of a child cannot be made in isolation, but must
be examined in the context of at least the immediate family, if not
also the broader framework of extended family and community.
How women and men feel as they come to terms with themselves as
new parents is greatly influenced by how their spouse feels and
what the relationship between them is like. It also is influenced by
characteristics of the baby. It has also become clear that to understand predictors of parents' experiences requires data from before
the birth of the baby, if not before the pregnancy. More studies have
to include control groups of adults who are not having babies, who
are followed over the same periods of time.

Finally, to look at strain in isolation is probably less fruitful than
to see individual's felt experiences as one part of a total manifestation of their reactions to early parenthood. It is entirely possible that
some parents express and experience their distress around the transition through feelings of inadequacy and depression, while others
express the same distress through constrictions of the parent-infant
relationship, or through fights with their spouse. It is only in the
context of studying a range of reactions that researchers will begin
to understand the meaning of strain in the transition to parenthood.

REFERENCES

Abiden, R.R. (1981). The Parenting Stress Index: A concurrent validity study using medical utilization data. Unpublished manuscript, Institute of Clinical Psychology, University of Virginia.

Belsky, J. (1985). Experimenting with the family in the newborn period. *Child Development, 56*(2), 407-414.

Belsky, J. & Benn, J. (1982). Beyond bonding: a family-centered approach to enhancing early parent-infant relations in the newborn period. In L. Bond & J. Joffe (Eds.) *Facilitating Infant and Early Childhood Development: Sixth Vermont Conference on the Primary Prevention of Psychopathology.* Hanover, New Hampshire: University Press of New England.

Belsky, J., Spanier, G. & Rovine, M. (1983). Stability and change in marriage across the transition to parenthood. *Journal of Marriage and the Family, 45*, 553-556.

Bem, S.L. (1974). The measurement of psychological androgyny. *Journal of Consulting and Clinical Psychology, 42*, 155-162.

Brazelton, T.B. (1973). *Neonatal Behavioral Assessment Scale.* Philadelphia: Lippincott.

Breskin, J.G. (1986). Marital satisfaction in couples with young children. Unpublished doctoral dissertation, Boston University.

Burke, W.T. & Abiden, R.R. (1980). Parenting Stress Index (PSI): a family system assessment approach. in R.R. Abiden (Ed.) *Parent Education and Intervention Handbook.* Springfield: Thomas.

Campbell, A. (1981). *The Sense of Well-being in America.* New York: McGraw-Hill.

Carlsson, S.G., Fagerberg, H., Horneman, G., Hwang, C.P., Larsson, K., Rodholm, M., Schaller, J., Danielsson, B. & Gundewall, C. (1978). Effects of amount of contact between mother and child on the mother's nursing behavior. *Developmental Psychology, 11*, 143-150.

Carlsson, S.G., Fagerberg, H., Horneman, G., Hwang, C.P., Larsson, K., Rodholm, M., Schaller, J., Danielsson, B. & Gundewall, C. (1979). Effects of various amounts of contact between mother and child on the mother's nursing behavior: a follow-up study. *Infant Behavior and Development, 2*, 209-214.

Cowan, P.A. & Cowan, C.P. (1983). Quality of couple relationships and parenting stress in beginning families. Presented at Meetings for the Society for Research in Child Development, Detroit.

Cowan, P.A. & Cowan, C.P. (1985). Pregnancy, parenthood, and children at three. Paper presented at Meeting of the Society for Research in Child Development, Toronto.

Cowan, P.A. & Cowan, C.P. (in press, a). Changes in marriage during the transition to parenthood: must we blame the baby? In G.Y. Michaels & W.A. Goldberg (Eds.) *Transition to Parenthood.* Cambridge, Massachusetts: Cambridge University Press.

Cowan, C.P. & Cowan, P.A. (in press, b). A preventive intervention for couples becoming parents. In C.F.Z. Boukydis (Ed.) *Research on Support for Parents and Infants in the Postnatal Period*. New Jersey: Ablex Pub. Co.

Cowan, C.P. & Cowan, P.A. (in press, c). Men's involvement in parenthood: identifying the antecedents and understanding the barriers. In P. Berman & F.A. Pedersen (Eds.) *Fathers' Transition to Parenthood*. Hillsdale, New Jersey: Erlbaum.

Cowan, C.P., Cowan, P.A., Coie, L. & Coie, J. (1978). Becoming a family: the impact of a first child's birth on the couple's relationship. In W. Miller & L. Newman (Eds.) *The First Child and Family Formation*. Chapel Hill: Carolina Population Center.

Cowan, C.P., Cowan, P.A., Homing, G., Garrett, E., Coysh, W.S., Curtis-Boles, H. & Boles III, A.J. (1985). Transition to parenthood: his, hers and theirs. *Journal of Family Issues, 6*(4), 451-481.

Cox, M.J. (1985). Progress and continued challenges in understanding the transition to parenthood. *Journal of Family Issues, 6*, 409-434.

de Chateau, P. & Wiberg, B. (1977a). Long-term effects on mother-infant behavior of extra contact during the first hours postpartum: 1. First observation at 36 hours. *Acta Paediatrica Scandinavica, 66*, 137-143.

de Chateau, P. & Wiberg, B. (1977b). Long-term effects on mother-infant behavior of extra contact during the first hours postpartum: 11. A follow up at three months. *Acta Paediatrica Scandinavica, 66*, 145-151.

Doering, S.G., Entwisle, D.R. & Quinlan, D. (1980). Modeling the quality of women's birth experience. *Journal of Health and Social Behavior, 21*, 12-21.

Durand, R. (1960). Rooming in — results of an inquiry. *New Zealand Journal of Medicine, 59*, 457-459.

Dyer, E. (1963). parenthood as crisis — a re-study. *Marriage and Family Living, 25*, 196-201.

Entwisle, D. & Doering, S. (1981). *The First Birth: A Family Turning Point*. Baltimore: Johns Hopkins University Press.

Fedele, N., Golding, E.R., Grossman, F.K. & Pollack, W.S. (in press). Psychological issues in adjustment to first pregnancy and early parenthood. In W. Goldberg & G. Michaels (Eds.) *Transition to Parenthood: Current Theory and Research*. Cambridge, Massachusetts: Cambridge University Press.

Feldman, S.S. (in press). Predicting strain in mothers and fathers of 6 month old infants: a short term longitudinal study. In F. Pedersen and P. Berman (Eds.) *Becoming a Father*. Hillsdale, New Jersey: Erlbaum.

Feldman, S.S. & Nash, S.C. (1984). The transition from expectancy to parenthood — impact of the firstborn child on men and women. *Sex Roles, 11*, 61-78.

Feldman, S.S., Nash, S.C. & Aschenbrenner, B.G. (1983). Antecedents of fathering. *Child Development, 54*, 1628-1636.

Greenberg, M., Rosenberg, I. & Lind, J. (1973). First mothers rooming-in with their newborns: its impact on the mother. *American Journal of Orthopsychiatry, 43*, 783-788.

Grossman, F.K. (in press). Separate and together: men's autonomy and affiliation in the transition to parenthood. In F. Pedersen and P. Berman (Eds.) *Men's Transition to Parenthood*. Hillsdale, New Jersey: Erlbaum.

Grossman, F.K., Eichler, L.S., Winickoff, S.A., et al. (1980). *Pregnancy, Birth and Parenthood*. San Francisco: Jossey Bass.

Hobbs, D. (1965). Parenthood as crisis: a third study. *Journal of Marriage and the Family, 27*, 367-372.

Hobbs, D. (1968). Transition to parenthood: a replication and an extension. *Journal of Marriage and the Family, 30*, 413-417.

Hobbs, D. & Cole, S.P. (1976). Transition to parenthood: a decade replication. *Journal of Marriage and the Family, 38*, 723-731.

Hobbs, D. & Wimbish, J.M. (1977). Transition to parenthood by black couples. *Journal of Marriage and the Family, 39*, 677-689.

Kach, J.A. & McGhee, P.E. (1982). Adjustment of early parenthood: the role of accuracy of preparenthood experiences. *Journal of Family Issues, 3*, 375-388.

Klaus, M.H. & Kennell, J.H. (1976). Labor, birth and bonding. In M.H. Klaus & J.H. Kennell (Eds.) *Maternal Infant Bonding*. St. Louis: Mosby.

Lacoursiere, R. (1972). Fatherhood and mental illness: a review and new material. *Psychiatric Quarterly, 46*, 105-124.

Leiderman, P.H., Leifer, A.D., Seashore, M.J., Barnnet, C.R., & Grobstein, R. (1973). Mother-infant interaction: effects of early deprivation, prior experience and sex of infant. *Early Development, 51*, 154-173.

LeMasters, E. (1957). Parenthood as crisis. *Marriage and Family Living, 19*, 352-355.

Lieberman, M. A. (1981). The effects of social support on responses to stress. In L. Goldberger & S. Breznitz (Eds.) *Handbook of Stress*. New York: Free Press.

Locke, H.J. & Wallace, K.M. (1959). Short marital adjustment and prediction tests: their reliability and validity. *Marriage and Family Living, 21*, 251-255.

Myers, B.J. (1982). Early intervention using Brazelton training with middle-class mothers and fathers of newborns. *Child Development, 53*, 462-471.

Pollack, W.S. & Grossman, F.K. (1985). Family interaction research. In L. L'Abate (Ed.) *Handbook of Family Psychology and Therapy*. Dow Jones-Irwin Press.

Riebstein, A. (1981). Cited in Lieberman, M.A. The effects of social support on responses to stress. In L. Goldberg and S. Brenitz (Eds.), *Handbook of Stress*. New York: Free Press.

Russell, C.S. (1974). Transition to parenthood: problems and gratifications. *Journal of Marriage and the Family, 36*, 294-302.

Seashore, M.J., Leifer, A.D., Barnett, C.R. & Leiderman, P.H. (1973). Effects of denial of early mother-infant interaction on maternal self-confidence. *Journal of Personality and Social Psychology, 26*, 369-378.

Shereshefsky, P.M. & Yarrow, L.J. (1973). *Psychological Aspects of a First Pregnancy and Early Postnatal Adaptation*. New York: Raven Press.

Sirignano, S.W. & Lachman, M.E. (1985). Personality change during the transition to parenthood: the role of perceived infant temperament. *Developmental Psychology, 21*, 558-567.

Sostek, A.M., Scanlon, J.W. & Abramson, D.C. (1982). Postpartum contact and maternal confidence and anxiety: a confirmation of short-term effects. *Infant Behavior and Development, 5*, 323-329.

Who Does What
When Partners Become Parents:
Implications for Men, Women,
and Marriage

Carolyn Pape Cowan
Philip A. Cowan

SUMMARY. Forty-seven couples who were first-time parents were assessed in late pregnancy and again at 6 and 18 months postpartum. Fifteen couples not yet decided about having a baby were assessed at equivalent times. Actual involvement in household, decision-making, and childcare roles was determined by responses to a 36-item "Who Does What?" questionnaire. Psychological involvement in parent, partner, and worker roles was also determined, as was each partner's satisfaction with behavioral and psychological involvement in each domain. On the basis of global analyses, previous studies have suggested that new parents adopt more traditional roles. Item analyses indicated that men's and women's roles change in both traditional and nontraditional ways during the transition to parenthood, depending on the item and the time of assessment. Measures of individual and couple adapation were also obtained: self-esteem, parenting stress, and marital satisfaction. Men's *involvement* in family tasks was uncorrelated with their own or their wives adaptation in pregnancy but became linked with adaptation at 6 months postpartum. However, at 18 months after birth husbands' involvement in family tasks was correlated only with wives' adaptation. For both parents, *satisfaction* with family task arrangements becomes correlated with self-esteem, parenting stress and marital quality after childbirth; these measures of adaptation are more

Carolyn Pape Cowan, PhD, is Research Psychologist and Lecturer, Department of Psychology; Philip A. Cowan, PhD, is Professor, Department of Psychology, University of California, Berkeley, CA 94720.

closely linked with role satisfaction than with actual sharing of family work.

Discussions of family roles in the early childrearing years almost inevitably focus on partners' division of household tasks, care of the children, and providing the family income. The ideology about how men and women should share these family roles appears to have shifted during the past three decades: women expect to work more outside the family while their children are young than their mothers did, while men are expected to participate in more of the family tasks than their fathers did. It is clear that women have entered the labor force in increasing numbers (Glick, 1979), but the expectation that husbands and wives will share family labor more equally appears to be ahead of current practices. Despite some recent indications that men are taking a significantly more active role in cooking, cleaning, and looking after their children (e.g., Pleck, 1981), women continue to bear the overwhelming responsibility for managing the household and the primary role in child care (Pleck & Rustad, 1980: Rapoport, Rapoport & Strelitz, 1977: Robinson, 1977), even when both partners work full time outside the home (Stafford, Backman, & Dibona, 1977: Szinovacz, 1977).

It is usually assumed that the tradition of gender-linked roles in young families is a continuation of earlier patterns of role socialization begun in the early years of marriage. But recent longitudinal studies support earlier cross-sectional findings: regardless of where couples begin on the traditional-to-egalitarian continuum, men's and women's family role arrangements become increasingly traditional after the birth of a first child (Belsky, Lang, & Rovine, 1985; Cowan & Cowan, 1981; LaRossa & LaRossa, 1981; McHale & Huston, 1985). Despite some uncertainties about the *magnitude* of the shift toward gender-linked division of labor during the transition to parenthood (e.g., Goldberg, Michaels & Lamb, 1985), the *direction* of the shift appears to have been clearly established (Belsky & Pensky, 1986).

Given the pervasiveness of mothers' central role in the rearing of young children, it is ironic that recent studies of new parents have tended to highlight *fathers'* involvement in child care. Some researchers deliberately choose samples of fathers who are primary caretakers of their children to examine men's changing parental role (Pruett, 1983: Radin, 1982; Radin, in press), while others describe more varied samples of men to search for predictive and concurrent correlates of men's participation in the care of their children (Barnett & Baruch, in press; Cowan & Cowan, in press[a]: Fein, 1978; Feldman, in press; Grossman, in press; Lamb, 1981; Palkovitz, 1984; Russell, 1982). The specific antecedents of fathers' family involvement seem to vary from one sample to another, although men's involvement in the care of their children seems to be predictable from a combination of measures of parents' individual characteristics, division of labor, and quality of marriage. There is substantial consensus across studies that the extent of father involvement, however large or small, is a product of both husbands' and wives' relationships with their families of origin and their coordination of current family and work roles.

In light of contemporary ideology emphasizing more egalitarian roles for men and women, the trend toward more traditional role arrangements after childbirth is usually interpreted as a negative and unfortunate outcome of becoming a family. We will argue that this conclusion is premature and incomplete. With data from our longitudinal study of partners becoming first-time parents, we will provide a detailed description of changes in men's and women's major roles during the transition to parenthood, and evaluate the impact of these role changes on men and women themselves, and on their relationships as couples.

In our examination of prior research we found five issues that require more systematic investigation:

1. The designation of role arrangements as traditional or egalitarian has been made by summarizing partners' division of labor across a wide variety of tasks. While we too have made generalizations based on summary data (Cowan & Cowan, 1983), our indepth interviews with the couples in our study led us to suspect that men's and women's mutual role arrangements change in different ways on different family tasks. Item analyses may provide a more accurate description of what happens to family roles during the transition to parenthood.

2. Studies of role arrangements in the early years of family formation focus almost exclusively on role performance—who actu-

ally does what in a list of household, child care, and income-providing tasks. This focus on behavior ignores an important psychological component of this central aspect of married life — how a given role (e.g., father, wife) fits into each partner's self-concept (Allen & van de Vliert, 1984; Sarbin & Allen, 1968).

3. Most researchers describe shifts in the role arrangements of new parents without presenting the participants' *evaluation* of their situation. A few recent studies (Cowan, Cowan, Heming, Garrett, Curtis-Boles, & Boles, 1985; McHale & Huston, 1985; White & Booth, 1985) do report pre- to postpartum changes in partners' satisfaction with their division of labor, but none has examined the connection between traditional or egalitarian role arrangements and men's and women's satisfaction with them.

4. As men and women acquire the role of parent, they experience significant changes in other major family roles, particularly those of spouse and worker. When mothers who were employed before they became parents tend to leave work for varying periods of time after giving birth, their husbands become the sole wage earners for the family. As partners shift these family and work roles, they spend more time with the newest member of the family and less time as a couple (McHale, Huston, & Macdermid, 1985). Perhaps as a consequence, there appears to be a decline in the quality of couple interaction (McHale & Huston, 1985; Raush, Barry, Hertel & Swain, 1974), and a small but significant reduction in overall satisfaction with the marriage (Belsky, Spanier, & Rovine, 1983; Cowan et al., 1985; Grossman, Eichler, & Winickoff, 1980; Feldman & Nash, 1984; Shereshefsky & Yarrow, 1973). In most of the research on the transition to parenthood, changes in parent, worker, and spousal roles have been described separately. What has been missing from these studies is a detailed examination of the way in which changing involvement in and satisfaction with household chores, nurturing the young child, and earning an income are connected with partners' feelings about themselves and about the quality of their relationship.

5. In a previous report of our study (Cowan et al., 1985), we described the fact that men and women change in different ways and at different rates as they become parents. Already different in late pregnancy, partners' descriptions become increasingly discrep-

ant — in their attitudes, perceptions, roles, and marital descriptions — during the year and a half after the birth of their first child. Earlier preliminary analyses of our data suggested that men and women may also show different patterns of correlation between changes in their roles and their marital satisfaction. It appears as if role arrangements, and especially satisfaction with the arrangements, may be more central to the marital satisfaction of women than of men.

In the present study of first-time parents, we address each of these issues by examining men's and women's role changes and their consequences. We examine parent, partner, and worker roles in terms of psychological salience and actual participation, and also assess each spouse's satisfaction with his or her level of involvement. Our first goal is simply to describe changes in these major adult roles from pregnancy to 18 months after the birth of a first child. We then examine the correlations between role arrangements and role satisfaction separately for men and for women. Next we investigate how involvement and satisfaction as parents, partners, and workers combine to account for variance in the personal, parental, and marital adaptation of new parents. We will test the hypothesis derived from our own preliminary results that role arrangements and satisfaction become increasingly more important in understanding women's adaptation than men's in the early years of becoming a family.

METHOD

Participants and Design

The data reported in this paper were gathered as part of a larger longitudinal research and intervention study of couple relationships during family formation and development (Cowan et al., 1985). From the practices of obstetrician-gynecologists in the greater San Francisco Bay Area, from a Health Maintenance Organization, and from community-wide newsletters, we recruited couples who were pregnant with their first child. Couples in the last trimester of pregnancy were invited to participate in a study of how marital relationships change during the transition to parenthood. The 72 couples who responded were interviewed and assigned randomly to one of three conditions:

I. The first 24 were invited to participate in one of six couples groups meeting weekly for six months with a male-female team of trained mental health professionals as co-leaders. Each partner filled out an extensive set of questionnaires and participated in a two-to-three-hour interview before the groups began. They were interviewed and assessed twice after the groups ended, when their children were 6 and 18 months old. The intervention is described in detail elsewhere (C. Cowan, in press [a], Cowan & Cowan, in press [b]).

II. Another 24 couples were assessed with interviews and questionnaires at the same points in their transition to parenthood, but they did not participate in a couples group. For most of the analyses reported in this paper, data from couples in Conditions I and II were combined.

III. A third sample of 24 couples was interviewed but not assessed in pregnancy, in order to examine the impact of the assessment. Fifteen of these couples who were available for follow-up were given full assessments at 6 and 18 months postpartum.

IV. Most previous studies of the transition to parenthood have not included a comparison sample of childless couples. In order to separate normal marital change over time from change attributable to becoming a family, we recruited couples from the same medical and community sources: they were not having fertility problems and had not yet decided whether to have a first child. Of these 24 couples, four separated or divorced over the next two years and five subsequently had children; the 15 who remained together and childless were assessed at Pretest, 9 months later, and again a year after that.

The participants ranged in age from 20 to 49 years: at the beginning of the study, the mean age of the men was 30.1 years, of the women 29.0 years. They live in 28 different communities within a 40 mile radius of Berkeley and Oakland. Total family income ranged from $7,000 to $70,000, with a mean of $25,500 when they entered the study. Eighty-five percent of the participants are Caucasian, and 15% are black, Asian, or Hispanic.

Measuring Instruments

Behavioral Role Performance and Satisfaction — Who Does What?

At each assessment period, both parents filled out the 36-item *Who Does What?* scale (Cowan, Cowan, Coie, & Coie, 1978). Three subscales of 12 items each ask partners to describe the couple's division of tasks in three areas of family life: (i) *household and family tasks* including laundry, cooking, care of plants or yard, and car maintenance: (ii) *family decisions* including plans for vacations, partners' involvement in work outside the family, and amount of involvement in the community; and (iii) *child-related tasks* such as feeding, dressing, bathing, arranging for child care or babysitting, and calling the doctor.

Each item was rated on a 1-9 scale for "How it is now," with 1 indicating that the woman does it all, 9 indicating that the man does it all, and 5 showing that partners share the task about equally. Partners also rated "How I'd like it to be" on each item. A simple average of the scores in each area of life reflected men's and women's *relative involvement* in household, decision-making and child care tasks.

A check on the potential bias of self-reported role arrangements is the correspondence between husbands' and wives' ratings. While each partner gave him or herself somewhat higher ratings of involvement than the spouse did, item correlations between spouses' ratings on household and child care scales averaged between .72 and .85 at all assessment periods. Item correlations between spouses' ratings of decision-making were lower (averaging .35 to .42), probably because the range of ratings on the decision-making items was quite restricted.

We created two indices of *satisfaction* within each area of "who does what?" The first was derived from a sum of the absolute discrepancies between ratings of "How it is" and "How I'd like it to be." The second was a simple rating made after filling out each subsection, in response to the question." In general, how satisfied are you with the way you and you partner divide the household, [or] decision-making [or] family tasks related to children?" Responses ranged on a five-step scale from very satisfied, through neutral, to very dissatisfied. The correlation between the two indices was generally significant but low (.30-.40). They seem to reflect different aspects of parents' satisfaction with their shared participation in the day to day tasks of managing a household and a family. The discrepancy measure may reflect how close parents come to meeting their ideals, while the overall rating may provide a more direct measure of how they feel about the current arrangements.

Psychological Role Involvement and Satisfaction – The Pie

Given a page with a circle 4" in diameter, each participant was asked to list the main roles in his or her life and to divide *The Pie* so that each section reflected the salience or importance of each aspect of self, not necessarily the time spent in the role (Cowan et al., 1978). Even in pregnancy, some expectant partners included a "parent" aspect of self. Involvement in each role was calculated from the degrees of the arc of the circle encompassed by the "piece" of *The Pie*. Content analysis yielded a coding scheme that included: family roles such as parent, partner/lover; worker and student roles: leisure roles such as artist, gardener; and self-descriptive statements such as "me" and "myself alone." In this report we focus on parent, partner, and worker aspects of self. Participants completed one *Pie* for "Me as I am" and another for "Me as I'd like to be" at each phase of the study. The discrepancy between degrees of the arcs drawn for actual and ideal pieces for each major role was interpreted as an index of satisfaction with that aspect of self the greater the discrepancy, the less the satisfaction.

Indices of Individual, Parental, and Marital Adaptation

1. *Self-esteem.* At each assessment period, participants completed two *Adjective Check Lists* (Gough & Heilbrun, 1980) describing "Me as I am" and "Me as I'd like to be." An index of self-esteem was derived from the discrepancy between the actual and ideal descriptions using 8 of the subscales (Gough, Fioravanti, & Lazzari, 1983).

2. *The Parenting Stress Index* (Abidin, 1980) contained 150 items in its fifth revision, which we used; Abidin now has a final version with 100 items. It provides a total Parenting Stress score

and subscale scores in the Parenting domain (depression, attachment to the child) and the Child domain (demandingness, mood). Many of the child items were adapted from infant temperament scales. The instrument has been shown to differentiate parents who abuse their children from those who do not (Abidin, 1980), and parents of children identified as having emotional problems from parents of normal children (Hamilton, 1980; Lafiosca, 1981; Zimmerman, 1979). It was filled out by both mothers and fathers when their children were 6 and 18 months old.

3. *The Short Marital Adjustment Test* (Locke & Wallace, 1959), one of the most commonly used indices of marital adaptation, was completed by each participant in late pregnancy and again at both 6 and 18 months postpartum.

Procedure

At each assessment period couples were interviewed by a male-female researcher couple at home or in the Psychology Clinic. They were given a packet of questionnaires to be filled out independently at home, and reinterviewed once the forms had been completed.

RESULTS

Role Change over Time

Household, Decision-Making, Child Care Tasks,
and Outside-the-Family Work

Involvement. Changes in men's and women's relative involvement in household, decision-making, and child care were analyzed in three, four-way mixed-model ANOVAs (Intervention × Time × Gender × Item). The intervention was treated as a between-subjects effect and the remaining variables as within-subjects effects. Different numbers of degrees of freedom associated with similar F-tests resulted from slightly different amounts of missing data in each analysis. Due to the complexity of the analyses, we did not include the nonparent couples, who, we know, remained relatively stable over time in these and other measures (Cowan et al., 1985). We investigated higher-order interactions, and then lower-order interactions and simple main effects, using Fisher's Least Significant Difference approach to correct for the possibility of family-wise error (Keppel, 1982). Since the patterns for couples with and without the intervention were not significantly different on these role variables, the results in this section are derived from 47 couples becoming families, 23 who participated in a couples group, and 24 with pre- and posttest measures but no intervention experience.

In *household task involvement* we found statistically significant gender × item (F = 3.99; df = 11/418) and time × item (F = 2.06; df = 22/418: p < .003) interactions, with no significant main effects for gender or time. Although the correlations reported in the Method section indicated that men and women tended to agree in their descriptions of their division of household tasks, in fact partners showed different levels of agreement on different items. Specifically, partners tended to agree most about who takes out the garbage, pays the bills, and keeps in touch with family and friends, and least about how the shopping, meal preparation, and looking after the car was divided.

The shifts in allocation of household tasks are more complex than we reported prior to these analyses of item differences (Cowan & Cowan, 1981). Earlier, we reported no significant change in the overall *Who Does What?* ratings for household tasks: *on the average*, there was no shift toward men or women taking more responsibility for the overall load of household and family tasks as they became parents than they had before the birth. Women were doing more of these tasks overall, and they continued to do so during the transition. We also reported a marked change in role specialization. During late pregnancy, there was a tendency for both partners to have some responsibility for each of the tasks, just as Goldberg and her colleagues suggested (1985). After the baby was born, fathers tended to do more of some household tasks, while mothers did more of others. That is, parents described their arrangements on the 12 household and family task items as farther away from 50:50 and closer to 1 ("she does it all") or 9 ("he does it all").

Item analyses clarify the meaning of these trends. From pregnancy to six months after birth, along with what may be characterized as traditional increases in men's responsibility for providing the family income, and decreases in their doing the laundry, men

showed significant *increases* in their participation in meal preparation, housecleaning, and food shopping. During the next year, from
6 to 18 months after birth, men's participation in shopping and gar-
dening increased significantly, but their contribution to meal preparation, housecleaning, and taking out the garbage declined. While
these latter changes in fathers' involvement in household work
could lead us to describe the couple as moving in a more traditional
direction, the fact that about two-thirds of the women were returning to work at least part-time, thus increasing *their* contribution to
the family income, would suggest a shift away from traditional arrangements. During the transition to parenthood, then, we see both
traditional and non-traditional role changes in both spouses at different times.

The ANOVA of *decision-making* patterns indicated a main effect
for items (F = 8.18; df = 11/319; p < .0001). According to both
men's and women's ratings, men tended to have slightly but consistently more responsibility for financial planning, decisions about
work outside the family, and when to initiate lovemaking, while
women tended to have slightly more responsibility for making social arrangements, and for deciding about participation in community activities and religious organizations. This pattern of family
decision-making in our sample of couples was unaffected by the
transition to parenthood, at least in the period from late pregnancy
to 18 months postpartum.

Recall that pre-birth ratings of *child-related tasks* were predictions of how the tasks would be divided after the child was born.
Here, there was a clear and significant main effect of time (F =
10.47; df = 2/60: p < .0001). The actual division of child care
tasks at 6 months postpartum indicated that men were doing much
less than they or their wives had expected they would during the
pregnancy assessment. There was, however, a significant increase
in men's participation in the daily tasks of child care between 6 and
18 months after birth.

Shifts over time in caring for the children were complicated by
both gender × item (F = 2.35; df = 11/330; p < .05) and time ×
item (F = 6.43; df = 22/660: p < .0001) interactions. As in the
ratings of household tasks, men and women had slightly different
perceptions of their involvement in the care of their child, depend-

ing on the item. They agreed most about who responded to the infant's cries, who bought toys, and who played with the child. They agreed least about who tended to take the child out, and who arranged babysitters and doctor's appointments.

The time × item interaction for child care tasks was relatively straightforward. The trend for mothers to be doing more of the care of the babies when they were 6 months old *than either parent had predicted* was evident for 8 of the 12 items. On four of the child care tasks, however, parents' expectations proved to be accurate: who would decide whether to respond to the child's cries: who would get up with the child in the middle of the night: who would do the child's laundry; and who would choose the baby's toys. It was predicted that these would be done more by mothers, and postpartum ratings showed that the predictions were correct.

Eight of the 12 items showed a significant increase in father involvement from 6 to 18 months postpartum, including bathing the baby and getting up during the night; fathers' participation in the other four tasks remained fairly constant: playing with the child, doing the baby's laundry, and arranging for babysitters and doctor's visits. Despite increases in fathers' involvement with their six-to-18 month olds, even the item with the highest father participation — playing with the child — received average ratings well below 5 ("we do this about equally") on the nine-point scale. Fathers are clearly taking part in their child's upbringing — perhaps more than their own fathers did — but mothers are carrying the major burden of child care.

Satisfaction with "who does what?" We considered including item differences in the ANOVAs of role satisfaction change, but decided that since they were based on discrepancy scores, compositing would be necessary to make them more reliable. Thus, we did three, mixed-model three-way ANOVAs (Time × Gender × Condition), with the condition variable comparing intervention parents, nonintervention parents, and couples not yet decided about having a baby (n = 62 couples).

Satisfaction with the division of household and family tasks showed a significant three-way interaction among gender, condition, and time (F = 3.15; df = 2/90: p < .05). As we have suggested elsewhere (Cowan & Cowan, in press [b]: C. Cowan, in press), the ongoing discussions in the couples' groups *during* the transition from couple to family seemed to keep partners' satisfaction with the shifts in household arrangements on a more even keel. Satisfaction remained stable for partners not having a baby, *and* for new fathers and mothers who had participated in the intervention. By contrast, fathers who had not been in a couples' group showed a decline in satisfaction with household division of labor over the 18 months of this study. Mothers without the intervention declined in household task satisfaction from pregnancy to 6 months after birth, but they returned to "baseline" one year later.

There were no statistically significant effects of gender, condition, or time on satisfaction with the arrangements for family decision-making over the transition to parenthood — not too surprising since partners described few changes in their patterns of making family decisions over the period of study.

Satisfaction with the division of child care tasks, assessed only in the 47 couples who had children, differed markedly for mothers and fathers at each assessment period (F = 28.56; f = 1/45; p < 0001). In both pre-birth expectations and post-birth realities, women described larger discrepancies between the actual and ideal division of child care tasks than men did. There was a trend (p < .11) toward a time effect, suggesting an increase in dissatisfaction at the 6-months-after-birth assessment with a return to pre-birth estimates of satisfaction when the babies were 18 months old. Is this increase-decrease pattern of satisfaction associated with the fact that fathers tend to decrease and then increase their level of participation in child care?

Involvement and satisfaction. Partners' style of dividing housework and family decisions was *not* correlated with men's satisfaction with those role arrangements at any of the three assessments. The more men expected to participate in the care of their babies, however, the more satisfied they anticipated they would be with the division of caring for the baby. The more involved fathers showed greater satisfaction with these arrangements at 6 months postpartum. By the time their babies had reached 18 months of age, similar to the findings in pregnancy, there was no longer a significant correlation between how involved they were in their children's day-to-day care and how satisfied they were with their involvement. Except for a brief period of time during the transition to parenthood, then, the extent of father involvement has little to do with men's satisfaction with the arrangement of family roles.

By contrast, men's level of involvement in family tasks mattered to *their wives'* satisfaction: the more fathers were involved in housework and caring for the children, the more mothers were satisfied with the couple's division of labor at all assessment periods. These findings will take on greater significance when we examine the different links for men and women between the couple's role arrangements and marital satisfaction.

Psychological Involvement in Partner, Parent, and Worker Roles

We have previously reported analyses of change in partner/lover, parent, and worker aspects of self as assessed by *The Pie* (Cowan et al., 1985). For the childless spouses, changes were evident in several aspects of sense of self over the two years of the study: the partner/lover aspects of self remained stable from pretest to the first posttest, and grew significantly larger from the first to the second posttest: parent was a very small aspect of self at each of the assessment periods: and men's psychological involvement in worker remained stable, while women's increased over time.

Not surprisingly, new parents showed very different trends in their self-descriptions over the first two years of the longitudinal study. For both new fathers and mothers, the partner/lover aspect of self declined — from 28% to 21% of *The Pie* for men and from 30% to 18% for women. Men's sense of self as parent increased from 5% to 24%, while women's increased from 11% to 38%. The greatest contrast between men and women showed in their sense of self as worker: for men, it increased from 28% to 33% of *The Pie* from pregnancy to 18 months postpartum, while for new mothers it decreased from 19% to 11% from pregnancy to 6 months after giving birth, with a rise to 17% one year later. What these data suggest is that as psychological involvement in parenthood increases, it is accompanied by a sense of decreasing involvement in the role of spouse and lover for both mothers and fathers, and contrasting changes in work involvement for husbands and wives. In each case women changed more than men, especially in the period from late pregnancy to 6 months postpartum. Certainly, these changes in the psychological sense of self are consistent with the behavioral role changes we have been describing.

The data from both behavioral and psychological involvement in family and work roles indicate that there is a complex set of interrelated changes occurring over the transition to parenthood that cannot be summarized on a single traditional-to-egalitarian dimension. The value of using both behavioral and psychological measures of role arrangements will become more apparent when we discuss the connection between these arrangements and measures of adaptation.

Consistency Over Time

Longitudinal studies of the transition to parenthood not only describe pervasive changes in mean scores and ratings: they also demonstrate remarkable consistency of individual differences over time (Belsky, Spanier, & Rovine, 1983; Cowan et al., 1985; Feldman & Nash, 1984: Grossman et al., 1980; Heinicke, 1984). By and large, individuals and couples adapting well to their first child are those who described less distress and more pleasure as individuals and couples before the baby arrived (Heming, 1985).

This same consistency can be seen in men's and women's perceptions of role arrangements and satisfaction on *Who Does What?* On household and decision-making involvement scales, correlations between pregnancy and 18 month postpartum ratings ranged from .56 to .81. Satisfaction in these two domains also showed reasonable consistency over the same time period (r = .46 to .56). There was very high consistency between 6 and 18 months measures of involvement in child care tasks (r = .67 for men and .76 for women), and low but significant correlations between parents' predicted involvement and satisfaction during pregnancy and their actual ratings almost two years later (see also Cowan & Cowan, in press [a]).

The Pie measures of psychological involvement in parent, partner, and worker roles also showed significant correlations over time, ranging from .31 to .61. The consistency of *Who Does What?*

involvement and satisfaction measures, and *The Pie* measures strongly suggest that despite important role changes during the transition to parenthood, there is an underlying continuity to couples' role arrangements. How men and women rearrange their family and work roles in response to the arrival of a baby grows out of the patterns they have already established in their individual lives and in their relationship.

In sum, we have shown that it is not possible to categorize behavioral and psychological changes in family roles as moving unequivocally in traditional or egalitarian directions during the transition to parenthood. The psychological changes appear to be more traditional, with women taking on more parent involvement and less partner/lover and worker involvement than men. The behavioral changes are mixed. Men's and women's role specialization increases. Midway through the first postpartum year men participate more actively in some household tasks and outside-the-family work than they did when they were expecting a baby, but they are less involved in child care than they or their wives expected them to be before the baby arrived. During the next year men's participation in household tasks decreases, but they become more active in the care of their children. All of these changes toward and away from egalitarian family role arrangements occur in a context in which women are still fulfilling their traditionally-defined family role as primary caretaker of the house and the child, and men are more involved in work outside the family. We now turn to the question of how variations in role arrangements and satisfaction during the transition to parenthood are related to other domains of family life.

Role Correlates of Individual, Parental, and Marital Adaptation

Our model of family functioning during a major life transition (Cowan & Cowan, 1985) has indicated that there are close connections among events in five family domains: individual, couple, parental, family of origin, and outside-the-family. As a partial test of that model, we examined a number of multiple regression equations linking new parents' behavioral and psychological role involvement and satisfaction with three indicators of adaptation: self-esteem, parenting stress, and marital satisfaction. As in any correlational analysis, multiple regression cannot determine causal connections, but it can show how behavioral and psychological measures of parent, partner, and worker involvement or satisfaction combine to account for variance in men's and women's adaptation at different points in the transition to parenthood.

Preliminary analyses indicated that *Who Does What?* ratings of child care involvement based on separate factor scores for daytime, evening and weekend, and nighttime periods provided more information than a single overall measure. These scores were based on items included in the 6 and 18 month postpartum follow-ups: they were not included in the pregnancy assessment. Eight variables representing aspects of role involvement were entered in each concurrent multiple regression equation: *behavioral involvement* in household, decision-making, daytime child care, evening and weekend child care, nighttime child care; *psychological involvement* in parent, partner, and worker aspects of *The Pie*.

As in a previous report (Cowan & Cowan [a]) global satisfaction ratings of household, decision-making, and child care were more strongly related to our adaptation measures than the actual-ideal discrepancies. These were entered into multiple regression equations along with discrepancy measures of satisfaction with parent, partner, and worker.

We chose the "backward elimination" technique to construct the multiple regression equations because it facilitated a test of our model. First, it entered into the equation all the measures that we expected would contribute to variance in the target. Then, it removed one measure at a time to assess whether the removal would significantly reduce the size of the multiple correlation. If the reduced correlation was still statistically significant, the variable was retained: if not, it was eliminated (Pedhazur, 1982). Beta weights describing the relative amount of variance explained are listed only when the variable was retained in the final step of the analysis (Table 1). We have included in Table 1 the more conservative *adjusted* R-squared estimates of variance accounted for by the combination of independent variables, to correct for the fact that the regression equations contain a relatively large number of variables relative to subjects.

Table 1

Role Correlates of Self-Esteem (SE), Parenting Stress (PS), and Marital Satisfaction (MS) during the Transition to Parenthood

	Pregnancy				6 months postpartum						18 months postpartum					
	Men		Women		Men			Women			Men			Women		
	SE	MS	SE	MS	SE	PS	MS	SE	PS	MS	SE	PS	MS	SE	PS	MS
Involvement																
household					-.31		-.29								-.43	.51
decisions					.16	-.28	.33								-.10	.07
child care																
- days					.16	-.27	.30								-.35	.58
- eves/weekends					.30	-.26	.29			.33					-.13	.14
- nighttime					.22	-.26	.23									
Parent					.38			-.39	.32	-.40					.29	
Partner																
Worker																
R			.27	.32*	.61**	.51	.65*	.39	.32*	.51*					.61*	.71***
Adj. R²			.06	.09	.20	.15	.27	.13	.08	.22					.31	.39
Satisfaction																
household			.27		.18		.57			.31		-.42			.47	.37
decisions		.37			.30					.33		-.21	.54		.18	.25
child care	.32	.25		.32	.31			.31	.32	.35	.35		.26		.34	
Parent					.25	-.26					.12	-.20	.30			
Partner						-.26						-.13			.17	
Worker						.51			.32			.49*	.67***		.59**	.69***
R	.32*	.37*	.27	.32*	.52*		.57			.77***	.50					
Adj. R²	.09	.11	.06	.09	.17	.15	.33		.08	.54	.15	.13	.37		.27	.40

* p < .05
** p < .01
*** p < .001

122

Pregnancy

The first general conclusion to be drawn from the upper left section of Table 1 is that neither psychological nor behavioral role *involvement* was related to self-esteem or marital satisfaction in expectant parents. Only a few single global ratings of satisfaction with *Who Does What?* were correlated with how satisfied men and women were with themselves and their marriage (lower left section of Table 1). In only one case did measures of role satisfaction combine in the regression equations and in no case did the single role satisfaction measure explain more than 11% of the variance in men's and women's adaptation during pregnancy.

Six Months After Birth

The picture changes graphically after the birth of a baby:

Men. Fathers of six-month-olds who were doing *less* housework and *more* child care than their peers, were feeling better about themselves and their marriages. In addition, the more psychological involvement men showed as parent, as measured by *The Pie*, the greater their self-esteem. Men's scores on the Parenting Stress Index were not correlated with involvement in caring for their child. However, the more satisfied they were with their involvement in caring for the baby, the less stress they experienced as a parent and the greater their self-esteem. Together, role satisfaction variables accounted for 15% of the variance in men's parenting stress and 17% of the variance in their self-esteem. Finally, men's satisfaction with the division of housework appeared to be the single most important ingredient of their marital satisfaction when their babies were six months old, accounting for 33% of the variance in their marital satisfaction scores.

Women. As we have come to expect, new mothers' patterns were somewhat different from new fathers'. Women with *less* psychological involvement as parent had higher self-esteem and lower parenting stress, although the correlations were quite small. This is in direct contrast with the trends for men. Further, when mothers with lower psychological *involvement* in the parent role had husbands who participated more often in looking after the child in the middle of the night, they were more satisfied with their marriage

(R = .51). A combination of satisfaction with several behavioral and psychological aspects of family roles was highly correlated with women's marital satisfaction (R = .77).

Eighteen Months After Birth

Midway through the second postpartum year, the difference between correlational patterns of men and women is even clearer.

Men. As in pregnancy, (a) men's behavioral involvement in household, decision-making, child care tasks: and (b) their psychological involvement in parent, partner, or worker roles were no longer connected with their self-esteem, parenting stress, or marital *satisfaction*. Different measures of role satisfaction combined to account for 15% of the variance in fathers' self-esteem, 13% of the variance in their parenting stress, and an impressive 37% of the variance in their marital satisfaction scores.

Women. At 18 months postpartum, none of the role involvement measures was associated with women' self-esteem, but *both* role involvement and satisfaction measures were highly correlated with parenting stress and marital satisfaction. Here again, mothers with smaller pieces of *The Pie* labeled parent experienced less parenting stress. In general, women were less stressed as parents when their husbands participated more in household tasks and care of the children, and when they themselves had more input in family decision-making.

Women's *psychological* involvement in or satisfaction with family roles did not seem to be an important factor in their satisfaction with marriage. Here, fathers' actual involvement in household and child care tasks accounted 39% of the variance in mothers marital satisfaction. Wives' satisfaction with the level of their husbands' involvement accounted for a similarly high 40% of the variance in their marital satisfaction scores.

DISCUSSION

The multiple regression analyses demonstrate clearly that behavioral and psychological aspects of being a parent, partner, and worker combine to account for a statistically significant amount of variance in new parents' adaptation as assessed by measures of self-esteem, parenting stress, and marital satisfaction. They also demonstrate that it is necessary to consider the status of all major mutual role arrangements and satisfaction in order to understand how individuals and couples adapt to becoming a family.

We were surprised that work involvement as measured by *The Pie* did not prove to be a significant correlate of adaptation either for fathers or mothers. Using a more behavioral index of work involvement (not employed, halftime, full time) added the information that men who worked half time or less at 6 months postpartum tended to have higher parenting stress ($r = -.44$), and lower marital satisfaction ($r = .22$) than men who worked full time. But the same work index was unrelated to adaptation for women at 6 months postpartum and unconnected with adaptation for either men or women at 18 months after birth. Thus, while work involvement cannot be ignored at 6 and 18 months postpartum, it does not seem to be as centrally linked to individual and marital adaptation as the division of labor in the home and the couple's psychological involvement in parent and partner roles. Perhaps the many other studies that find work effects are focusing on families with older children and families with more than one child (e.g., Bronfenbrenner & Crouter, 1982; Hoffman, 1979).

Is it possible to find out whether role arrangements influence adaptation or whether adaptation leads to specific role arrangements and satisfaction? Supplementary multiple regression analyses indicate that the findings reported above do not simply reflect associations between variables at a static point in time, but are a consequence of the fact that role arrangements and adaptation are tightly interlocked. *Changes* in role involvement from pregnancy to 18 months after birth account for about the same amount of variance in 18 month adaptation as concurrent correlates. Conversely, changes in adaptation predict role involvement and satisfaction at 18 months postpartum. Finally, pregnancy to 18 month postpartum changes in role arrangements and satisfaction are highly correlated with changes in adaptation especially for women. Role arrangements and individual or couple adaptation appear to move in tandem.

In our view, these findings support a family system model of circular rather than linear causality. We believe that the role changes accompanying the transition to parenthood affect how men and women feel about themselves and their marriage. But partners' self-esteem and marital satisfaction in pregnancy also influence the way in which they arrange their roles and how satisfied each partner becomes with how family labor is divided. What these data add to the existing family system models developed by therapists working with dysfunctional families is the importance of "Who Does What?" issues in understanding both individual and marital adaptation during the period of family formation.

The fact that role arrangements and adaptation become linked only after the birth of a baby is one example of what major life transitions do—they create functional relationships that were not present before, and they "unhook" functional relationships that existed before the life change occurred. Individual and family development, we are suggesting, is not simply a matter of change in average scores but also a change in the pattern of connections among variables. Given these shifting links between men's and women's roles and adaptation during the transition to parenthood, it is no wonder that babies tend to be blamed for causing parents' distress (Cowan & Cowan, in press [c]). Our data suggest that it is not the arrival of a child *per se* but the changes in parent, partner, and worker roles as they interact with feelings about oneself and one's marriage that create disequilibrium in the family system.

The data also suggest that disequilibrium does not inevitably lead to distress or dysfunction. While some couples make changes in role arrangements that lead to distress, others manage to become satisfied with their roles and to feel more positively about themselves and their marriage. It is noteworthy that men who participate actively in the care of their children show greater adaptation at 6 months after birth, and that their wives show greater adaptation at both 6 and 18 month follow-ups. Similarly, it is important to understand that women who manage to limit some of their psychological involvement in the parent role, and to maintain their investment in the spousal role, experience less parenting stress and greater satisfaction with their marriage. How some couples manage to arrange their roles in this fashion will be the subject of some of our future research.

The results of the multiple regression analyses also emphasized a theme of our previous reports (Cowan et al., 1985) and those of other researchers studying couples becoming families (e.g., Feldman & Nash, 1984). Just as in Bernard's observation that there are "his and hers" marriages, we find his and her transitions to parenthood. At 6 months after birth some aspects of role arrangements and adaptation are correlated for both men and women, but one year later only women appear to link the couple's division of labor with their stress as parents and as spouses. It seems likely that at least part of the reported decline in marital satisfaction during the early years of family formation may result from the fact that new mothers and fathers are experiencing these major role changes in different ways.

Implications for Family Policy

We have underlined the fact that women are still assuming the major responsibility for family work in the early childrearing years. Nevertheless, our more detailed item analyses suggest that men increase their participation in specific aspects of family life during this time and women begin to move back to work outside the family. Based on our extensive interviews with men and women over the past 12 years, we believe that the usual tendency to describe men's family involvement in terms of psychological motivation (willingness or resistance) is an oversimplification (Cowan & Cowan, in press [a]).

In fact, there are many *barriers* to fathers' involvement in the care of their young children. Because women tend to reduce their involvement in outside-the-family work and are deprived of a major source of self-esteem, they are often reluctant to give up their special role, to "let men in." Men's increased involvement in the workplace is often a result and not a cause of their reduced opportunities for involvement in the parent role.

Furthermore, businesses are still reluctant to support men's paternal role beyond the first few weeks. When both partners work outside the home, men are very unlikely to stay home when the child is sick or child care arrangements go awry. And, since the Presidential veto of federal support for child care centers, no legislation has been passed to provide both men and women with options to share work inside and outside of the family.

Our data do not suggest that increased father involvement in household tasks decision-making, and child care will inevitably lead to higher levels of individual and marital adaptation. Except in the first few postpartum months, men's level of involvement in the family is relatively independent of their self-esteem, parenting stress, and marital satisfaction. For women the correlations between role involvement and adaptation are higher but far from perfect. However, both men's and women's *satisfaction* with the who does what of life are consistently related to individual and couple adaptation during the first year and one half of family life. These findings suggest to us that family policies enacted by business and government will be most effective if they offer couples a choice about how to balance their work and family arrangements.

The case for increased support to couples so that they can adopt more satisfying role arrangements can be strengthened by considering the welfare of both parents and children. If 37% to 40% of the variance in men's and women's satisfaction with marriage at 18 months can be explained by satisfaction with role arrangements, then we have identified a key ingredient in the emotional climate of new parents' lives. But the ultimate pay-off for supporting more flexible family roles goes beyond the adaptation of the couple. Preliminary data from our assessments of the families when the children are three and one half (Cowan & Cowan, 1985) indicate that parents' individual adjustment and marital satisfaction are strongly connected with the quality of their parenting styles (e.g., authoritative, authoritarian, permissive). In turn, these styles are linked with the children's cognitive, personality, and social development, and the early emergence of internalizing or externalizing behavior problems. The findings suggest that parents who feel more stressed as individuals and as couples are less able to be warm, responsive, limit-setting and structuring as parents, and more likely to report difficulties in their children's adjustment. Thus, support for shifts in the division of family tasks toward arrangements more satisfying to the parents may ultimately facilitate adaptation in the development of their children.

While our data do not support ideological statements that the division of family tasks *must* be egalitarian, they do indicate that families may benefit from a reconsideration of current role arrangements. This reconsideration could be facilitated by new and more flexible family policies in government and in the workplace. We are concerned, however, with one sobering implication of our findings. Women's postpartum adaptation appears to be more sensitive to role arrangements than men's. We wonder whether this fact makes it more difficult for men to understand the need for changes in the who does what of family life. As long as the vast majority of policy-makers are male, change in new parents' provisions for balancing employment and family work may occur more slowly than would be ideal for men's, women's, and children's adaptation during the early years of family life.

REFERENCES

Abidin, R. (1980). *Parent education and intervention handbook.* Springfield: Thomas.

Allen, V. L. & van de Vliert, E. (1984). A role theoretical perspective on transitional processes. In V.L. Allen & E. van de Vliert (Eds.). *Role transitions: explorations and explanations.* New York: Plenum.

Barnett, R.C. & Baruch, G.K. (1983, August). Determinants of fathers' participation in family work. Paper presented at the meeting of the American Psychological Association, Anaheim, CA.

Belsky, Jay, Spanier, Graham B., & Rovine, Michael. (1983). Stability and change in marriage across the transition to parenthood. *J. of Marriage and the Family*, 45 (August): 567-577.

Bronfenbrenner, U. & Crouter, A. (1982). Work and family through time and space. In S.B. Kamerman & C.D. Hayes (Eds.), *Families that work: Children in a changing world.* Washington, DC: National Academy Press.

Cowan, C. Pape. (in press). Working with couples during family formation: Effects on new fathers. In P. Bronstein & C. Pape Cowan (Eds.), *Fatherhood Today: Men's changing role in the family.* New York: Wiley.

Cowan, C. Pape, Cowan, P.A., Coie, L., & Coie, J.D. (1978). Becoming a family: The impact of a first child's birth on the couple's relationship. In W.B. Miller and L.F. Newman (Eds.) *The first child and family formation.* Chapel Hill, NC: Carolina Population Center.

Cowan, C. Pape, & Cowan, P.A. (1983, August). Conflicts for partners becoming parents: Implications for the couple relationship. Paper presented at the meeting of the American Psychological Association, Los Angeles, CA.

Cowan, C. Pape, & Cowan, P.A. (1981, April). Couple role arrangements and satisfaction during family formation. Paper presented at the Society for Research in Child Development, Boston, MA.

Cowan, P.A. & Cowan, C. Pape (1985, May). Risks to the marriage when partners become parents. Paper presented at the meetings of the American Psychiatric Association, Washington, DC.

Cowan, C. Pape, & Cowan, Philip A. (in press-a). Men's involvement in parenthood: Identifying the antecedents and understanding the barriers. In Phyllis Berman & Frank Pedersen (Eds.), *Men's transition to parenthood*. Hillsdale, NJ: Lawrence Erlbaum Associates.

Cowan, C. Pape & Cowan, P.A. (in press-b). A preventive intervention for couples becoming parents. In C.F.Z. Boukydis (Ed.) *Research on support for parents and infants in the postnatal period*. NJ: Ablex.

Cowan, C. Pape, Cowan, P.A., Heming, G. Garrett, E., Coysh, W.S., Curtis-Boles, H. & Boles, A.J. (December, 1985). Transitions to parenthood: His, hers, and theirs. *Journal of Family Issues*.

Coysh, W.S. (1983). Factors influencing men's roles in caring for their children and the effects of father involvement. Doctoral dissertation, University of California, Berkeley.

Fein, R.A. (1978). Consideration of men's experiences and the birth of a first child. In W.B. Miller and L.F. newman (Eds.) *The first child and family formation*. Chapel Hill, NC: Carolina Population Center.

Feldman, S. Shirley & Nash, Sharon C. (1984). "The transition from expectancy to parenthood: Impact of the firstborn child on men and women." *Sex Roles*, 11 (July): 61-78.

Garrett, Ellen T. (1983). Women's experiences of early parenthood: Expectations vs. reality. Paper presented at American Psychological Association Meetings, Anaheim, CA.

Gough, Harrison G. & Heilbrun, Alfred B. Jr. 1965, 1980. The Adjective Check List Manual. Palo Alto: Consulting Psychologists Press.

Gough, Harrison G., Fioravanti, Mario, & Lazzari, Renato. (1983). "Some implications of self versus ideal congruence on the revised Adjective Check List." *J. of Personality and Social Psychology*, 44 (June): 1214-1220.

Grossman, F.K. (in press). Separate and together: men's autonomy and affiliation in the transition to parenthood. In P. Berman & F.A. Pedersen, (Eds.) *Father's Transition to Parenthood*. Hillsdale, NJ: Erlbaum.

Grossman, F., Eichler, L. & Winickoff, S., et al. (1980). *Pregnancy, birth, and parenthood*. San Francisco: Jossey-Bass.

Heinicke, C.M. (1984). Impact of prebirth personality and marital functioning on family development: A framework and suggestions for further study. *Developmental psychology, 20*, 1044-1053.

Heming, Gertrude. (1985). Predicting adaptation during the transition to parenthood. Unpublished dissertation, University of California, Berkeley.

Hoffman, L.W. (1979). Maternal employment. *American Psychologist, 34*, 859-865.

Keppel, Geoffrey. (1982). Design and analysis: A researcher's handbook (2nd ed.). Englewood Cliffs, NJ: Prentice-Hall.

Lafiosca, T. (1981). The relationship of parent stress to anxiety, approval motivation, and children's behavioral problems. Unpublished doctoral dissertation, University of Virginia, Institute of Clinical Psychology. .

Lamb, M.E. (Ed.). (1981). *The role of the father in child development*. (2nd ed). New York: Wiley.

Locke, H. & Wallace, K. (1959). Short marital adjustment and prediction tests: Their reliability and validity. *Marriage and Family Living, 21,* 251-255.

Palkovitz, R. (1984). Parental attitudes and fathers' interactions with their 5-month-old infants. *Developmental Psychology,* 20, 1054-1060.

Pedhazur, E.J. (1982). *Multiple Regression in Behavioral Research: Explanation and Prediction.* Second Edition. New York: Holt, Rinehart, & Winston.

Pleck, J.A. (1981, August). Changing patterns of work and family roles. Paper presented at the meeting of the American Psychological Association, Los Angeles.

Pleck, J.A. & Rustad, M. (1980). Husbands' and wives' time in family work and paid work in the 1975-1976 study of time use. Unpublished manuscript. Wellesley MA.: Wellesley College Center for Research on Women.

Radin, N. (1982). Primary caregiving and role-sharing fathers. In M.E. Lamb (Ed.), *Nontraditional families*. Hillsdale, NJ: Erlbaum Associates. 173-204.

Radin, N. (in press). Primary caregiving fathers of long duration. In P. Bronstein & C.P. Cowan (Eds.), *Fatherhood Today: Men's changing role in the family.* NY: Wiley.

Radloff, L. (1977). Sex differences in depression: The effects of occupation and marital status. *Sex Roles, 1,* 249-265.

Rapoport, R., Rapoport, R.N. & Strelitz, Z. (1977). *Fathers, mothers and society*. New York: Basic Books.

Rossi, Alice S. (1977). A biosocial perspective on parenting. *Daedalus, 106* (Spring): 1-31.

Russell, G. (1982). Effects of maternal employment status on fathers' involvement in child care and play. *Australian & New Zealand Journal of Sociology, 18,* 172-179.

Russell, G. (1983). *The changing role of fathers?* St. Lucian, Qld: University of Queensland Press.

Sarbin, T.R. & Allen, V.L. (1968). Role theory. In G. Lindzey & E. Aranson (Eds.) *Handbook of social psychology*. (Vol I). Reading, MA: Addison-Wesley.

Shereshefsky, Pauline M., & Yarrow, Leon J. (1974). *Psychological aspects of a first pregnancy*. New York: Raven Press.

Stafford, R., Backman, E., & Dibona, P. (1977). The division of labor among cohabiting and married couples. *Journal of Marriage and the Family, 39,* 43-57.

Marital Change Across
the Transition to Parenthood

Jay Belsky
Emily Pensky

SUMMARY. Recent studies of the transition to parenthood which advance understanding over to earlier, cross sectional and retrospective investigations are examined with regard to what they indicate about how marriages change across the transition to parenthood. Before summarizing changes that occur in marital activities/interactions and sentiments, design issues pertaining to this recent research are considered, specifically the need for and meaning of a childless comparison group. An analysis of studies which employ and do not employ such contrast groups indicates that across the transition household division of labor becomes more traditional, couple leisure activities become less frequent, positive interchanges decrease whereas conflict increases, and overall satisfaction with the marriage and feelings of love for the spouse decline, especially in the case of wives. It is observed, however, that these changes are modest in magnitude (at least as currently measured) and probably represent the accentuation of changes that typically take place in marital relationships over time. The need to study the multiple determinants of individual differences in marital change across the transition to parenthood is considered in the concluding section of this paper, as are implications for practice.

Prior to the transition to parenthood the nuclear family is synonymous with the marital dyad. With the addition of another individ-

Jay Belsky, PhD, is Professor of Human Development; Emily Pensky is a graduate student in the Department of Individual and Family Studies, Penn State University, University Park, PA 16802.
Work on this paper was supported by grants from the National Institute of Child Health and Human Development (R01HD 15496) and from the National Institute of Mental Health (K02MH 00486).

133

ual, however, the family system increases in complexity; as one new, relatively helpless individual (i.e., the infant) is added to the preexisting marriage, the number of interpersonal relationships in the family triples. Presumably, this dramatic change in family structure alters the functioning of the husband-wife relationship. How so? That is the question we address in this paper. Drawing upon research findings from the several recent longitudinal studies of the transition to parenthood, we consider the basic — and often most obvious — changes that take place in the marriage when a first child is added to the family unit. We should note at the outset that we exclude from consideration what most would still regard as non-traditional families, even though from a standpoint of sheer numbers it is clear that what is normative has undergone dramatic change over the past two decades.

Investigation of the transition to parenthood also has changed dramatically in the last decade, as implied by the oft repeated criticisms of the early, pioneering work of Hobbs (1965, 1968). Contemporary research on this period of family formation has totally — and wisely — forsaken past concerns with crisis and, in so doing, has abandoned methodologically flawed, cross sectional and retrospective research designs in favor of prospective, longitudinal ones. Rather than directing attention to whether sufficient change has been experienced by the family to merit the (impossible-to-define) label of "crisis," contemporary investigators have concerned themselves with chronicling changes in self, marriage, and family functioning, and with understanding the determinants and consequences of the changes that are associated with the transition to parenthood.

As students of this transition we have found it useful to think about the process of becoming parents in terms of "an emergent family system," which we conceptualize as a developing set of interdependent interpersonal relationships. The functioning of this system is considered to be a product of the individual and relationship histories of the spouses and a source of influence on future individual and relationship functioning and family development. As should be evident, one basic, working assumption of this perspective is that continuity characterizes the family across major epochs of individual, relationship, and family system development. A second basic assumption is that family systems are open to change, particularly in terms of how relationship subsystems function, and that lawful processes which account for such change are empirically knowable; that is, they *are* measurable and subject to scientific scrutiny. A third assumption which, like the first, is mostly untested is that how the marriage functions, and how the family develops, will exert important influence on the future functioning of the marriage and the family and its constituent elements (i.e., individuals and relationships).

Our focus in this paper, then, on what is currently known about how marriages *change* across the transition to parenthood is motivated by a larger concern for how the family system works. It is noteworthy that all of the longitudinal investigations to be considered in this summary of characteristics of marital change across the transition to parenthood are concerned with this same general issue. This period of individual, relationship, and family development is thus widely recognized by a number of contemporary students of individual and family development as significant in its own right and of considerable importance from a more general perspective.

CURRENT LONGITUDINAL WORK:
DESIGN CONSIDERATIONS

It is incontestable that the research designs routinely employed today which include repeated measurements of families over time represent a significant advance over the first wave of investigation in which studies routinely consisted of the assessment of families at a single point in time—and often years after the birth of the first child. This does not mean that longitudinal designs, in and of themselves, are not without their limitations. Criticism has been wielded against research designs in which childless comparison groups have not been studied along with families expecting, bearing, and rearing first and later born children (e.g., Belsky et al., 1983, 1985). How are we to know, White and Booth (1985) recently asked, whether findings resultant from investigations that focus only upon couples having children are a function of the transition to parenthood or of marital time more generally? Without a "control" group, it is argued, how can we be sure that the changes that take place would not have occurred without the "experimental treatment," i.e., had no child been born?

As evidence that changes attributed to the transition to parenthood are indeed the result of marital time, White and Booth (1985) report the results of analyses of survey data gathered on some 220 individuals interviewed first in 1980 and again in 1983. Comparison of those who became parents (n = 107) between the two data collections and those who did not (n = 113) revealed no differences; regardless of parental status, overall marital happiness and frequency of marital interaction (actually joint marital activity) declined, whereas marital problems and disagreements increased.

Before it is inferred that the inclusion of control groups in research designs reveals the transition to parenthood to be a time of no special change, several points must be noted. The first is that even in the White and Booth (1985) study trends in the data indicated that "the presence of a new baby does seem to result in slightly greater increases in problems and disagreements than one would expect otherwise" (p. 147). One is thus left to wonder whether the telephone-interview, survey methodology employed in this investigation might have been insensitive to reliable changes in the marriage associated with the transition to parenthood. That this might indeed be the case is suggested ever so strongly by a more extensive interview and questionnaire-based study carried out by Cowan et al. (1985) which also utilized a childless-couple comparison group yet discerned consistent and highly reliable effects of the transition to parenthood. Also showing significant effects with a so-called control group is McHale and Huston's (1985) investigation, though not so extensively as did Cowan et al. (1985). The limited size of the McHale and Huston sample of parents (n = 28) and the fact that they were studying newlyweds in their first year of marriage raises the possibility that effects of becoming a parent might have been even more pronounced had statistical power not been so limited and had the transition to parenthood not been confounded with the transition to marriage. The fact that in both the White and Booth (1985) and McHale and Huston (1985) studies age of child varied across couples (and by as much as three years in the former study) leads us also to wonder whether this factor might affect the results obtained. In the Cowan et al. (1985) work, like that of Belsky et al. (1983, 1985), assessments of marriage are tied to the age of children, with resultant changes clearly being associated with time since the birth of the child.

The fact that the results of the Belsky and Cowan projects, conducted as they are in different parts of the country (Pennsylvania and California), using different research instruments, are in substantial agreement with each other—one with a comparison group and one without—leads us to believe that White and Booth (1985) may have overstated the case in arguing that the apparent effects of having a child on the marriage are principally the product of marital time, with all relationships deteriorating to the same extent irrespective of parental status. We do not mean to imply, though, that those changes in marriage associated with the transition to parenthood which we will consider in this paper are not somewhat a function of time. That this is indeed the case is clearly revealed by the Cowan et al. (1985) data which indicate that couples with children differ from childless couples in the degree, and usually not the direction, of change, with the transition to parenthood seeming to accelerate and conceivably accentuate changes that are observed in couples not bearing and rearing children.

A point that should not be lost in this brief discussion of research design and its implications for the assessment of marital change concerns the utility of childless comparison groups. The inclusion of such subjects in research on the transition to parenthood presumes that couples not bearing children provide an appropriate contrast for couples having children. Yet there would seem to be grounds for questioning this assumption and the very research designs that include "matched" groups or statistically control for pre-existing differences between groups. Families not expecting or rearing a baby differ from those that are in a variety of important ways above and beyond the mere status of parenthood or even the very demographic factors on which they are most likely to be compared for purposes of establishing their similarity and presumed equivalence. Most importantly, many couples today choose to have a child, and, even among those that do not willfully plan to have a first born yet nevertheless do, many do not "work" as hard as others to avoid pregnancy and childbirth. Thus, even when differences emerge in a comparative study using a two-group design, it would seem impossible to determine whether it was the actual transition to parenthood, or the motivation to become (or not to become) parents, which was responsible. In fact, unless a comparison group was comprised of couples trying to conceive a baby, and thus evincing a motive similar to those bearing a child, it is doubtful that an appropriate comparison group would be available. And, of course, the experience of couples desirous of becoming pregnant but not succeeding is likely to make them functionally quite different from those with a similar motive that are successful. The point to be made is simply that one needs to recognize limits inherent in quasi-experimental designs and not presume that a between-group comparison provides the most valid assessment of the effects of parenthood on the marital relationship.

CHARACTERIZING MARITAL CHANGE

There are a variety of ways to conceptualize marriages and, as a result, a myriad of ways to measure them. In this analysis of marital change across the transition to parenthood we follow Huston and Robins (1982) in distinguishing marital behavior, interactions, and activities from more subjective feelings and attitudes regarding one's spouse and the marital relationship. To be recognized, in this regard, is the fact that behavioral events and subjective feelings are reciprocally and causally related; that is, it is not simply the case that spousal interactions generate marital sentiments or that feelings about the spouse and the marriage affect what transpires behaviorally between spouses, but rather that over time both of these processes occur.

Activities and Interactions

Studies of the transition to parenthood address three distinct, yet interrelated aspects of the marital relationship as considered from a behavioral perspective: division of labor, leisure activities, and affectively-toned interactions. Each of these will be considered in turn.

Division of Labor

It is commonly assumed that one effect of having a baby is the traditionalization of the household division of labor. In order to address this issue investigators have typically queried spouses about "who does what," usually using a list of traditionally female activities (e.g., preparing the meals, making the beds, cleaning the home, doing the laundry, etc.). The specific method employed in various studies has ranged from reliance on a single question (White & Booth, 1985), to a series of task-related questions addressed to each spouse individually (Cowan et al., 1985) or to the couple (Belsky et al., 1983, 1985), to telephone reports of exactly who did what on a given day (McHale & Huston, 1985).

In general, the evidence tends to indicate that wives assume more household tasks such as doing dishes and laundry, preparing meals and cleaning house after the arrival of the first child than before (Belsky et al., 1985; LaRossa & LaRossa, 1981; Cowan et al., 1976). This should not be read to imply, though, that prior to the child's birth husbands perform more such duties than wives or that responsibilities are roughly equivalent, only that the absolute burden on women in the household seems to increase across the transition (even when not considering child care tasks). For example, Cowan et al. (1985) found that not only were couples bearing children more traditional in their household division of labor than couples not having children, but that this was also true with respect to their division of labor prenatally and with their expectations regarding how things would be once the baby was born. These results are consistent with those reported by McHale and Huston (1985) in their small sample study of newlyweds; as they noted,

Sex role patterns became more traditional inside the home with parenthood. The transition to parenthood increased the work load at home for both husbands and wives, but the increase was considerably greater for wives. The proportion of instrumental activities carried out by wives remained stable over the year for nonparents, but women who became mothers experienced a substantial increase in their relative responsibilities (from 67% to 79%). . . . Thus the data taken as a whole suggest that the transition to parenthood traditionalizes sex role patterns not so much by reducing the tendency of men and women to take on tasks typically done by members of the other sex but rather by an increase in the extent to which women carry out the kinds of tasks that traditionally have been done by women. (p. 422)

This seemingly consistent finding that the transition to parenthood exerts a traditionalizing impact on household division of labor has not gone unchallenged. In their longitudinal analysis of a large, nationally representative sample, White and Booth (1985) reported no differences in the manner in which or extent to which division of labor changed for childless couples and couples bearing children. Important to note, however, in evaluating the meaning of these findings is the fact that traditionalism was measured by only a single item in the telephone survey.

The traditionalizing effect of the transition to parenthood has been called into question by Goldberg et al. (1985) also, but for different reasons. Most assessments of change in the division of labor, they note, rely upon comparisons of "who does what" *late* in pregnancy and again sometime following the baby's birth. Upon measuring division of labor *early* in pregnancy as well as at these other two points in time, Goldberg et al. discovered a curvilinear pattern of change — with the least sex-typed arrangements occurring late in pregnancy, something Rausch et al. (1974, cited in Power and Parke, 1984) noted more than a decade ago. Because this is often the initial time of assessment in many study designs, Goldberg et al. argue that findings such as those summarized above represent statistical artifacts; that is, the reason that division of labor appears to become more traditional is that baseline measurements are made at that pint in the transition process when couples are *least* traditional and this is not necessarily representative of the family at other points in time — even during pregnancy.

In making this useful observation, Goldberg et al. fail to stress the fact that even their data tend to indicate that the traditional nature of the division of labor increases from early in pregnancy to the period after the child's arrival. So even through baseline measurements obtained late in pregnancy may *inflate* the degree to which to division of labor becomes more traditional, the *direction* of change is still accurately depicted. In actuality, what may be most significant from a phenomenological perspective, especially for a wife, is the pattern of change in which she has the opportunity to do less late in pregnancy only to do more afterwards. Could it be that the very assistance which she receives toward the end of pregnancy makes the return to the old pattern, even if not a more traditional pattern, particularly noticeable and more disturbing than it might otherwise be? In view of the fact that in most households it is the wife who assumes the lion's share of child care tasks (e.g., bathing, feeding), this seems quite possible. Thus the very inflated effect which Goldberg et al. (1985) contend many investigators are chronicling may well reflect the point of comparison that wives use when appraising their own and husband's contribution postnatally. While distorting the size of the effect of the transition to parenthood on the division of labor, research designs which assess family functioning in late pregnancy for the first time may nevertheless accurately characterize the phenomenological experience of the family, or at least that of wives.

Leisure Activities

When one considers the extensive needs of the newborn infant and young baby, the additional costs incurred in rearing a child, and the fact that many young families today are physically distant from their own parents (who are potential babysitters), it might be expected that the transition to parenthood decreases the amount of time the couple has to engage in recreational activities together and/ or alters the way in which spouses spend their time together. Even though this area of marital activity has not been studied as extensively as division of labor, there does exist empirical support for each of these propositions.

In order to address the issue of frequency of joint leisure, Belsky et al. (1983, 1985) asked their working- and middle-class couples how often they engaged in joint leisure activities, such as going out to dinner, to the movies or just watching television. Results revealed a significant decline from the last trimester of pregnancy through three-months postpartum and a leveling off thereafter. Because McHale and Huston (1985) did not discern a similar pattern of change in either their sample of parents or nonparents, we are led to wonder whether the number of years of marriage may mediate this effect somewhat; the couples in the Belsky et al. investigations had been married for more than four years on average, whereas those in the McHale and Huston study were in their first year of marriage.

What McHale and Huston did observe in their sample of newly-weds, however, was that what husbands and wives did when they were together changed across the transition to parenthood. Specifically, and in contrast to those couples that did not become parents, "couples who became parents increased in the proportion of joint activities that centered around household tasks and child care responsibilities" (p. 420). Thus, even though the absolute amount of time that newlyweds spent together did not seem to change, relative to childless couples, those that experienced the transition to parenthood spent a smaller *proportion* of their time in the very recreational activities that the Belsky et al. studies found to decrease in absolute frequency following the transition among couples that had been married for a number of years. From a phenomenological standpoint, it is important to recognize that this *relative frequency* may have the same, if not greater, psychological impact on the couple as a change in absolute frequency. That is, all time which husbands and wives spend together is not the same, and the relative decline in joint leisure time may not compensate for the other time that is spent together in more instrumental activities. Indeed, this may be one reason why couples in the Belsky et al. (1983, 1985) studies characterized their marriages as more of a partnership and less of a romance following the transition than they did before.

It remains unclear at the present time whether the change under consideration in the things which couples do together is characteristic of all married couples or just those rearing young children. Recognizing the need for future research to resolve this issue, it seems reasonable for the time being to draw the tentative conclusions that, with the possible exception of newlyweds, absolute time spent in joint leisure activity declines across the transition to parenthood and that, probably for all couples, the relative time spent in recreational activities also decreases. What is also unclear at present and just as much in need of future attention is whether rates of joint leisure activity ever return to prechild levels and, if so, when. Also to be addressed are the multiple determinants of change sin this domain of marital activity. Money, energy, availability of babysitters, and the employment status of mothers are a few of the factors that may determine the extent to which leisure activities change with the onset of parenthood.

Consideration of these potential determinants of change in leisure activities serves to raise a series of additional questions. For example, if husband and wife feel differently about leaving their baby with a sitter, do changes in leisure result in marital stress and conflict? If this is indeed the case, changes in leisure activity may have implications which are more serious than the dissatisfaction resulting from the mere change in time spent together. Indeed, the exact meaning of these changes most likely varies from couple to couple. Consider in this regard the significance of getting out of the house during the evening for a woman who is at home all day with her baby in contrast to one whose daily routine involves separating from the child each working day in order to pursue a career or earn needed income for the family.

Affectively-Toned Interactions

In view of the changes that seem to occur following the transition to parenthood in household division of labor and leisure activities, it stands to reason that the behavioral interactions that take place between spouses would also change with the onset of parenthood. That this might indeed be the case was suggested in Ryder's (1973) early longitudinal study in which it was found that new mothers, in contrast to childless women, were significantly more likely to report that their husbands were not paying enough attention to them. Consideration of more recent longitudinal work reveals that this is not the only aspect of marital interaction that changes across the transition to parenthood.

Several studies report that the frequency, nature and/or quality of positively-toned interactions between husband and wife change over time. In their first longitudinal investigation, Belsky et al. (1983) discerned a significant decline in the expression of positive affection from the last trimester of pregnancy through nine months postpartum as reported by both husbands and wives. In their second study, substantially similar results were chronicled using a different measurement system, one developed by Huston (1983; Huston, McHale, & Crouter, in press) which assessed the extent to which spouses would like positive events to occur more often than they do (Belsky et al., 1985). Specifically, from the last trimester of pregnancy through nine-months postpartum, husbands and wives alike experienced decreasing levels of positive interactions; that is, over time they expressed an increasing desire for such events to occur more frequently than they actually did. It is important to note that these questionnaire-based findings from both studies are in perfect agreement with observational data collected in the same two investigations which indicated that the expression of positive affect between spouses during the course of one-hour visits to the family declined in frequency of occurrence from the first to third to ninth postpartum month.

McHale and Huston's (1985) comparison of newlywed couples with and without children indicates that this change in positive interaction over time is not restricted to only those couples experiencing the transition to parenthood. This is not to say, however, that the experiences of parents and nonparents are exactly the same. In fact, McHale and Huston (1985) discovered that the change experienced by parents was more pronounced; that is, even though newlywed couples bearing and not bearing a first child exchanged fewer positive behaviors over time, the degree of decline was greater for those couples that became parents than for those that did not. Important to note, though, is the fact that this change resulted principally from the elevated levels of positive interaction that occurred during pregnancy rather than as a result of different levels of such events following the birth of the infant.

Consideration of negative as opposed to positive interactions between spouses, and particularly marital conflict, presents a picture of the transition to parenthood that is quite consistent with the one we have just considered. Unpublished data from our lab on some 180 couples, for example, indicates that conflict between spouses increases from the last trimester of pregnancy through the ninth postpartum month. And the work of the Cowans further reveals that it is not the case that childless couples and couples with children both experience an increase in conflict over time, with the experience of the latter group being simply more pronounced than that of the former (Cowan et al., 1985). In fact, in their longitudinal study, it was discovered that while frequency of conflict increased for those experiencing the transition to parenthood, frequency of conflict actually decreased for those who did not become parents. To be noted, however, is the fact that White and Booth (1985) report distinctly different results using their nationally representative sample, with conflict being found to increase — and to the same extent — for parents and nonparents alike.

How are we to reconcile the differences between these two studies? Upon considering the volunteer nature of the Cowan et al. sample and the nationally representative nature of the White and Booth sample, one might be led to conclude that the results of the latter are likely to be more generalizable. Before such conclusions are drawn, however, it is important to note the potential limits of the survey methodology employed by White and Booth and their implications. In fact, because the survey included only four items related to conflict, with two of these involving the use of violence during an argument and the presence of an alcohol problem in the family, we are inclined to question the sensitivity of White and Booth's measure and, as a consequence, the conclusions that can be drawn from their work with respect to the effect of the transition to parenthood on marital conflict.

To the extent that positive interactions decrease following the transition to parenthood and marital conflict increases, there is reason to consider the cause of these changes. Once again it is likely to be the case that changes such as those just discussed are multiply determined. The wife's work status, differences in childrearing attitudes and practices of the parents, and changes in the couple's sexual relationship all seem worthy of attention in future research designed to address this question. Our own experience studying couples going through the transition leads us to believe that it is the division of labor, or "who does what," that is the greatest source of conflict in the marriage. Invariably, wives assume more household burdens than do men, and at least two studies indicate that family roles turn out to be more traditional postnatally than couples anticipated prenatally (Belsky, Ward, & Rovine, 1986; Cowan et al., 1985). Not only does it seem likely that these violated expectations breed difficulty, but also likely to be contributing are the different points of view that husbands and wives hold within a family. Wives, we suspect, often view their husbands as not doing nearly enough at the same time that husbands may well regard themselves as making a considerable, even if not equivalent, contribution to the household division of labor. Whereas husbands are likely to evaluate their contribution in terms of what their own fathers did in their families of origin or in terms of what their friends and coworkers contribute, wives probably evaluate their husbands' contributions in terms of their own role performance. The husbands who considers himself, then, to be somewhat nontraditional in preparing a meal or two each week, helping to get the baby dressed in the morning, and getting up periodically at night to change a diaper may well encounter a wife who (legitimately) accuses him of not doing anything, or at least very little, and certainly not enough.

This scenario strikes us as one that may well go on in many middle-class homes today since many women have been led to believe that sex roles have changed a great deal more than they actually have. That such a situation could breed conflict is not difficult to envision. And the fact that "who does what" is an issue which a couple must confront, either explicitly or implicitly, each and every day, makes it an arena of marital activity that may well have as much if not more to do with how the transition to parenthood affects the marriage than anything else.

Subjective Feelings and Attitudes

In view of the changes that we have considered in marital activities and interactions that accompany the transition to parenthood, it seems reasonable to expect that the feelings that husband and wife have for each other and for their marital relationship should also be affected by the experience of becoming parents. In order to explore this possibility, most investigations of the transition have employed some standardized and well utilized measures of overall marital quality, routinely labeled marital satisfaction. The Locke-Wallace (1959) Marital Satisfaction Scale and the Spanier (1976) Dyadic Adjustment Scale are two of the more commonly used measurements. It should be noted that these assessment devices have been criticized in recent years due to the fact that they assess, and routinely combine in their scoring system, both interactive processes (e.g., frequency of conflict) and subjective feelings (e.g., feelings of closeness to spouse) (Huston & Robins, 1982). In response to this criticism, efforts have been made in studies of the transition to parenthood to assess overall satisfaction with the marriage at a more subjective level (Belsky et al., 1985; McHale & Huston, 1985) or to focus upon particular feelings toward the spouse, such as love and ambivalence (Belsky et al., 1985).

As indicated at the outset of this paper, many of the earliest studies assessing change in the marital relationship across the transition to parenthood focused on marital satisfaction and were somewhat consistent in showing a general decline in retrospectively evaluated marital quality (LeMasters, 1957; Hobbs, 1965; Hobbs & Wimbish, 1979; Glenn & McLanahan, 1982). Ryder's (1973) early longitudinal study, in which marital satisfaction was assessed (using the Locke-Wallace scale) prenatally and again at three-months postpartum, provided support for conclusions drawn from retrospective studies, namely, that the transition to parenthood adversely affects the marital relationship. In contrast to a comparison group of nonparents, he found that wives, though not husbands, significantly declined in self-reported satisfaction with their marriage.

More than a decade later, using a design quite similar to Ryder, Cowan et al. (1985) replicated and extended his findings. Also using the Locke-Wallace instrument, Cowan et al. (1985) found that

within the first six months of the infant's life women who had become parents showed a significant — and negative — change in overall marital satisfaction and that this was not the case for their husbands or for childless spouses. By the time assessments of the
marriage were made for the third time, when children were 18
months of age, husbands who had become fathers also evinced a
significant and pronounced decline in marital satisfaction with
wives continuing to decline, too, though not as steeply as did husbands from 6-18 months postpartum. Once again, husbands and
wives who remained childless did not display the same degree of
change. These data led Cowan et al. to conclude not only that it was
the transition to parenthood and not simply marital time which exerted an effect, but also that men and women differ in their "journeys into parenthood," such that "the impact of becoming a parent
is felt first by women" and "only later do men feel the negative effects . . ." (p. 469). To be noted is the fact that this heightened
susceptibility to negative change by women has been a persistent
finding in the transition to parenthood literature for decades (e.g.,
Waldron & Routh, 1981; Hobbs, 1965; Hobbs & Wimbish, 1977;
Russell, 1974; see also Rossi, 1968).

Also consistent with the patterns of change chronicled by Cowan
et al. in their middle- and working-class, volunteer sample in California is evidence obtained by Belsky and his colleagues on some
250 Pennsylvania families participating in three longitudinal investigations. Although the first study chronicled modest, but ever so
reliable declines in overall marital adjustment for husbands and
wives alike through the first nine months of parenthood (using the
Spanier scale), one of our subscales, that measuring cohesion or
closeness, revealed significantly different patterns of change for
husbands and wives, with wives displaying more pronounced
change than their spouses (Belsky et al., 1983). The remaining two
samples, which responded to completely different self-report instruments at the same times of measurement (prenatal, three-month and
nine-month postpartum), displayed a similar pattern (Belsky et al.,
1983, unpublished). Specifically, overall satisfaction assessed using a semantic differential procedure developed by Campbell, Converse, and Rogers (1976), on which individuals evaluated their
marriages in terms of a series of bipolar adjectives (e.g., miserable-

enjoyable, rewarding-disappointing, boring-interesting), declined more for wives than husbands, though significantly so for both. The same was true for feelings of love for the partner and ambivalence about the relationship, though, in the case of ambivalence, feelings tended to increase over time rather than decrease (as with love and satisfaction). In view of all these findings, it is little wonder that Miller and Sollie (1980) observed that marital stress increased to a much greater extent in the case of wives in comparison to husbands from the first through eighth postpartum month.

Despite this apparent consistency across studies, both with childless comparison groups (Ryder, 1973; Cowan et al., 1985) and without (Belsky et al., 1983, 1985, unpublished; Miller & Sollie, 1980), the change patterns just detailed and attributed to the transition to parenthood have not been observed on each and every occasion on which they have been studied longitudinally. White and Booth (1985), we indicated earlier, found that marital happiness and satisfaction, measured via 11 questions in their nationally representative telephone survey, changed in the same direction and virtually (though not completely) to the same degree in the case of individuals having children or remaining childless. Recall, however, that nonsignificant trends in the data indicated that the decline in marital quality was greater for individuals going through the transition to parenthood. McHale and Huston (1985), too, found no differences in change patterns in their sample of newlyweds who became and did not become parents using the very same marital satisfaction instrument employed by Belsky et al. (1985) and described above.

What are we to make of these two "dissenting" studies. First, it should be clear, as we hope it has been throughout this assessment of marital change across the transition to parenthood, that whatever the effects of having a baby on the marriage are they are not always distinguishable from those associated with the mere passage of time. The fact that the McHale and Huston (1985) investigation was of a small sample of parents quite distinct from those assessed in other investigations (i.e., newlyweds) leads us to believe that, in many respects, just being married for the first year results in as much marital change as does combining this experience with the rearing of a newborn infant. It is more difficult to decipher the meaning of the survey findings reported by White and Booth (1985). The fact that other studies using childless-couple comparison groups discern effects attributable to the transition to parenthood per se, when coupled with the possibility that the telephone survey assessment of individuals with children of widely varying ages may be somewhat insensitive to change in the first place, leads us to conclude that it is probably not just the passage of time that is responsible for the changes in marital activities, interactions, and sentiments that are associated with the transition to parenthood. In all likelihood, though, and as noted earlier, these changes probably reflect the accentuation of developments that occur in marriages with the passage of time regardless of parental status.

CONCLUSION

It is highly likely that anyone who has read what we have written through this point would be ready to conclude that both time and the transition to parenthood take their toll on marriages, especially as experienced by wives. This is certainly what the data consistently seem to indicate. Although it is true that there are undeniable benefits or gratifications associated with the transition (Russell, 1974; Sollie & Miller, 1980), these have not been studied as extensively as the costs associated with the experience. Why this is the case is not entirely clear to us, but it may well have something to do with the more-difficult-to-measure nature of the good things or the fact that when it comes to marriages, are outweighed and thus overshadowed by the difficulties that are encountered.

Despite the changes associated with the transition to parenthood and a variety of domains of the marital relationship, it would be a mistake to conclude that the changes that have been reported in the literature are striking in magnitude. Although this may indeed be the case phenomenologically, the actual degree of change discerned in most studies is rather modest, even when ever so reliable from a statistical standpoint. The reliability of the change, we are convinced, stems from the virtual universality of the experience. The limited magnitude of the change, on the other hand, may well be a function of the fact that individuals in these longitudinal investigations are asked to share a good deal of private experience and personal feelings, something that may be difficult for even volunteer subjects to do. Thus the measured changes may underestimate the experienced changes.

Whatever the size of the changes under consideration, it must be kept in mind that everything which we have discussed up to this point has been concerned with central tendencies, that is, the average experience. All comparisons have involved mean scores from two or more points in time. This, however, is not the only way to conceptualize and measure change. Another way is to think in terms of the rank ordering of individuals and thus whether having a baby turns a good marriage into a bad one or a bad marriage into a good one. Although it may be the case that this is sometimes true, the available evidence suggests otherwise. That is, studies which have compared the rank ordering of marriages in terms of a variety of indices of general quality routinely report that, to a highly significant extent, those marriages that appear to be most harmonious before the child's arrival continue to look that way afterwards; conversely, those couples that seem most dissatisfied with the functioning of their marriages before the transition are more than likely to feel similarly afterwards (Belsky et al., 1983, 1985, unpublished; Cowan et al., 1985; McHale & Huston, 1985). So, even as marital quality is declining, with individuals becoming less satisfied over time, those involved in more satisfying relationships initially remain generally more satisfied subsequently.

Once again, it is important not to overstate the case. Some reshuffling of individuals and couples in terms of their rank ordering does take place over time, though in the only study that has conducted the appropriate comparison, such instability in individual differences is no greater among individuals who become parents than it is among those who do not (McHale & Huston, 1985). Nevertheless, this change at the level of individuals would seem to be one of the most intriguing aspects of the transition to parenthood. Put another way, why are some individuals and couples more affected by the experience of becoming parents than are others? The research that is available to address this question underscores the fact that individual differences in marital change and in the experience of the transition to parenthood more generally are multiply determined. In this regard, characteristics of individual parents, such as their self-esteem and their expectations have been found to relate to variation in the transition experience (Belsky, Ward, & Rovine, 1986; Cowan & Cowan, 1983; Kach & McGhee, 1982). So too have characteristics of the marriage prior to the child's arrival, including level of marital satisfaction and cohesion (Wandersman & Wandersman, 1980; Ryder, 1973) and even number of years married (Russell, 1974). Differences in infants' health and temperament also have been implicated as factors affecting the degree to which the transition is stressful and the marriage is strained (Belsky, Ward, & Rovine, 1986; Hobbs, 1965; Russell, 1974). The fact that experience which adults report having had in their families of origin, including how they were reared and the quality of their parents' marriage (Belsky & Isabella, 1985; Cox et al., 1985), also relates to variation in the transition experience raises in our mind the possibility that developmental experiences, by influencing one's personality development and even mate selection, may also affect the way the marriage functions prior to and during pregnancy and how it develops and changes across the transition to parenthood.

At multiple levels of analysis, then, individuals and relationships may be more or less vulnerable or resistant to the marital stress that seems to be normatively associated with the transition to parenthood. That this might be the case is certainly consistent with the emergent-family system perspective outlined briefly in the introduction to this paper. This is not meant to imply, however, that the past is fully deterministic of how the transition to parenthood is experienced by the couple, but rather simply that the past is prologue to the future. The exact extent to which this is the case must await future study not only of marital changes across the transition to parenthood but of the multiple determinants of such change as well.

Even though future study is called for, efforts can be undertaken at this point in time to support couples as they approach and navigate the transition to parenthood. Many expectant parents are hungry for information and assistance that might make the transition less stressful. It would seem helpful simply to disseminate the message, both to parents-to-be and to nonparents entertaining the possibility of becoming parents, that marriages do change with the advent of the parenting role, and that these changes are similar to those that are likely to ensue with time anyway. Further, making it clear to couples that parenthood does not save poor marriages, or seem to seriously harm good marriages, might well alleviate the anxieties that some couples have while simultaneously educating those who are wishfully expecting the shared activity of parenting to make a stressed relationship more harmonious.

As we have noted elsewhere (Belsky, in press), childbirth education classes would seem to be an ideal place for intervention efforts to be undertaken, particularly because large numbers of families voluntarily enroll in these community sponsored programs. Unfortunately, it is all too often the case that these classes devote themselves virtually entirely to the birth event itself, with relatively little attention paid to the period which follows the child's arrival. By using part of the childbirth class as a period for couples to talk in small groups about their expectations, it is conceivable that anticipatory socialization might take place that would otherwise not occur. To the extent that such discussion could be focused on salient issues like the division of labor, feelings about responding to a crying baby, and the involvement of parents and in-laws in the emerging family system, it is likely that effects of such intervention would be greater. By learning not only about what their spouses might be thinking, but what others who are also awaiting the arrival of a baby are anticipating, it seems possible that individuals and couples might develop more realistic expectations regarding the transitional pressures they are likely to encounter.

If any such efforts were built into existent childbirth classes, we would want to discourage the relabeling of these classes as preparation for parenthood programs. We suspect that such an explicit focus might well discourage some couples from participating who now participate because the title and reputation of the classes suggest a more limited focus. Although this might be regarded by some as deceptive, our experience suggests that once in these programs parents-to-be may be more willing to participate in activities such as those suggested above than they would otherwise have been if asked initially to enroll in a program that explicitly emphasized marital change and the more general nature of the transition to parenthood. In other words, we feel that for such preparatory efforts to be effective and attract a maximum number of families they must be subtle in their orientation. Individuals, we feel, while willing to admit to their ignorance regarding the birth event and to seek assistance in the service of avoiding pain, are probably far less inclined to seek support in negotiating the transition to parenthood as this might make them feel like they were admitting to being in trouble and needing help. Programming thus needs to be sensitive to the sensitivities of parents-to-be who, like many others, often regard participation in interventions that are nonmedical in nature as admissions that there is something wrong or problematical with them.

REFERENCES

Belsky, J. (in press). Marital change and the transition to parenthood. *Childbirth Education.*

Belsky, J., & Isabella, R. A. (1985). Marital and parent-child relationships in family of origin and marital change following the birth of a baby: A retrospective analysis. *Child Development, 56,* 342-349.

Belsky, J., Lang, M. E., & Rovine, M. (1985). Stability and change in marriage across the transition to parenthood: A second study. *Journal of Marriage and the Family, 47,* 855-865.

Belsky, J., Spanier, G. B., & Rovine, M. (1983). Stability and change in marriage across the transition to parenthood. *Journal of Marriage and the Family, 45,* 553-556.

Belsky, J., Ward, H., & Rovine, M. (1986). Prenatal expectations, postnatal experiences and the transition to parenthood. In R. Ashmore & D. Brodzinsky (Eds.), *Perspectives on the family* (pp. 119-146). Hillsdale, NJ: Lawrence Erlbaum, Assoc.

Campbell, A., Converse, P., & Rodgers, W. (1976). *Quality of American life: Perception, evaluation and satisfaction.* New York: Russell Sage.

Cowan, C., Cowan, P., Core, L., & Core, J. (1978). Becoming a family: The impact of a first child's birth on the couple's relationship. In L. Newman & W. Miller (Eds.), *The first-child and family formation* (pp. 296-326). Chapel Hill, NC: Carolina Population Center.

Cowan, C. P., Cowan, P. A., Heming, G., Coysh, W. S., Curtis-Boles, H., & Boles, A. J. (1985). Transition to parenthood: His, hers, and theirs. *Journal of Family Issues, 6*(4), 451-481.

Cox, M. J., Owen, H. T., Lewis, J. H., Reidel, C., Scalf-McIver, C., & Suster, A. (1985). Intergenerational influences on the parent-infant relationship in the transition to parenthood. *Journal of Family Issues, 6*(4), 543-564.

Glenn, N. D., & McLanahan, S. (1982). Children and marital happiness: A further specification of the relationship. *Journal of Marriage and the Family, 44*, 63-72.

Goldberg, W. A., Michaels, G. Y., & Lamb, M. E. (1985). Husbands' and wives': Adjustment to pregnancy and first parenthood. *Journal of Family Issues, 6*(4), 483-503.

Hobbs, D. (1965). Parenthood as crisis: A third study. *Journal of Marriage and the Family, 27*, 367-372.

Hobbs, D., & Wimbish, J. (1977). Transition to parenthood by black couples. *Journal of Marriage and the Family, 39*, 677-689.

Huston, T. (1983, July). *The topography of marriage: A longitudinal study of change in husband-wife relationships over the first year*. Plenary address to the International Conference of Personal Relationships, Madison, WI.

Huston, T. L., McHale, S., & Crouter, A. (in press). When the honeymoon's over: Changes in the marriage relationship over the first year. In R. Gilmour & S. Duck (Eds.), *The emerging field of personal relationship*. Hillsdale, NJ: Lawrence Erlbaum, Assoc.

Huston, T., & Robins, E. (1982). Conceptual and methodological issues in studying close relationships. *Journal of Marriage and the Family, 44*, 901-925.

Kach, J., & McGhee, P. (1982). Adjustment to early parenthood: The role of accuracy of preparenthood expectations. *Journal of Family Issues, 3*, 361-374.

LaRossa, R., & LaRossa, M. M. (1981). *Transition to parenthood: How infants change families*. Beverly Hills, CA: Sage Publications.

LeMasters, E. E. (1957). Parenthood at crisis. *Marriage and Family Living, 19*, 352-355.

Locke, H. J., & Wallace, K. M. (1959). Short-term marital adjustment tests: Their reliability and validity. *Journal of Marriage and Family Living, 21*, 251-255.

McHale, S. M., & Huston, T. L. (1985). The effect of the transition to parenthood on the marriage relationship. *Journal of Family Issues, 6*(4), 409-433.

Miller, B. C., & Sollie, D. L. (1980). Normal stresses during the transition to parenthood. *Family Relations, 29*, 459-465.

Power, T. G., & Parke, R. D. (1984). Social network factors and the transition to parenthood. *Sex Roles, 10*, 949-972.

Rausch, H., Barry, W., Hertel, R., & Swain, M. (1974). *Communications, conflict, and marriage* . San Francisco: Jossey-Bass. Cited in T. G. Power & R. D. Parke (1984), Social network factors and the transition to parenthood. *Sex Roles, 10*, 949-972.

Rossi, A. (1968). Transition to parenthood. *Journal of Marriage and the Family,* *30,* 26-39.

Russell, C. S. (1974). Transition to parenthood: Problems and gratifications. *Journal of Marriage and the Family, 36,* 294-302.

Ryder, R. (1973). Longitudinal data relating marital satisfaction and having a child. *Journal of Marriage and the Family, 35,* 604-607.

Sollie, D. L., & Miller, B. C. (1980). The transition to parenthood as a critical time for building family strengths. In N. Stinnet, B. Chesses, J. DeFrain, & P. Kraus (Eds.), *Family strengths: Positive models of family life.* Lincoln: University of Nebraska Press.

Spanier, G. B. (1976). Measuring dyadic adjustment: New scales for assessing the quality of marriage and similar dyads. *Journal of Marriage and the Family, 38,* 15-28.

Waldron, H., & Routh, D. (1981). The effect of the first child on the marital relationship. *Journal of Marriage and the Family, 43,* 785-788.

Wandersman, L., Wandersman, A., & Kahn, S. (1980). Social support in the transition to parenthood. *Journal of Community Psychology, 8,* 332-342.

White, L. K., & Booth, A. V. (1985). The transition to parenthood and marital quality. *Journal of Family Issues, 6*(4), 435-449.

Changes in
Parent-Child Relationships
with the Birth of
the Second Child

Kurt Kreppner

INTRODUCTION

Hill and Aldous (1969) wrote that "parenthood rather than marriage appears to be the crucial role transition point that marks the entrance into adulthood status in our society." This means that the arrival of a child changes existing relationships not only among spouses but also among the new parents and the outside world. Clearly, it is the first child's arrival that is mostly thought of as having the greatest influence on the young couple's life and status. The arrival of the second child is not seen as having a comparably far-reaching impact. This article's aim, however, is to show that aspects of the second child's arrival deserve particular attention as far as family formation and changes in parent-child relationships are regarded under a family-developmental perspective.

The entry into parenthood after the first child's birth and its potential crises has been described by a number of interview and

Kurt Kreppner, PhD, is Senior Research Specialist, Max Planck Institute for Human Development & Education, 94 Lentzealle, D-1000, Berlin 33, Germany.

The empirical research reported in this article is part of a project which is carried out in collaboration with Yvonne Schuetze. I gratefully acknowledge the helpful contributions of Alexander von Eye to the statistical analysis of the data. I want to thank Christiane Brunke and Holger Wessels for their assistance in computing the data and I appreciate all the raters who helped to produce the data from the videotapes.

checklist studies concerning general changes of the spouses' assessment of family satisfaction during pregnancy and after birth (LeMasters, 1957; Dyer, 1963; Hobbs, 1965). Methodologically more sophisticated research was conducted in recent years as to how stressful pregnancy and the first child's first months in the family are experienced by the young couple (Ryder 1973; Cowan et al., 1978; Jaffe & Viertel, 1979; Entwisle & Doering, 1980; Miller & Solling, 1980). Aside from some divergent results concerning the depth of crises experienced by mothers and fathers or the degree of prepartum and postpartum marital satisfaction, these studies' common results point to a general crisis for mothers after the birth and during the first months of the infant's life. A few months after birth, an intensified crisis was found to occur for both parents in many couples. During this time, fathers are more involved in experiencing crises than during the time of pregnancy.

In recent years only a few studies investigated how a second child aggravates or ameliorates the crises that have been reported as occurring when the first child arrives. This handful of studies will be discussed later, after reviewing the domain in developmental psychology which to date has generated the richest stock of material concerning second born children, the sibling studies.

The following article will center on three aspects. First, the second child's actual status in psychological and sociological studies will be briefly reviewed, second, a framework will be discussed which may help to conceptualize the structural and family-developmental implications of a second child's arrival in terms of problems and crises, and third, some results from an empirical study will be presented which can elucidate general trends in changes concerning family interaction patterns after the birth of a second child.

THE SECOND CHILD AS A SIBLING AND A SOURCE OF STRESS

Sibling Studies

To become a full-fledged subject in sociological and psychological research, the second child had to make its way to scientific attention through the sibling status. Three main strains of research can be followed while regarding the role of the second child as an object of sibling studies: first, as product of specific family constellations, second, as a target of particular parent-child interaction likened to the older sibling, and third, as a producer of specific intellectual and social capacities in reaction to a particular interaction milieu.

Constellation

The second child attained a prominent role when being considered a product of a specific sibling constellation within the family in respect to sex, age, and interval (spacing), which endow him or her with specific personality characteristics (Koch, 1955a,b, 1956; Sutton-Smith, & Rosenberg, 1970). Depending on whether the second child is a boy or a girl, a same-sex or an opposite-sex sibling, and whether siblings are closely (less than two years), moderately (2 - 4 years), or widely (more than 4 years) spaced, his or her behavior will differ from the older sibling's. For example, according to Sutton-Smith and Rosenberg (1970), second born boys display a greater amount of aggressivity and peer orientation than their first born male sibling. In cases in which the older sibling was a sister, these boys showed a considerable degree of dominant behavior. In general, spacing was analyzed as to how it might influence similarity and dissimilarity among siblings: Whereas moderate spacing seems to enlarge differences between siblings, narrow spacing diminishes differences, especially when both siblings are female.

Interaction

Parent-child interactions and their differences concerning first and second born children were the second prominent issue in sibling research. The longitudinal study of Lasko (1954) focused on parental, mostly maternal behavior to first and second born siblings over a longer period of time. The most outstanding result in this study was the abrupt change of parental interaction with the first born after the second year — usually the time when the sibling is born — compared to the greater continuity of parental behavior towards the second born child. In addition, mothers showed a greater degree of warmth toward their second children. Studies conducted by Jacobs and Moss (1976), Kendrick and Dunn (1980), and Abramovitch et al.(1982) indicate that particularly during the first months after the birth of a second child the mother is absorbed in caretaking activities for the new child and decreases her activities with the first child. Spacing played a crucial role in maternal caretaking activities for first and second born children: Widely spaced as well as closely spaced second infants received more material attention than middle-spaced children (Lewis & Kreitzberg, 1979). Jacob and Moss' (1976) investigation unveiled that mothers spent significantly less time in social, affectionate, and caretaking interactions with their second borns compared to the time they spent with the first child. This replicated earlier results by Rotbarth (1971) and Thoman et al. (1972) indicating that primiparous mothers provided more stimulation to their newborn infants than multiparous mothers.

Milieu

A third series of studies began to investigate the specific milieus that are created for first or later born children as to the development of motivational or intellectual capacities (Adams & Philips, 1972; Zajonc & Markus, 1975), or the quality of parent-child and child-child relationships (Abramovitch et al., 1982; Lamb, 1978a, b; Ward, Malone & DeAngelo, 1983). Continuities and changes of maternal behavior towards the firstborn and secondborn children as well as the process of integrating the younger sibling into the existing mother-older sibling relationship were analyzed in studies by Bryant and Crockenberg (1981), Zahn-Waxler, Radke-Yarrow, and King (1979), and a whole series of studies conducted by Judy Dunn and her coworkers (Dunn & Dale, 1984; Dunn & Kendrick, 1982; Dunn & Munn, 1985, 1986). Changes in the sibling-sibling interaction during the younger sibling's second year were depicted in respect to characteristics such as antagonistic as well as prosocial behavior between siblings, transmission of rules, and the learning of sanctions against transgressions of rules.

In sum, these sibling studies indicate that second children are regarded implicitly as agents who might promote change in an extant parent-child relationship in their role as siblings, as persons with specific characteristics, as targets of particular contextual influences, or as producers of distinctive patterns of mother-child and sibling-sibling interaction. They have not been analyzed so far, however, according to their unique effects as being a fourth member in a former triadic family system.

Source of Stress

Only a very limited number of studies attempted to analyze the second child's arrival and development during the first years in terms of increased or decreased stress in regard to marital and family satisfaction. Feldman (1974) found out that the birth of the second child generates a deeper crisis of the same kind that has been reported as prevailing the parents' life after the first child's birth. La Rossa and La Rossa (1981) discovered that not only in families with an individualistic or an extreme husband-wife orientation the second child was experienced as being a threat to the existing system, but also, contrary to the general belief, in familistic families, that is, in families with a high innergroup orientation, the second child was experienced as a potential intruder into the family jeopardizing the balance among the various family members. In sum, these studies have begun to look at the second child's arrival from a more family-oriented point of view, and the findings might shed new light on the specific conditions into which a second child, compared to the first, is being born.

CONCEPTUALIZING FAMILY TRANSITION

Family Conflicts and Problems

In order to conceptualize discontinuities in the young couple's experiences, some attempts have been made to construct a suitable framework for the results that have been found so far. La Rossa and La Rossa (1981) have proposed a "conflict sociological model of the transition to parenthood" for delineating the impact of crises that are likely to occur in various areas of the parents' new roles as responsible caretakers for the dependent and helpless infant and as crisis managers of their new life in a triadic family. Another way of looking at this period of transition to parenthood is to isolate a series of problems that have to be resolved by the parents during this period of change. For example, Belsky (1984) has conceptualized a process model describing the transition from being spouses to being parents. The model takes into account different sources of stress during the young couple's transition such as personal resources of the parents, temperamental characteristics of the child, and the context's contribution of stress and support.

The newer empirical studies investigating parental adaptation to the first child's arrival clearly outdo the concepts of parents' retrospective self-descriptions. Osofsky and Osofsky (1984), in a summarizing article, point to some new trends concerning this research: After having dealt with retrospective and clinical-descriptive studies, now "a research perspective with careful specification of variables often prospective in nature studied within a developmental framework appears to be emerging. Further, more focus is being placed on the success of the individual and couple in accomplishing necessary tasks during the period of expectant and new parenthood that may have an important impact on their parenting ability and the developing parent-child relationship" (p. 391-392).

Although these new approaches represent a growing sophistication in theoretical and empirical handling, they still lack a sound family-oriented approach which perhaps could reach both beyond a traditional parental-marital relationship dichotomy, and beyond a path-analytical study of variables. A systems-oriented approach could consider behavioral as well as attitudinal continuities and discontinuities under an "extension-of-the-family" perspective. The enlargement of the family usually does not come about without crises, and it demands a common adaptation effort involving all members to cope with them. However, descriptions of these crises should not be likened to the parents' experiences after the birth of the first child. A broader frame of reference is needed for describing transition from a one-child to a two-child family. Whereas, from a parent-child relationship perspective, the second child's arrival should not shake the young family fundamentally because the basic change from spouses to parents has already been carried out successfully, things look quite different when one looks at changes in family relationships under a structural perspective.

Conceptions for Transition

For analyzing the second child's specific role for the expansion of the family system, three conceptions are introduced which may help to study processes of family change after the second child's arrival under a crises perspective and to embed these changes into a wider development framework: Structural change, family tasks, and family development.

Structural Change

Regarding schematically possible relationships in a triadic and tetradic family, the family's structure is dramatically changed after the second child's arrival. In a triad, a one-child family, the unique dyadic relationship between the spouses (marital relationship) has been supplemented with two other dyadic relationships, the mother-child relationship and the father-child relationship. In addition, a triadic constellation is possible in which the new parents have a common interaction with their child. Regarding a tetradic formation, six possible dyadic, four triadic constellations, and one tetradic constellation can be found. (See Figure 1.)

The arrival of a second child thus dramatically enhances the chances for mutual communicative exchange in different constellations, but at the same time this may advance the giving up of old patterns of interaction and the search for new balances. Changes in

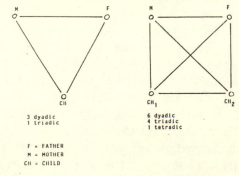

3 dyadic
1 triadic

6 dyadic
4 triadic
1 tetradic

F = FATHER
M = MOTHER
CH = CHILD

FIGURE 1: POSSIBLE CONSTELLATIONS IN TRIADIC AND
TETRADIC FAMILIES

the family's structure may not become visible immediately after the new child's arrival, but only as the second child develops, particularly during the first two years.

Family Tasks

Havighurst's (1953) notion of a "developmental task" as a sequence of problems that every human individual encounters during his or her growth (e.g., to walk, to talk, to form concepts of physical and social reality, to find an identity, etc.) can be transferred to the family, which is taken as a kind of developing system during its phase of enlargement. As the individual has to accomplish a series of tasks during his or her development, the family as a group also must achieve a set of tasks during its "course of development." The notion of "family tasks" has been introduced by family researchers like Rodgers (1973), Duvall (1977), and Aldous (1978) for describing specific problems and their solutions under a life span perspective. Here, the notion of task is used for depicting the family's efforts to cope with the problems that emerge when a new member is added to the family group and consequently a new balance has to be found. Under a socialization perspective, the integration of the child into the existing family system can also be taken as a process involving the transmission of cultural norms and the teaching of social skills.

Family Development

Heinz Werner (1948, 1957) created a comparative approach for the study of development by emphasizing the "orthogenetic principle"—known in biology and evolution theory as a basic rule dominating growth in every organism—and transferring it to developmental psychology. Accordingly, the notion that there is a process of *differentiation, specification*, and *hierarchical integration* within a growing individual has been used to delineate a kind of inner mechanism of organismic development. According to Werner, the integration of new capacities that emerge during human development may be compared to the emergence of new "organs," which have to be integrated in any developing organism and which may thus spur further development. Using this concept in a family oriented context, one may describe the integration of a new child into an existing family system by comparing this process to the emergence of a new ability or skill within an individual developing organism. The process of an *enlarging* family after the birth of a second child thus might be conceptualized as being different from a process of a *beginning* family. Whereas new roles and relationships have to be established by the couple when the first child's arrival begins the new family, the arrival of a second child seems to be more important for the family's "development." With a second child, the extant parent-child system has to be differentiated and specified according to parent-child 1 and parent-child 2 relationships, and it must be hierarchically integrated. For example, the mother takes over the responsibility as being a mother of two children, and the father has to build up a more specific relationship with the first child than was the case before. The hierarchical integration in a family can be taken as a kind of prerequisite for a developmental process, organizing, for example, complex patterns of relationships as to the different power status of members within the family.

Interplay Between Individual and Family Development

Although this may not be typical of the second child, an additional aspect should be mentioned which plays an important role while family changes are investigated: variations of the infants' behaviors due to their individual development. Specifically, during the first two years, the children run rapidly through a series of developmental steps on various levels. For example, the motor development allows the infants to progress from grasping to sitting, from rotating to crawling, and from standing to toddling and walking.

The second child's ontogenetic steps per se are not particularly interesting in this context, but they can be taken as additional factors which intervene with the general task to enlarge the family system. Thus, adaptation to the changing abilities of the new member may at times intensify crises within the family.

In sum, attempts to conceptualize a frame of reference for studying the second child's specific function for transition are encompassed by the following aspects: First, crises were taken as pointing to a conflict between parents' and growing children's interests, and second, structural and family developmental components were suggested as being helpful for analyzing the crises associated with the

second child's arrival. In addition, the individual child's development is interpreted as intervening with these structural rearrange-
ments thus creating a family dynamic of its own and triggering family changes which in turn may influence the child's development.

EMPIRICAL STUDY OF FAMILY CHANGES

The following considerations stood at the beginning of the study:

— The arrival of growth of the second child during the first two
  years was taken as a kind of "natural experiment" according
  to which the families could be compared.
— The family's everyday life and behavior in the natural environment should serve as a basis for the empirical study of family
  changes and continuities.
— The triadic family with father, mother and one child should be
  taken as the original unit, to which a fourth member is added.
— The whole family system is to be observed regularly after the
  birth of a new member over a longer period of time.
— Various methodological approaches should be used to opti-
  mize the interpretation and evaluation of the material.

Many questions can be raised about the interplay of family interaction and individual development, but only a few problems can be
studied within the context of this contribution. The focus here will
be upon the structural and dynamic perspective regarding the time
specific course of the rearrangement of the family balance during a
two year period.

Design and Analysis

Sample and Observation Technique

Sixteen families with a first child between one and four years old
and a second child born just at the beginning of the study were
selected from the Berlin area. The families were visited in their
homes every month over a two year period after the birth of the
second child. Observations (videotaped) were made in unstructured, everyday situations when one or both parents were dealing
with one or both children. The main "product" of this study was

the store of about 28 hours of videotapes from every family, encompassing two years of family interaction.

Qualitative Analyses of the Raw Material

As an initial step to analyzing the videotapes, a hermeneutic approach was used to describe recurring patterns of family interaction, that is, events from observations were transcribed and interpreted on the basis of structural and functional aspects of interaction between family members. As a main result of this analysis, a three phase model was proposed for exploring changes and continuities of the developing family in order to depict a series of tasks which are common to all families (Kreppner, Paulsen, Schuetze 1982). (See Figure 2.)

Phase 1 (0-8 months): Integration of the new member
Phase 2 (9-16 months): Achieving for new calibration
Phase 3 (17-24 months): Generation differentiation

Aside from a number of tasks that are associated with the family's procedures of coping with the normal developmental steps of every child such as "introduction of the new child," "transmission of rules," "setting of sanctions against transgression of rules" or "affirmation of parents' interests," there are a series of other tasks which emphasize the second child's unique function for family development. Among those are "distribution of attention," "involvement of father," "handling of sibling rivalries," and establishment of parent and sibling subsystems.

Quantitative Analysis

For supplementing the interpretations of the changes in family interaction that were found after the first series of qualitative analyses, a subsample of 7 families was drawn from the 16 families and studied quantitatively. To achieve this, the two year period was partitioned into seven segments (6/8 weeks, 4/5 months, 8/9 months, 12/13 months, 16/17 months, 20/21 months, and 23/24 months after the birth of the second child). Two different observations, each lasting about 30 minutes, were selected from each segment for balancing situational effects of observation. The segment-specific observations were then split into short episodes, each

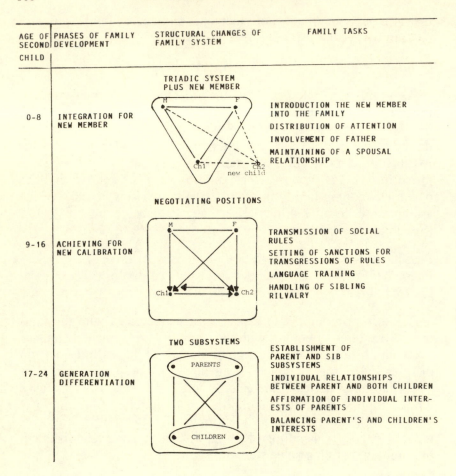

AGE OF SECOND CHILD	PHASES OF FAMILY DEVELOPMENT	STRUCTURAL CHANGES OF FAMILY SYSTEM	FAMILY TASKS
		TRIADIC SYSTEM PLUS NEW MEMBER	
0-8	INTEGRATION FOR NEW MEMBER		INTRODUCTION THE NEW MEMBER INTO THE FAMILY DISTRIBUTION OF ATTENTION INVOLVEMENT OF FATHER MAINTAINING OF A SPOUSAL RELATIONSHIP
		NEGOTIATING POSITIONS	
9-16	ACHIEVING FOR NEW CALIBRATION		TRANSMISSION OF SOCIAL RULES SETTING OF SANCTIONS FOR TRANSGRESSIONS OF RULES LANGUAGE TRAINING HANDLING OF SIBLING RILVALRY
		TWO SUBSYSTEMS	
17-24	GENERATION DIFFERENTIATION		ESTABLISHMENT OF PARENT AND SIB SUBSYSTEMS INDIVIDUAL RELATIONSHIPS BETWEEN PARENT AND BOTH CHILDREN AFFIRMATION OF INDIVIDUAL INTERESTS OF PARENTS BALANCING PARENT'S AND CHILDREN'S INTERESTS

FIGURE 2:   FAMILY DEVELOPMENT DURING THE FIRST TWO YEARS

lasting between 20-40 seconds. Thus, each family was represented by about 160-180 episodes per segment, yielding about 1100 episodes per family for the whole period.

Every episode was scored according to a number of categories encompassing structural, dynamic, and socialization aspects of family interaction (Kreppner 1984). Only structural and dynamic aspects of these analyses will be reported here. In the structural domain, every episode was scored as to the specific family constellation in the 20-40 second interval, yielding the mean number of different constellations found per family in each time segment. For example, the number of family members present in each episode is scored along with the member's specification (mother, father, child 1, child 2), and relationships among them (for example, family members are not interacting at all, or, another example, dyads are formed, mother-second child, father-first child, or father-mother, child 1-child 2 etc.). The dynamics inside the family are depicted by two other categories, one of which delineates who is taking the initiative in an episode, the other who is the target of this initiative. For example, in one episode the mother is turning to child 2, and in the next episode child 2 is turning to child 1 etc.

Statistical analyses of frequency tables were conducted by the method of log-linear models (Fienberg, 1980) for each family separately. The following dimensions and categories were included: age of second child (A), initiative in an episode (I), target in an episode (T), and, in addition, a category describing structural aspects of family socialization (S). For all families, a similar model (AI, ITS) describing the single family's interaction changes over time could be found. (See Table 1.)

The term ITS indicating a triadic interaction between initiative, target, and socialization activity such as taking up the other member's activity on trying to exert control, will not be interpreted in more detail in this context, for the specific family socialization aspects (S) were not included in those overall analyses that are pre-

TABLE 1: LOG-LINEAR ANALYSIS
CHISQUARES AND PROBABILITIES FOR MODEL AI, ITS

FAMILY	DF	CHISQ. (L - R)	PROB.	CHISQ. (PEARSON)	PROB.
1	486	408.41	.9955	428.87	.9705
2	486	427.31	.9740	440.12	.9331
3	486	419.50	.9867	446.69	.8989
4	486	463.24	.7644	489.72	.4441
5	486	479.78	.5710	512.85	.1929
6	486	390.27	.9995	393.82	.9992
7	486	368.80	1.0000	386.22	.9997

sented here. As time-specific changes of family dynamics are of specific interest in this context the term AI, which indicates a kind of age-dependent initiative pattern in all families will be considered more specifically below.

Overall trends of changes in family dynamics can reveal, for example, at what periods the second child is being preferred over the first child by the mother or the father.

Interrater reliabilities (Cohen's Kappa) for these dimensions describing structural and dynamic aspects of family interaction were between .98 and .81.

RESULTS

Changes in Family Constellation

Trends in changing family interaction over the two year period are unveiled by the mean number of *different* constellations in every family found in the seven time segments. (See Figure 3.)

The general trend over the two year period clearly points to an

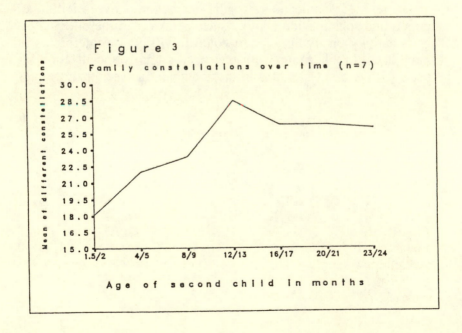

Figure 3

Family constellations over time (n=7)

Mean of different constellations

Age of second child in months

increase in the mean number of constellations during the first year, reaching a peak at about 12 months. After this time, frequencies decrease slightly, pointing perhaps to a new stabilization in the families.

Interestingly, the frequencies indicate a process of family expansion that does not occur immediately after the second child's arrival, but begins smoothly and lasts about 1-1/2 years. Whereas during the first months the families seem to be restrained to a small set of constellations, perhaps depending on the new member's helplessness, a steep increase in the number of different constellations beginning at the eighth month might signal the family's efforts to cope with the second child's integration. The initial number of constellations is nearly doubled by 12 months. After this, at about 16 months and later, the number of different constellations remains constant, perhaps indicating a certain degree of stabilization.

Changes in Family Dynamics

To illustrate another general trend in family interaction during the two year period, the changes of a few single dyadic relationships in the families will be depicted below.

The parents' different ways to deal with their two children are delineated in Figures 4 and 5.

The big difference of the mother's initiatives toward their two children during the first 4-5 months reveals a dramatic phenomenon concerning the first child's difficult adaptation task after the birth of the second child. Even after the first phase of intensive care for the helpless baby, when mothers seem to return more and more to normal routines, they continue to show a higher rate of initiatives toward their second children compared to their first children for the rest of the two year period.

The father-child 1 and father-child 2 interactions appear to be quite different from both the mother-child 1 and mother-child 2 relationships. However, it should be kept in mind that the absolute amount of frequencies for mothers and fathers varies strongly (a maximum of over 200 for mothers compared to over 90 for fathers) so that the father's initiatives toward the first child are about the same as the mother's. However, looking at these frequencies and

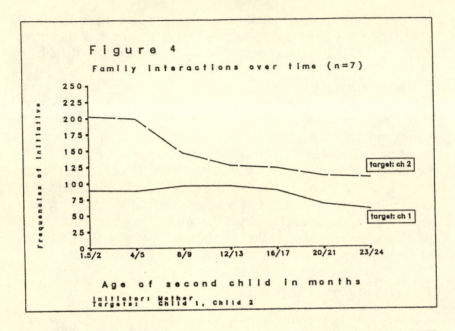

Figure 4

Family interactions over time (n=7)

target: ch 2

target: ch 1

Frequencies of initiative

Age of second child in months

Initiator: Mother
Targets: Child 1, Child 2

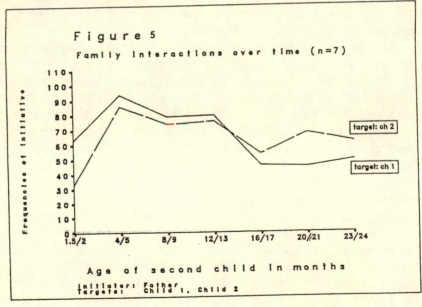

Figure 5

Family interactions over time (n=7)

target: ch 2

target: ch 1

Frequencies of initiative

Age of second child in months

Initiator: Father
Targets: Child 1, Child 2

their course over time, during the first year the father turns out to be the person who initiates interactions with the first child more often than with the second child. After a general drop in father's activities during the first half of the second year, he begins to prefer the second child over the first one, thus producing a trend in family interaction that is similar to that displayed by the mother's behaviors.

Whereas these trends represented the parent-children directed interaction, the Figures 6 and 7 illuminate the children's own changing initiative toward both parents.

Figure 6 shows that the first child, perhaps as he or she tries to compensate the loss of maternal attention, very distinctly turns to the father at 4-5 and 8-9 months; during the second year, however, especially in the second half, the mother is preferred over the father. The second child shows continuously increasing initiatives toward both parents; his or her increasing cognitive and social skills may in a way counteract the decreasing parental initiatives during the second year.

The family as a whole would not be completely depicted without

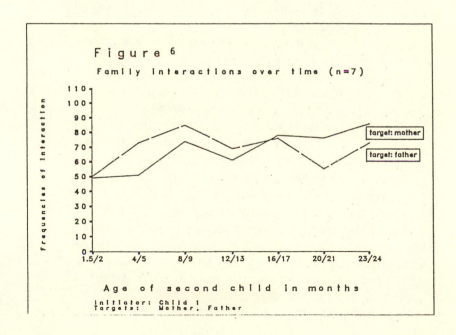

F i g u r e 6

Family Interactions over time (n=7)

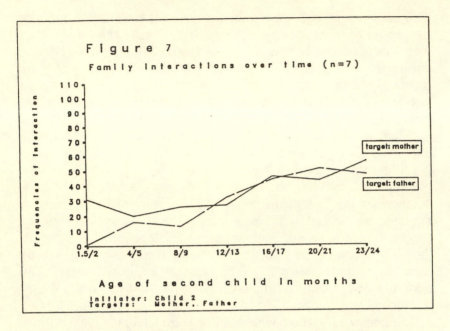

Figure 7

Family Interactions over time (n=7)

Frequencies of Interaction

target: mother

target: father

Age of second child in months

Initiator: Child 2
Targets: Mother, Father

having a look at the remaining other relationships, the sibling and the parent relationships.

In Figure 8, the first child shows various ups and downs concerning his or her initiatives toward the younger sibling. Initiatives increase at about 12-13 months, when the second child has gained new competencies, and again toward the end of the second year. Most interestingly, there is a short overlap of both children's curves at 1-17 months, pointing perhaps to the reaching of a balanced interaction at this time. The second child shows a slight but continuous increase in his or her initiatives toward the older sibling up to the 16-17 month with a decrease thereafter.

Finally, the two parents' curves depicting mutual relationships (Figure 9) during the time after the birth of the second child reveal an overall slightly higher rate of mother's initiatives toward the father compared to the father's own initiatives. Immediately after birth, during the first 4-5 months, both parents turn to each other more frequently than during the rest of the first year. However, mothers turn to fathers more intensely again at 16-17 months, and fathers show a slightly increased tendency to take initiative toward

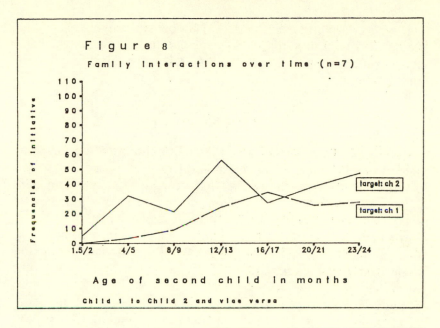

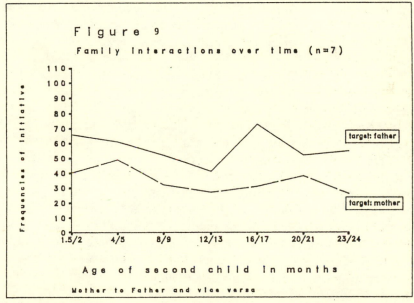

their wives during the next period. This perhaps might indicate an attempt to find a new rapprochement during this phase when the second child in a way has found his or her place in the enlarged family system.

DISCUSSION

Results can be discussed under a structural and family-development viewpoint. First, the increase of different constellations found in family interaction during the first year and the levelling of a higher rate of different constellations during the second year can be interpreted as indicating a time-specific expansion of the triadic family system. It seems as if the family remains with a comparably small number of constellations during the first half year leaving the extant family network untouched. Then a sharp increase in different constellations at the end of the first year is obvious. This change coincides with marked developmental progressions of the new member. Toward the end of the second year, a kind of stabilization of the number of different constellations occurs which seems to signal the family's rearrangement. Second, regarding changes in family dynamics during the entire two year period, the mother's extensive interaction with the new child during the first 8-9 months contrasts with a clearly lower rate of attention given to the first child during this time. The father, starting with a rather low rate of interactions, increases his initiatives to both children during the first year. By paying more attention to the first child, he takes over a supplementary function to compensate for the mother's increased involvement in caretaking activities with the new child. However, the father also begins preferring the second child after the 16-17th month. Thus, the first child is in a difficult position when the second child is about one and a half years old. When one interprets these changes not from a single member's point of view, but tries to look at them under a family system perspective, these results can be interpreted in different ways; data point to a number of time-specific crises where parents have to accomplish the task of integrating a new child, and all members have to find new ways of interacting with each other. In addition, the growing abilities of the second child lead to a series of interactions between the siblings and might confront parents with tasks that are completely new namely the handling of the sibling rivalry. The increases in parents' initiatives to turn to one another at different times during the expansion period can be taken as indicating a kind of rearrangement of parental relationships.

Looking at these results from a systems point of view, data suggest that new balances are formed especially during the second year and that a certain degree of stabilization or "new calibration" (Watzlawick, Beavan, & Jackson, 1967) is found in the tetradic constellation. Comparing one-child parents with two-child parents, the latter experience a situation at the end of the two year period which is completely new to them. As the second child gains an own and equal position in the family group, they are no longer parents of an older child and a new baby, but parents of "children." This might have far reaching consequences not only for the family as a whole, but for the parents as adult individuals. The parents begin to understand their roles as being mother and father not only as caretakers and teachers for individual children but, in addition, they realize that they now are belonging to a group of "adults" in the family in contrast to the other group, the "children." This may widen the parents' view of self and others and can, in a way, contribute to their individual development.

Thus, by embedding the second child's arrival and integration into a frame of reference in which the rearrangement of the family is taken as a developmental process of its own, crises often attributed to personal or contextual factors can be interpreted from the perspective of changing relationships in an enlarging system.

A focus on relationships rather than on personal attributes leads one to consider the implications of these results for possible supports or intervention programs for parents involved in this transitional process. Whereas several programs exist that are targeted to young parents expecting their first child and intended to provide them with physiological growth data and their child's changing needs and abilities in both cognitive and social areas, no specific programs can be found for parents expecting their second child. In most cases, no guidelines are given about the structural changes involving the *relationships* among all family members and the crises that have to be expected after the arrival of the new member.

The task of establishing a whole set of new relationships and rearranging existing ones is very seldomly brought up, and more importantly, the specific role of the first child in this period of family enlargement is not sufficiently underscored. Providing parents have a second child with knowledge about the many facets of these emerging problems could lead to better coping with possible relational crises that most likely aggravate the already tense interaction climate within the family during this difficult period. If the parents had available a plan or blueprint which depicted the sequence of necessary relational changes and concomitant crises as part of a *normal* enlargement process of the family, at least some of the frustrations and the sudden disruptions of emotional relationships could be avoided. The importance of buffering activities and supplementary attention from one parent when the other is occupied with care of the new child could be made more obvious.

To give a trenchant metaphor for describing how, for example, the first child might experience the arrival and the growing importance of a sibling in the family in which he or she has been the only child and therefore had held a unique position, one could compare this event and its emotional implications with the arrival and growing importance of a new wife in the home from the present wife's perspective. The permanent demands of the husband to enjoy the new and nice family member and to show consideration for her specific needs most likely would not sufficiently soothe the present wife's emotional disturbance and distress.

Because the first child seems to be affiliated with the father during the first months after the second child's arrival, a certain kind of buffering function of this relationship can be assumed. It can ameliorate the first child's difficult situation. From a comparison of the trajectories of the various dyadic relationships during the two year period, it seems as if the first child, by turning to the father during the first months, is willing to accept the mother's increased attention to the newly-arrived sibling during the first months when the baby obviously needs help and resembles more a disabled person than a rival. Things change dramatically when the growing abilities and skills of the new child signal his or her competence in competing for the parents' attention intentionally. As data have shown, the first child now turns more often to the mother than to the father, but does not receive a higher amount of the mother's attention. The balancing of the parents' attention between their two children is one of the relevant tasks that the young adults have to accomplish in their own passage to being parents.

In the last years we have gained some insight into general trends of changes within the family. In the future, family researchers should strive to provide windows to differences among families in dealing with these "normal" crises during the transition to parenthood. In addition, the study of critical points in relational changes and necessary adaptations to new demands might shed some light upon possible maladaptive processes leading to pathological development. The concept of these passages as being necessary for both children and parents in their own individual development suggests that monitoring the establishing and arranging of relationships in times of necessary changes could be a productive focus for future investigation of the family over the life span.

REFERENCES

Abramovitch, R., Pepler, D., & Corter, C. (1982). Patterns of sibling interaction among preschool-age children. In M.E. Lamb & B. Sutton-Smith (Eds.). *Sibling relationships: Their nature and importance across life span* (pp. 61-86). Hillsdale, N.J.: Lawrence Erlbaum.

Adams, W.J., & Phillips, B.N. (1972). Motivational and achievement differences among children of various ordinal birth positions. *Child Development, 43*, 155-164.

Aldous, J. (1978). *Family careers*. New York: Wiley.

Belsky, J. (1984). The determinants of parenting: A process model. *Child Development, 55*, 83-96.

Bryant, B.K., & Crockenberg, S.B. (1980). Correlates and dimensions of prosocial behavior: A study of female siblings with their mothers. *Child Development, 51*, 529-544.

Cowan, C.P., Cowan, P.A., Coie, L., & Coie, J.D. (1978). Becoming a family: The impact of a first child's birth on the couple's relationship. In W.B. Miller & L.F. Neuman (Eds.), *The first child and family formation* (pp. 296-324). Chapel Hill, N.C.: Carolina Population Center.

Dunn, J., & Kendrick, C. (1980). The arrival of a sibling. Changes in patterns of interaction between mother and firstborn child. *Journal of Child Psychology and Psychiatry, 21*, 119-132.

Dunn, J., & Dale, N. (1984). I a daddy: 2 year old's collaboration in joint pretend play with sibling and with mother. In I. Bretherton (Ed.), *Symbolic play: The development of social understanding* (pp. 131-158). New York: Academic Press.

Dunn, J., & Munn, P. (1985a). Becoming a family member: Family conflict and the development of social understanding in the second year. *Child Development, 56,* 480-492.

Dunn, J., & Munn, P. (1985b). *Sibling quarrels and maternal intervention: Individual differences in understanding and aggression.* MRC Unit on the Development and Integration of Behaviour, University of Cambridge, England.

Duvall, E. (1977). *Marriage and family development.* New York: Lippincott.

Dyer, E. (1963). Parenthood as crisis: A restudy. *Marriage and Family Living, 25,* 196-201.

Entwisle, D.R., & Doering, S.G. (1980). *The first birth.* Baltimore, M.D.: The Johns Hopkins University Press.

Feldman, H. (1974). Change in marriage and parenthood: A methodological design. In E. Peck & J. Senderowitz (Eds.), *Pronatalism: the myth of mom and apple pie.* (pp. 206-226). New York: Thomas V. Crowell.

Fienberg, S.E. (1980). *The analysis of cross-classified categorical data.* Cambridge, MA: The MIT Press.

Havighurst, R.J. (1953). *Human development and education.* New York: David McKay.

Hill, R., & Aldous, J. (1969). Socialization for marriage and parenthood. In D.A. Goslin (Ed.), *Handbook of socialization theory and research* (pp. 885-950). Chicago: Rand McNally.

Hobbs, D.F. (1965). Parenthood as a crisis: A third study. *Journal of Marriage and the Family, 27,* 367-372.

Jacobs, B.S., & Moss, H.A. (1976). Birth order and sex of sibling as determinants of mother-infant interaction. *Child Development, 47,* 315-322.

Jaffe, S.S., & Viertel, J. (1979). *Becoming parents: Preparing for the emotional changes of first-time parenthood.* New York: Atheneum.

Koch, H.L. (1955a). Some personality correlates of sex, sibling position, and sex of sibling among five and six year old children. *Genetic Psychology Monographs, 52,* 3-50.

Koch, H.L. (1955b). The relation of certain family constellation characteristics and the attitudes of children towards adults. *Child Development, 26,* 13-40.

Koch, H.L. (1960). The relation of certain formal attributes of siblings to attitudes held toward each other and toward their parents. *Monographs of the Society for Research in Child Development,* Serial No. 78, Vol. 25, No. 4.

Kreppner, K. (1984). *Kategoriensystem zur Beschreibung familialer Interaktionen.* Manuscript, Max Planck Institute for Human Development and Education, Berlin.

Kreppner, K., Paulsen, S., & Schuetze, Y. (1982). Infant and family development: From triads to tetrads. *Human Development, 25,* 373-391.

Lamb, M.E. (1978a). Interactions between 18-month-olds and their preschool-aged siblings. *Child Development, 49,* 51-59.

Lamb, M.E. (1978b). The development of sibling relationships in infancy: A short-term longitudinal study. *Child Development, 49,* 1189-1196.

LaRossa, R., & LaRossa, M.M. (1981). *Transition to parenthood. How infants change families.* Beverly Hills: Sage.

Lasko, J.K. (1954). Parent behavior toward first and second children. *Genetic Psychology Monographs, 49,* 97-187.

LeMasters, E.E. (1957). Parenthood as crisis. *Marriage and Family Living, 19,* 352-355.

Lewis, M., & Kreitzberg, V.S. (1979). Effects of birth order and spacing on mother-infant interactions. *Developmental Psychology, 15,* 617-625.

Miller, B.C. & Sollie, D.L. (1980). Normal stresses during the transition to parenthood. *Family Relations, 29,* 459-465.

Osofsky, J.D., & Osofsky, H.J. (1984). Psychological and developmental perspectives on expectant and new parenthood. In R.D. Parke (Ed.), *Review of child research, Vol. 7, The family,* (pp. 372-397). Chicago: The University of Chicago Press.

Rodgers, R.H. (1973). *Family interaction and transaction. The developmental approach.* Englewood Cliffs, N.J.: Prentice-Hall.

Rothbart, M.K. (1971). Birth order and mother-child interaction in an achievement situation. *Journal of Personality and Social Psychology, 17,* 113-120.

Ryder, R.G. (1973). Longitudinal data relating marriage satisfaction and having a child. *Journal of Marriage and the Family, 35,* 604-607.

Sutton-Smith, B., & Rosenberg, B.G. (1970). *The sibling.* New York: Holt, Rinehart & Winston.

Thoman, E.B., Barnett, C.R., & Leiderman, P.H. (1971). Feeding behaviors of newborn infants as a function of parity of the mother. *Child Development, 42,* 1471-1483.

Ward, M.J., Malone, S.M., & DeAngelo, E.J. (1983). *Patterns of maternal behavior with first- and second born children: Evidence for consistency in family relations.* Paper presented at the Biennial Meetings of the Society for Research in Child Development, Detroit.

Watzlawick, P., Beavin, J.H., & Jackson, D.D. (1967). *Pragmatics of human communication.* New York: Norton.

Werner, H. (1948). *Comparative psychology of mental development.* New York: International University Press.

Werner, H. (1957). The concept of development from a comparative and organismic point of view. In D.B. Harris (Ed.), *The concept of development* (pp. 125-148). Minneapolis: University of Minnesota Press.

Zahn-Waxler, C., Radke-Yarrow, M., & King, R.A. (1979). Child rearing and children's prosocial initiations toward victims of distress. *Child Development, 50,* 319-330.

Zajonc, R.B., & Markus, G. (1975). Birth order and intellectual development. *Psychological Review, 82,* 74-88.

Changes in Attitudes, Beliefs and Expectations Associated with the Transition to Parenthood

Rob Palkovitz
Marcella Copes

INTRODUCTION

"Dad, is it confusing to be a grown-up?" my six-year-old wondered aloud as we sat in the lobby of a bank, waiting to see a loan officer about a construction mortgage.

"What do you mean, son?" (This seemed like a safe response at the time.)

"It just seems like there's a lot to figure out . . . so many plans and all."

"Yeah, sometimes it *is* hard, especially when your plans don't work out the way you expected . . . "

This brief excerpt from a conversation with my son serves to introduce the topic of this paper . . . the relationships between parents' expectations, their perceptions of reality, their behavior, and the continual adjustment of the relationship between these.

Within each stage of the family life cycle individuals respond to

---

Rob Palkovitz, PhD, is Assistant Professor, Department of Individual and Family Studies, College of Human Resources, University of Delaware, Newark, DE 19716. Marcella Copes is Assistant Professor and Chairperson of Nursing, Delaware State College, Dover, DE 19901.

The data reported in this paper were collected and analyzed by the first author while supported by a grant from the University of Delaware's General University Research Fund.

183

new social conditions and roles that promote change within and between individuals (Feldman & Nash, 1984). It is speculated that within each stage there are specific tasks to accomplish (Duvall, 1971), with an accompanying redefinition of behaviors and beliefs (Parsons & Bales, 1955). One of the more dramatic lifecourse transitions within the family lifecycle is the transition to parenthood (Feldman & Nash, 1984, Miller & Sollie, 1980). In assuming the roles of parenthood, a wide range of affective and cognitive experiences are realized: joy, gratification, personal growth, stress and marital change (Belsky & Pensky, this issue; Hill, 1949; Hobbs, 1965, 1968; Hobbs & Cole, 1976; LaRossa, 1986; LeMasters, 1957; Newman & Newman, this issue; Russell, 1974). The beliefs and expectations of parents are important determinants of the subjective experience of parenthood (Palkovitz, 1985, 1987a, 1987b), and reciprocally, parents' experiences influence their beliefs and expectations (McGillicuddy-DeLisi, 1980; Palkovitz, 1987a, 1987b). Further, parents are instrumental in facilitating their children's development and endowing them with a rational system of beliefs, religious values, attitudes, and personality attributes. As children develop through adolescence and become young adults, the attitudes, beliefs, values and related behaviors they carry with them will influence their decisions to marry or to remain single, to parent or to be childless. As generations physically reproduce, social reproduction occurs as well (Erikson, 1959).

To what extent are parental beliefs and attitudes fluid during the transition to parenthood? If parental beliefs, attitudes and behaviors change during the course of the transition, what factors predict positive adaptation, and which predict risk? Are fathers' and mothers' transitional experiences similar or dissimilar?

The present chapter addresses the importance of beliefs, attitudes, and expectations as they relate to parental experiences during the transition to parenthood.

TRANSITION TO PARENTHOOD

Family scholars view the family as a social system of interrelated roles and statuses (Dyer, 1963; Hill, 1949; LeMasters, 1957). Any addition or deletion of family members requires change and reorganization of interaction patterns and roles which may result in either temporary or long-term stress (Dyer, 1963; Hill, 1949; LeMasters, 1957). The effect of introducing a new family member into the system through birth has been a research topic for over 25 years. The resulting literature has been inconclusive, and at times, contradictory. Initial investigations of the transition to parenthood described the transition to be problematic, causing a state of crisis (Dyer, 1963; LeMasters, 1957). LeMasters (1957) interviewed 48 couples to ascertain whether the arrival of their first child was viewed as a critical life event, or "crisis." LeMasters concluded that the transition to parenthood was, indeed, difficult and was appropriately viewed as a crisis. Couples who reported the transition to be "no crisis," a "slight crisis" or "moderate crisis" were clearly in the minority (comprising only 17% of the total sample), and were considered to be deviants.

Dyer (1963) replicated LeMaster's study and supported the previous findings. Dyer advanced the literature base by noting a relationship between marital state prior to the birth of the child and the amount of crisis afterwards. Specifically, those couples with stronger marriages and more resources to draw upon experienced less crisis after the delivery.

Later studies by Hobbs and his associates (Hobbs, 1965, 1968, 1976; Hobbs & Wimbish, 1977) suggest that although the transition to parenthood is somewhat stressful, it should not be viewed as a crisis. Similarly, Russell (1974) reported a range of parents' transitional feelings from stressful to satisfying to gratifying. Russell (1974) concluded that the first year of parenthood is a time of moderate stress, tempered by numerous rewards.

The operation of cohort effects may offer the most parsimonious explanation for the observed discrepancy between earlier versus later research findings. Cohort effects are likely to continue exerting influences on future findings concerning the transition to parenthood. Three or more cohorts (teen parents, parents in their twenties, and those in their thirties), although concurrently experiencing the transition to parenthood, may be approaching it in distinctly different manners. Some differences could reasonably be expected because persons of different ages face different developmental tasks and may bring different developmental skills (and different sets of age-related circumstances) to the transition. That is, some cohort differences are primarily explainable in terms of age differences. It is equally likely, however, that history effects are in operation. Specifically, it may have been the case that earlier generations of parents viewed the transition to parenthood to be more of a crisis than more recent first-time parents. Although there is no documentation to support this assertion, documentable shifts in family role patterns make this explanation plausible. Because increasing numbers of families are dual career families, those experiencing the transition to parenthood are more likely to purchase services routinely performed by the family (mother?) in the past (e.g., diaper service, day care) (Palm, 1986). When mothers return to work four to six weeks after the birth of their first child, and services are purchased, the overall transition experience is buffered by a relatively greater degree of stability in circumstances and roles. Focused research is needed to adequately compare adjustment to transitional experiences, comparing families with employed and nonemployed mothers.

Finally, another explanation exists for the observed discrepancy between early and recent research findings. As research methods and family theory have advanced, refinements in measurement techniques and interactive models, coupled with differences between samples may be moderating the findings.

Despite the differences observed between studies, a major consistency exists. Common to *all* studies on the topic is the finding that the transition to parenthood involves change of a considerable magnitude. Because change is associated with stress (Holmes & Rahe, 1967) one would expect to observe some degree of stress during the transition to parenthood. It is likely that individual differences in coping skills, access to supports, and presence or absence of other stressors mediate individual parents' subjective experiences of adjustment to the changes required by assuming the roles associated with parenting. Thus, variability in the degree of subjective stress is mediated by a number of interacting factors.

Quite aside from the obvious behavioral changes required in making the transition to parenthood (e.g., few nonparents elect to expend large sums on diapers or to invest significant time in children's activities), it is legitimate to question, from a theoretical basis, why one would expect attitudes and beliefs to change across the transition to parenthood.

THEORETICAL UNDERPINNINGS

Two disparate developmental perspectives can offer useful frameworks for considering changes in beliefs and attitudes across the transition to parenthood. First, the concept of the critical period, as applied to physical development connotes the time of most rapid growth or change in a system. Because development does not occur in a vacuum, rapid changes in one system subsequently influence other systems. For example, environmental influences during the critical period for the development of the optic nerve at 6 weeks postconception (at the estimated rate of 30,000 eye-brain connections per minute) will have profound, life-long effects on the functioning of sensation, perception, cognition and some aspects of motor coordination. Similarly, because the transition to parenthood involves a large number of major shifts in behavior and thinking during the relatively short span of pregnancy and the neonatal period, it can be argued that the transition to first-time parenthood is the time of most rapid changes in parenting behavior and thinking. Anecdotal evidence suggests that changes associated with the births of the second and subsequent children are less dramatically perceived by the parent. While the first transition to parenthood represents a time of rapid change or growth, it is not, however, to be likened directly to a critical period.[1] Clearly, there is no brief, circumscribed time period within which an all-or-nothing parenthood experience must occur, with irreversible consequences. However, the extensive and rapid evolution of roles, beliefs and attitudes *does* exert a long-lasting impact on parental behaviors in a wide array of areas of functioning.

Alternately, Erikson's conception of the epigenetic principle offers a useful description of forces operating upon development during the transition to parenthood. In his classic description of the epigenetic principle, Erikson (1959) posits that maturational readiness and societal construction interact so as to direct the rate and sequence of an individual's passage through a series of psychosocial crises, or turning points. Although Erikson did not provide de-

---

1. It must be firmly stated that there is *no* consensus that psychological critical periods exist. While we are not advocating the adoption of a critical period model for the transition to parenthood, the model serves as a useful analogy.

tailed elaborations concerning the epigenetic principle's functioning at each juncture throughout the lifespan, this concept can be directly applied to the transition to parenthood. Both physical readiness and societal guidance are easily observed. Maturational readiness, in the case of pregnancy, is represented through a host of hormonal changes in the mother, physical "showing," new limitations on activities, greater susceptibility to fatigue, the possibility of morning sickness, and changes in routine due to physical conditions. These changes provide an undeniable foreshadowing that further change is forthcoming, and is, in fact, already under way. While these changes are primarily associated with expectant mothers, fathers indirectly experience the changes as their spouses alter their behaviors and their appearances are gradually transformed. Further, in an interesting review of the couvade syndrome, Bogren (1986) reported that approximately 20% of all fathers experience physical symptoms of pregnancy during their infant's gestation.

The social structure places demands on the expectant couple as well. Friends, relatives and even strangers begin to query the expectant couple concerning the impending change of status. "Have you picked names yet? What do you want, a boy or a girl? Are you going to breast or bottle feed? Will you be going back to work, or will you 'just' be staying home?" Thus, society plays a role in challenging prospective parents to formulate and defend their thoughts on such issues, whether they have been prepared in advance or not. The net result is that couples begin to assume a more child-centered set of attitudes prior to the child's arrival. This assertion is corroborated by expectant couples' perception that parenting represents a portion of their role responsibilities (see Cowan & Cowan, this issue). Often times, pregnancy is the first time that important parenting and role assignment issues receive serious consideration.

As such, it is not surprising that it is during the transition to parenthood, that prospective parents frequently search for "new data" on parenting, provided within the societal context. It is common for expectant parents to observe experienced parents with their children, to hold the infants of others (so long as they are content), to have dialogue with one another concerning the parenting styles and skills of others they have observed, and for middle-class couples, to read (at the minimum, about pregnancy and delivery, preferably, about parenting in general) and attend childbirth preparation or childcare classes. Thus, prospective parents are expecting in more ways than one. They form expectations about appropriate parenting behavior by observing others, through compiling the abundant advice of experienced parents, and by wrestling with the issues raised in conversations about impending parenthood.

This discussion clearly demonstrates that the transition to parenthood begins prior to the birth itself, and may, for some couples begin well in advance, through their discussions concerning the desire for and timing of offspring. Clearly, each couple's transition through this extensive array of physical and attitudinal metamorphoses will vary uniquely. A complex interaction of factors is likely to influence parental adjustment at each phase of the transition. For instance, the experience of a couple who plans and attempts to achieve pregnancy (perhaps with the assistance of a fertility clinic and in vitro techniques) will be distinctly different than that of couples who, to their disappointment, discover that they are pregnant, and need to decide "what to do about it." Parents' age, SES, marital and occupational status, job satisfaction, work hours, peer group, and educational achievement will each exert an influence, however subtle (and these factors are likely to interact, as well). Is it any wonder that independent studies have produced discrepant results?

Clearly, as reflected in the number of chapters in this issue devoted to specific aspects of the transition to parenthood, the transition involves rapid and extensive change. The more resources and supports one has to face the changes, the greater the relative stability one can experience through the transition. The more effective the coping styles of the individual, the less the level of subjective stress and the more positive the adjustment to the entire process.

Roles, Attitudes and Behavior

Although greater flexibility in roles and less rigid adherence to traditional roles is called for in contemporary America, there is still considerable evidence that adherence to traditional roles persists to a significant degree, particularly with reference to household chores and parenting roles (Palkovitz, 1987b, Pleck, 1985). Traditionally, roles have been assigned on the basis of gender with husbands acting as the breadwinner and wives as homemakers; mothers generally responsible for caregiving activities and fathers interacting with their children primarily through play activities (Belsky, 1985; McHale & Huston, 1984). Russell (1978, 1982a, 1982b) found that fathers who were primary caregivers placed greater emphasis on interpersonal sensitivity and expressiveness than did fathers in traditional family constellations. Fathers who were highly involved in childcare also described themselves to be high in instrumentality. These findings, along with questionnaire data reported by Baumrind (1982) and DeFrain (1979) support the notion that androgynous fathers are more extensively involved in some aspects of child rearing than are sex-typed fathers. Palkovitz (1984) reported data from a home-based observational study where paternal sex role orientation emerged as an important predictor of both quantity and quality of fathers' affective and behavioral involvement with their infants. Specifically, 21% of the variability in paternal involvement scores was accounted for by sex role orientation classification. Androgynous fathers were the most involved fathers as a group, displaying high frequencies of both typical masculine behaviors (e.g., rough and tumble play) *and* traditionally feminine behaviors (e.g., caregiving). Fathers who were characterized by undifferentiated sex role orientations were the least involved with their infants, corroborating Fein's (1976) assertion that the existence of a well-defined paternal role is more important than the precise characteristics of the role definition in facilitating fathers' adjustment to parenthood.

Lamb (1978) reported that parents' sex roles become redefined after the birth of a child. Similarly, Feldman and Aschenbrenner (1983) documented changes in masculinity and femininity in a longitudinal study covering the transition to parenthood. Both investigations can be interpreted to support the notion that assuming the parental role exerts a traditionalizing effect on couples' sex roles.

Recently, researchers have focused on the way that parents view their roles and its relation to parental behavior (McHale & Huston, 1984; Palkovitz, 1980, 1984, 1987b). Home-based naturalistic observations have documented a strong relationship between both parents' views of the father's role and fathers' behavioral and affective involvement with their young infants (Palkovitz, 1980, 1984). Specifically, the mother's view of the role of the father predicts paternal behavior in the mother's presence, but not in her absence. When alone with his infant, the father's view of his role is a better predictor than the mother's view of the father's role. It should be noted, however, that there are significant positive within-couple correlations between maternal and paternal prescriptions for the father's role. Thus, it appears that fathers may behaviorally conform to their wives' parenting expectations in their presence, but act somewhat more independently in their absence.

Moss (1967) found that maternal responsiveness to infants at age three months could be predicted by attitudes as much as two years in advance of the child's birth. Similarly, McHale and Huston (1984) found that sex role patterns of couples before birth predicted role preferences after birth. Fathers' role preferences are characterized by relative stability before and after the birth, with mothers' being less stable (McHale & Huston, 1984). Fathers' role preferences prior to the birth are predictive of maternal preferences after the birth. This finding stands in marked contrast to the common assertion that fathers are involved with their infants to the extent that mothers "grant permission" for their involvement. Further, McHale and Huston (1984) investigated the way that parental sex role orientation and amount of involvement in the paid labor force jointly and independently contributed to parenting activities. The data suggested that the amount of maternal involvement with children is influenced by the amount of paid labor force participation. In comparison, a father's involvement is affected by his attitudes about his wife.

During the course of their development, men and women accumulate information that shapes their perceptions of their roles as men and women, their roles as parents, their behaviors, their attitudes and their belief systems. The transition to parenthood represents a period of developmental readiness for growth/change in these areas. More precisely, independent of the level of personal maturity, the transition to parenthood requires adjustments to each of the above attributes.

Persons enter the transition to parenthood with a wealth of expectations based on both direct and indirect experience with parents, through which they filter their perceptions. During and after the transition to parenthood, parents continue to develop their belief systems from their expectations, perceptions and interpretations of events related to their own children (McGillicuddy-DeLisi, 1980). Parents' beliefs are challenged by their perceptions of reality: some beliefs are retained, some are altered, and others are abandoned as new experiences with parenting are accumulated. Depending on the speed and scope of change, parents' attitudinal evolution could be likened to an assimilatory process (see Piaget, 1952), dissonance reduction (see Festinger, 1957), or a revolution (see Kuhn, 1963).

Few longitudinal studies have traced the changes in beliefs and attitudes associated with the transition to parenthood. Up to this point, much of the literature concerning attitudinal shifts through the transition is derived from speculations based on theory or extrapolated from analogous situations. The data reported in this paper represent a portion of a larger longitudinal study, following 35 couples from the last trimester of pregnancy into the first month of parenthood. This report will focus on changes in couples' beliefs and attitudes concerning the role of the father in childcare, sex role orientation and self-esteem.

METHOD

Sample Characteristics

Thirty-five married couples expecting their first child served as subjects in the study. Mothers averaged 26.45 years of age (range 21-32) and fathers 27.81 years (range 23-37). A vast majority (84%) of the couples represented dual earner families. The sample tended to be well-educated (mean 14.88 years of education for women and 15.45 years for men), and had an average family income of $36,702 (s.d. = 14,000, range 9,000-65,000). Seventy-eight percent (78%) of the couples indicated that the pregnancy was planned and 22% said that it was not. The current pregnancy was reported to be the first for 76% of the couples, while 19% (N = 7) reported one previous pregnancy, and 5% (N = 2) had experienced 2 previous pregnancies. Of the previous pregnancies, 7 were miscarried and 2 aborted. In every couple, the father was planning to attend the birth of the child, and each couple had enrolled for childbirth education classes.

Procedure

Subjects were recruited via telephone after a list of potential participants was received from obstetricians and childbirth education providers. The researcher phoned the couple, described the study (as being focused on the changes that people go through when they have their first child) and arranged a time for the first visit.

Each couple was seen at two different times. The initial visit was scheduled during the third trimester of pregnancy, but before childbirth education classes had begun. The follow-up visit occurred after delivery when the baby was three weeks old (x = 21.8 days of age, s.d. = 4.5 days). Each visit consisted of an open-ended couple interview and the administration of a series of questionnaires, independently filled-out by husbands and wives. Each visit required approximately one hour to complete.

Measures

At each visit, the Bem Sex Role Inventory (BSRI) (Bem, 1974), the Coopersmith Self Esteem Inventory, short form (Coopersmith, 1981), The Role of the Father Questionnaire (ROFQ) (Palkovitz, 1980), and a bonding beliefs questionnaire (Palkovitz & Cannon, in press) were administered to both husbands and wives. Further questionnaire and interview items focused on the couples' estimations of who would be performing specific child care tasks, and in what proportions, expectations for the delivery, satisfaction with the birthing experience, etc. A complete set of questionnaire items and an interview agenda are available from the first author. For the purposes of this report, we will focus attention on those items reflecting changes in parents' beliefs, attitudes and expectations during the transition to parenthood.

RESULTS AND DISCUSSION

Data were analyzed to examine intraindividual stability/change as well as intra-couple consistency. Paired t tests were employed in order to facilitate these analyses. Results will be discussed in terms of intra-individual change for fathers, mothers, and intra-couple comparisons, respectively.

Comparing data from before and after the birth through paired t tests, it can be shown that fathers experience significant increases in masculinity [$t(34) = 3.15$ p < .003], femininity [$t(34) = 2.23$, p < .03] and self-concept [$t(34) = 3.14$, p < .004] across the transition to parenthood. Fathers also manifest a small increase in their perceptions of the role of the father from the prenatal to the postpartum period [$t(34) = 1.99$, p < .055]. The fathers in the sample manifested a dramatic drop [$t(34) = -6.94$, p < .0001] in their beliefs concerning the importance of father-infant bonding across the transition to parenthood (the change score averaged -12.26 points per father).

In contrast, mothers experience no change in masculinity [$t(34) = -.08$, n.s.]. Mothers parallel their husbands by manifesting significant increases in self-esteem [$t(34) = 2.13$, p < .04] and femininity [$t(34) = 2.03$, p < .05]. Following the birth, mothers exhibit significantly lower beliefs about the importance of father-infant bonding (change scores averaged -15.54 points) [$t(34) = -9.11$, p < .0001] and the role of the father [$t(34) = -4.74$, p < .0001].

In order to interpret the magnitude of change and to illuminate probable family dynamics, it is necessary to present the results of paired t tests on couples before and after the birth of their child on these measures. Before the birth, mothers and fathers do not differ in their masculinity scores [$t(34) = 0.80$, n.s.] or self-concepts [$t(34) = 0.63$, n.s.]. Mothers were more feminine [$t(34) = -3.42$, p < .002] and held stronger beliefs about the importance of father-infant bonding [$t(34) = -2.76$, p < .01] and the role of the father [$t(34) = -5.35$, p < .0001] than their husbands did.

In contrast, the profile of couples' beliefs and attitudes after the birth are quite different. The only factors that remain the same in intra-couple comparisons are that mothers remain more feminine than fathers [$t(34) = -3.23$, p < .003], and parents' self-concepts are not significantly different from one another [$t(34) = 0.71$, n.s.]. In post-birth assessments, fathers were significantly more masculine than mothers [$t(34) = 2.48$, p < .02]. Follow-up visits also revealed that mothers and fathers no longer differed in their beliefs about the role of the father [$t(34) = 1.36$, n.s.] or the importance of father-infant bonding [$t(34) = -0.79$, n.s.].

These findings are prone to several conflicting interpretations. Specifically, it may be the case that the transition to parenthood has fewer significant impacts on the father than on the on the mother's belief systems. It appears that mothers adjust their prescriptions of the role of the father to conform to their spouses'. This finding stands in stark contrast to the common assertion that women socialize men into the role of fathering. On the contrary, these data indicate that mothers adjust their beliefs in this important area to conform to their husband's belief systems. It may be the case that mothers' expectations are not met in terms of paternal involvement. Prospective mothers may hold unrealistic views, and may adjust to more realistic levels in the neonatal period. It should be noted that in every couple, mothers were primary caregivers during the follow-up visit, as they were still on pregnancy leave, and fathers were working full-time. As such, the circumstances may have dictated greater role specialization than anticipated in prenatal projections of role assignment and childcare tasks.

Overall, fathers showed somewhat more attitudinal stability than mothers. This may be due to the fact that they have experienced less change in the physical realm (hormonally, weight, body image, milk production, bleeding, appetite, bladder capacity) than their wives. They are also less likely to experience major shifts in time distributions (home/work time ratios) and employment status. In contrast, mothers involuntarily go through all of these changes in rapid succession. In addition, if they are cast in the role of primary caregiver, they are experiencing another major change in distributions of responsibility, autonomy and commitment. The typical father in the sample, although involved and supportive, was clearly an assistant parent or traditional father (see Palm and Palkovitz, this issue). As such, greater change in roles and circumstances was experienced by the mother. Therefore, it is not surprising to find that maternal attitudes, beliefs and expectations changed to a greater extent than fathers'.

Fathers exhibit a marginally significant increase in their beliefs about the role of the father. It may be that their early experience with their infants concretize their responsibilities. Interview responses spontaneously offered by fathers support this assertion, as do the findings of Greenberg and Morris (1976). Mothers may have greater feelings of responsibility during the pregnancy because they are responsible for the safety and well-being of the infant through nutritional intake and avoidance of teratogens and physical trauma. Fathers apparently experience a heightened realization that they are responsible for their infants once they see them. In this sense, although no convincing evidence exists to support the notion of father-infant bonding (Palkovitz, 1985), early paternal involvement and experience may be important for facilitating fathers' role adjustments.

In many regards, the transition to parenthood can be viewed to exert a positive influence on the beliefs and attitudes of both mothers and fathers. Mothers realize enhanced self-esteem and femininity. Although their estimations of the importance of fathers' role and father-infant bonding decrease, this may be a function of their own feelings of importance and competence in caregiving. Similarly, fathers increase in masculinity, femininity and self-esteem. Again, these are positive changes for most men. The average father also realizes a modest increase in his estimation of the importance of his role in fostering child development.

It must be noted that first-time parents may be particularly at risk for disappointment around the birth of their children, in that both mothers and fathers expressed dramatically significant drops in their beliefs about the importance of father infant bonding. The data collected in this study are unable to address whether parents adjusted their expectations in a downward direction prior to the delivery, or after it.

The possibility exists that parents took the opportunity to discuss their feelings, beliefs, attitudes and expectations concerning parenting as a result of the first visit. As such, this research project may have served as an intervention program for participants by stimulating communication and or negotiation concerning their relative roles, beliefs, and expectations. Future studies should employ adequate controls to assess this possibility. It is an important issue to address for the sake of parent support and education programming.

A systematic examination of the body of literature (see Palkovitz, 1987a), and the data presented in this paper, makes it clear that the relationship between parental attitudes, beliefs, expectations and parental behaviors is not as straightforward as researchers and family interventionists may desire. Although attitudes influence the manifestation of behaviors, maximum adaptability requires that parents respond appropriately to situational cues. As such, parents' perceptions of situational variables exert significant impact on the expression of their behaviors, and may serve to obscure the relationships between attitudes and behaviors. When things don't go as we expect them to, we (as parents, researchers and practitioners) need to rise above the "confusion of being grown-ups" and respond by drawing upon our resources, supports, and accumulated experiences.

REFERENCES

Baumrind, D. (1982). Are androgynous individuals more effective as persons and parents? *Child Development, 53,* 44-75.

Belsky, J. & Pensky, E. (1988). Marital change across the transition to parenthood. *Marriage and Family Review,* 12, 3/4.

Bem, S.L. (1974). The measurement of psychological androgyny. *Journal of Consulting and Clinical Psychology, 47,* 155-162.

Bogren, L.Y. (1986). The couvade syndrome. *International Journal of Family Psychiatry,* 123-136.

Coopersmith, S. (1981). Coopersmith inventory, adult form. Palo Alto, CA: Consulting Psychologists Press.

Cowan, C.P. & Cowan, P.A. (1987). Who does what when partners become parents: Implications for men, women and marriage. *Marriage and Family Review, 13.*

DeFrain, J. (1979). Androgynous parents tell who they are and what they need. *Family Coordinator, 28,* 237-243.

Duvall, E.M. (1971). *Family Development* (4th ed.). Philadelphia, PA: Lippincott.

Dyer, E.D. (1963). Parenthood as crisis: A re-study. *Marriage and Family Living, 25,* 196-21.

Erikson, E.H. (1959). Identity and the life cycle: Selected papers. *Psychological Issues Monograph Series, I*(no. 1). New York: International Universities Press.

Fein, R.A. (1976). Men's entrance to parenthood. *Family Coordinator, 25* (4), 341-348.

Feldman, S.S. & Aschenbrenner, B. (1983). Impact of parenthood on various aspects of masculinity and femininity: A short-term longitudinal study. *Developmental Psychology, 19,* 278-289.

Feldman, S.S. & Nash, S.C. (1984). The transition from expectancy to parenthood: Impact of the firstborn child on men and women. *Sex Roles, 11,* 61-78.

Festinger, L. (1957). *A Theory of Cognitive Dissonance.* Stanford, CA: Stanford University Press.

Greenberg, M. & Morris, N. (1974). Engrossment: The newborn's impact upon the father. *American Journal of Orthopsychiatry, 44,* 520-531.

Hill, R. (1949). *Families under Stress.* New York: Harper and Brothers.

Hobbs, D.F. (1965). Parenthood as crisis: A third study. *Journal of Marriage and the Family, 27,* 367-372.

Hobbs, D.F. (1968). Transition to parenthood: A replication and an extension. *Journal of Marriage and the Family, 30,* 413-417.

Hobbs, D.F. (1976). Transition to parenthood: A decade replication. *Journal of Marriage and the Family, 38,* 723-731.

Hobbs, D.F. & Wimbish, J.M. (1977). Transition to parenthood by black couples. *Journal of Marriage and the Family, 39,* 677-689.

Holmes, T. & Rahe, R. (1967). The social readjustment rating scale. *Journal of Psychosomatic Research, 11,* 213-218.

Kuhn, T.S. (1962). *The Structure of Scientific Revolutions.* Chicago: University of Chicago Press.

Lamb, M.E. (1978). Influence of the child on marital quality and family interaction during the prenatal, perinatal, and infancy periods. In R.M. Lerner and G.B. Spanier (Eds.), *Child Influences on Marital and Family Interaction: A Lifespan Perspective.* New York: Academic Press.

LaRossa, R. (1986). *Becoming a Parent.* Beverly Hills, CA: Sage Publications.

LeMasters, E.E. (1957). Parenthood as crisis. *Marriage and Family Living, 19,* 352-355.

McGillicuddy-DeLisi, A.V. (1980). The role of parental beliefs in the family as a system of mutual influences. *Family Relations, 29,* 317-323.

McHale, S.M. & Huston, T.L. (1984). Men and women as parents: Sex role orientations, employment and parental roles with infants. *Child Development, 55,* 1349-1361.

Miller, B.C. & Sollie, D.L. (1980). Normal stresses during the transition to parenthood. *Family Relations, 29,* 459-465.

Moss, H. (1967). Sex, age and state as determinants of infant reaction. *Merrill Palmer Quarterly, 13*, 19-36.

Newman, P.R. & Newman, B.M. (1988). Parenthood and adult development. *Marriage and Family Review*, 12, 3/4.

Palkovitz, R. (1980). Predictors of involvement in first time fathers. *Dissertation Abstracts International, 40*, 3603b-3604b. (University Microfilms no. 8105035).

Palkovitz, R. (1984). Parental attitudes and fathers' interactions with their five-month-old infants. *Developmental Psychology, 20*, 1054-1060.

Palkovitz, R. (1985). Fathers' birth attendance, early contact, and extended contact with their newborns: A critical review. *Child Development, 56*, 392-406.

Palkovitz, R. (1987a). Consistency and stability in the family microsystem environment. In D.L. Peters and S. Kontos (Eds.), *Annual Advances in Applied Developmental Psychology, Vol. II*. Norwood, NJ: Ablex Publishing Co.

Palkovitz, R. (1987b). Fathers and families: Facts, fictions and fantasies. Paper presented at the Third Annual Parenting Symposium, International Society for Parenting Research, Los Angeles, CA, March.

Palkovitz, R. & Cannon, M. (in press). Popular beliefs about father-infant "bonding": A survey. *Parenting Studies*.

Palm, G. (1986). The challenge of educating fathers. Paper presented at the Second Annual Parenting Symposium, International Society for Parenting Research, Philadelphia, PA, March.

Parsons, T. & Bales, R.F. (1955). *Family Socialization and Interaction Process*. New York: Free Press.

Piaget, J. (1952). *The Origins of Intelligence in Children*. New York: International Universities Press.

Pleck, J.H. (1985). *Working Wives/Working Husbands*. Beverly Hills, CA: Sage Publications.

Russell, C.S. (1974). Transition to parenthood: Problems and gratifications. *Journal of Marriage and the Family, 30*, 294-301.

Russell, G. (1978). The father role and its relation to masculinity, femininity and androgyny. *Child Development, 49*, 1174-1181.

Russell, G. (1982a). *The Changing Role of Fathers*. St. Lucia, Queensland, Australia: University of Queensland Press.

Russell, G. (1982b). Highly participant Australian fathers: Some preliminary findings. *Merrill Palmer Quarterly, 28*, 137-156.

The Influence of Kin
on the Transition
to Parenthood

Lucy Rose Fischer

Most of the research literature on the transition to parenthood has little to say about nonhousehold kin. Families are studied *as if* they exist within household boundaries. In fact, however, the birth of a child is a family event which affects and is affected by family members who not only do not share a common residence with the new parents and their child but who even may live thousands of miles away.

One of the first acts of a new parent after the umbilical cord is cut is to share the "news"—usually first with the parents on both sides (the new grandparents) and then with other kin and close friends. Thus, the newly born child, within a hour or so after his or her birth, has been incorporated into a network of kin. In many cultures, within the child's first month of life, there is some form of ritual that brings together the child's kin—for example, a christening, a brit milah, or a naming ceremony. These rituals create a social identity for the infant, who is given a "name" and whose arrival is thus officially and symbolically announced to family and community. Relatives sometimes travel considerable distances to participate in such rituals. These ceremonies are marker-events not just for the child and his/her parents—but also for other kin. The birth of a child creates new role relationships for a whole set of family members who become grandparents, aunts, uncles, etc.

The inattention granted to the study of kinship by family sociolo-

---

Lucy Rose Fischer, PhD, is Associate Professor, Department of Sociology, St. Olaf College, Northfield, MN 55057.

gists might lead us to believe that ties with kin are merely symbolic — that is, that kin have little real influence on parents and children. But it appears that this is not so. Research on grandparenthood has documented that there often are strong emotional ties between grandparents and grandchildren (cf. Robertson, 1976; Hagestad, 1985). Moreover, personal accounts of family life suggest that many individuals grow up with strong attachments to and involvement with grandparents and other kin. There is considerable variability in relationships with kin, of course. Some grandparents and some grandchildren barely know one another. In contrast, some grandparents rear their grandchildren as if they were their own children. Families vary in the importance that they place on kinship. Individuals also give selective attention to certain kin. Thus, for example, a child may select a "favorite aunt" from a network of relatives. Factors such as gender and geographical distance appear to be predictive of such selective attention: Grandchildren tend to have closer ties with maternal grandmothers than with their other grandparents (Willmott and Young, 1960; Kahana and Kahana, 1971; Hoffman, 1979-80). Relatives who are geographically proximate are more likely to be familiar than distant kin (Klatsky, 1968).

RESEARCH ON INTERGENERATIONAL
FAMILY RELATIONSHIPS

I have done three studies on intergenerational relationships and the transition to parenthood. One project examined how relationships between adult daughters and their mothers change when daughters become mothers themselves. This study is discussed in *Linked Lives: Adult Daughters and their Mothers* and in other papers (Fischer, 1986; 1981; 1983b; 1983c). A second study, using some of the same instruments and therefore paralleling the first, focused on mens' relationships with their mothers, father and other kin (Fischer, 1983a). These first two projects were based on cross-sectional and retrospective research designs. The mother-daughter study, for example, compared dimensions of mother-daughter relationships where the daughter was married with an oldest child around two years old; married but childless; and single. The daughters and mothers also were asked to reflect on changes in their relationships over the years. Similarly, the second project, on married men and their relatives, entailed interviews with a sample of married men who had been married about three years; the sample was divided into those with and those without children. The third project concerned "role conceptions" of grandparenthood from the paired perspectives of young mothers and grandmothers. That project was based on interviews with mothers and grandmothers about grandparental interactions with the particular grandchild (Fischer and Silverman, 1982).

This chapter will draw on findings from my research and from other studies and will suggest conceptual frameworks for further research. The chapter begins with a discussion of how variability in kinship structure affects the transition to parenthood. Next, the two recipients of influence from kin will be discussed separately: the children and the parents. Finally, there will be an analysis of the limitations of influence by kin. This is largely a concept-paper and is intended to stimulate future research agendas about the influence of kin on the socialization of parents and the development of children.

KINSHIP: THEMES AND VARIABILITY

Families vary along a number of dimensions: size, spacing (or birth order), geographical dispersion, emotional closeness, etc. Research on family structure is made difficult by the enormous range of this variability. For example, family scholars who have attempted to study birth order as a variable have noted the complexity of such research (cf. Schvaneveldte and Ihinger, 1979). Most birth order research compares first-borns with later-borns (for instance, in studies of achievement). However, the position of first-borns can vary markedly by such factors as gender, gender of later-born siblings, spacing between siblings, and family size. Compare, for instance, the family positions of the following first-born sons: (a) the older of two sons where there are four years between the sons; (b) the oldest in a family of eight who is one year older than the next sibling, a daughter; and (c) an only son. All of these are first-borns; and yet their family structures and their specific positions are strikingly different. These three illustrations reflect a small portion of the variability among first-borns. There is even more variability among later-borns.

If there is so much complexity in depicting household-nuclear-family structure, a discussion of variability in kinship structure is even more complicated. Kinship structure consists of combinations and permutations of individuals and households. Any particular set of kin are defined around one individual (or "ego") — so that when a child is born, s/he shares that set of kin only with unmarried siblings. As the child ages, kin are gained and lost as s/he moves up the generational gradient. Thus, kinship structure varies not only from one individual to another, but even for the same individual over the life course.

Several variables in kinship structure are likely to be particularly important in influencing both the new parents and the developing child: (a) size and dispersion (geographic location) of "acknowledged" kin; (b) age differences between generations; and (c) attachments to maternal versus paternal kin.

Size and Dispersion

Kinship exists not simply as a matter of "blood" ties but through a process of social acknowledgement — that is, people are kin because we recognize them as such. When we talk about the size and geographical dispersion of a set of kin, the reference, then, is to the set of acknowledged kin — those people whom we count as an interact with as kin. For heuristic purposes, we can dichotomize both of these variables, as shown in the following table:

	Dispersion:	
Size:	*Concentrated*	*Dispersed*
Small Kin Network	I. "Limited"	II. "Isolated"
Large Kin Network	III. "Insulated"	IV. "Separated"

The combination of these two dichotomous variables creates four "types" — or conceptual categories. What is suggested by the names in the four cells are the ways that these combinations affect the transition to parenthood.

Type I: Limited. When new parents have a small set of kin who live nearby, they may or may not be involved with those kin, but in any case their options for interactions with kin are limited by the small numbers of individuals available.

Type II: Isolated. When new parents have a small set of kin who are geographically dispersed, their interactions with kin are far more limited than in the first type of kinship system. New parents in this type of kinship setting are essentially "isolated" from their kin and their close ties need to come from non-kin.

Type III: Insulated. When new parents have a large set of kin by whom they are surrounded — that is, there are lots of kin nearby — they are likely to be "insulated" by their kinship set. In effect, their ties with kin will place so many demands on their time, that (unless they break these ties) they will tend to find themselves preoccupied by interactions with kin and having limited time to develop other ties.

Type IV: Separated. When new parents have a large set of kin from whom they are geographically separated, they will need to find substitutes for kin (like Type II families) but their symbolic universe will nonetheless incorporate their distant kin.

The most striking contrast is between Type II ("Isolated") and Type III ("Insulated"). For new parents with "isolated" kinship structures, there are no kin around to help with childcare, to ask advice from, to celebrate with, etc. For the child, there is no one (that is, no one — aside from parents — readily familiar to the child) to whom the child is automatically attached by birth, no one who will necessarily be part of the child's universe indefinitely, no one who has an irrevocable stake in that child. In contrast, new parents with "insulated" kinship structures begin the process of childrearing in a very different kind of social environment. New parents who live near many kin have large numbers of potential helpers — their parents, in-laws, siblings, aunt, uncles, cousins, etc. In family celebrations (holidays or special events), kin are likely to be invited first — with friends being given a "place at the table" only when there happens to be room. The new child is born into this universe of kin and grows up surrounded by layer upon layer of relatives.

It might be argued, of course, that small, geographically dispersed families can be emotionally close with individuals can live near large numbers of kin and yet rarely see them. Even so, the size and dispersion of the kinship setting constitute an important dimension of the social environment in which a child is reared. Families with "isolated" kinship structures simply do not have the opportunity to be influenced by kin that potentially exists for young families who are "insulated" by a large network of kin.

Age Differences Between Generations

The preceding section discussed horizontal dimensions of kinship — that is, size and dispersion. Much of the literature on American "kinship" actually is limited to vertical, or intergenerational, relationships. An important dimension of intergenerational ties is the age gap between generations. Statistically, the narrower the age differences, the longer the overlapping lives across generations (cf. Hagestad, 1985; Burton and Bengtson, 1985). Let us look at two hypothetical examples: In Lineage I, every generation has a teenage mother who is fifteen at the birth of her first child. In Lineage II, in each generation women postpone first childbirth until age thirty. The following table shows the age of one individual at various family transitions:

	Lineage I	Lineage II
Birth of first child	15	30
Birth of first grandchild	30	60
Birth of first greatgrandchild	45	90
Birth of first greatgreatgrandchild	60	120
Birth of first greatgreatgreat-grand-child	75	150

The Lineage II woman has a good chance to live to become a grandmother and a much smaller chance to be a greatgrandmother and be part of a four-generation family. In contrast, in a family with teenage mothers, the generations are much closer together so that survival into a six-generation family is quite likely and it is even possible to become part of a seven-generation family.

The child of a close-gap lineage would be much more likely than the child of a large-gap lineage not only to have grandparents and greatgrandparents at birth but also to have a large portion of their lives overlapping with grandparents, greatgrandparents, grand-aunts and grand-uncles, etc. Of course, there are other factors besides age at first birth that affect age differences between generations — such as birth order and longevity. The oldest child of an oldest child is more likely than a youngest sibling to spend a large portion of their lives with grandparents. Moreover, the lengthening life expectancy that has occurred recently also increases the overlap between generations.

The age gap between generations is a factor which affects but is nonetheless distinct from the size of the kinship group. Obviously, more overlap tends to lead to a larger network of kin. But vertical ties also may be particularly important. Most research on American kinship suggests that the closest "kin" are (for young adult children) parents and (for immature children) grandparents (Troll, Miller and Atchley, 1979). Thus, the most likely kin to influence new parents and young children are the parents/grandparents.

The implications of spacing between generations are complex. There are some advantages for children in close-gap lineages. Not only do relatively close-gap grandparents and grandchildren share overlapping lives, but also some research suggests that younger grandparents (for example, those who are 45-55) may have more energy and be more involved in their grandchildren's lives than are grandparents who enter this role when they are much older — such as in their 60s (cf. Neugarten and Weinstein, 1964; Johnson, 1985). Moreover, there is less of a historical or cohort gap for grandparents and grandchildren who are closer in age. On the other hand, grandparents who are retired are likely to have more time to devote to grandparenting than "middle-aged" grandparents who tend to be pressed by competing demands for their time. It is also clear that a very close generational pattern, which results from teenage parenting (often replicated across generations), is usually seen as problematic (cf. Burton and Bengtson, 1985).

Attachments to Maternal versus Paternal Kin

Most studies of kinship in American and British societies have shown a tendency toward stronger ties with maternal than with paternal kin. For the most part, the explanation for the maternal bias relates to gender roles in families. Women tend to be in charge of "family business" — so that family roles are more likely to bring together mothers and daughters than mothers and sons (Willmott and Young, 1960; Hagestad, 1985). Several studies have found, in fact, that women often maintain contact not only with their own kind, but also with their husbands' relatives (Adams, 1968; Fischer, 1983a, 1983b, 1986). Women, since they are the prime caretakers for their children, tend to be "gatekeepers" who largely determine their relatives' access to their children. Moreover, another gender-related factor is that, because men tend to be somewhat older than their wives, their kin also are older and may be more likely to be deceased at an earlier stage in the child's life.

But despite a tendency toward greater involvement with maternal kin, families vary considerably in terms of their interactions with and attachments to "her" kin versus "his." They may live near to one side, both sides or neither side. Their relationships may be closer or more strained with one set of their relatives. There may be competition between grandparents on both sides — and/or the young parents may perceive a competition.

My research indicates that both married daughters and married sons have more contact with their parents once they have children. Both sons and daughters with children talk about their need for face-to-face visits with their parents — at least for the purpose of developing relationships with the children. However, paternal grandparents are less likely to "drop in" for informal visiting in the homes of their children than are maternal grandparents (Fischer, 1983a).

These findings suggest that new parents who live near to maternal kin are likely to be more involved with relatives than those who live near paternal relatives only. An issue that needs further study is how new parents balance their attachments to the two sides of kin. My research indicates that married daughters with children who live near to their husbands' family but distant from their own families are concerned about issues of "equity." These daughters talk of wanting to ensure that their parents have access to their children and say they want to give "equal time" to their own mothers. For example, one daughter/daughter-in-law, who lives down the road from her mother-in-law and 90 miles away from her mother, commented: "I want him [the child] to have as much exposure to my mother as he does to Tom's mother. She tends to come over here a lot." (Fischer, 1983b:191) Of course, this daughter could not, literally, give "equal" access; her children saw their paternal grandparents frequently and their maternal grandparents infrequently. What these daughters wanted to ensure, nonetheless, was that their children would be *also* — if not equally — attached to their maternal grandparents. And this required effort and mediation.

Although most studies of grandparents have noted that the parents are in a mediatory position, there has been little research on *how* parents mediate between their children and their other relatives (including grandparents). Do parents use special names for favorite relatives? Do parents actually monitor the amount of time that is spent with the two sides of kin? Are sons, as well as daughters, concerned about giving "equal time" to their own families or orientation? In order to begin to understand the dynamic nature of relationships with kin, we need both in-depth, qualitative research to examine the nature of negotiations with kin and more quantitatively designed research so that we can see how variability in kinship structure affects these interactions.

KIN IN THE CHILD'S WORLD

In discussing the influence of kin on the transition to parenthood, we need to make a distinction between two recipients of influence: the children and the parents. Kin potentially affect the developing child in three distinct ways: (1) as audience; (2) through influence; and (3) in terms of the allocation of resources.

Kin as Audience to the Child's Selfhood

In my interviews with adult daughters and their mothers, I often heard statements which illustrated the "audience" function of kin. For example, one young mother, who lived far from her parents, talked about the importance of sustaining face-to-face contact between her parents and her child: "I would like them to see her. I would like to show her off and have them see how she's grown and everything." A grandmother, in another family, described her grandparenting role by noting that it's "fun to see them growing . . . you show pictures . . . and everybody had to look at the picture whether they wanted to or not . . ." (Fischer, 1986, p. 142).

Even if certain sociologists are right when they argue that grandparents often are largely symbolic figures, the "audience" function provided by grandparents and other kin is important in itself. As audience for the child's emerging sense of self, relatives can demonstrate in concrete ways that the child is important and is the center of a universe of people. Through praise, attention, special names of affection, and (in some families — an endless stream of) photographs or snapshots of the child, the grandparents and other relatives buttress the child's ego. If a child at a certain age believes himself or herself to be the "center of the universe," surely this belief often is reinforced not just by parents, but even more explicitly by other doting relatives.

Of course, not all developing children are surrounded by loving relatives. And that is just where research questions arise: To what extent do the number and nature of ties with relatives affect a child's self-esteem? Under what circumstances can positive and warm ties with aunts, grandparents or other relatives compensate for lack of nurturance from parents? In what ways do children "need" kin (or substitute kin) to serve as an audience for their "performances" as children?

The Influence of Relatives on Children

Much has been said, and refuted, about the so-called "isolated" nuclear family (cf. Sussman and Burchinal, 1962). Despite the fact that children, particularly white, middle-class children, rarely live in the same household with relatives (other than parents and siblings), most children have at least some measure of contact with kin and many have close ties with their grandparents and other relatives. Kin provide two general kinds of influence on children: (1) they are often involved directly or indirectly in childrearing and (2) they can serve as additional role models of adult behavior.

Findings from my research and other studies show that some grandparents, particularly grandmothers, give advice to parents, serve as co-discipliners with parents, provide direct care on short-term bases, and give advice directly to children (cf. Fischer, 1982, 1983a, 1986; Cherlin and Furstenberg, 1985). Although there is less evidence in the research literature about other kin, it is likely that other relatives "influence" children in similar ways. Advice, disciplining and direct care all can be construed as "influence" in the sense that these behaviors affect, and are intended to affect, the child's actions and situation. Grandmothers and other relatives often give advice (and are asked for advice) on such issues as toilet-training, feeding, and health care. It must happen occasionally, to give an extreme example, that a grandmother's expertise averts disaster—for instance by telling a new mother that formula in a bottle needs to be lukewarm rather than scalding hot. More commonly perhaps, the influence of relatives may be subtle. The child who has an aunt or grandparent who believes in "health foods" is probably more likely than other children to be given and be knowledgeable about certain kinds of diets.

In addition to directly influencing behavior through advice and contact, relatives also serve as "role models" for growing children. Relatives can be models in a generic sense—that is, as people whom children may want to emulate. In my interviews with young adult daughters, I asked if there were anyone whom, as children and adolescents, they wanted to be like. A number of the daughters mentioned relatives—such as aunts or uncles—whom they admired either for their personal qualities or their achievements.

Relatives also provide family role models. Thus, relatives, or other adults, may provide children with additional images of how "mothers" and "fathers" are supposed to act in families. Children who have a considerable amount of contact with their relatives may have an opportunity to see other family systems from the inside. For example, they may stay overnight in their relatives' homes and watch the customs that are taken for granted inside those families. Of course, the same type of exposure to other family cultures can and does occur with friends. But contact with relatives may lie on the borderline between family and friend. it is likely that children are more often exposed to "backstage" behavior among kin than friends. "Backstage" behavior refers to a concept from Goffman's (1959) dramaturgy framework—that is, that certain kinds of behavior are reserved for those who know us well, like our families, and who see us when we are behind the scenes and setting the stage for a performance given to outsiders. When kin get together, some of the participants have grown up together, have lived in the same household at some time, and/or have a sense of familiarity with one another. For example, a mother and aunt who are sisters may tease or fight with one another—as "family." Because of the sense of familiarity that often pervades the world of kin, children who are involved with their kin may be witnesses to the insider-interactions of a multiple family household.

Margaret Mead, in her autobiographical book *Blackberry Winter*, describes the great influence that her grandmother and other relatives had on her development. She commented that she had several models of "strong women" in her family. Mead's background may be unusual, but even so it is likely that many people grow up with relatives who are important and influential in their lives.

In my research on mothers and daughters, I found that daughters, in various idiosyncratic ways, seemed to replicate their mothers' mothering style. Often the daughters would describe negative qualities that they had picked up. One daughter, for instance, said: "I'll hear myself saying, for example, as I was never allowed to get dirty as a child and Christine will come and I will say, 'Oh look at you, you're so dirty.' And I feel like a parrot" (Fischer, 1986, pp. 89-90). To what extent do individuals who are cared for by other relatives, in addition to their parents, *also* pick up parenting styles from these other role models? One type of research design that might be useful would be to compare the "mothering" styles of two groups of women: one group that had grown up essentially isolated from kin and another that had been cared for by other relatives in addition to their mothers. Do people who are reared by multiple "mothering" figures have greater range and flexibility in their own mothering styles?

The Allocation of Resources

A final and important way that kin potentially have an impact on the developing child concerns the distribution of money, goods and services. Many studies have shown that kin are involved in networks of exchanges (cf. Sussman and Burchinal, 1962; Hill et al., 1970). Documenting exactly what and how much is exchanged among kin, however, has proved to be a difficult task—in part, perhaps, because no one quite keeps track of what passes back and forth among their relatives. It is clear that a child who has a wealthy grandparent or rich aunt may sometimes (but not necessarily) benefit from that relative's largesse.

In my interviews with young married women and men, I was struck by the *lack* of economic or material dependence on parents. A few had received substantial gifts or loans (most commonly—help with a mortgage or in the purchase of a major piece of furniture, like a dining room or bedroom set). Most had received small gifts—a living room lamp or chair that was no longer needed in someone's home (given by the relative rather than sold) or a gift of food. But most of the adult daughters and sons that I interviewed stated that they expected to be financially independent and that, in any case, their parents could not afford to help them in any substantial way.

Actually, the impact of kin on the allocation of resources vis-à-vis the developing child might be either positive or negative—that is, through kin resources might be concentrated around the child or deflected from the child (or both—with different relatives, or at different times). Thus, grandparents and other relatives (possibly those who are at the peak of their life earnings) may help to enrich the child's financial and material environment. And/or needy relatives may siphon off resources—money, goods, or services (time and labor). The point is—in order to assess the material environment of the developing child, we need to understand the wider family setting rather than just the economic position of the household-family.

NEW PARENTS AND THEIR RELATIVES

Relatives may help to socialize first-time parents into their new roles in two ways: First, relatives may help to mute, or soften, the responsibility of parenting. Second, and more speculatively, it is possible that relatives—most particularly the mother of a new mother—may help to facilitate "bonding" with the child.

Sharing the Burden

Being a parent is an awesome responsibility. Parenthood — particularly motherhood — is an irrevocable role: You cannot "divorce" your children and no one who has living children really can be called a "post-parent" (cf. Rossi, 1968; Hagestad, 1981; Fischer, 1986). The young mothers and grandmothers whom I interviewed spoke of the immense change that comes with parenthood. Their portrayals suggested that motherhood is an "all-consuming role" — in two senses. First, mothers are required to be experts in the special needs and behaviors of their own children (Fischer, 1986); and, second, mothers almost always take "psychic responsibility" for their children — that is, ensure that they are cared for all the time — by themselves or someone else, whose services they have arranged for (cf. Boulton, 1983).

When daughters become mothers they often find themselves with a new need for their mothers.

> It is not only during the emotionally charged postpartum period that daughters need their mothers' help. The birth of a child brings rising costs and a drop in income, since most new mothers drop out of the labor force at least temporarily. At the same time, the "work" of mothering entails continuous and often heavy responsibilities. Daughters with children are much more likely both to need and to receive help from their mothers than are married daughters without children. This does not mean that all or most daughters are given a lot of help by their mothers. To the contrary, not all daughters receive baby-sitting or other kinds of help, only one daughter relied on her mother as a fulltime baby-sitter. But at least for some of the daughters, both living near to and far from their mothers, there were occasional opportunities to go "home" — to become a daughter again, letting their mothers provide a temporary respite from the responsibilities of adulthood. (Fischer, 1986, p. 81-2)

The older generation of mothers (the grandmothers) expressed a keen awareness that new parents need help now and then with the work of parenting. Many of the mothers of the adult daughters told of services they provided when the daughters came home after childbirth and they said explicitly that they wanted to help their daughters—not just do things for the new baby. Many of the mothers brought food, did laundry, helped with the cleaning, etc.—all to lessen the burden in the first few weeks of parenthood. There was great variability in how much the mothers/grandmothers helped subsequently. Some of the mothers more or less took over childcare when their daughters (or daughters-in-law) were around; others told their adult children that they were "finished" with childrearing and insisted that they would do virtually no babysitting. Other relatives also helped—particularly the sisters of the new parents. Some of the young mothers in my interviews talked wistfully about the help they wished for but did not receive. What became clear in my research is that, while the new parents generally have the great weight of responsibility for their children, actively involved grandparents and other relatives can help to ease the transition to parental responsibility.

Facilitating Mother-Child "Bonding"

Several psychologists have talked about new mothers, in the postpartum period, wanting to be "mothered" by their own mothers (Bibring et al., 1959; Deutsch, 1944; Leifer, 1980). A number of the daughter/mothers whom I interviewed recalled a similar feeling—wanting their mothers to come and "take care" of them (Fischer, 1986). It is this observation that leads to an hypothesis about how the presence or absence of daughters' mothers may affect the socialization of new mothers—that is, the maternal grandmother may facilitate bonding between mother and child. If this hypothesis is correct it would be through an interesting process of emotional transmission: The mothering of the adult daughter would reinforce her position as "object" of maternal love and help her to identify with her child, who is, in turn, the "object" of her mothering-attachment. Thus, when daughters become mothers they understand simultaneously what it is to be both the subject (the mother) and the object (the one who is mothered). In support of this hypothesis is the finding that daughters, when they become mothers, tend to develop a new identification with and understanding of their mothers as mothers — that is, they come to understand the role positions of *both* mother and child (Fischer, 1981; 1986).

WHEN DOORS ARE CLOSED AGAINST KIN

Interactions with kin are to a large extent voluntary. Therefore, the extent of involvement is far more a matter of choice than is the commitment of parents to their immature children. There is a quasi-theory about "pressure" from grandparents to have children; my research indicated that this quasi-theory is exaggerated. In my mother-daughter study,

> None of the mothers tried to exert positive, direct, and specific influence on their daughters concerning having children. A few of the mothers, and only a few, talked a little with their children about having children in general . . . Two mothers and a few fathers joked about having grandchildren . . . But more than three-quarters of the mothers said absolutely nothing to their daughters that could be construed as influence . . . (Fischer, 1986, p. 72)

If influence on daughters is minimal, there is likely to be even less attempted influence on sons — concerning such issues as the number or timing of children. Grandparents generally are not obligated, either legally or normatively, to provide care for their grandchildren. If grandparents, and other kin, are supposed to have the "fun without the responsibility," this is also a good indicator of the limitations around their rights in terms of influencing the new parents or the child: The limited stake (responsibility) entails restricted rights in terms of influence and involvement.

One of the characteristics of relationships with kin is a sense of caution — particularly for in-law relationships. In my research, I have found mothers-in-law placing emphasis on what they do *not* do — that is, specifically, that they do not interfere. One mother-in-law, for example, said that she has tried to make her relationship "friendly . . . but not overbearing, inquisitive or possessive." Another said: "I don't want her to feel because she lives close that I am going to bother her all the time." Another commented: ". . . I try not to pry into any of their affairs." Another, referring to advice about children, remarked: "I'm careful how I say things to my daughter-in-law because I know the reputation of a mother-in-law" (Fischer, 1986, pp. 134, 149).

In two separate research projects, where I had data from two generations, I found that daughters-in-law (especially those with children) and their mothers-in-law often perceive their relationships very differently: The mothers-in-law see themselves as having been asked for advice while the daughters-in-law say that their mothers-in-law give them unsolicited advice. Moreover, the daughters-in-law tend to impute much more conflict and strain to those relationships than do the mothers-in-law (Fischer, 1986).

Ties with kin, directly or indirectly, involve in-law relationships, since it is largely through marriages that kinship networks are expanded. The constraints that are placed on in-law bonds are suggestive of the limitations that are placed on influence by kin. Relatives, by definition in this culture, are people who may be invited as guests into the household. They have more of a "right" to be included in family events than others — in the sense that invitations do not necessarily require prompt reciprocity. Nonetheless, in most families, the extended kin are not involved in day-to-day childcare.

The recent literature on family violence has noted the difficulty of getting data on the actual incidence of various forms of abuse — because these problems occur "behind closed doors" (cf. Strauss et al., 1980). Kin have an interesting position vis-à-vis those "closed doors." In one sense, they are likely to be uninvolved — as are neighbors and friends. They are not around when the day-to-day interactions occur between parents and children; they are not likely to be direct witnesses to abuse. But, in another sense, they are far more involved than neighbors or others. Because they are kin, they have a stake — often an emotional stake — in the children. Kin also are more likely than strangers to be perpetrators of child abuse.

Research on kin and their influence on new parents and children may help to provide answers for questions about human development. For example, studies have shown that there is a high correlation between being an abused child and growing up to be an abusive parent or spouse; however, there is not a one-to-one correlation. If the nature of kinship relationships were examined and included in these equations, possibly the correlations would be considerably stronger. In a similar way, the correlation between educational/occupational attainments of adult children and the attainments of their parents might be further specified if the achievements (and influence) of other relatives were included in the research questions.

I am not arguing that ties with kin determine developmental outcomes for either children or their parents. What I am saying is that the involvement of kin is one factor — potentially an important factor — that ought to be considered. The emphasis of family research on nuclear-family-households has obscured an important source of variability in family behavior and life course development.

REFERENCES

Adams, B. (1968). *Kinship in an urban setting*. Chicago: Markham Publishing Co.

Bibring, G., Dwyer, T., Huntington, D., and Valenstein, A. (1959). Considerations of the psychological processes in pregnancy, *The Psychoanalytic Study of the Child, 15*, 113-21.

Boulton, M. G. (1983). *On being a mother: A study of women with pre-school children*, London: Tavistock Publications.

Burton, L. and Bengtson, V. (1985). Black grandmothers: Issues of timing and continuity of roles, in V. Bengtson and J. Robertson, eds. *Grandparenthood*, Beverly Hills: Sage Publications, 61-77.

Cherlin, A. and Furstenberg, F.F. (1985). "Styles and strategies of grandparenting," in V. Bengtson and J. Robertson, eds. *Grandparenthood*, Beverly Hills: Sage Publications, 97-116.

Deutsch, Helene (1944). *The psychology of women*, New York: Grune and Stratton.

Fischer, L.R. (1986). *Linked lives: Adult daughters and their mothers*, New York: Harper and Row.

Fischer, L.R. (1983a). Married men and their mothers, *Journal of Comparative Family Studies, 14*, 393-402.

Fischer, L.R. (1983b). Mothers and mothers-in-law, *Journal of Marriage and the Family, 45*, 187-192.

Fischer, L.R. (1983c). Transition to grandmotherhood, *International Journal of Aging and Human Development, 16*, 67-78.

Fischer, L.R. (1981). Transitions in the mother-daughter relationship, *Journal of Marriage and the Family, 43*, 613-22.

Fischer, L.R., and Silverman, J. (1982). Grandmothering as a "tenuous" role, paper presented at the annual meetings of the National Council on Family Relations, Washington.

Goffman, E., (1959). *The presentation of self in everyday life*, New York: Doubleday.

Hagestad, G. O. (1985). Continuity and connectedness, in V. Bengtson and J. Robertson, eds., *Grandparenthood*, Beverly Hills: Sage Publications, 31-48.

Hagestad, G.O. (1981). Problems and promises in the social psychology of intergenerational relations, in R. Fogel, E. Hatfield, S. Kiesler, and E. Shanas, eds., *Aging: stability and change in the family*, New York: Academic Press, 11-46.

Hill, R., Foote, N., Aldous, J., Carlson, R., and MacDonald, R. (1970). *Family development in three generations*. Cambridge, MA: Schenkman.

Hoffman, E. (1979-80). Young adults' relations with their grandparents: An exploratory study, *International Journal of Aging and Human Development, 10*, 299-310.

Johnson, C. (1985). Grandparenting options in divorcing families: An anthropological perspective, in V. Bengtson and J. Robertson, eds., *Grandparenthood*, Beverly Hills: Sage Publications, 81-96.

Kahana, E. and Kahana, B. (1971). Theoretical and research perspective on grandparenthood, *Aging and Human Development, 2*, 261-68.

Klatsky, S. (1968). *Patterns of contacts with relatives*, Washington, D.C.: American Sociological Association.

Leifer, M. (1980). *Psychological effects of motherhood: A study of first pregnancy,* New York: Praeger.

Mead, M. (1972). *Blackberry Winter*, New York: William Morrow & Co.

Neugarten, B. L., and Weinstein, K. K. (1964). The changing American grandparent, *Journal of Marriage and the Family, 26*, 199-204.

Robertson, J. (1976). Significance of grandparents: perceptions of young adult grandchildren, *The Gerontologist, 16*, 137-40.

Rossi, A. (1968). Transition to parenthood, *Journal of Marriage and the Family, 30*, 26-39.

Schvaneveldt, J. D., and Ihinger, M. (1979). Sibling relationships in the family, in W. R. Burr, R. Hill, F. I. Nye, and I. Reiss, eds., *Contemporary Theories About the Family, 1*, New York: The Free Press, 453-67.

Strauss, M. A., Gelles, R., and Steinmetz, S. K. (1980). *Behind closed doors: Violence in the American family*, New York: Doubleday/Anchor Press.

Sussman, M. B. and Burchinal, L. (1962). Kin family network: unheralded structure in current conceptualizations of family functioning, *Marriage and Family Living, 24*: 231-40.

Troll, L. E., Miller, S. J., and Atchley, R. C. (1979). *Families in later life*, Belmont, CA: Wadsworth Publishing Company.

Willmott, P., and Young, M. (1969). *Family and class in a London suburb*, London: Routledge & Kegan Paul.

Disappointment:
When Things Go Wrong in
the Transition to Parenthood

Ross D. Parke
Ashley Beitel

The transition to parenthood is a complex and multi-determined process that significantly affects and is altered by family relationships as well as the social system within which the family is located. The process is not always smooth and predictable and instead may be marked by unexpected and often difficult events that make the transition a major stressor in the lives of families. The purpose of this review is to explore the ways in which families adapt when non-normal events occur during pregnancy and childbirth and by examining differences in how mothers and fathers manage stressful transitions, to gain new insights into the nature of maternal and paternal roles. Specifically, the impact of early detection of abnormality will be considered as well as the ways in which parents cope with the transition to parenthood when an infant is born prematurely or with various kinds of handicapping conditions. By an examination of how the transition to parenthood is modified or exaggerated by unusual events, insight into the normal change process of families may be increased.

Ross D. Parke, PhD, is Professor in the Department of Psychology, University of Illinois at Champaign-Urbana; Ashley Beitel has a PhD in clinical psychology, University of Illinois, Champaign, IL 61820.

The preparation of this paper and our research on preterm infants was supported, in part, by NICHD grant HD 05951 to the first author and NICHD Training Grant HD 07225. Thanks to Barbara Tinsley for comments on the manuscript and to Kae Helms and Ria Merriman for their assistance in manuscript preparation.

THEORETICAL ASSUMPTIONS

First, to fully understand the family, it is necessary to recognize the interdependence among the roles and functions of all family members (Parke & Tinsley, 1981, 1987). It is being increasingly recognized that families are best viewed as social systems. Consequently, to understand the behavior of one member of the family, the complementary behaviors of other members also need to be recognized and assessed. For example, as men's roles in families shift, changes in women's roles in families must also be monitored.

Second, family members indirectly influence each other, in addition to their direct influence through interaction. For example, fathers may indirectly impact mother-child relationships by their level of participation in family tasks. In turn, women affect their children indirectly through their husbands by modifying both the quantity and quality of father-child interaction (Lewis & Fiering, 1981; Parke, 1979, 1981; Parke, Powers, & Gottman, 1979). In addition, recognition is being given to the embeddedness of families within a variety of other social systems, including both formal and informal support systems as well as the cultures in which they exist (Bronfenbrenner, 1979; Cochran & Brassard, 1979; Parke & Tinsley, 1982, 1987).

Another assumption concerns the role of cognitive factors in understanding family reaction to unexpected negative events. Specifically we assume that the ways in which parents anticipate, perceive, organize and understand both the nature of the event, and the reasons for its occurrence will determine the type and severity of their reaction and subsequent coping and adaptation (Parke, 1978; Parke & Tinsley, 1982; 1987).

A TAXONOMY OF STRESSFUL EVENTS

A variety of factors determine the degree of stress associated with the transition to parenthood. Table 1 outlines these dimensions and suggests the manner in which they vary across normal and different types of non-normal birth outcomes. As the table illustrates these parameters form a heuristic framework for organizing the current

TABLE 1

Dimensions which define the degree of stress associated with normal and non-normal transitions to parenthood

	NORMAL	PRETERM INFANT	STILLBORN	DOWNS SYNDROME INFANT	PHYSICALLY HANDICAPPED INFANT
Violation of Expectations	Low	Medium	Highest	High	Medium to High
Severity	Low	Medium	Very high	Variable	Variable
Chronicity	Low	Medium (Acute but not chronic)	Low-Medium (Acute)	High (Chronic)	Acute, but varies with condition
Predictability of outcome (a) Birth outcome	High	Low	Low	Low (potentially high if prenatal screening)	Low (varies with prenatal screening)
(b) Long-term outcome	High	High	-----	Mixed	Low
Controllability	High	Low	Low	Low	Low
Modifiability	No necessity to correct	Often self-correcting	-----	Non-modifiable (potential can be increased with limits)	Varies, depends on condition
On time vs off time	One time	Off time	-----	Varies	Varies
Single vs multiple event	Single	Stress is higher if preterm and ill	-----	Higher if combined with other perinatal complications	One vs multiple handicaps

literature and alert us to the necessity of carefully distinguishing among various types of stress-inducing conditions.

In the present context the importance of distinguishing among different types of birth outcomes is illustrated by this table as well. The transition to parenthood will vary considerably depending on whether the birth is normal and predictable or whether there are problems in either timing or the health status of the infant.

Severity. The severity or magnitude of the medical problem of the infant will be an important determinant of the degree of stress.

Significance. The degree of importance of the event is a central determinant of stress. While all families view the transition to parenthood as important, the level may vary as a result of such factors as the age of the parents (i.e., opportunities to continue to reproduce), the prior number of children, the degree to which the pregnancy was planned, and the degree of difficulty with prior pregnancies.

Expectations. A parents' beliefs about the course of the pregnancy, the ease or difficulty of the birth and the developmental progress of the infant will be an important determinant of their reaction when these expectations are violated by non-normal outcomes. These expectations are determined by a variety of prior experiences and knowledge such as earlier pregnancies, family history as well as current attitudes concerning the capabilities of medical professionals.

Chronicity. Events vary in terms of their chronicity or their probable duration. Compare the impact of a stillborn infant, a healthy preterm infant and a physically handicapped infant. Each of these events will be stressful, but the impact will vary, in part, due to the length of time that the event continues. The magnitude is higher in the case of the stillborn infant but the mourning process may be of limited duration and the family in turn, adapts to this loss. In the case of the preterm infant, there is initial shock and worry, but the long-term prognosis is often good. Finally in the case of the handicapped infant, there is not only initial upset, but there is the demand of continuous adaptation to the changing problems of caring for a handicapped infant and child. In this case, there is both initial and sustained difficulty, which, in turn, requires not a single response but a continuing series of adaptations to the stress that reappears at different points throughout the child's development (Wilker, 1981).

Controllability. The extent to which a person perceives that he/ she can control the onset and duration of the event is another important determinant of reaction to an event. To the extent that the event is controllable, the amount of stress may be less. For example, a planned vs. unplanned pregnancy is associated with different degrees of perceived control. Similarly the availability of the option to continue or discontinue a pregnancy after learning of a potential fetal problem increases the amount of perceived control.

Predictability. The degree to which an event is expected or anticipated is a further determinant of stress. Events that are anticipated, expected or predictable are in general less stressful than events that are unanticipated and occur suddenly and without warning. A planned pregnancy and the subsequent transition to parenthood is probably less stressful than an unplanned pregnancy. A birth defect that is unanticipated and diagnosed only at the time of delivery or shortly afterward may be more stressful than a previously diagnosed problem. In part, the increased impact is due to the lack of planning that may involve making adjustments to ease the difficulties associated with the event.

Modifiability. Some events are stressful but may be modified to reduce their negative impact. For example, an infant who is born with a visual problem (e.g., strabismus) may be able to undergo corrective surgery. The extent to which an event is viewed as modifiable as opposed to uncorrectable will determine the reaction to the event by modifying their perception of the severity of the event and their control of the event.

On time vs. off time event. As Neugarten (1979) has noted, the timing of events in terms of their occurrence in relation to other life tasks is an important determinant of the reaction to the event. Childbirth, for example, is expected to occur after marriage and after completion of education. Adolescent parenthood is often a stressful event due to its early "off time" onset as well as to the increased risk of complications (McCluskey, Killarney, & Papini, 1983). Similarly, late-timing of parenthood can be distressing as well in view of the increasing biological risks to the developing fetus in women over 40 years of age (Daniels & Weingarten, 1981). Finally, within the context of the timing of birth itself, preterm birth or post-term birth (Field, 1987) can be viewed as off-time events and therefore more stress-producing than an on-time birth.

Single vs. multiple events. It is increasingly recognized that the impact of a stressful event will depend, in part, whether it occurs singly or in combination with other events (Rutter, 1983). For example, the family that experiences both the birth of a preterm infant and the mother delivering by C-section, will clearly be under more severe stress than if only one of these stressors occurred. These dimensions are not independent of each other and interact in complex ways in defining the degree of stress produced by different birth outcomes. For example, perceived severity of outcome will vary depending on whether or not the condition is modifiable which, in turn, would alter both the perceived controllability and the level of chronicity. If the condition was not correctable by medical intervention, perceived control would be lower, the chronicity and severity ratings higher and the level of stress for the family higher than in the case where a condition was modifiable. The ways in which these factors interrelate for different outcomes associated with the transition to parenthood are only beginning to be understood and throughout the review these connections are illustrated as the available literature permits.

EARLY WARNING:
DETECTION DURING PREGNANCY

Advances in medical technology allow prenatal diagnosis of fetal abnormality, which, in turn, redefines the degree of predictability, controllability, and even modifiability associated with prenatal and postnatal events. As indicated in Table 1, reducing uncertainty may modify the degree of stress experienced by families of preterm and handicapped infants. The aim of this section is to examine the methods of early detection of fetal risk and the implications of these advances for family adaptation. These methods of diagnosis vary greatly in their invasiveness, and consequently their risk to the fetus, their cost, their ability to predict certain abnormalities, and their accuracy.

Despite the limitations of this technology, it may be valuable to consider those anomalies we can detect and consider the implication of this knowledge. In turn we can contrast these handicaps/problems with others for which we have no technological insights. Not only can we learn how the technology affects our reactions by exploring these issues, but it will be useful in guiding our pursuit of further advances. For instance we need to know what impact advanced knowledge and preparation have on families of Down's syndrome children and to contrast those who had prior testing with those who did not. What use do individuals make of forewarning, such as the use of abortion? Finally, it is important to explore the impact of this prior knowledge on family coping and adaptation.

Methods of Screening

Family history continues to be the basis with which to begin an assessment of risk for an abnormal pregnancy. Peripheral measures, such as blood tests, are noninvasive and relatively inexpensive. They can be used to screen specific high risk populations, such as for Tay Sachs. The combination of history taking, blood tests, amniocentesis, and counseling has led to dramatic success with Tay Sachs. Tests such as serum levels of alpha-fetoprotein (AFP) can also be used to screen the general population for neurotube damage, 90% of which occurs with no prior family history (Chamberlain, 1978; Milunsky, Alpert, Neff, & Frigoletto, 1980).

Ultrasonography appears to be such a safe means of detecting gross anatomical abnormalities (ie., anencephaly or hydrocephaly) that many physicians now routinely include it in their prenatal care package. This test can also detect specific defects, such as menigomyelocele, when prior history or testing has led the physician to suspect this possibility.

Amniocentesis, usually done in the 16th week, is recommended whenever the couple has had a previous abnormal birth, when there is a family history of a defect, or the mother is over 35 years of age. Results for the test are usually available three to four weeks later, which is not long before the date when the fetus becomes potentially viable (at 24 weeks the fetus is sufficiently developed to possibly survive if born prematurely). Few physicians condone abortions after 20 weeks. Therefore a couple is afforded little time in which to decide about aborting an abnormal pregnancy. Abortion at this late date is complicated and not without physical risk for the mother. The decision is made even more difficult since quickening usually occurs between the 16th to 18th week, a time when many parents begin to name their baby and form a special attachment (Shereshefsky & Yarrow, 1973; Grossman et al., 1980).

The risk of spontaneous abortion as a result of amniocentesis has been reported to be .5% (Charrow, 1985) to 1% (Finegan et al., 1984) beyond the normal baseline rate of 3-3.5% in the second trimester. In addition, Finegan et al. (1984) reports that the procedure may result in a 1% risk of premature birth. These are exceptionally high rates for a general population where NTD occurs at a ratio of .1 to .2% and when 35- year-old women are still at a .15% risk for a serious chromosomal anomoly. The risk of having a child with any congenital defect may be as high as 3 to 5% (Charrow, 1985), but this would include benign problems such as a cleft lip or an extra digit, and 80% of fetuses with serious anomalies are spontaneously aborted during pregnancy.

Chorionic villi sampling (CVS) may prove to be an alternative to amniocentesis. This procedure samples chorionic villi cells with a syringe from the placenta, allowing the same chromosome analysis as amniocentesis, yet earlier (8-11 weeks gestation age). The procedure is done under ultrasound guidance and results are available within hours. The major advantage is that it would allow for 1st trimester abortion of abnormal fetuses with much less risk and discomfort, medically and probably psychologically.

Fetoscopy affords close examination of the fetus via fiber optics through an incision in the amniotic wall during the 14-20th week. It is unclear whether fetal death rates of 5% can be improved on sufficiently to make this a viable means of diagnosis.

Comparison of Problems

Contrasting neurotube damage and Down's syndrome provides a means of contrasting the relative impact of families of prenatal diagnosis. NTD, which includes anencephaly, spina bifida, and menigomyelocele has an incidence rate in the general population of .1 to .2% (Charrow, 1985). Ninety percent of NTD's are born to couples with no prior family history of this abnormality. An elevation of AFP serum level suggests NTD, but has a false positive rate of 7% and 2-3% on repeat screening. Therefore some would argue that 97% of all women who tested positive would have been needlessly alarmed (Charrow, 1985).

The AFP test is also dependent upon accurate gestational age, since the serum level increases with age. Therefore the best results are achieved when the test is linked with ultrasonography, frequently used in dating pregnancies.

Linked with ultrasound, which may allow for visual detection of the suspected abnormality under close inspection, and amniocentesis, this process can result in detection of 85% of NTD's. This would certainly argue for general screening of all pregnant women with the AFP test. As stated above, amniocentesis is not risk-free, but by the time a women is recommended to have amniocentesis because the prior tests have suggested NTD, her risk of having such an anomoly has risen to 10% rather than the .1 to .2% risk group she was in prior to preliminary screening. Given the worst case scenario for iatrogenic complications, the couple would still have to consider fetal death 10 times worse as an outcome than the birth of a NTD infant before they would choose not to have amniocentesis at this point.

Down's syndrome results from chromosomal aberrations that increase in likelihood exponentially once women reach their thirties. Some have suggested that low serum levels of AFP indicate Down's, but at this point the research is equivocal, especially since many of the AFP screenings, designed to detect NTDs, are rather insensitive in the lower ranges. Although there may be preliminary peripheral tests for Down's in the future, the current selection criteria for amniocentesis is based on family history and maternal age.

Unlike the relative risks and benefits for amniocentesis with NTD, screening for Down's represents a risk of spontaneous abortion very comparable to the risk of the disorder itself. Therefore for a couple that has delayed having children until their thirties, or for couples who have tried a number of years to get pregnant, the possible loss of the fetus becomes increasingly significant in their decision.

Early diagnosis affords the parents choice, but not without risk to the fetus. General use of amniocentesis is unwarranted because the probability of spontaneous abortion, which may be as high as one percent (Finegan et al., 1984) and the risk of premature delivery outweigh the probability of a serious handicap being detected by amniocentesis.

Implications of Prior Knowledge

The psychological impact of various screening programs are only beginning to be understood. Since many screening methods have a high rate of false positives, many women with unaffected fetuses will be unnecessarily alarmed. Very little is known about the psychological harm that could ensue from large scale screening, such as AFP screening (Chamberlin, 1980). Recent reports indicate that reports of elevated serum AFP levels can cause anxiety and emotional distress. Fearn, Hibbard, Laurence, Roberts & Robinson (1982) found all women to be extremely anxious at the time of reassessment of the AFP concentration, and even women who did not require further evaluations (e.g., amniocentesis) after reassessment continued to have some residual anxiety. Others report similar results. Berne-Fromell, Uddenberg and Kjessler (1983) found that there were wide individual differences ranging from panic and concern to denial of fear after disclosure of abnormal serum AFP levels, with the majority experiencing considerable anxiety, but relatively short-lived distress. All women shared their concern with their spouses and 86% discussed this situation with others, especially the women's own mother. While the study did not examine the relationship between emotional support from significant others and reported anxiety, this issue merits examination. However, evidence of the impact of screening is far from conclusive since others (Berne-Fromell & Kjessler, 1984) have found less anxiety in the screened group than in nonscreened pregnant women. Burton, et al. (1985a,b) did not find differences in anxiety, depression, marital discord, work attendance, or work productivity between unscreened women and those with initially high alpha-fetoprotein levels.

Ultimately the risk to benefit decision is a personal one for each couple. However, there is considerable evidence (Blake, 1981) that parents have great concern for the health or "quality" of their children and may reduce their family size in order to ensure the birth of healthy offspring. In one recent survey of over 2000 women, Roghmann and Doherty (1983) reported that 62% of the sample thought that they would terminate the pregnancy if this was a diagnosed defective fetus. However, these figures need to be interpreted with caution. Just as attitudes and behavior do not necessarily correspond, prior knowledge of an actual abnormality may result in a decision by parents which differs from the decision made in a hypothetical situation. More information is need to understand the impact of prior knowledge, not only on the rate with which couples choose to continue or abort pregnancies, but also on the ways in which the knowledge modifies parental adaptation to the birth of an abnormal infant. Prior knowledge of an anomoly increases the predictability of the outcome and may increase the couple's sense of control over the situation, which, in turn, may help the couple adapt more successfully. In addition, prior information provides the couple with more time not only to accept and understand the implications of the information but to actively begin to prepare for the birth of the child in new ways. This may include increased vigilance in the choice of a medical team and hospital delivery site, as well as planning for the expenses involved in the delivery and postnatal care of a sick or disabled infant. Solicitation of support from members of the family's social network at an earlier stage may ensure more adequate and sustained social support.

The determinants of effective utilization of early warning information at this stage are not known, nor has the impact of various strategies on later adaptation been systematically explored.

In summary, considerable advances have been made in the early detection of possible fetal abnormalities; however, much more information is needed concerning the impact of these procedures on the psychological adaptation of the family. More is known about the reactions of families to the birth of preterm and handicapped infants, and next, we turn to our review of this literature.

THE STRESSFUL NATURE OF NON-NORMAL BIRTH

Deviations from a normal birth sequence can be a significant source of stress for families due, in part, to the violations of their prior expectations. In this section we examine the degree of stress associated with preterm birth and with the birth of a handicapped infant.

(A) Preterm Infant

The birth of a premature infant is often a stressful event. A number of investigators have isolated several themes that characterize the experience of having a premature infant. Parents are often described as angry, shocked and emotionally distraught (Kennedy, 1973; Slade, Redl, & Masguten, 1977). In contrast to mothers of full-term infants, Trause and Kramer (1983) found that mothers in a sample of relatively low risk premature infants recalled crying more and feeling guilty, helpless, and worried about future pregnancies. These earlier studies are limited by their retrospective methodology, which may have distorted the response of the participants.

Further documentation that the birth of a premature infant is stressful comes from a recent study by Pederson, Jenkins, Evans, Chance and Fox (1985), in which mothers were interviewed near the end of the premature infant's hospitalization — a methodological advance over earlier reports which were based on retrospective reports well after the hospitalization period. These investigators found that having a premature infant is emotionally stressful for most mothers but the degree of upset was modified by the illness status of the infant. Emotional stress was indexed by crying, feelings of emotional upset, disappointment, uncertainty about the infant's prognosis, alienation from the infant, psychosomatic symptoms, inconvenience in visiting the infant, resentment over separation from the infant, and anticipation of special care after discharge. While inconvenience and resentment were moderately high for both groups (36% & 17%) of mothers, mothers of ill and well preterms did not differ along these dimensions. The modifying impact of the illness of the infant on parental anxiety confirms earlier findings (Harper, Sia, Sokal, & Sokal, 1976).

Trause and Kramer (1983) assessed the reactions of both mothers and fathers to the birth of preterm and full-term infants. Parents of preterms were more distressed (higher helplessness, worry, crying, and concern about coping) than parents of full-terms. However, mothers' negative reactions to birth (pre- and full-term) were greater than fathers' both immediately after birth and one month after discharge. Even at seven months after discharge, mothers of preterms cried more, thought about the baby more and worried about future pregnancies more than did fathers. Fathers, on the other hand, were more concerned than mothers about their spouse's ability to cope at one and seven months. Similarly, Phillip (1983) found that mothers recalled having experienced more anxiety than fathers in response to the birth of a low birthweight infant perhaps because of women's greater sense of responsibility for infants in general (Russell, 1983). This study is only suggestive due to its reliance on retrospective reports. In spite of these parental sex differences, the study suggests that fathers show similar but attenuated reactions to the birth of a preterm infant.

However, some (e.g., Kaplan & Mason, 1960) have argued that the experience of premature birth is for most parents an acute crisis that diminishes after hospital discharge. For example, Trause and Kramer (1983) found that differences in anxiety between parents of preterm and full-term infants disappeared one month after discharge, at least in the case of healthy infants. However, as noted below, the continuing demands of caregiving may be a source of continuing stress — although at a lower level than during the hospitalization period. Moreover, the patterns of interaction established among family members as a result of the earlier illness may persist even after the crisis has passed.

The birth of a low-birthweight premature infant violates many parental expectations. In addition to arriving early, often before parental preparations for birth are completed, these infants differ from full-terms in their appearance, cries, feeding needs, interactional demands, and developmental progress, which, in turn, can contribute further to the stress associated with their arrival (Brooks & Hochberg, 1960; Frodi, Lamb, Leavitt, Donovan, Neff, & Sherry, 1978). For example, Frodi et al. documented that in addition to their appearance, the high-pitched cry patterns of the premature infant are rated by parents as more disturbing, irritating, and annoying. In addition, the parents reporting found premature infants less pleasant and less attractive to interact with than full-term infants. More recently, Stern and Hildebrant (1984) found that mothers rated term infants labeled premature as less physically developed, less attentive, slower, less intelligent, quieter, more sleepier, and more passive than were the same infants labeled full-term. These studies provide support for the existence of a prematurity stereotype among adults. In turn, these biased perceptions may lead to a self-fulfilling prophecy whereby the premature infant comes to exhibit less optimal behavior patterns. These findings underscore the value of a cognitive mediational approach in attempting to understand the impact of infant behavior on parents (Parke, 1978).

In addition to violating parental expectations, the birth of a premature infant exacerbates the disequilibrium initiated by any birth (e.g., additional tasks associated with caregiving, modifications of schedules and activities, readjustment of the marital relationship) (Cowan & Cowan, 1987; Entwisle & Doering, 1981). The immature development of the infant may require special medical neonatal support procedures, which in turn may lead to separation of the mother and her infant. While early separation may cause short-term stress on the family, follow-up studies indicate no long-term impact (i.e., two years) of this type of separation on the development of these infants (Leiderman, 1981, 1982). However, the increased medical support may, in turn, impose increased financial strains on the family.

Preterm infants place greater demands on their caregivers than term infants. For example, feeding disturbances are more common among low birthweight infants (Field, 1987; Klaus & Fanaroff, 1979). Moreover, premature infants are behaviorally different than their term peers; premature infants spend less time alert, are more difficult to keep in alert states, are less responsive to sights and sounds than term infants, and provide less distinctive cues to guide parental treatment (Goldberg, 1979; Goldberg & DiVitto, 1983; Field, 1987). In view of these behavioral characteristics, it is not surprising that parents have to work "harder" when interacting with a premature infant. Brown and Bakeman (1980) have documented that preterm infants are more difficult and less satisfying to feed than term infants; during feeding interactions, preterms contributed less to maintenance of the interactive flow than term infants and the burden of maintaining the interaction fell disproportionately on the mothers of these preterms.

In summary, there is considerable evidence that preterm infants place greater demands on the family than their full-term counterparts.

(B) Handicapped Infants

The birth of a handicapped infant is associated with similar indications of stress on the family. Parents of handicapped infants express a similar emotional sequence of disappointment, denial, anger, and guilt (Holt, 1958; Legeay & Keogh, 1966; Klaus & Kennell, 1981; Marion, 1981). Drotar et al. (1975) have described a series of stages that parents pass through in adapting to the birth of a handicapped infant: shock, denial, anger, sadness or anxiety, and finally, adaptation. Unfortunately couples may not progress through the stages of adaptation in synchrony. For instance if one spouse is in the angry stage while the partner persists in denial, this disequilibrium could increase the tension within the family. Handicapped infants violate parental expectations for rearing a normal well-functioning child as well (Canning & Pueschel, 1978). Interaction patterns between parents and infants are more problematic than with preterms as a result of the limited capacities of the handicapped infants. Observational studies of Down's syndrome children (Vietze, Abernathy, Ashe, & Fault-Stich, 1978), or severely handicapped infants (Walker, 1982) report a similar pattern of reduced responsiveness during social interchanges. (These studies are discussed in more detail below.) Together, these studies confirm that children with a variety of limiting conditions are less responsive during parent-child interaction.

There are other factors affecting families with handicapped infants, such as the increased burden of caregiving that may be required for handicapped infants. In contrast to preterm infants, the chronicity of handicapped conditions may impose long-term and continuing caregiving demands and/or result in possible institutionalization. In either case, there are increased concerns about the cost of providing for the child (Gumz & Gubrium, 1972). Fathers, in particular, express more concern over future problems such as economic and social dependence and legal and educational issues than fathers of nonhandicapped infants and children (Meyer, Vadasy, Fewell, & Schell, 1982). The form of concern varies by the sex of the parent as well. Fathers express instrumental concerns, especially cost issues and the ability of the child to be self-supporting. In contrast, mothers experience an expressive crisis and indicate concern about the emotional stress of caring for a handicapped child (Gumz & Gubrium, 1972). This matches the pattern of the role differentiation that seems to accompany the transition to parenthood (Cowan & Cowan, 1987). If parental roles become less traditional and more overlapping, there may be less distinctive styles of expressing concern across mothers and fathers. In fact, even in the Gumz and Gubrium study, there was overlap across parents in their concerns.

Finally, it is important to note that the ways in which the event is perceived is an important determinant of how well the parent(s) may adapt to the stressful event. Specifically the pattern of attributions concerning the causes of perinatal problems may play an important role in parental adaptation and coping. Affleck and his colleagues have explored this hypothesis with parents of infants with perinatal complications (Affleck, Allen, McGrade, & McQueeney, 1982). Mothers of infants with severe perinatal complications were interviewed at hospital discharge about three major categories of information: mothers' expressed beliefs about the causes of the infants medical problems, mothers' self-reported mood, and mothers' expectations of the extent of caretaking-related difficulties the infant would present. Three types of attributions were common and these indicated the degree to which the infants' difficulties were the result of (a) something the mother did or did not do (e.g., sex during pregnancy, excessive exertion, smoking), (b) something someone else did or did not do (e.g., obstetric error, insufficient stimulation in the intensive care unit), and (c) chance (e.g., "a one in a million chance," "a fluke," "just one of those things that happens"). Of interest is the fact that those who gave self-blame as the cause of their infant's problems reported a stronger conviction that their infant's current recovery and future outcomes were dependent on their own actions and that similar problems could be prevented in future deliveries. Mothers who attributed a greater role to chance reported less personal control over their infant's recovery and over prevention of similar problems in the future. Blaming others was unrelated to control cognitions (Tennen, Affleck, & Gershman, 1986).

Together these findings support a model that suggests that greater perceived severity produces greater self-blame, which in turn, plays an indirect role in emotional adaptation through its association with the belief that a recurrence of the negative event could be prevented. Although this pattern merits replication and further work is needed to understand the underlying processes, the implications for the interplay between institutions and families are interesting. It brings into question whether the professional management of parents of ill infants, namely the discouragement of self-blame attributions and the encouragement of attributions to chance is beneficial. Although it has been argued that parental self-blame signals poor coping, the present results bring this view into question. Instead, self-blame has a "potential healing role for some victims of aversive life events" (Tennen et al., 1986, p. 695).

IMPACT OF PRETERM AND HANDICAPPED INFANTS ON PARENT-INFANT RELATIONSHIPS

In this section, the effects of a preterm and handicapped infant on parental familial roles as well as styles of parent-infant interaction are examined. It is assumed that the family is best understood as a system and shifts in the demands imposed on the system will, in turn, elicit different degrees of involvement by mothers and fathers.

Parental Roles: Quantitative Effects

(A) Preterm Infants

In light of the increased demands placed on parents by the birth of a preterm infant, the usual pattern of shifting to more traditional roles for mothers and fathers after the birth of a full-term infant (Cowan & Cowan, 1987) may not be as evident.

Evidence indicates that fathers of preterms are interested and active interactive agents in the early postpartum period. Marton, Minde and Perrotta (1981) examined the visitation patterns of fathers when their preterm was hospitalized during the postpartum period. In their sample, fathers visited an average of 2.5 times prior to the mother's first visit with the infant. Particularly in transport situations, where the infant may be moved to an intensive care nursery at a centralized perinatal unit without the mother, the father may often have the earliest contact with the infant. In this study, however, father involvement, as indexed by the visitation patterns, did not diminish after mother visitation became possible. Both parents visited an average of three to four times each week during the infants' average 6-7 week hospital stay.

There is some support for the proposition that the birth of a premature infant elicits greater father involvement in caregiving; this heightened involvement may, in part, be due to the additional time, energy, and skill required to care for preterm infants. A recent investigation by Yogman (1985) will illustrate. Twenty preterm and 20 full-term infants were followed longitudinally from birth to 18 months. On the basis of father reports of routine caregiving at 1, 5, and 18 months, Yogman found that fathers of preterm infants reported engaging in more of the caregiving tasks at each age than the comparison group of fathers of full-term infants. The differences were especially marked and statistically significant by 18 months, when fathers were more likely to take the infant to a physician, to bathe the infant, and to get up at night to console their infant. In summary, the birth of an infant prematurely appears to elicit greater father participation in caregiving.

However, it is not clear that these early caregiving arrangements are stable over long periods of time; instead as the preterm infant "catches up" developmentally and becomes less burdensome for the family, the father's level of participation may decrease. A pattern of early father involvement which decreases by the end of the first year is evident in the studies of C-section delivery on father participation as well (Vietze et al., 1980).

Although the birth of an infant prematurely appears to elicit greater father participation in caregiving, not all investigators find such a relationship. In our recent short-term longitudinal study of the development of preterm infants (Parke, 1984), we followed 44 families — 24 full-term and 20 preterm infants from birth to 12 months of age. Families were observed at the hospital, at three weeks, three months, eight months, and 12 months. The preterm infants were less than 2500 grams (x = 2000 grams) and less than 37 weeks gestation (x = 32 weeks gestation). As a sample, they were a relatively healthy set of preterm infants; in contrast to the Yogman sample, the infants in our sample were less at risk. As part of our assessment battery, parents were asked to record the amount of caretaking they provided their infants during the course of one week following each of the home visits using a specially-prepared diary provided by the project staff. Parents recorded the amount of time mother and father each spent in feeding, diapering, and bathing. Independent methodological work (Anderson, 1984), in which independent observers' ratings of these caregiving activities were compared with parental diary records indicates that parents are moderately reliable recorders of these types of caregiving activities. In spite of early trends which suggested that fathers of preterms engaged in more caregiving than fathers of full-terms, a recent analysis of the families across eight months indicated only one main effect for all contexts (feeding, diapering, and bathing); namely, sex of parent. Mothers were consistently more involved in all facets of caregiving across all time points and all full-term and preterm conditions than fathers.

Marton et al. (1981) similarly found that fathers of preterms contributed significantly less to routine caregiving (feeding, diapering, bathing, comforting) than mothers, but the unavailability of a full-term group does not allow us to determine whether these fathers of preterms were still performing at higher rates than the fathers of full-term infants.

How do we reconcile these discrepancies? The Yogman data on fathers of preterms as well as the extensive data on fathers of infants delivered by C-Section (Vietze, MacTurk, McCarthy, Klein, & Yarrow, 1980; Grossman, Eichler, & Winickoff, 1980) both suggest that fathers modify their levels of involvement to assist mothers when she is unable to cope, due either to her own condition or to the increased demands imposed by the infant. In the Parke study, the relatively healthy status of our infants may have obviated the necessity of increased father involvement which suggest that fathers become involved mainly when there is an acute crisis to be managed by the family.

(B) Handicapped Infants

Does father participation increase with the increased need created by the birth of a handicapped infant? Although the data is neither abundant nor entirely consistent, research suggests that fathers of retarded infants and children tend *not* to show increased involvement in child care. In fact, the level of participation in caregiving of fathers of retarded children is low (Holt, 1958; Andrew, 1968). In one of the rare observational studies in this area, Stoneman, Brody, and Abbott (1983) found that mothers assumed the role of teacher more frequently in a structured interaction situation than did fathers when there was a handicapped infant in the family. Mothers and fathers did not differ in their level of teaching in families of nonhandicapped children. Unfortunately, the level of father involvement in routine caregiving activities of handicapped children was not assessed in this investigation,

In a recent study, Bristol and Gallagher (1986) found that both mothers and fathers reported that fathers assume less responsibility for total tasks in families of developmentally disabled children than do fathers in families of nonhandicapped children. Specifically fathers of developmentally disabled children assume substantially less responsibility for the care of the child than do fathers in families of nonhandicapped children. However, the lack of paternal involvement with children in these families is specific to the disabled child, since father assistance with nonhandicapped siblings did not differ across family types.

Lamb (1984) suggests that "this reflects the fact that fathers obtain less satisfaction from retarded than normal children (Cummings, 1976) and the fact that paternal involvement — unlike maternal involvement is discretionary. The paternal role is defined in such a way that fathers can increase or decrease their involvement depending on their preferences and satisfactions whereas traditionally mothers are expected to show equivalent commitment to all their children — regardless of personal preferences or the individual characteristics of their children" (p. 16-17). However, not all investigators find this pattern of low involvement. In an early study, Tallman (1965) found that fathers of handicapped children became highly involved in child care, but only with boys. This heightened involvement of fathers with their sons is consistent with earlier studies of nonretarded infants (Parke & Sawin, 1976, 1980). Others find no differences in the level of father involvement with handicapped and nonhandicapped children.

Parent-Infant Interaction Patterns: Qualitative Effects

(A) *Preterm Infants*

As already noted, parent-infant interaction patterns are different for the preterm and full-term infant, in part, due to the reduced responsiveness of the preterm infant.

Although less research has been devoted to describing father-preterm infant interaction, recent studies indicate that the father-infant relationship is modified when the infant is born prematurely. In a comparative observational investigation of the interaction patterns of fathers with premature and term infants in the high-risk nursery and at home over the first year of life, styles of father-infant play with the preterm and full-term infants differed (Parke, 1984). Fathers exhibited their characteristic higher rate of physical play (bounce-stretch) than mothers — but only when the infant was born at term. When the infant was born prematurely, there was no mother-father difference in play style. On the other hand, mothers were more verbal and affectionate and provided more caregiving than fathers — for both full and preterm infants. Mothers treated full and preterm infants differently and were more verbal with their preterm and more affectionate with their full-term infants — a pattern which may, in part, be due to the greater difficulty of maintaining the attention of pre vs. full-term infants.

Other evidence is consistent with these findings. Yogman (1985) studied fathers of preterm and full-term infants during a three-month episode of face-to-face play in the laboratory. The games were then categorized as arousing if they involved proximal activities such as tactile and limb movement games, or as non-arousing if they were assumed to maintain rather than arouse the infant's attention such as verbal and visual games. Fathers of preterm infants played fewer and shorter games and fewer arousing games than did fathers of full-term infants. Fathers were less able to directly engage their preterm infants in play compared to the full-term infants. Possibly, fathers assume that the premature infant is fragile and unable to withstand robust physical stimulation which, in turn, leads to an inhibition of fathers' usual play style. Moreover, since preterm infants have more difficulty with motor activity and tone and with state regulation and hypersensitivity, vigorous stimulation may stress and disorganize an already vulnerable infant. Fathers, in turn, in view of this feedback may not only shift their play style to a less stressful mode but may interact less. In view of the important role of physical play in the development of social competence, ways to increase the degree of physical play interaction between preterm infants and their parents may be worthwhile (MacDonald & Parke, 1984; Parke, MacDonald, Beitel, & Bhavnagri, 1987). It is assumed that this differential treatment of preterm infants continues well beyond the time when the infant's condition necessitates a less vigorous play style. However, some evidence (Wasserman, Solomon-Scwerzer, Spicker, & Stern, 1980) suggests that interactions between preterm infants and their parents are more like full-term dyads during the second year.

(B) *Handicapped Infants*

Relatively few observational studies have been conducted with parents and their handicapped infants to determine if there are stylistic differences between mothers and fathers, in how they interact with handicapped and nonhandicapped infants. Observational studies by Walker (1982) of the social interactions between mothers and handicapped infants suggest that the handicapped infant is less reinforcing, less interesting, and more difficult as a social partner. In her studies, mothers accounted for a large share of the playful stimulation, while the infant contribution was severely limited. Similarly, observational studies of parent interaction with Down's syndrome infants in comparison to parents of normal infants of comparable developmental level indicates that parents of Down's infants are more active and move directive (Berger & Cunningham, 1983). Moreover, mothers of Down's children reported that their interaction goal was to teach, while the goal of the mothers of able-bodied infants was to "have fun" (Jones, 1980). Parallel work with fathers using an observational strategy would help illuminate further the father's role in the early development of handicapped infants. Some suggestive evidence comes from Gallagher et al. (1981), who found that fathers of handicapped children did not engage in the usual kinds of physically playful interaction. Together these findings suggest that there are significant alterations in the interactive styles of parents with different types of conditions.

BEYOND THE DYAD: THE LINK BETWEEN THE MARITAL RELATIONSHIP AND PARENTING

Models that limit examination of the effects of interaction patterns to only the father-infant and mother-infant dyads and the direct effects of one individual on another are inadequate for understanding the impact of social interaction patterns in families (Belsky, 1981, 1984; Lewis & Feiring, 1981; Parke, Power & Gottman, 1979). The full family group must be considered. Second, parents influence their infants indirectly as well. A parent may influence a child through the mediation of another family member's impact (e.g., a father may contribute to the mother's positive affect towards her child by praising her caregiving ability). Another way in which one parent may indirectly influence the child's treatment by other agents is by modifying the infant's behavior. Child behavior patterns that develop as a result of parent-child interaction may, in turn, affect the child's treatment by other social agents. For example, irritable infant patterns induced by an insensitive and impatient mother may, in turn, make the infant more difficult for the father to handle and pacify. Thus, patterns developed in interaction with one parent may alter interaction patterns with another caregiver. In larger families, siblings can play a similar mediating role. The marital relationship can be viewed from two perspectives, namely the buffering impact of the marriage on the couple's ability to deal with the "disappointment," and alternatively the impact of the unexpected events on the marital relationship itself.

(A) Healthy Full-Term Infants

A number of recent studies have demonstrated that spousal support is an important correlate of both parental competence and infant outcome. In their interview study of parents of preterm and full-term infants, Trause and Kramer (1983) found that maternal adjustment difficulty was related inversely to fathers' sensitivity to their spouses' needs and feelings.

In a recent study of four- to eight-month-old infants and their parents, Dickie and Matheson (1984) examined the relationships between parental competence and spousal support. Parental competence was based on home observations and involved a variety of components such as emotional consistency, contingent responding, and warmth and pleasure in parenting. Emotional support — a measure of affection, respect, and satisfaction in the husband-wife relationship, as well as cognitive support — an index of husband-wife agreement in child care — were positively related to maternal competence. These same investigators found that maternal emotional support and cognitive support were related to paternal competence. In fact, spousal support was even a more important correlate of competence in fathers than mothers. The level of emotional and cognitive support successfully discriminated high and low competent fathers, but failed to do so in the case of mothers. In short, successful paternal caregiving may be particularly dependent on a supportive intra-familial environment.

Lamb and Elster (1985) recently addressed a similar question in a sample of adolescent mothers and their male partners. Using an observational scheme similar to Belsky et al. (1984), mother, father, and infant were observed at home in an unstructured context for approximately one hour. As in earlier studies, father-infant interaction was significantly and positively related to the level of mother-father engagement. By contrast, mother-infant interaction was unrelated to measures of mother-father engagement.

Those findings suggest that the maternal caregiving system can benefit from spousal support, but it is a buffered system which is not critically dependent on this support. In contrast, paternal caregiving appears to be less buffered and less overdetermined by cultural demands and socialization experiences and therefore more dependent on spousal support for successful enactment of this role.

(B) *Preterm Infants*

Spousal support is important in preterm groups as well. Crnic, Greenberg, Ragozin, Robinson, and Basham (1983a), in a study of 105 four-month-old preterm and full-term infants, found that support from an intimate (spouse, partner) was strongly and consistently related to a variety of measures of maternal parenting attitudes and behavior. Intimate support was related to satisfaction with parenting, as well as maternal behavior (a composite index of responsiveness, affection, and gratification from interaction with infant). Moreover, intimate support was related to infants' responsiveness to the parent as well as a cluster of positive infant behaviors during maternal face-to-face interaction. The impact of support on infants was indirect since intimate support modified maternal behavior, which in turn related to infant behavior.

Unfortunately, stressful events such as the birth of a premature or retarded infant may often have a disruptive impact on the marital relationship. In turn, this disruption may reduce the level of mutual support which spouses provide each other in stressful circumstances. Of relevance to this issue is the work of Leiderman (1981) and Leiderman and Seashore (1975). These investigators examined the relationship of prematurity to marital stability. In the two-year period following hospital discharge, marital discord, often leading to separation or divorce, was higher for the families of preterm infants who were initially separated from their mothers. As Leiderman and Seashore suggest, "separation in the new born period does have an effect, albeit non-specific, by acting through the family as a stress that creates disequilibrium in the nuclear family structure" (Leiderman & Seashore, 1975, p. 229-230). While the Leiderman work provides further support for considering the family unit, the specific ways in which the birth of a preterm infant affect relationships among family members remains unclear.

However, this disruptive impact on marriage does not always occur. Trause and Kramer (1983), for example, in their study of preterm infants, found no separation or divorce in any of their families eight to 26 months postpartum. The discrepancy, in part, may be due to the relatively good health of the infants and the social and economic stability of the families.

(C) *Handicapped Infants*

Just as in the case of preterm infants, the birth of a handicapped infant often has a negative impact on the marital relationship. Specifically, a number of investigators have found extensive marital and family disruption as a result of the birth of a retarded or handicapped child (Holt, 1957; Farber, 1959, 1960; Lonsdale, 1978; Tew, Lawrence, Payne, & Rawnsley, 1977).

In a recent study, Bristol and Gallagher (1986) found that mothers of developmentally disabled children reported less satisfactory marital adjustment than mothers of nonhandicapped children; fathers in the two groups did not differ. This dissatisfaction may, in part, be mediated by the lower level of expressive support—emotional, intellectual and recreational—the mothers of developmentally disabled children perceive that they receive from their husbands. Moreover, rates of marital separation and dissolution are higher in families with a handicapped child. Among United States parents of children five years old or less, divorce and separation rates for parents of handicapped children were 14% compared to 8% for parents of normal children. In fact, the rates were highest among families with low income and low education levels. However, as Bristol (1985) cautions:

> . . . separation and divorce are seldom due entirely to the stress of the handicapped child. It appears that marital breakdown is most likely to occur in families which are experiencing personal or financial difficulty before the birth of the child, in those in which the child was conceived premaritally, in those in which the care of a defective child is not a shared value or in those where the demands of the handicapped child outstrip the available resources of the family and the services found in the community. (p. 3)

Other comparisons suggest that the disappointment of bearing and then losing a handicapped child is highly stressful for the couple's relationship, but that the burden of continued care has an additional impact on the marriage. For example, Tew et al. (1977) found that parents of spina bifida infants were divorced nine times more often than their cohort in England, assessed 10-12 years after delivery, while couples whose spina bifida infants were stillborn had rates three times as high as their age cohort. In light of the recent work by Affleck et al. (1982) concerning the attributions that parents make when an infant is born with a handicapping condition, it would be worthwhile to examine how the marital disruption rates are affected by the types of parental attributions.

In addition, Tew reports that divorced fathers are likely to remarry, while their ex-wives who usually retained custody of the handicapped child do not. It is clear that women, in particular, assume a disproportionate share of the burden. They feel ultimately responsible for the child, whereas for fathers it is a matter of choice. Moreover, nonretarded siblings tend to be negatively affected (Farber, 1960; Holt, 1957) and further childbearing tends to cease (Carver & Carver, 1972).

A supportive spousal relationship can serve to buffer or diminish the negative impact of giving birth to a handicapped or retarded infant. Support for this hypothesis comes from a study of maternal adjustment to having a handicapped child (Friedrich, 1979). Marital satisfaction was found to be the best predictor of maternal coping behavior.

Further support comes from Bristol and Gallagher (1986), who found that maternal perceptions of expressive support received from their husbands were positively related to better marital adjustment and to better in-home ratings of quality of parenting in both developmentally disabled and non-handicapped groups. In addition, expressive spousal support was related to fewer reported symptoms of depression among the mothers with a handicapped child. In contrast, a different picture emerged for fathers. Fathers of developmentally disabled children who felt emotionally supported by their wives were less depressed (marginally), more happily married and were providing their children with higher quality of care.

In light of this evidence concerning the disruptive impact on marriage of a handicapped birth, it would be interesting to examine the potentially ameliorative effect of early diagnosis of fetal abnormality. Since parents would be afforded a choice of taking the pregnancy to term or aborting it, this may reduce the sense of uncontrollability; if they decided to continue the pregnancy, the forewarning provides the opportunity to prepare and plan for the birth and seek information about the special problems associated with caring for a handicapped infant.

The importance of these findings is clear: in order to understand either the mother-infant or father-infant relationship, the total set of relationships among the members of the family needs to be assessed. Although interviews are helpful, they are not sufficient; rather, direct observations of both mother *and* father alone with their infants, as well as the mother, father and infant together are necessary.

BEYOND THE TRIAD: EXTRAFAMILIAL SUPPORT SYSTEMS AND THE PRETERM AND HANDICAPPED INFANT

A further extension of our theoretical framework — from the dyad to the triad to the family in its ecological context — is needed to understand the environment and the development of either the preterm or retarded infant. Families do not exist as units independent of other social organizations within society. Thus, families need to be viewed within their social context and recognition of the role of the community as a modifier of family modes of interaction is necessary for an adequate theory of early development.

To understand the specific functions that extrafamilial support systems play in modulating interaction patterns in families of premature and/or handicapped or retarded infants, an appreciation of the problems associated with the care of these types of infants is necessary. Infants who are born prematurely or with a handicapping condition may be at-risk for later parent-child relationship problems as a result of (a) limited knowledge of development on the part of parents, (b) inappropriate infant care or skill, and/or (c) the stress associated with the care and rearing of a preterm infant. Extrafamilial support systems can function to alleviate these problems by (a) providing accurate timetables for the development of infants with special problems, (b) monitoring current infant care practices and provide corrective feedback in order to improve infant care skills, and (c) providing relief from stress associated with the birth and care of the preterm and/or handicapped infant.

There are a variety of support systems of special relevance to at-risk infants and their families. Two kinds of support systems operate: formal (e.g., health care facilities, social service agencies, recreational facilities), and informal (e.g., extended families, neighbors, and co-workers). These programs serve the educational function of providing child care information, as well as alleviating stress associated with premature or ill infants. Support systems which serve an educational function include: hospital-based courses in child care and childrearing, visiting nurse programs, well-baby clinics, follow-up programs, and parent discussion groups. Some other supportive programs that offer stress relief are: family and group day-care facilities, babysitting services, mother's helpers, homemaker and housekeeping services, drop-off centers, crisis nurseries, and hot lines.

Patterns of Utilization of Informal and Formal Support Systems

In view of the stressful nature of a premature birth, it is expected that parents would utilize informal social networks for support purposes. Evidence of utilization patterns comes from a number of recent studies.

Social support was measured by Pederson et al. (1985) in their study of preterm infants. During the period of hospitalization, husbands, the mother's own parents, and church groups (for church members), were viewed as major sources of support during the crisis period. Although there was a tendency for mothers of ill infants to perceive their own parents and in-laws as more supportive, only in-laws, in fact, differed in level of support that they provided for mothers of ill vs. well preterms. More support was given in the case of ill infants. A small percentage of mothers (12-15%) saw the hospital medical staff as major sources of emotional support; however, one-third reported that neonatologists and nurses provided informational support.

In our recent longitudinal project (Parke & Tinsley, 1984), we found a number of differences in the patterns of social support utilization among families of preterm and full-term infants. At each time point, parents completed a social support questionnaire which tapped the extent to which families used either informal or formal support agents. Second, the purpose of this use was separately evaluated (i.e., social, emotional, informational, or physical). A number of findings are noteworthy.

First, there were clear sex differences. As is often found, mothers visit and phone relatives and friends more than fathers. When examined by the purpose of the contact, mothers again were higher than fathers, in contact with informal networks for information purposes, for assistance with home baby care, for alleviating worry or upset about their baby, and for relaxation and enjoyment. In general, mothers utilized informal networks more than fathers.

Second, there was a trend indicating that parents of preterms report seeking information more often from professional or social service agencies than parents of full-term infants. This was qualified by the fact that fathers of preterms sought information more often from formal support agencies than fathers of full-terms at the hospital period. Over time and presumably as the crisis has passed, fathers decrease their reliance on formal agencies. Mothers of preterms, in contrast to fathers of preterms, do not differ from mothers of full-terms in their use of formal agencies for information in the early postpartum period. Fathers and mothers, in short, appear to have distinctive styles of support seeking. Possibly males view information seeking from formal sources as role-consistent, whereas females are more comfortable utilizing informal social networks. Alternatively, fathers may not have as well-established informal social networks upon which to rely in times of crisis. Finally, parents of full-term infants report more frequent contact with friends for purposes of babysitting than do parents of preterm infants. This finding implies a more protective attitude on the part of parents of preterm infants. Overall, the results underscore the importance of distinguishing formal and informal support systems and suggest the necessity of providing formal support systems, especially for fathers. Further analysis will indicate the impact of these patterns of support utilization for family functioning and infant development. Next we turn to the examination of the impact of support systems on family interaction patterns.

The Impact of Informal Support Systems

A number of studies have suggested that there is a positive relationship between informal social networks and family's adaptation to stressful events (Parke & Tinsley, 1982). Of particular relevance are recent investigations concerning the relationship between social networks and mother-child interaction.

(A) *Preterm Infants*

A number of investigators have examined the impact of social networks on mother-infant interaction and found a positive relationship between the level of maternal social support and subscales from the HOME scale (Pascoe, Loda, Jeffries & Earp, 1981). For example, Pascoe and Earp (1984) investigated the relationship between mothers' life changes, social support and the preschool child's home environment three years after discharge from a neonatal intensive care unit. While the number of reported life changes occurring to the mothers since the birth of the children was not related to the amount of home stimulation mothers provided their children (Home Scale), mothers reporting more social support (an index of the caregivers' perceptions of daily task-sharing among family members, satisfaction with relationships, availability of emergency help, and degree of community involvement) provided a more stimulating home environment for their children. In view of the relationships between the Home Scale and social and cognitive development, these findings assume importance.

A number of studies have examined the impact of informal social support on parent-infant interaction in *both* preterm and full-term infants. Crnic, Greenberg, Ragozin, Robinson, and Basham (1983), using samples of both preterm and full-term four-month-old infants, reported positive relationships between informal social support and a variety of measures of parenting attitudes and behavior — regardless of the birth status of the infant. In addition to the importance of the spousal relationship discussed earlier, these investigators found that community or neighborhood support was modestly predictive of satisfaction with parenting (borderline effect),(while more strongly predictive of mothers' behavior in free play, imitation and vocalization-elicitation situations. Mothers with higher levels of community support were more responsive, gratified with the interactions, and affectionate, as were their infants; perhaps these mothers were more successful in eliciting social support outside the family.

Although social support did not differentially affect parents of preterm and full-term infants, later research suggests that differential effects can be found if a wider range of infant health status is examined. Perhaps the levels of social support that are necessary for adequate childrearing differ for families with problems of different degrees of severity. This is illustrated in a recent study of the relationship between mother-infant interaction and social support networks of mothers with high-risk infants. Feiring, Fox, Jaskin, and Lewis (1987) found a strong relationship among high-risk birth, postnatal illness, mothers' social networks, and mother-infant interaction patterns. Healthy and sick preterms and healthy and sick full-term infants were studied. Results indicated that at three months mothers of sick preterm infants reported few friends and fewer total support agents contributing goods than mothers in the other groups, while mothers of both sick preterm and sick full-term infants reported receiving fewer services than mothers of healthy preterm and term infants. Differences in social support and infant birth status varied along three dimensions of mother-infant interaction: proximal, distal, and play behaviors. For all families, mothers who received more services from support agents were more proximal with their infants. Mothers of sick preterm infants were most distal with their infants, although receipt of goods by these mothers was associated with reduced distal behavior. Mothers who received the most services engaged in the most play with their infants, especially for families with healthy preterm and term infants. The authors of this study suggest an interpretive pattern in the data. They suggest that the network response to sick preterms is cautious, which leads to less proximal and more distal maternal behavior while the network response to sick term and healthy preterm and term infants is more positive, leading to increasing proximal and decreasing distal mother behavior. A possible model suggests that the support received by the mother was mediated by the birth status of the infant, which in turn modified mother-infant interaction behavior. These findings suggest that the degree of severity is an important factor to be considered in studies of the impact of social networks on family interaction patterns.

(B) *Handicapped Infants*

In the case of families with handicapped infants and children, social networks are particularly important aids to successful coping and adaptation. However, a number of studies have documented that these families are socially isolated (Carver & Carver, 1972;

Illingworth, 1967; Birenbaum, 1970). In a recent study, McDowell and Gabel (1981) found significantly small social networks for parents of mentally retarded infants as compared to a contrasting group of parents of normally developing infants; the difference was due to smaller extended kinship networks. There are many reasons for this isolation. First, the families may be too emotionally and physically exhausted to maintain ties with friends and relatives, due in part to the heavy caregiving demands placed on parents by a handicapped infant. In turn, this may further restrict the amount of time available to spend with friends and relatives. Second, the assumed stigma of a retarded child in the family may lead parents to avoid outside social contacts. Third, others may ostracize the family of a retarded person due to lack of acceptance and understanding. Fourth, relatives such as grandparents may be less able to provide emotional support in the case of the birth of a retarded or handicapped infant, due in part, to their own upset and grief over the discovery that their grandchild is handicapped (Berns, 1980; Solnit & Stark, 1961). Moreover, the grandparents, themselves, may need support and may become an additional burden for the parents (Gabel & Kotsch, 1981). Finally, many potential social support agents in the informal network, such as friends or relatives may be less capable of providing assistance in child care when the child is handicapped due to the need for specialized arrangements for these kinds of children (Gabel & Kotsch, 1981). In view of the heavy reliance on professional assistance in the case of retarded and handicapped children, we turn next to examine the role of formal support systems.

The Impact of Formal Support Systems on Families

In recent years, a number of investigators have used the hospital to provide social support for parents and, in particular, the postpartum period as a convenient time point for initiating supportive services for parents of infants. Parents are accessible at this point and often motivation for learning about infant development and caregiving skills is high during this time.

These studies illustrate that educational intervention can effectively modify levels of parental involvement and the quality of parent-infant interaction (see Parke & Beitel, [1986] for a recent review of this work). To cite an illustrative example, Whitt and Casey

(1982) found that mothers who were provided with an office-based pediatric intervention program emphasizing physical and preventive child care, developmental norms, and information on infant communication abilities during well-baby exams, demonstrated a more positive relationship with their infants. Again, given the problematic medical status of many premature infants, utilization of pediatric visits as support mechanisms for families of premature infants appears to be a promising form of supportive intervention. Together, these intervention studies illustrate the ways in which formal institutions, such as hospitals and other health care facilities, can potentially affect infants through the modification of the skills of mothers, fathers, or both parents.

There are many intervention programs for retarded and handicapped infants and children (see Fewell & Vadasy, 1986, for a review). However, few of these programs are family focused and instead are focused primarily on the mother. Even though many programs are ostensibly for parents, they are functionally "mother programs" because they are often held at times inconvenient for fathers and they tend to reflect mothers' concerns" (Meyer, 1986, p. 241). In view of this lack of specific attention to fathers, it is not surprising that father participation in programs is very low (Meyer, Vadasy, Fewell, & Schell, 1982). Since fathers have difficulties in adjusting to and accepting the birth of a retarded or handicapped child, it is important to include fathers in future intervention efforts. There are signs that fathers are finally being targeted. For example, the University of Washington's Supporting Extended Family Members (SEFAM) is specifically organized to assist fathers of handicapped infants (Meyer, Vadasy, Fewell, & Schell, 1982; Vadasy, Fewell, Meyer, Schell, & Greenberg, 1984). Based on a weekly program in which fathers and children meet with male teachers, "fathers learn activities and games that they can enjoy with their children, share their concerns with other fathers, and learn how to help their family cope effectively with the responsibilities of caring for and educating a child with special needs" (Vadasy et al., 1984, p. 14). A sample of fathers of handicapped children who had participated in a program for one to three years were compared with fathers who had just entered the program (Vadasy, Fewell, Meyer, & Greenberg, 1985). Fathers who had been in the program reported less depression, less fatigue, less pessimism over future concerns, less guilt, fewer total problems, more satisfaction and better decision-making ability than did newly enrolled fathers. Program fathers also reported greater satisfaction than new fathers with their level of religious involvement, neighborhood involvement, and people with whom they could share private feelings. Moreover, consistent with a family systems view, fathers' participation had second-order effects on their wives who experienced greater support in their role. Wives of men who had been enrolled in the program reported fewer feelings of failure, more positive feelings of attractiveness, less stress due to child's characteristics, and more satisfaction with the time they had to themselves than did wives of newly enrolled fathers. Although these findings are tentative and need comparisons with comparable, nontreated controls, they provide strong support for viewing intervention from a family perspective in which fathers as well as mothers are included.

CONCLUSIONS AND UNRESOLVED ISSUES

A variety of issues remain to be addressed in this area. First, the role of historical change needs to be given more attention in our studies of the transition to parenthood. Recent advances in medical technology over the past two decades have significantly altered our capability for the early detection of fetal abnormalities. Psychological evaluation of the impact of these diagnostic screening programs on families has not kept pace with the medical advances. Much more needs to be learned about the impact of early screening on maternal and family adaptation during pregnancy and ways to decrease the negative emotional side-effect of early detection as well as to increase ways of assisting families to more effectively cope by preparing for the birth of an at-risk infant.

Similarly, medical advances have altered our definition of the preterm infant. Increasingly small infants are surviving, who in earlier eras may have died shortly after birth. These new survivors, however, may have a variety of short-term and long-term developmental problems that may, in turn, place new and extraordinary demands on parents to care for these infants. The viability of these infants also raises a host of new ethical and legal questions that both parents and the medical community must face, particularly whether or not severely handicapped infants with uncertain futures should, in fact, be kept alive (see Palkovitz & Wolfe, 1987; Shelp, 1986, for discussion of these issues).

Finally we need to learn more about the determinants of parental attitudes concerning the responsibility of medical science for different birth outcome and the expectations of the infallibility of physicians. In light of the work by Affleck and his colleagues (Affleck, Allen, McGrade, & McQueeney, 1982) attribution of blame to medical experts for non-normal outcomes may, in fact, be undermining adaptation. Ways of modifying parental attributions through education in both the pre and postnatal period would be worthwhile, since reliance on external sources (remedical professionals) is not necessarily the most adaptive response.

Similar related legal and ethical issues concerning the termination of a fetus with a suspected or diagnosed problem are arising as a result of recent advances in early detection techniques.

Moreover, the ways in which families respond to the transition to parenthood have changed as well. A number of changes have taken place over the last two decades that have altered the ways in which mothers and fathers define their family roles. Shifts in sex role ideology, work patterns for men and women, and age of timing of parenthood, have combined to alter the climate in which men and women are immersed as they undergo the transition to parenthood. In turn, the reactions of men and women to the birth of a preterm infant may have changed over this time period. Would the increased paternal involvement in infant care have been seen in at least some fathers of preterm infants or in the case of infants of C-section deliveries in earlier cohorts of fathers? For example, in a more traditional era, characterized by more rigid gender roles for mothers and fathers, the transition to parenthood involving a preterm infant may not necessarily have led to increased paternal involvement. Female members of the family's social network such as relatives or friends may have been enlisted to assist the new mother during this transition. However, in light of decreased geographical proximity between families and extended kin in the current era, relatives are often less available, which, in turn, increases the likelihood of father involvement. In light of the fact that the use of social network agents outside the nuclear family is negatively correlated with the father's involvement in child care (Bloom-Feshbach, 1979), the current unavailability of kin may increase father participation. Thus, several societal trends converge to create a situation in which fathers are naturally encouraged to increase their participation in caregiving.

Another issue that merits more attention in future studies is the impact of adult development on the ways in which the transition to parenthood, especially in situations where problems arise, is handled. A life span perspective (Elder, 1974; Parke & Tinsley, 1984, 1987) suggests the importance of examining developmental changes in the adult since parents continue to change and develop during the adulthood years. Evidence is accumulating that the age of the adult at the time of the onset of parenthood can have important implications for how females and males manage their maternal and paternal roles (Daniels & Weingarten, 1982). In view of the fact that the probability of having an at-risk infant increases with parental age (Charrow, 1985), it is particularly important that the issue of the timing of parenthood be examined in families with at-risk infants. In light of the greater financial and career security of older couples, as well as the more stable self-definitions of older individuals, the late-timed couples may be better able to cope with the emotional and financial stresses associated with a preterm and handicapped infant, in comparison to younger couples. On the other hand, the reduced opportunity to have children among older couples due to maternal age may make the decision to abort a handicapped fetus problematic for these couples. It is clear that these issues need to be examined by exploring ways in which adults of differing ages handle tasks of adulthood, such as self-identify, education and career and, in turn, examine the relationship between the management of these tasks and the transition to parenthood in families of both non-risk and at-risk infants.

More attention needs to be given to describing the impact of infants who are at different degrees of risk for later developmental problems. Terms such as preterm infants and handicapped infants represent categories that are no longer sufficient since they mask a considerable degree of variability that exists among infants subsumed by these categories. Studies that organize their samples around the types of risk factors outlined earlier in this paper represent one step in this direction.

Finally, longitudinal studies of the transition to parenthood in families of non-risk and at-risk infants are necessary in order to adequately describe the similarities and differences in this transition process for different risk groups. By understanding this process better, we will be better able to provide effective support and intervention to help families cope with this important life transition.

REFERENCES

Affleck, G., Allen, D., McGrade, B.J. & McQueeney, M. (1982). Maternal causal attributions at hospital discharge of high risk infants. *American Journal of Mental Deficiency, 86*, 575-580.

Anderson, E. (1984). The father's role in the development of preterm infants. Unpublished honors thesis, University of Illinois.

Andrew, G. (1968). Determinants of Negro family decisions in management of retardation. *Journal of Marriage and the Family, 30*, 612-617.

Annas, G. J. & Sherman, E. (1985). Maternal serum AFP: Educating physicians and the public. *American Journal of Public Health, 75*, 1374-1375.

Belsky, J. (1981). Early human experience: A family perspective. *Developmental Psychology, 17*, 3-23.

Belsky, J. (1984). Determinants of parenting: A process model. *Child Development, 55*, 83-96.

Belsky, J., Gilstrap, B., & Rovine, M. (1984). The Pennsylvania Infant & Family Development Project, I: Stability & change in mother-infant and father-infant interaction in a family setting at one, three & nine months. *Child Development, 55*, 692-705.

Berger, J. & Cunningham, C. (1983). Development of early vocal behaviors & interactions in Down Syndrome and non-handicapped infant-mother pairs. *Developmental Psychology, 19*, 822-831.

Berne-Fromell, K. & Kjessler, B. (1984). Anxiety concerning fetal malformations in pregnant women exposed or not exposed to an antenatal serum alpha-fetoprotein screening program. *Gynecology & Obstetrics Investigations, 17*, 36.

Berne-Fromell, K., Uddenberg, N. & Kjessler, B. (1983). Psychological reactions experienced by pregnant women with an elevated serum alpha-fetoprotein level. *Journal of Psychosomatic Obstetrics & Gynecology, 2-4*, 233-237.

Berns, J.H. (1980). Grandparents of handicapped children. *Social Work, 25*, 238-239.

Birenbaum, A. (1970). On managing a courtesy stigma. *Journal of Health and Social Behavior, 11*, 196-206.

Blake, J. (1981). Family size and the quality of children. *Demography, 18*, 421.

Bloom-Feshbach, J. *The Beginnings of Fatherhood*. Unpublished Doctoral Dissertation, Yale, 1979.

Bristol, M. (1985, April). A series of studies of social support, stress & adaptation in families of developmentally disabled children. Paper presented at the biennial meeting of the Society for Research in Child Development. Toronto, Ontario Canada.

Bristol, M. & Gallagher, J. (1986). Variation in adaptation in families of young developmentally disabled and non-handicapped children: The role of current and expected spousal instrumental and expressive support. Unpublished manuscript. University of North Carolina.

Bronfenbrenner, U. (1979). *The ecology of human development*. Cambridge: Harvard University Press.

Brown, J.V. & Bakeman, R. (1980). Relationships of human mothers with their infants during the first year of life: Effects of prematurity. In R.W. Bell and W.P. Smotherman (Eds.), *Maternal influences and early behavior*. Holliswood, NY: Spectrum.

Brooks, V. & Hochberg, J. (1960). A psychological study of "cuteness." *Perceptual and Motor Skills, 11*, 205.

Burton, B.K., Dillard, R.G. & Clark, E.N. (1985a). The psychological impact of false positive elevations of maternal serum alpha-fetoprotein. *American Journal of Obstetrics and Gynecology, 151*, 77-82.

Burton, B.K., Dillard, R.G. & Clark, E.N. (1985b). Maternal serum alpha-fetoprotein screening: The effect of participation on anxiety and attitude toward pregnancy in women with normal results. *American Journal of Obstetrics and Gynecology, 152, 5*, 540-543.

Canning, C.D. & Pueschel, S.M. (1978). An overview of developmental expectations. In S.M. Pueschel (Ed.), *Down Syndrome children: Growing and learning*. New York: Andrews & McMeel.

Carver, N. & Carver, J. (1972). *The family of the retarded child*. Syracuse, NY: Syracuse University Press.

Chamberlain, J. (1978). Human benefits and costs of a national screening program for neural-tube defects. *Lancet, ii*, 1293-1297.

Charron, J. (1985). Genetic counseling and prenatal diagnosis. *The Child's Doctor, 5*, 11-19.

Cochran, M.M. & Brassard, J.A. (1979). Child development and personal social networks. *Child Development, 5*, 601-616.

Cowan, P.A. & Cowan, C.P. (1987). Becoming a family: Couple relationships during family formation. In P. Berman & F. Pederson (Eds.), *Transition to fatherhood*. New York: Academic Press.

Crnic, K.A., Greenberg, M.T., Rogozin, A.S., Robinson, N.M. & Basham, R.B. (1983). Effects of stress and social support on mothers and premature and full-term infants. *Child Development, 54*, 209-217.

Cummings, S.T. (1976). The impact of the child's deficiency on the father: A study of fathers of mentally retarded and of chronically ill children. *American Journal of Orthopsychiatry, 46*, 246-255.

Daniels, P. & Weingarten, K. (1982). *Sooner or later: The timing of parenthood in adult lives*. New York: W. W. Norton.

Dickie, J. & Matheson, P. (1984). Mother-father-infant: Who needs support? Paper presented at the Annual Meeting of the American Psychological Association, Toronto.

Drotar, D., Baskiewicz, B.A., Irvin, N., Kennell, J. & Klaus, M. The adaptation of parents to the birth of an infant with a congenital malformation: A hypothetical model. *Pediatrics, 56*, 710-717.

Elardo, R., Bradley, R. & Caldwell, B. (1975). The relations of infants' home environments to mental test performance from 6 to 36 months: A longitudinal analysis. *Child Development, 46*, 71-76.

Elder, G.H. (1974). *Children of the Great Depression*. Chicago: University of Chicago Press.

Entwisle, D. & Doering, (1981). *The first birth*. Baltimore, MD: Johns Hopkins University Press.

Farber, B. (1959). Effects of a severely retarded child on family integration. *Monographs of the Society for Research in Child Development, 24*, whole number 71.

Farber, B. (1960). Family organization and crisis: Maintenance of integration in families with a severely mentally retarded child. *Monographs of the Society for Research in Child Development, 25*, whole number 75.

Fearn, J., Hibbard, B.M., Laurance, K.M., Roberts, A. & Robinson, J.O. (1982). Screening for neural-tube defects and maternal anxiety. *British Journal of Obstetrics & Gynecology, 89*, 218-221.

Feiring, C., Fox, N., Jaskir, J.O., Lewis, M. (1987). The relationship between social support, infant risk status and mother-infant interaction. *Developmental Psychology, 23*.

Ferwell, R.R. & Vadasy, P.F. (1986). *Families of handicapped children: Needs and supports across the life span.* Austin, TX: Pro-Ed.

Field, T. (1987). Affective and interactive disturbances in infants. In J. Osofsky (Ed.), *The handbook of infant development*. 2nd ed. New York: Wiley.

Finegan, J.K., Quarrington, B.J., Hughes, H.E., Rudd, N.L., Stevens, L.J., Weksberg, R. & Doran, T.A. (1984). Midtrimester amniocentesis: Obstetric outcome and neonatal neurobehavioral status. *American Journal of Obstetrics and Gynecology, 150*, 989-999.

Frederich, W.N. (1979). Predictions of the coping behavior of mothers of handicapped children. *Journal of Consulting and Clinical Psychology, 47*, 1140-1141.

Frodi, A.M., Lamb, M.E., Leavitt, L.A., Donovan, W.L., Neff, C. & Sherry, D. (1978). Fathers' and mothers' responses to the faces and cries of normal and premature infants. *Developmental Psychology, 14*, 490-498.

Gabel, H. & Kotsch, L.S. (1981). Extended families and young handicapped children. *Topics in early childhood special education, 1*, 29-36.

Gallagher, J., Cross, A. & Scharfman, W. (1981). Parental adaptation to a young handicapped child: The father's role. *Journal of the Division for Early Childhood, 3*, 3-14.

Goldberg, S. (1979). Premature birth: Consequences for the parent-infant relationship. *American Scientist, 67*, 214-220.

Goldberg, S. & DeVitto, B. (1983). *Born too soon: Preterm birth and early development*. San Francisco: Freeman.

Grossman, F.K., Eichler, L.S. & Winickoff, S.A. (1980). *Pregnancy, birth and parenthood*. San Francisco: Jossey-Bass.

Gumz, E.J. & Gubrium, J.F. (1972). Comparative parental perceptions of a mentally retarded child. *American Journal of Mental Deficiency, 77*, 75-180.

Harper, R.G., Sia, C., Sokal, S. & Sokal, M. (1976). Observations on unrestricted parental contact with infants in the neonatal intensive care unit. *Journal of Pediatrics, 89*, 441-445.

Hersey, D.W., Crandall, B.F. & Schroth, P.S. (1985). Maternal serum alpha-fetoprotein screening of fetal trisomies. *American Journal of Obstetrics and Gynecology, 153*, 224-225.

Holt, K.S. (1957). The impact of mentally retarded children upon their families. Unpublished doctoral dissertation, University of Sheffield, England.

Hook, E.B., Cross, P.K. & Schreinemachers, D.M. (1983). Chromosomal abnormality rates at amniocentesis and in live-born infants. *Journal of American Medical Association, 249*, 2034-2038.

Illingworth, R.S. (1967). Counseling the parents of the mentally handicapped child. *Clinical Pediatrics, 6*, 340-348.

Jones, O.H.K. (1980). Prelinguistic communication skills in Down's syndrome and normal infants. In T. Field, S. Goldberg, D. Stern & A. Sostek (Eds.), *High-risk infants and children: Interactions with adults and peers*. New York: Academic Press.

Kaplan, D.M. & Mason, E.A. (1960). Maternal reaction to premature birth viewed as an acute emotional disorder. *American Journal of Orthopsychiatry, 30*, 539-552.

Klaus, M.H. & Fanaroff, A.A. (1979). *Care of the high-risk neonate* (2nd edition). Philadelphia, PA: Saunders.

Klaus, M.H. & Kennel, J.H. (1982). *Parent-infant bonding*. St. Louis, MO: Mosby.

Kennedy, J. (1973). The high risk maternal infant acquaintance process. *Nursing Clinics of North America, 8*, 549-556.

Lamb, M.E. (1984). Fathers of exceptional children. In M. Seligman (Ed.), *A comprehensive guide to understanding and treating the family with a handicapped child*. New York: Grune & Stratton.

Lamb, M.E. & Elster, A.B. (1985). Adolescent mother-infant-father relationships. *Developmental Psychology, 21*.

Legeay, C., & Keogh, B. (1966). Impact of mental retardation on family life. *American Journal of Nursing, 66*, 1062-1065.

Leiderman, P.H. (1981). Human mother-infant social bonding: Is there a sensitive phase? In K. Immelman, G.W. Barlow, L. Petrinovich, and M. Main (Eds.), *Behavioral development*. New York: Cambridge.

Leiderman, P.H. (1982). Social ecology and childbirth: The newborn nursery as environmental stressor. In N. Garmezy and M. Rutter (Eds.), *Stress, coping, and adaptation*. New York: McGraw-Hill.

Leiderman, P.H. & Seashore, M.J. (1975). Mother-infant separation: Some delayed consequences. *Parent-infant interaction*. CIBA Foundation Symposium 33. Amsterdam: Elsevier.

Lewis, M. & Feiring, C. (1981). Direct and indirect interactions in social relationships. In L. Lipsitt (Ed.), *Advances in infancy research*, (Vol. 1). New York: Ablex Publishing Corporation.

Lonsdale, G. (1978). Family life with a handicapped child: The parents speak. *Child: Care, Health, and Development, 4*, 99-120.

MacDonald, K. & Parke, R.D. (1984). Bridging the gap: Parent-Child play interaction and peer interactive competence. *Child Development, 55*, 1265-1277.

Marion, R.L. (1981). *Education, parents, and exceptional children*. Rockville, MD: Aspen Systems Corporations.

Marton, P., Minde, K. & Perrotta, M. (1981). The role of the father for the infant at risk. *American Journal of Orthopsychiatry, 51*, 672-679.

McCluskey, K.A., Killarney, J., & Papini, D.R. (1983). Adolescent pregnancy and parenthood: Implications for development. In E.C. Callahan & K.A. McCluskey (Eds.), *Life-span developmental psychology: Non-normative life events*. New York: Academic Press.

McDowell, J. & Gabel, H. (1981). Social support among mothers of retarded infants. Unpublished manuscript, George Peabody College, Nashville.

Meyer, D.J. (1986). Fathers of children with mental handicaps. in M.E. Lamb (Ed.), *The father's role: Applied perspectives*. New York: Wiley, pp. 227-254.

Meyer, D.J., Vadasy, P.F., Fewell, R.R. & Schell, G. (1982). Involving fathers of handicapped infants: Translating research into program goals. *Journal of the Division for Early Childhood, 5*, 64-72.

Milunsky, A., Alpert, D.C.H., Neff, R.K. & Frigoletto, F.D. (1980). Prenatal diagnosis of neural tube defects. IV Maternal serum alpha-fetoprotein screening. *Obstetrics & Gynecology, 55*, 60-66.

Neugarten, B. (1979). Time, age and the life cycle. *American Journal of Psychiatry, 136*, 887-894.

Palkovitz, R. & Wolfe, C.B. (1987). Rights of children born with disabilities: Issues, inconsistencies & recommendations. *Marriage & Family Review, 11*(1/2), 83-103.

Parke, R.D. (1978). Parent-infant interaction: Progress, paradigms, and problems, In G.P. Sackett (ed.), *Observing behavior: Theory and applications in mental retardation*. Baltimore: University Park Press.

Parke, R.D. (1979). Perspectives on father-infant interaction. In J. Osofsky (Ed.), *The handbook of infant development*. New York: Wiley, 549-590.

Parke, R.D. (1981). *Fathers*. Cambridge, MA: Harvard University Press.

Parke, R.D. (1984). The development of preterm infants: the role of the family. Progress report to NICHD, Washington, DC.

Parke, R.D. & Anderson, E. (1987). Fathers and at-risk infants: Empirical and conceptual analyses. In P. Berman & F. Pedersen (Eds.), *Men's transition to parenthood: Longitudinal studies of early family experience*. Hillsdale, NJ: Erlbaum.

Parke, R.D. & Beitel, A. (1986). Hospital-based intervention for fathers. In M.E. Lamb (Ed.) *The father's role: Applied perspectives*. New York: Wiley.

Parke, R.D., MacDonald, K., Beitel, A. & Bhavnagri, N. (1987). The interrelationships among families, fathers and peers. In R. Peters (Ed.), *New approaches to family research*. New York: Brunner/Mazel.

Parke, R.D., Power, T.G. & Gottman, J.M. (1979). Conceptualizing and quantifying influence patterns in the family triad. In M.E. Lamb, S.T. Soumi & G.R. Stephenson (Eds.), *Social interaction analyses: Methodological issues*. Madison, WI: The University of Wisconsin Press.

Parke, R.D. & Swain, D.B. (1976). The father's role in infancy: A re-evaluation. *The Family Coordinator, 25*, 365-371.

Parke, R.D. & Swain, D.B. (1980). The family in early infancy: Social interaction and attitudinal analyses. In F.A. Pedersen (Ed.), *The father-infant relationship*. New York: Praeger.

Parke, R.D. & Tinsley, B.R. (1981). The father's role in infancy: Determinants of involvement in caregiving & play. In M.E. Lamb (Ed.), *The role of the father in child development*. (2nd ed.) New York: Wiley.

Parke, R.D. & Tinsley, B.R. (1982). The early environment of the at-risk infant: Expanding the social context. In D. Bricker (Ed.), *Intervention with at-risk and handicapped infants: From research to application*. Baltimore, MD: University Park Press.

Parke, R.D. & Tinsley, B.R. (1984). Historical & contemporary perspectives on fathering. In K.A. McCluskey & H.W. Reese (Eds.), *Life-span development psychology: Historical & generational effects in life-span human development*. New York: Academic Press, 203-248.

Parke, R.D. & Tinsley, B.J. (1987). Family interaction in infancy. In J. Osofsky (Ed.), *The handbook of infant development*. 2nd ed. New York: Wiley.

Pascoe, J.M. & Earp, J.A. (1984). The effect of mothers' social support and life changes on the stimulation of their children in the home. *American Journal of Public Health, 74*, 358-360.

Pascoe, J.M., Loda, F.A., Jeffries, V. & Earp, J.A. (1981). The association between mothers' social support and provision of stimulation to their children. *Developmental and Behavioral Pediatrics, 2*, 15-19.

Pederson, D.R., Jenkins, S., Evans, B., Change, G.W. & Fox, A.M. (April, 1985). Maternal responses to the birth of a preterm infant. Paper presented at the biennial meetings of the Society for Research in Child Development, Toronto.

Phillip, C. (1983). The role of recollected anxiety in parental adaptation to low birth weight infants. *Child Psychiatry and Human Development, 13*, 239-248.

Roghmann, K.J. & Doherty, R.A. (1983). Reassurance through prenatal diagnosis and willingness to bear children after age 35. *American Journal of Public Health, 73*, 760-762.

Russell, G. (1983). *The changing role of fathers?* St. Lucia, Queensland: University of Queensland Press.

Rutter, M. (1983). Stress, coping and development: Some issues and some questions. In N. Garmezy & M. Rutter (Eds.) *Stress, coping & development in children*. New York: McGraw-Hill.

Shelp, E.E. (1986). *Born to die?* New York: Free Press.

Shereshefsky, P.M. & Yarrow, L.J. (1973). *Psychological aspects of a first pregnancy and early postnatal adaptation*. New York: Raven.

Slade, C.I., Redl, O.J. & Manguten, H.H. (1977). Working with parents of high-risk newborns. *Journal of Obstetric and Gynecologic Nursing, 6*, 21-26.

Solnit, A.J. & Stark, M.H. (1961). Mourning and the birth of a defective child. *Psychoanalytic Study of the Child, 16*, 523-537.

Stern, M. & Heldebrandt, K.A. (1984). Prematurity stereotype: Effects of labelling on adults' perceptions of infants. *Developmental Psychology, 20*, 360-362.

Stoneman, Z., Brody, G.H. & Abbott, D. (1983). In-home observations of young Down Syndrome children with their mothers and fathers. *American Journal of Mental Deficiency, 87*, 591-600.

Tallman, I. (1965). Spousal role differentiation and the socialization of severely retarded children. *Journal of Marriage and the Family, 27*, 37-42.

Tennen, H., Affleck, G. & Mershman, K. (1986). Self-blame among parents of infants with perinatal complications: the role of self-protective motives. *Journal of Personality and Social Psychology, 50*, 690-696.

Tew, B.J., Lawrence, K.M., Payne, J. & Rawnsley, K. (1977). Marital stability following the birth of a child with spina bifida. *British Journal of Psychiatry, 131*, 79-82.

Trause, M.A. & Kramer, L.L. (1983). The effect of premature birth on parents and their relationship. *Developmental Medicine & Child Neurology, 24*, 459-465.

Vadasy, P.F., Fewell, R.R., Meyer, D.J. & Greenberg, M.T. (1985). Supporting fathers of handicapped young children: Preliminary findings of program effects. *Analysis & Intervention in Developmental Disabilities, 5*, 151-163.

Vadasy, P.F., Fewell, R.R., Meyer, D.J., Schell, G. & Greenberg, M.T. (1984). Involved parents: characteristics and resources of fathers and mothers of young handicapped children. *Journal of the Division of Early Childhood, 8*, 13-25.

Vietze, P.M., Abernathy, S.R., Ashe, M.L. & Faulstich, G. (1978). Contingent interaction between mothers and their developmentally delayed infants. In G.P. Sackett (Ed.), *Observing behavior: Theory and applications in mental retardation*. Baltimore, MD: University Park Press.

Vietze, P.M., MacTurk, R.H., McCarthy, M.E., Klein, R.P., & Yarrow, L.J. (1980, April). Impact of mode on delivery on father- and mother-infant interaction at 6 & 12 months. Paper presented at the International Conference on Infant Studies, New Haven, CT.

Wasserman, G., Soloman-Scwerzer, C.R., Spicker, S. & Stern, D. (March, 1980). Maternal interactive style with normal and at-risk toddlers. Paper presented at the International Conference on Infant Studies, New Haven.

Walker, J.A. (1982). Social interactions of handicapped infants. In D. Bricker (Ed.), *Intervention with at-risk and handicapped infants*. Baltimore, MD: University Park Press.

Wilker, L. (1981). Chronic stresses of families of mentally retarded children. *Family Relations, 30*, 281-288.

Whitt, J.K. & Casey, P.H. (1982). The mother-infant relationship and infant development: The effect of pediatric intervention. *Child Development, 53*, 948-956.

Yogman, M.W. (1985). The father's role with preterm and fullterm infants. In J. Call, E. Galenson & R. Tyson (Eds.), *Frontiers in infant psychiatry*. NY: Basic Books.

Transition to
Adoptive Parenthood

David M. Brodzinsky
Loreen Huffman

SUMMARY. The present paper presents a conceptual and empirical overview of the transition to adoptive parenthood. It is argued that prospective adoptive couples confront not only the universal problems faced by other adults in the transition to parenthood, but a host of challenges and hurdles that are unique to adoptive family life. It is also noted, however, that contrary to expectations, adoptive parents and their children appear to handle these additional stresses quite well, at least in the early period of the family life-cycle. Speculations are offered on the relationship between early and later patterns of adjustment within the adoptive family, as well as an overview of some of the methodological problems confronting researchers who undertake to study this area of family life.

Becoming a parent is a goal that most young adults expect to achieve. It is a goal, that for most of us, first emerged as a germ of an idea in fantasy-based play during the preschool years. From this early, unpretentious beginning, our thoughts, feelings, fantasies, and plans about marriage, parenthood, and family life are shaped by myriad social and cultural forces. Yet for all the variability in socialization to which we are exposed, relatively few individuals enter adulthood doubting their ability to be parents—at least in a biological sense. We come to expect that at a time chosen by us, we will be able to conceive and bear children, and thus become parents, like

David M. Brodzinsky, PhD, is Associate Professor of Clinical and Developmental Psychology and Loreen Huffman is a graduate student in developmental psychology, Department of Psychology, Tillett Hall, Rutgers University, New Brunswick, NJ 08903.

the majority of our peers. However, for some 10-15% of adults, this is not to be. One or both partners have a fertility problem that prevents normal conception (Rathus, 1983). In response to this medical and personal crisis, a number of options become available for the couple, including surgery (when appropriate), drug treatment, artificial insemination by donor, in vitro fertilization, surrogate childbearing, and adoption.

Much has been written about adoptive family life from social casework, clinical, and research perspectives. A great deal of this work has focused on the increased vulnerability of the adopted child to psychological and academic problems (Bohman, 1970; Bohman & Sigvardsson, 1982; Brodzinsky, in press a, in press b; Brodzinsky, Radice, Huffman, & Merkler, 1986; Brodzinsky, Schechter, Braff, & Singer, 1984; Brodzinsky, Schechter, & Brodzinsky, 1986; Deutsch, Swanson, Bruell, Cantwell, Weinberg, & Baren, 1982; Feigelman & Silverman, 1983; Hoopes, 1982; Nickman, 1985; Schechter, 1960; Singer, Brodzinsky, Ramsay, Steir, & Waters, 1985; Stein & Hoopes, 1985). Other researchers and theorists have dealt with the adjustment of adoptive parents and the unique personal and interpersonal issues that impact upon adoptive family members (Blum, 1983; Brinich, 1980; Brodzinsky, in press; Hoopes, 1982; Kirk, 1964; Sorosky, Baran, & Pannor, 1979; Schechter, 1970). Yet despite the rather large literature on adoption, we actually know very little about the experiences of adults in the course of their transition to adoptive family life. We also lack understanding of the short-term and long-term impact of this transitional process on parent, child, and family adjustment. In keeping with the theme of this special volume, the present paper will examine some of the issues involved in the transition to adoptive parenthood. Unlike the other authors, however, our analyses and speculations do not rest upon a well validated base of empirical data, for such data are meager in this substantive area. Our goal, therefore, is primarily to present a conceptual overview of the issues involved in the transition to adoptive parenthood and to speculate on the linkage between this adult life transition and the eventual adjustment of adoptive family members. It is our hope that such an analysis will stimulate much needed research in this area of parenthood and family life.

TRENDS IN ADOPTION

Each year tens of thousands of children are adopted. Most are the product of out-of-wedlock pregnancies. However, an increasing number are the result of court intervention terminating the rights of biological parents because of abuse or neglect. Other children became available for adoption because of abandonment, parental death, and voluntary relinquishment. Finally, an increasing number of foreign-born children are being adopted (Feigelman & Silverman, 1983).

Accurate figures on the current incidence and prevalence of adoption in the United States are lacking because the federal government no longer compiles such statistics. However, a recent national health survey suggests that there are approximately 1.3 million children under 18 years of age (or 2% of the population of children) who have been adopted by adults unrelated to them (Zill, 1985).

One of the more important trends in adoption is the decline in healthy infants available for adoption, especially white infants. This decline is directly related to the increased availability of abortion and contraception, and to the greater acceptance by society of young women rearing their out-of-wedlock babies. At the same time, the demand for adoptable children continues unabated and has resulted in a greater willingness to adopt "special needs" children— that is, older children, minority children, sibling groups, physically handicapped children, medically ill children, emotionally disturbed children, etc. Thus, the transition to adoptive parenthood potentially entails a wide range of complicating factors— in fact, a much wider range than we can hope to cover in this paper. To simplify our task, we will focus on a single type of adoption: infant and early child placements, the traditional, and typically most preferred form of adoption.

ADOPTIVE PARENTHOOD: NORMATIVE TRANSITIONAL ISSUES

Ever since the work of Hill (1949), family sociologists and psychologists have been interested in the impact of parenthood on the married couple. The early research and theoretical writings emphasized that becoming a parent was a "crisis" for the couple, albeit a "normative life crisis." More recently, the emphasis has shifted away from crisis models of parenthood toward a view of parenthood as a normal transition in the family life-cycle process (Belsky, 1984; Cox, 1985; Rossi, 1968; Russell, 1974).

As the literature on transition to parenthood has grown, so too has our appreciation for the impact of this life-cycle transition on the couple. Among the more important stress-related outcomes associated with becoming a parent are increased fatigue, decreased social relations, increased conflict between work and family roles (particularly for women, but increasingly for men, as well), increased financial strain on the family, decreased sexual relations between the couple, and a heightened sense of responsibility for another person (which at times is experienced as a burden). It is these types of stressors, among others, that have been suggested to underlie the decline in marital satisfaction that emerges with the transition to parenthood (Belsky, Spanier & Rovine, 1983; Glenn & McLanahan, 1982; Miller & Sollie, 1980). In turn, a decline in marital satisfaction, as well as incongruence between prebirth parental expectations and postbirth experiences, may lay the groundwork for increased problems in family relationships (Belsky, Ward & Rovine, 1986; Isabella & Belsky, 1985; Oates & Heinicke, 1985; Palkovitz, 1985).

Adoptive parents, like their nonadoptive counterparts, must adapt to the increased personal and interpersonal strains that accompany parenthood. Unlike nonadoptive parents, however, adoptive parents experience a number of challenges and hurdles that complicate this already stressful life transition. These complexities, and the way they are confronted and resolved, are thought to play an important role in the increased vulnerability of the adopted child to psychological problems.

Adopting Infants and Young Children

Traditionally, the most common and certainly most preferred type of adoption involved the placement of an infant, often only a few weeks to a few months of age, in the home of an infertile couple. Such placements were thought to mirror the natural or biological family as closely as possible. In fact, parents were often encouraged to forget their adoptive status once the placement was made. In this social climate, few professionals paid much attention to the inherent differences of adoptive and nonadoptive family life. This began to change, however, with a landmark publication by H. David Kirk (1964). Kirk, and more recently, Brodzinsky (in press a), have argued that the transition to adoptive parenthood, and adoptive family life, in general, is characterized by a number of complications that may interfere with the development of a warm, relaxed, growth-producing family environment. Kirk, in particular, has suggested that adoptive parents are burdened by a number of "role handicaps" that make the transition to parenthood potentially more problematic.

Consider first the issue of infertility. As noted previously, because most couples simply presume the capacity for reproduction, the realization that one, or both, partners have a fertility problem is experienced most often as a medical and personal emergency. Researchers have long known that infertility poses increased risk for a host of psychological problems for the individual and married couple (Kraft, Palumbo, Mitchell, Dean, Meyers, & Schmidt, 1980; Shapiro, 1982). A devaluated self-image, distortions in body concept, anxiety, depression, disruptions in marital communication, a decline in marital sexual relations, and increased feelings of resentment toward one's spouse are just some of the more common problems associated with this condition. When these problems are not resolved adequately — that is, when adoptive parents are unable to work through their narcissistic injuries and mourn the loss of their fantasized biological child — the likelihood of fostering intrafamilial trust, security, and unity is thought to be decreased (Blum, 1983; Brinich, 1980; Brodzinsky, in press a; Kirk, 1964; Schechter, 1970).

A second complication in the transition to adoptive parenthood is the uncertainty in the timing of the process. Unlike pregnancy, which lasts nine months, the adoption process is highly variable. In private, or independent, adoptions it may be as short as a few months; in agency-based adoptions, particularly in cases where the couple wishes only to adopt a healthy, white baby, it may be as long as six or seven years. The lack of a clear time table may well inhibit the couple from effectively planning for the arrival of the child. Furthermore, the absence of the usual cues associated with pregnancy (e.g., changes in the woman's body shape, clothes styles, etc.) make it more difficult for others to begin altering their perceptions and expectations of the couple as "soon-to-be parents."

In addition to the uncertainty of the waiting period, most adoptive parents must also undergo an indepth evaluation process — that is, they must prove their worthiness to be parents to social service caseworkers. This process is often experienced as intrusive, demeaning, and anxiety arousing for prospective parents.

Adoption also is associated with social stigma in our society (Kirk, 1964). It is viewed as a "second best route to parenthood." As a result, adoptive parents are less likely to receive wholehearted support from significant others when they announce their intention to adopt a child. This is particularly true when the couple adopt across racial/ethnic lines (Singer, Brodzinsky, Ramsay, Steir, & Waters, 1985). Thus, unlike nonadoptive parents, whose parental status is likely to be warmly welcomed by others, adoptive parents frequently must justify why they have made their particular decision — a process that not only is likely to facilitate parental anxiety and resentment, but that accentuates for them their "differentness."

A further complication for many adoptive parents is the lack of readily available role models. Because only a small percentage of the adult population choose adoption as a means of achieving parenthood, there area, relatively speaking, few individuals to whom the adoptive couple can turn in time of need for information, advice, and support regarding adoption-related issues. In the absence of appropriate role models, individuals are more likely to have a difficult time developing realistic expectations concerning the transition to adoptive parenthood. In turn, unrealistic and/or disconfirmed expectations can make the transition even more stressful than it need be (Belsky et al., 1986; Palkovitz, 1985, 1987).

The timing of the adoption placement can also complicate the transition to adoptive parenthood, particularly as it relates to the development of attachment bonds between parents and children. Bowlby (1973, 1980), among others, has argued that children who experience disruptive early caregiving are likely to display acute distress reactions, which under appropriate conditions can lead to more insidious forms of maladjustment (e.g., personality disorders). This pattern is more likely to occur when children experience multiple separations and losses in the first year or so — as in the case of successive foster placements — and consequently, are unable to form a secure and trusting relationship with any caregiver. Acute distress is also expected to occur in situations where the child has formed a secure attachment to a caregiver, only to have the relationship severed because of subsequent removal from the home. Least vulnerable, according to Bowlby, is the child who is removed from the home very early in his/her life (e.g., before 4-6 months) and placed in a warm, loving, and consistent substitute caregiving environment. Under these conditions, separation distress is expected to be minimal, and subsequent attachment relationships with the new caregivers should develop accordingly. Support for this position, with respect to adoptive family relationships, has been found by two separate groups of researchers. In a recent study, Singer et al., (1985) reported that when children are placed for adoption within the first few months of life, they develop secure attachments with their mother in much the same way as do nonadopted infants. Similarly, Yarrow and his associates (Yarrow, 1965; Yarrow & Goodwin, 1973; Yarrow, Goodwin, Manheimer, & Milowe, 1973) noted that socioemotional difficulties following separation of adopted infants from their biological and/or foster mothers primarily occurred in cases where the separation took place after 6-7 months of age.

One final factor that may affect the transition to adoptive parenthood is the increased biological risk associated with adoption. A growing body of research suggests that adopted children are more likely than nonadopted children to be born to adults who manifest various psychopathological conditions thought to have some genetic component (Bohman, 1978; Loehlin, Willerman, & Horn, 1982). Furthermore, adopted children more often experience prenatal and birth complications than their nonadopted counterparts (Bohman, 1970; Losbough, 1965; Hoopes, 1982). Both types of biological vulnerabilities could produce more difficult temperament patterns and early developmental delays in young adopted children, which in turn, could adversely affect the early parent-child relationships and the couple's attributions concerning parenthood.

In summary, we have argued that in adopting infants and young children, adoptive parents confront a number of challenges and hurdles that interact with and complicate the more universal problems faced by other adults who become parents biologically. Given the reality of this situation, one must question how the adoption experience impacts on the couple and/or young child. Do the complications involved in the transition to adoptive parenthood adversely affect adoptive family members? On the one hand, one might expect that adoptive parents, because of the increased stress associated with the transitional process, would display greater dissatisfaction with their family life, or at the very least, greater marital dissatisfaction. One might also expect more adverse consequences for the child's adjustment and the parent-child relationship.

Research on Early Adoptive Family Life and Children's Adjustment

Examination of the few studies available in the area of early adoptive family life and children's adjustment fails to support the position that the transition to parenthood has more negative short-term consequences for adoptive couples compared with nonadoptive couples. In fact, the trend appears to be in the opposite direction, at least in relationship to marital satisfaction and caregiving quality. For example, Humphrey (1975) found that adopting couples scored higher on measures of affection given and received (to one another) than a matched sample of nonadoptive couples, most of whom were at the preschool phase of their family life-cycle. In a nine year follow-up study, intergroup comparisons in marital adjustment still favored the adoptive parents (Humphrey & Kirkwood, 1982).

A more comprehensive analysis of early adoptive family life and parental and child adjustment was reported recently by Hoopes (1982). This study was part of a comparative longitudinal investigation of adoptive and nonadoptive family functioning. Multiple assessments of the quality of family life and family members' adjustment were taken from the infancy period through the early elementary school years. Results generally suggested that adoptive parents were rated more positively than their nonadoptive counterparts. For example, during infancy and the preschool years there was less marital conflict among adoptive couples compared with nonadoptive couples. By the elementary school years, however, no differences in marital adjustment were noted between the groups. In addition, adoptive parents, especially mothers, reported being more protective and careful with their children than nonadoptive parents. They also were rated higher in areas such as parent-child relatedness, acceptance of child, praising of child, affection and warmth, and handling the child. Interestingly, they also were found to foster more dependency in their children and to be rated lower on equalitarianism (i.e, allowing for individual points of view) and higher on anxiety regarding parenthood. By contrast, biological parents, especially fathers, were found to be somewhat less gentle with their children. That is, they more often suppressed affection and used harsh discipline; they also forced independence and attempted to accelerate development. Biological mothers, in turn, compared with their adoptive peers, acknowledged greater feelings of irritability with their children and greater feelings of martyrdom (i.e., self-sacrifice). During the elementary school years, these general patterns were still evident. As a group, adoptive parents were less intrusive, less controlling, and less authoritarian than nonadoptive parents. In summarizing the attitudes of adoptive parents regarding their children, Hoopes stated that the adopted children were "likely to be especially cherished and protected because they were not easily acquired and their advent into the family certainly was not taken for granted" (p. 98).

In another recent study, Plomin and DeFries (1985) also failed to find evidence suggesting that the short-term impact of the transition to adoptive parenthood has adverse consequences on family life. Using objective measures such as the Home Observation for Measurement of the Environment (Caldwell & Bradley, 1978) and the Family Environment Scale (Moos, 1981), among others, these researchers observed few, if any, meaningful differences between adoptive and nonadoptive families at 12 and 24 months of age in the quality of home environment and in the interpersonal relationships among family members.

Failure to support the expectations concerning the short-term adverse consequences of the stresses associated with the transition to adoptive parenthood also can be found in the patterns emerging with respect to the psychological adjustment of adoptees in the early years of life. In reviewing the literature on adoption adjustment, Brodzinsky (in press a) noted that although adoptees appear to be at risk for a variety of psychological and academic problems, on the average, they do not begin to manifest these difficulties until the school age years. For example, no differences have been noted between adoptees and nonadoptees in infancy and the early preschool years in areas such as developmental quotient, communicative behavior, temperament, and attachment (Carey, Lipton, & Myers, 1974; Greenbaum, Auerbach, & Frankel, 1983; Plomin & DeFries, 1985; Singer et al., 1985). Although Plomin and DeFries (1985) did find some minor differences between adopted and nonadopted infants in areas of adjustment, the vast majority of comparisons between these groups failed to yield significant results. Moreover, for those few differences that did emerge, it is important to note that adoptees generally displayed more favorable adjustment.

To summarize, although adoptive parents would appear to experience increased stress in the transition to parenthood compared with nonadoptive parents, there is no evidence to suggest that this stress impacts adversely on family interaction and parent's and children's adjustment, at least in the first few years of the family life-cycle. To explain this discrepancy, one must look to other factors that buffer or protect adoptive parents from the stresses associated with this transitional process.

PROTECTIVE FACTORS IN THE
TRANSITION TO ADOPTIVE PARENTHOOD

One factor that may buffer the impact of the stresses associated with the transition to parenthood for the adoptive couple is their age (Kadushin, 1980). Adoptive parents, on the average, are six to seven years older than nonadoptive parents when their first child arrives. Being older, they are likely to have developed a greater number and more effective array of coping skills to handle the various stresses associated with family life, in general, and parenthood, in particular. Furthermore, they also are more likely to be settled in their career tracks and to have greater financial security.

Not only are adoptive couples older when they achieve parenthood, but they also generally have been married longer. Being together for an extended period of time prior to the arrival of their first child, may foster greater sensitivity, empathy, and communication between spouses, which in turn, may explain the more positive marital adjustment found among adoptive couples in the research literature.

Adoptive couples also achieve parenthood after an extended period of deprivation. They have experienced the pain and stigma of infertility and the many months, and even years, of uncertainty associated with infertility treatment and/or the adoption process. Having waited so very long and having felt so deprived of the most basic of human roles — parenthood — the adoptive couple is likely to feel an overwhelming sense of fulfillment with the arrival of their child. In turn, this sense of fulfillment is likely to overshadow not only the unique stresses associated with adoptive parenthood, but the more universal stresses of parenthood as well.

One final factor that is likely to protect the adoptive couple from the stresses and strains involved in the transition to parenthood is the development of specific adoption-related coping patterns. David Kirk (1964) has identified two primary ways in which adoptive parents handle the inherent differences of adoptive family life. By differences, Kirk means the unique challenges, hurdles, and life-cycle tasks that interact with and complicate the more universal tasks of family life (cf. Brodzinsky, in press a). According to Kirk, some parents attempt to cope with the role handicaps associated with adoption by simulating nonadoptive family life as closely as possible. Thus, they rigorously deny or reject the inherent differences of being adopted or of being an adoptive parent. In fact, they tend to encourage their children to forget about being adopted, and all that goes with it — as they themselves try to do. Kirk has referred to this coping pattern as *rejection-of-difference* (RO). By contrast, other parents more openly confront the differences associated with adoptive parenthood. They attempt to resolve their internal conflicts and role handicaps by more active confrontation. Thus, they allow themselves and their children the freedom and opportunity to ex-

plore the ambivalent feelings associated with being different. Kirk
has referred to this pattern as *acknowledgment-of-difference* (AO).

Rejection-of-difference and acknowledgment-of-difference, according to Kirk, do not represent disjunctive attitudes and/or styles
of responding, but rather endpoints on a continuum of adoption-
related beliefs and behavior (see Brodzinsky, in press a and Brodzinsky & Reeves, 1986 for a more detailed consideration of this
continuum). The RO end of the continuum, Kirk suggests, is less
beneficial for the family's adjustment because it tends to inhibit the
development of an accepting and trusting family atmosphere—one
that is conducive to open the honest dialogue between parents and
children regarding adoption. Brodzinsky (in press a) also has suggested that in such an environment, children will be less able to
effectively cope with their grief associated with adoption-related
losses (cf. Nickman, 1985), as well as with their feelings of being
different and out-of-place. By contrast, an AO strategy, according
to Kirk, is thought to create a more likely context for positive psychological growth and development. Within this type of family environment, one might expect parents to be more empathic regarding
their children's ambivalent feelings associated with adoption. One
might also expect such parents to more often encourage their children to explore the meaning of adoption in their lives.

But must a RO coping strategy necessarily lead to more adverse
patterns of adjustment? Is it not possible that denying or rejecting
the differences associated with adoption could have some beneficial
effects for the family, at least during certain phases of the family
life-cycle? For example, if the RO coping strategy is more common
in the early phases of the family life-cycle (which recent pilot data
collected by us suggests), it could explain the relative ease with
which the adoptive couple makes the transition to parenthood. In
other words, adoptive parents who adhere to a RO coping strategy
may be less affected by the complications associated with the transition to adoptive parenthood, primarily because these complications
are less likely to be acknowledged in the first place. To the extent
that they are not acknowledged, they are less likely to be experienced as stressful. Thus, as the couple adjusts to their new roles as
adoptive parents, a RO coping strategy may serve to offset the uncertainty and anxiety that ordinarily would be expected in response

to the many challenges and hurdles that inevitably accompanies this transitional process.

Still, one must question whether the RO approach is really adaptive. Although initially it may serve the couple as a means of handling the stress associated with adoptive parenthood, in the long run it may actually hinder family members' adjustment. We would speculate that unless adoptive parents are able to gradually shift toward the "acknowledgment" end of the coping continuum, as the family moves through its life cycle, they will very likely create a caregiving environment that places the entire family at risk for adjustment problems. For example, if parents rigidly maintain a RO attitude, we would expect them to have more difficulty and be more anxious when they begin to disclose adoption information to their children—which usually occurs in the preschool years. Similarly, as children begin to understand the meaning and implications of being adopted—usually in the elementary school years (Brodzinsky, in press a; Brodzinsky et al., 1984; Brodzinsky et al., 1986)—we would expect them to have more difficulty resolving their confusion and ambivalence about being adopted if they live in a family environment characterized by a "rejection-of-difference" attitude. Thus, although we concur with Kirk's general position regarding the relationship between AO and positive psychological adjustment, we also suggest that this coping strategy is more likely to emerge as the family moves through its life cycle and confronts increasingly more complex adoption-related tasks (Brodzinsky, in press a). By contrast, a RO attitude is likely to be more prevalent in the early phase of the family life-cycle, when the tasks of building basic family unity and security are most salient.

CONCLUSIONS AND RECOMMENDATIONS FOR FUTURE RESEARCH

In this paper, we have argued that adoptive couples experience a number of challenges and hurdles that interact with and complicate the more universal tasks usually associated with this role transition. We also have noted, however, that these additional stresses apparently do not impact adversely on adoptive parents and their children in the early phase of the family life-cycle, except possibly in rather subtle ways (e.g., fostering of dependency and overprotection of children, and increased anxiety regarding parenthood). These seemingly incongruent patterns raise a number of questions regarding the short-term and long-term impact of the transition to adoptive parenthood on the couple, their children, and the family system, as a whole. For example, given the relatively positive atmosphere characterizing the adoptive family in the early phase of its life-cycle, how are we to explain the increased problems manifested by adopted children as they enter the school age years (cf., Brodzinsky, in press a, in press b)? One possibility is that the problems of adopted children simply are unrelated to the type of caregiving environment in which they are raised. This explanation, however, generally is contradicted by the bulk of the research on adoption (Feigelman & Silverman, 1983; Kadushin, 1980; Mech, 1973). A second possibility is that the quality of the caregiving environment may change as the family moves through its life-cycle. To the extent that adoptive parents and their children become more anxious and/or ambivalent with the passage of time regarding adoption-related issues, they could eventually create an environmental context conducive to the type of adjustment problems generally associated with adoption. A third possibility is that the early, protective, caregiving environment of adoptive families, while conducive to resolving certain basic life-cycle tasks (e.g., promoting attachment and family unity), may become maladaptive as children get older. Thus, adults who are anxious regarding their parental status and who foster dependency and are overprotective of their children (cf., Hoopes, 1982), might be expected to adhere to a RO coping strategy regarding adoption-related issues. To the extent that this strategy is maintained in a rigid way as the children enter the preschool and school age years, one might also expect these individuals to have a more difficult time disclosing adoption information to their children, as well as helping their children cope with ambivalent feelings associated with being adopted. In turn, these difficulties could very well lead to adjustment problems among adopted children. In this context, it is interesting to note that Hoopes (1982) reported that although adoptive parents were quite well adjusted (although somewhat defensive) in the early years of the family life-cycle, by the time their children were 5 years old, they (the children) were already beginning to manifest increased problems compared with their nonadopted peers (e.g., greater fearfulness, less confidence in their ability, less attention to tasks). In the elementary school years, the adjustment problems among adoptees were even more evident, both in self-reports and teacher ratings (but not in parent ratings).

Another important question centers on the factors that buffer or protect adoptive parents and their children from the stresses associated with adoptive family life. Although a number of possible protective factors were suggested in this paper, it is important to note that our ideas are purely speculative at this time. To date, there has been no empirical research on the role of mediating factors in family members' adjustment to adoption. In fact, research on the transition to adoptive parenthood is, itself, only just beginning. Thus, the most immediate goal for researchers is to collect baseline comparative data on the relative impact of parenthood on the adoptive and nonadoptive couple (and their children). We need to determine whether the trends in adjustment reported by Humphrey (1975), Hoopes (1982), and Plomin and DeFries (1985), among others, are in fact replicable and valid. If they are, we need to isolate those factors that foster such a favorable adjustment pattern for adoptive parents and their children in the early phase of the family life-cycle. In addition, we also need to examine parent and child attribution patterns and interactive behaviors within adoptive and nonadoptive families over extended periods of time. Such an approach is likely to have a significant impact on our understanding of the increased vulnerability of adopted children to psychological and academic problems.

Finally, in suggesting the need for increased attention on the adjustment patterns of adoptive families, it is important to note certain methodological problems that inevitably arise in working with this population. First, adjustment to adoptive parenthood is most often confounded by infertility problems. Consequently, it would be important to control for this factor, if at all possible. Including groups of individuals who are infertile, but have chosen to remain childless, as well as couples who are fertile, but still have chosen to adopt, would constitute an important methodological advance in this area. One problem is that the latter group—fertile couples who choose to begin their family by adopting—are relatively rare. A second methodological issue that needs addressing is the differences in ages and length of marriage prior to parenthood for adoptive and nonadoptive couples. As noted previously, adoptive parents generally are older and have been married longer prior to the arrival of their first child. One possible control is to include a group of nonadoptive couples who have delayed childbirth until later in their marriage—although this, in itself, may introduce other complicating factors associated with motivations for delayed parenthood. A third complication in this area is the uncertainty in the timing of the adoption placement. Adoptive couples achieve parenthood after highly variable periods of waiting—from a few months to six or seven years. To the extent that length of waiting impacts on personal and familial patterns of adjustment, as well as on attributions and expectations concerning parenthood, it is important that this factor be taken into consideration—if only as a variable to be controlled during statistical analyses. A fourth factor that needs to be considered in understanding the transition to adoptive parenthood is the age of the child at the time of placement. In this paper, we have emphasized infant and early child placements. Even in the first year or so, however, age of placement, as well as continuity between biological/foster homes and adoptive homes, are important variables mediating adoption adjustment (Yarrow & Goodwin, 1973; Yarrow et al., 1973; Yarrow & Klein, 1980). As the reader might imagine, the complications associated with placing older children (e.g., beyond 3-4 years) for adoption are even greater (cf. Fanshel, 1972; Feigelman & Silverman, 1983; Jewett, 1978; Kadushin, 1970; Tizard, 1977).

In summary, transition to adoptive parenthood and its relationship to parental and child adjustment remains largely an unexplored area of family life. To a great extent this neglect stems from the traditional association of adoption with social casework as opposed to research-based disciplines such as psychology or sociology. The lack of interest in this area also has been related to the historical assumption that placement of a young infant with adoptive parents simulates the "natural" family to such a degree that there is little, if any, reason to expect differences in the development and adjustment of adoptees compared to their nonadopted counterparts. As we have noted, however, this assumption is being challenged by a growing body of research documenting the increased vulnerability of adopted children to a variety of psychological and academic problems. Although extremely valuable, this body of research represents only a first level analysis of the issues involved in this substantive area. Future research must begin to explore in detail those factors underlying the adoptee's vulnerability. To date, attempts to disentangle the many personal, interpersonal, and contextual factors contributing to the problems of adopted children (and their families) have been limited. Our own belief is that the experiences, expectations, and attributions of parents in the early phases of the family life-cycle (including the initial transition to adoptive parenthood) play a crucial role in the later adjustment patterns and problems of adoptive family members. Accordingly, we see our future research, and hopefully, the efforts of other adoption investigators, becoming increasingly involved in the type of research represented by the many contributors to this volume. We expect the outcome of these efforts to be particularly fruitful, not only for our understanding of adjustment to adoption, but more importantly, for our understanding of broader issues in human development and family socialization.

REFERENCES

Belsky, J. (1984). The determinants of parenting: A process model. *Child Development, 55*, 83-96.

Belsky, J., Spanier, G.B., & Rovine, M. (1983). Stability and change in marriage across the transition to parenthood. *Journal of Marriage and the Family, 45*, 553-566.

Belsky, J., Ward, M.J., & Rovine, M. (1986). Prenatal expections, postnatal experiences, and the transition to parenthood. In R.O. Ashmore & D.M. Brodzinsky (Eds.), *Thinking about the family: Views of parents and children* (pp. 119-145). Hillsdale, NJ: Lawrence Erlbaum Associates.

Blum, H.P. (1983). Adoptive parents: Generative conflict and generational continuity. *Psychoanalytic Study of the Child, 38*, 141-163.

Bohman, M. (1970). *Adopted children and their families: A follow-up study of adopted children, their background environment, and adjustment*. Stockholm: Proprius.

Bohman, M. (1978). Some genetic aspects of alcoholism and criminality. *Archives of General Psychiatry, 35*, 269-277.

Bohman, M. & Sigvardsson, S. (1982). Adoption and fostering as preventive measures. In E.J. Anthony & C. Chiland (Eds.), *The child in his family* (Vol 7, pp. 171-180). New York: Wiley.

Bowlby, J. (1973). *Attachment and loss. Vol 2: Separation*. New York: Basic Books.

Bowlby, J. (1980). *Attachment and loss. Vol 3: Loss*. New York: Basic Books.

Brinich, P.M. (1980). Some potential effects of adoption on self and object representation. *Psychoanalytic Study of the Child, 35*, 107-133.

Brodzinsky, D.M. (in press a). Adjustment to adoption: A psychosocial perspective. *Clinical Psychology Review*.

Brodzinsky, D.M. (in press b). Looking at adoption through rose colored glasses: A critique of Marquis and Detweiler, "Does adoption mean different? An attributional analysis." *Journal of Personality and Social Psychology*.

Brodzinsky, D.M., Radice, C., Huffman, L., & Merkler, K. (1986). *Incidence of clinically significant symptomatology in a nonclinical sample of adopted and nonadopted children*. Manuscript submitted for publication.

Brodzinsky, D.M. & Reeves, L. (1986). *Relationship between adoptive parents' coping strategies and their children's adjustment to adoption*. Unpublished manuscript.

Brodzinsky, D.M., Schechter, D.E., Braff, A.M., & Singer, L.M. (1984). Psychological and academic adjustment in adopted children. *Journal of Consulting and Clinical Psychology, 52*, 582-590.

Brodzinsky, D.M., Schechter, D., & Brodzinsky, A.B. (1986). Children's knowledge of adoption: Developmental changes and implications for adjustment. In R.D. Ashmore & D.M. Brodzinsky (Eds.), *Thinking about the family: Views of parents and children* (pp. 205-232). Hillsdale, NJ: Lawrence Erlbaum Associates.

Caldwell, B.M. & Bradley, R.H. (1978). *Home Observation for Measurement of the Environment*. Little Rock: University of Arkansas.

Carey, W.B., Lipton, W.L., & Myers, R.A. (1974). Temperament in adopted and foster babies. *Child Welfare, 53*, 352-359.

Cox, M.J. (1985). Progress and continued challenges in understanding the transition to parenthood. *Journal of Family Issues, 6*, 395-408.

Deutsch, C.K., Swanson, J.M., Bruell, J.H., Cantwell, D.P., Weinberg, F., & Baren, M. (1982). Overrepresentation of adoptees in children with the attention deficit disorder. *Behavior Genetics, 12*, 231-238.

Fanshel, D. (1972). *Far from the reservation*. Metuchen, NJ: Scarecrow Press.

Feigelman, W. & Silverman, A.R. (1983). *Chosen children: New patterns of adoptive relationships*. New York: Praeger Press.

Glenn, N.D. & McLanahan, S. (1982). Children and marital happiness: A further specification of the relationship. *Journal of Marriage and the Family, 44*, 63-72.

Greenbaum, C.W., Auerbach, J., & Frankel, D. (1983). *Effects of intervention and adoption on child development*. Annual Scientific Report, Bi-National Science Foundation, Hebrew University, Jerusalem, Israel.

Hill, R. (1949). *Families under stress*. New York: Harper & Row.

Hoopes, J.L. (1982). *Prediction in child development: A longitudinal study of adoptive and nonadoptive families*. New York: Child Welfare League of America.

Humphrey, M. (1975). The effect of children upon the marriage relationship. *British Journal of Medical Psychology, 48,* 273-279.

Humphrey, M. & Kirkwood, R. (1982). Marital relationship among adopters. *Adoption and Fostering, 6,* 44-48.

Isabella, R.A. & Belsky, J. (1985). Marital change during the transition to parenthood and security of infant-parent attachment. *Journal of Family Issues, 6,* 505-522.

Jewett, C. (1978). *Adopting the older child*. Cambridge, MA: Harvard Common Press.

Kadushin, A. (1970). *Adopting older children*. New York: Columbia University Press.

Kadushin, A. (1980). *Child welfare services* (3rd ed.). New York: Macmillan.

Kirk, H.D. (1964). *Shared fate*. New York: Free Press.

Kraft, A.D., Palombo, J., Mitchell, D., Dean, C., Meyers, S., & Wright, A.W. (1980). The psychological dimensions of infertility. *American Journal of Orthopsychiatry, 50,* 618-628.

Loehlin, J.C., Willerman, L., & Horn, J.M. (1982). Personality resemblances between unwed mothers and their adopted-away offspring. *Journal of Personality and Social Psychology, 42,* 1089-1099.

Losbough, B. (1965). Relationship of EEG neurological and psychological findings in adopted children. *Medical Journal of EEG Technology, 5,* 1-4.

Mech, E.V. (1973). Adoption: A policy perspective. In B. Caldwell & H. Ricciuti (Eds.), *Review of child development research* (Vol 3, pp. 467-508). Chicago: University of Chicago Press.

Miller, B. & Sollie, D. (1980). Normal stresses during the transition to parenthood. *Family Relations, 29,* 459-465.

Moos, R.H. (1981). *Family Environment Scale Manual*. Palo Alto, CA: Consulting Psychologists Press.

Nickman, S.L. (1985). Losses in adoption: The need for dialogue. *Psychoanalytic Study of the Child, 40,* 365-398.

Oates, O.S. & Heinicke, C.M. (1985). Prebirth prediction of the quality of the mother-infant interaction. *Journal of Family Issues, 6,* 523-542.

Palkovitz, R. (1985). Fathers' birth attendance, early contact, and extended contact with their newborns: A critical review. *Child Development, 56,* 392-406.

Palkovitz, R. (1987). Consistency and stability in the family microsystem environment. In D.L. Peters and S. Kontos (Eds.), *Annual Advances in Applied Environmental Psychology, Vol. II*. Norwood, NJ: Ablex Publishing Co.

Plomin, R. & DeFries, J.C. (1985). *The origins of individual differences in infancy: The Colorado Adoption Project*. New York: Academic Press.

Rathus, S.A. (1983). *Human sexuality*. New York: Holt, Rinehart, & Winston.

Rossi, A.S. (1968). Transition to parenthood. *Journal of Marriage and the Family, 30*, 26-39.

Russell, C. (1974). Transition to parenthood: Problems and gratifications. *Journal of Marriage and the Family, 36*, 294-301.

Schechter, M. (1960). Observations on adopted children. *Archives of General Psychiatry, 3*, 21-32.

Schechter, M. (1970). About adoptive parents. In E.J. Anthony & T. Benedeck (Eds.), *Parenthood: Its psychology and psychopathology* (pp. 353-371). Boston: Little, Brown & Co.

Shapiro, C.H. (1982). The impact of infertility on the marital relationship. *Social Casework*, Sept., 387-393.

Singer, L.M., Brodzinsky, D.M., Ramsay, D., Steir, M., & Waters, E. Mother-infant attachment in adoptive families. *Child Development, 56*, 1543-1551.

Sorosky, A.D., Baran, A., & Pannor, R. (1979). *The adoption triangle: The effects of the sealed record on adoptees, birth parents, and adoptive parents*. Garden City, NY: Anchor Books.

Stein, L.M. & Hoopes, J.L. (1985). *Identity formation in the adopted adolescent*. New York: Child Welfare League of America.

Tizard, B. (1977). *Adoption: A second chance*. New York: Free Press.

Yarrow, L.J. (1965). Theoretical implications of adoption research. In *Perspectives on adoption research*. New York: Child Welfare League of America.

Yarrow, L.J. & Goodwin, M.S. (1973). The immediate impact of separation: Reactions of infants to a change in mother figure. In L.J. Stone, H.T. Smith, & L.B. Murphy (Eds.), *The competent infant: Research and commentary* (pp. 1032-1040). New York: Basic Books.

Yarrow, L.J., Goodwin, M.S., Manheimer, H., & Milowe, I.D. (1973). Infancy experiences and cognitive and personality development at 10 years. In L.J. Stone, H.T. Smith, & L.B. Murphy (Eds.), *The competent infant: Research and commentary* (pp. 1274-1281). New York: Basic Books.

Yarrow, L.J. & Klein, R.P. (1980). Environmental discontinuity associated with transition from foster to adoptive homes. *International Journal of Behavioral Development, 3*, 311-322.

Zill, N. (1985). *Behavior and learning problems among adopted children: Findings from a U.S. national survey of child health*. Paper presented at the meetings of the Society for Research in Child Development, Toronto, Canada.

Normal Parents:
Institutions and the Transition
to Parenthood

Raymond G. DeVries

SUMMARY. Institutions influence the transition to parenthood in two ways: they affect the timing of the decision to have children and they shape the experience of parenting. This paper explores both types of influence focusing on educational, economic, medical, legal and religious institutions. After looking at the role of institutions in delaying childbirth, examination focuses on the response of institutions to today's older new parents and consideration is given to normal (i.e., typical) parent roles are created. The article concludes by analyzing the importance of "experts" in the lives of new parents.

In certain high schools around the country, those who teach courses on "health" or "personal hygiene" — euphemisms for sex education — are given to having students pair off and take care of an uncooked egg for a week. The egg must be accompanied at all times by one member of the couple; if this is impossible the egg must be placed in the care of a suitable "eggsitter." The point of this eggciting exercise is to impress on students the adjustments that accompany the move from non-parent to parent. Caring for an egg gives students a general sense of the increased responsibility that comes with parenting, but fails to convey the social evolution of parent-

Raymond G. DeVries, PhD, is Associate Professor of Sociology, Westmont College, Santa Barbara, CA 93108.

This paper benefited from the assistance of C. A. DeVries and Rebecca Davis as well as the editorial comments of two anonymous reviewers.

hood, the ways in which parenting is shaped by society and its institutions.

If I were having my sociology students carry eggs around, I would want them to understand that 30 years ago, caring for their egg would have been an entirely different experience. There would be less question about who had primary responsibility for the egg, it would be easier to arrange for relatives to "eggsit," and most couples would begin their parenting experience in their early twenties. By way of contrast, couples today are more likely to negotiate care-taking roles, rely heavily on professional child care, and delay parenting until their late twenties and early thirties. These variations call attention to the power of society to create the experience of parenting. Society influences the decision when (or if) to have children, the manner in which the children will be born, the effect of children on the careers of parents, and how we think about children.

Modern life is situated in the context of institutions. As the influence of the extended family wanes, formal institutions—including medicine, the economy, religion, education, law, and government—become more important in the lives of individuals. These institutions play a vital role in the decision to become a parent as well as the nature of the experience of new parents. In this paper, I explore both types of influence. I begin by looking at the decision to have children in order to identify the unique features of the transition to parenthood in the last decade. Having described the new parents of the eighties and identified their peculiar problems, I take a close look at the ways institutions shape the parental role.

I. OF INFANTS AND INSTITUTIONAL TIMETABLES

It is by now common knowledge that women are choosing to delay childbirth until their late twenties and early and mid-thirties.[1] Data from the National Center for Health Statistics show that while the first birth rate for women between the ages of 15 and 24 dropped since the early seventies, the first births for women aged 25 to 39 increased dramatically. For women 25-29 years, the first birth rate jumped nearly 30% in a 12 year period—from 29.4 per 1000 women in that age group in 1972 to 37.9 in 1983. The first birth rate for women 30-34 years more than doubled in that same period, moving from 7.0 in 1972 to 15.4 in 1983. The same is true of women aged 35-39 with the rate increasing from 1.8 in 1972 to 3.7 in 1983 (Ventura, 1982; National Center for Health Statistics, 1985).

Figures 1 and 2 offer a picture of this trend and present some additional information about those who are choosing to delay child-

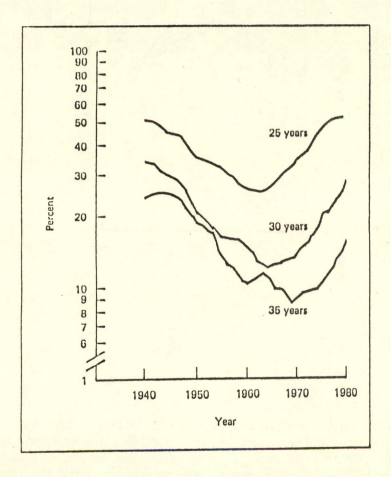

FIGURE 1: PERCENT OF WHITE WOMEN WHO ARE CHILDLESS AT EXACT AGES 25, 30, AND 35 YEARS: UNITED STATES, JANUARY 1, 1940-80 (from Ventura, 1982, p.3).

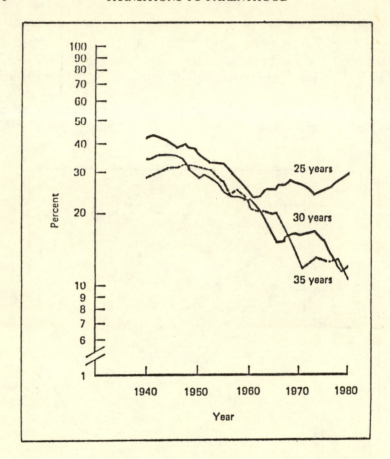

FIGURE 2: PERCENT OF ALL OTHER WOMEN WHO ARE CHILDLESS AT EXACT AGES
25, 30, 35 YEARS: UNITED STATES, JANUARY 1, 1940-80
(from Ventura, 1982, p. 4).

birth. Figure 1 shows the marked increase in white women choosing to remain childless in their twenties and thirties. Figure 2 indicates that delayed childbearing is not as evident among non-white women. This white/non-white difference suggests that the postponement of parenting is more common among the middle and upper-middle classes.

The Role of Institutions in Delaying Childbirth

How can we account for this trend? One obvious place to look is age at first marriage. When we look at changes in the median age at first marriage over the last fifteen years we discover that marriage, like childbirth, is being postponed. For women the median age at first marriage increased from 20.8 in 1970 to 23.3 in 1985; for men there was an increase from 23.2 in 1970 to 25.5 in 1985 (Bureau of the Census, 1985a). But age at first marriage has limited power in explaining delayed childbirth because birth rates to unmarried women have increased in recent years and because the postponement of marriage itself needs explanation.

On the most general level the postponement of marriage and childbirth can be understood as a manifestation of the trend toward individualism chronicled by several observers of the American social landscape (see Yankelovich, 1981; Bellah et al., 1985). The pursuit of individual goals displaces the commitment to marriage and children. This is where institutions play their part in delaying childbirth: the realization of individual goals requires accommodation to institutional timetables.

The data we have on women who delay childbearing indicate that they are allowing established educational and employment patterns to set the agenda for childbearing. Table 1 shows the proportion of first-time mothers over the age 25 with college degrees rose sharply between 1970 and 1979 (see Bureau of the Census, 1985b; Happel et al., 1984). Further evidence confirms that this trend is not an artifact of general improvement in educational levels. The first birth

TABLE 1: PERCENT OF WOMEN EXPERIENCING FIRST BIRTH BETWEEN THE AGES OF 25 - 39 WHO COMPLETED 16 OR MORE YEARS OF SCHOOLING, 1970, 1975, 1979 (Ventura, 1982, p. 12).

	YEAR		
AGE	1970	1975	1979
25 - 29 YEARS	33.5	37.3	37.1
30 - 34 YEARS	28.3	39.9	47.8
35 - 39 YEARS	22.0	31.5	40.3

rates for well-educated women 30-34 years old increased significantly between 1970 and 1979 (Ventura, 1982, p. 5). Bureau of the Census (1985c) data show that women aged 25-29 who have completed 4 years of college have a fertility rate (119.3 per 1,000) about twice that of those with five or more years of college (60.5 per 1,000), the latter group postponing parenthood to continue their education or career.

The evidence suggests that institutions structure the decision to bear children: in this case established patterns of schooling, and the flow of schooling into employment, work to delay or in some cases eliminate parenting (see Houseknecht, 1982; Faux, 1984; Bram, 1984). The transition to parenthood is itself in transition—new parents in this decade are different from earlier generations of new parents and as such they face new problems.

New Parents, New Problems

The changing character of new parents poses problems not only for the parents themselves, but for the institutions that surround them. For parents, the problems center on the lack of models to offer guidance in their new role. The parents of this decade's new and older parents typically had their children at a younger age and did not face the struggle of a two career marriage, hence there is little they can offer in the way of practical advice. The new generation of parents must look to mass-market instruction available in self-help books and packaged seminars on improving yourself and your baby. The lack of established models for new parents leaves them hungry for advice and particularly susceptible to the influence of institutions.

For institutions the new parents of this decade present both problem and potential. New parents represent problems to the extent that they place new demands on institutions. New parents demand new institutions for child care,[2] they want medical organizations to provide them with a safe *and* pleasurable birth experience, and they expect employers to accommodate to their new roles. But new parents also represent new markets to exploit, a fact that has not gone unnoticed by America's entrepreneurs.

The boom in magazines offering advice in the art of parenting provides an apt illustration of the problems and potentials of new parents. 1985 was a good year for magazines targeted toward parents. While advertising revenues for all magazines declined 1.4 percent, *Parents* magazine enjoyed a 13.9 percent increase. In that same year five new national magazines intended for parents were created. A researcher at the Magazine Publishers Association in New York called 1985 "the Year of the Baby" (Fuller, 1985). This trend in magazine publishing testifies to the symbiotic relation between new parents (with their unique problems) and business institutions (with their marketable solutions). New parents, with few models to guide them, are looking for advice, and the entrepreneur stands ready to capitalize on this need. These parents are an attractive market because they are impressionable and—having established themselves in their careers—they have ample money to meet their needs.[3]

The recent success of parenting magazines hints at the power of institutions, not only to influence the decision when to parent, but also to shape the experience of parenting. Institutions that play a part in defining the parenting role—medicine, religion, the economy, and the law—have had to respond to the demands of today's new parents. The nature of their response will shape the future of parenting.

II. RESPONSE OR RESISTANCE? INSTITUTIONS AND TODAY'S NEW PARENTS

Because they are unlike previous generations of new parents, today's new parents pose a challenge to institutions. They place unfamiliar demands on institutions, demands which require change in routines. Employers are asked to respond to the needs of pregnant workers and to grant extended maternity and paternity leaves. Hospitals are asked to make room for fathers who want to assist in the birth or perhaps record the event on videotape. When the demands of these new parents clash with the needs of institutions, who accommodates?

To answer this question we must consider the varied costs of accommodation. For institutions the costs are measured either in terms of money or ideology. Some adjustments affect the "bottom line,'' requiring either capital investments (as in the creation of birthing rooms in hospitals) or reducing resources (as in the loss of productivity during maternity or paternity leaves). Other adjustments are costly to important ideologies. For example, parents' demands in childbirth challenge scientific views of birth held by obstetricians and other birth assistants.

Parents pay the price of accommodation in the currency of satisfaction. As the needs of institutions overwhelm the desires of parents, their satisfaction with parenting is diminished. Parents are at a disadvantage in the conflict with institutions. Because they approach the institution as ''one-shotters'' — Galanter's (1974) phrase for those who place only sporadic demands on institutions — their demands lack the force that comes with organization and consistency. The demands of parents are both immediate and transient — they need the hospital to change for their birth, they need their employer to be sensitive to their desire to be with their infant. Once they have passed a particular stage of parenting new parents have little need to see policies in that realm altered.

Given these parameters, I explore the response of four institutions — medicine, the economy (specifically, the workplace), religion and the law — to the changing character of new parents. As I measure the response of each institution, I also look for the ways these institutions shape the transition to parenthood.

Medicine and the Experience of Birth

Medicine is perhaps the single most important institution in the transition to parenthood. The move into parenthood occurs under the watchful eye of medicine beginning (for some) with genetic counseling, on to prenatal care, through the birth and into the first year of the infant's life. Because new parents rely heavily on them for guidance, the agents of medical institutions (doctors, midwives, nurses and others), play a key role in shaping the transition.[4]

The nature of medicine's involvement in the transition to parenthood changed significantly during this century. Several excellent histories document the most notable aspects of this change including the rise in popularity of hospital birth, the demise of home birth, and the decline and halting re-emergence of the American midwife (see Wertz and Wertz, 1977; Litoff, 1978). The past half century in America is marked by the proliferation of new techniques for intervening in and controlling the birth process and a sharp increase in the number of surgical deliveries.

Beginning about fifteen years ago, the medicalization of birth was met with a call to humanize birth. An important source of this resistance to medicalization lies in the nature of new parents. The generation giving birth over the last fifteen years lived through an era marked by civil disobedience, race riots, public protests over the war in Vietnam, and the call "back to nature." The resulting sensitivity to the abuse of power by institutions, sexism in medicine, and the benefits of naturalness led to questions concerning the medical routines for birth (see Arms, 1977).

The plea to humanize birth reflects a shift in focus from the *product* to the *experience* of birth. Among earlier generations, the primary concern in birth was with the health of mother and child. This attitude allowed obstetric science to flourish because the scientific approach was product oriented—promising better techniques for healthier babies. As birth became less dangerous and yielded better results, and as the nature of parents changed, there was growing concern with the experiential elements of birth. Birth became not just a way to produce an heir, but a key experience for personal growth. Obstetric routines that hindered that experience were challenged.

The growing interest in fathers at birth offers ample evidence of the new emphasis on experience. The focus on experience provides a primary place in the delivery room for fathers. When the overriding concern is to produce a healthy baby, fathers have no rightful place at birth. But when concern shifts to the experience of birth, the participation of fathers is vital. The shift to an experiential view of birth allows discussion of the "pregnant male" (Jones, 1982) and explains the growth in literature examining participation of fathers at birth (see Phillips & Anzalone, 1982; Robinson & Barret, 1986; Greenberg, 1985; Palkovitz, 1985).[5]

The institution of medicine is challenged on two levels by new parents. On a superficial level they present a new and unusual population of birthing women—women over thirty having their first baby. On a deeper level they fault the medical treatment of birth for being sexist (see Ruzek, 1978; Dreifus, 1978), costly (see Parfitt, 1977), over-dependent on technology (see Arms, 1977; Stewart and Stewart, 1976; 1977), potentially dangerous (see Haire, 1972), and for failing to attend to the experiential dimension of birth.

The response of medicine to these challenges illustrates the nature of flexibility in medicine: changes are made as long as the underlying ideology of medicine is not threatened. For instance, change in the type of women giving birth requires accommodation on the part of medicine, but that accommodation does not call into question the basic model of medicine. The aging of first time mothers led medicine to redefine pregnancies of women over 35. Pregnant women over 35 used to be considered "elderly," and "high risk." As physicians began to see more women in this category and as the nature of these women changed, evidence was collected confirming that birth after 35 is not riskier than birth at younger ages (Parachini, 1986).

It is more difficult for medicine to change in response to claims that it is sexist, costly, overly technological, dangerous, and ignorant of the social, psychological and spiritual needs of its patients. To do so would be to admit that the philosophy of medicine is flawed. Medicine is product oriented, not experience oriented. Focus on experience cannot coexist with a focus on a healthy product: one or the other must take precedence. Writing in the *Journal of the American Medical Association*, two physicians note:

> We believe that certain priorities in the birthing process must be maintained if rational decisions regarding birth environments are to be made. The first priority is a live and healthy mother; the second, a live and healthy baby; and *third*, a psychologically rewarding experience for the parents and the baby. (Adamson & Gare, 1980, emphasis added)

When the demands of consumers conflict with the tenets of scientific medicine, medicine cannot give in.

The predictable reaction to this situation is an attempt by medicine to transform the desires of new parents into medically recognizable terms. New parents come to medicine wanting to enhance the experience of birth, demanding less use of technology, more contact with their infant, and more emphasis on the relational aspects of birth. Medicine responds by "scientizing" experience, treating experience as any other variable that influences the outcome of birth. Experience becomes a quantifiable, clinical variable subject to careful randomized trials to measure efficacy (see Chalmers, 1986). Arney and Bergen (1984) regard medicine's new found interest in experience as a logical consequence of the evolution of medical technique. As the utility of looking into the body to solve health problems diminished, attempts to more fully understand and promote health adopted an ecological approach. The medical gaze was shifted from the body to the environment, to experience.

Medicine's concern with experience extends medical control over parenting. The history of bonding and alternative birth centers (ABC's) offers a case in point (see DeVries, 1979; 1980; 1983; 1984). Faced with a bevy of criticism and a small but worrisome trend toward home birth, medicine needed an acceptable avenue of response. Study of the bonding process—early attachment between parent and infant—provided that avenue. Attachment was easily subjected to scientific study and led researchers to the conclusion that there were important clinical reasons to focus on the experiential aspects of birth (see Klaus and Kennell, 1976; 1981; Klaus et al., 1972; Ringler et al., 1975; Kennell et al., 1975). This evidence gave key medical organizations acceptable grounds for restructuring hospital birth. In their "Statement on parent and newborn interaction," the American Medical Association (1977) said:

> . . . increasing evidence has accumulated to support the concept of an "attachment and bonding" process in the human race. It is timely to review all hospital procedures and professional practices for their appropriateness and thereby encourage the hospitals to reassess their policy in support of the bonding principle.

The sentiments of the AMA were mirrored in a 1978 report, "The development of family centered maternity/newborn care in hospitals," prepared by an Interprofessional Task Force comprised of obstetricians, pediatricians, hospital representatives, and nurses.

Thus was born the ABC. ABC's typically include a queen sized bed located in a room with a "homey look" created by carpeting, hanging plants, pictures, overstuffed chairs, and perhaps a dining table. Women labor and give birth in the same bed, and family and friends are allowed to participate. ABC's promise enhanced parental control over birth, but in fact they function to increase medical control of the experience; in ABC's birth becomes a routinized event and patients are ultimately subject to medical authority (see DeVries, 1980; 1983).

Other developments are working to increase medical control over birth. The legitimation through licensure of nurse midwifery — and in some states, lay midwifery — puts midwifery under the supervision of medicine and reduces the alternative nature of midwifery care (DeVries, 1985). The insurance industry has an important influence on birth, shaping the decisions of parents with patterns of reimbursement and with prohibitive rates for liability insurance. Third party payers typically do not reimburse consumers for care outside of hospitals, even though out-of-hospital settings are less expensive and are desired by parents seeking more control over the birth of their children. The crisis in malpractice insurance closes off options for parents by creating the need for defensive, often intrusive, medicine and by forcing some practitioners, including midwives and physicians, out of business.

The response of medicine to the demands of new parents created new forms of control (Oakley, 1980; Romalis, 1981). The rise of humanized, alternative methods for managing birth gives medicine new freedom to direct and shape early parenting experiences. Nelson (1982) discovered that childbirth education, often seen as a program promoting resistance to medicine, actually increases openness to medical intervention (see also Rothman, 1981). Medical professionals become "experts," not only on physical matters, but on the experiential dimension of birth. For instance, in the case of attachment, physicians suggest that they must be consulted to achieve proper attachment — in the words of an anonymous editorial in the British Medical Journal (1977) — physicians are the ones who can "help mothers to love their babies." Nurses also see themselves as key facilitators of relationships between parents and their newborn children (Jenkins & Westhus, 1981; Rising, 1974; Woolery & Barkley, 1981). New professions which direct parenting are emerging under the aegis of medicine. Perhaps the best example is provided by "lactation consultants" who are establishing themselves as experts in matters of breastfeeding, necessary adjuncts for every nursing mother.

The concern with bonding — as well as other recent changes in the medical handling of childbirth — display a tendency to move from innovation to regimen. Seiden (1978, pp. 99-100) observes, "Many mothers have complained of having to fight for the privilege of seeing their babies born or of rooming-in; yet a few years later, every mother in the same hospital will be pressed to participate regardless of her preference." Widespread emphasis on the importance of bonding creates feelings of guilt or anxiety in those unwilling or unable to participate in the experience (Palkovitz, 1985). This process was observed with regard to natural childbirth: women trained in natural childbirth often feel like failures if they choose pain relieving medications to assist in birth. Wertz and Wertz (1978, p. 191) note the negative consequences of imposed models of birthing. With regard to natural childbirth they comment:

> Not surprisingly, some women who felt pain [in birth] pretended they did not, hoping that eventually they could replace their real memories with textbook memories of "what it should be like." Some, expecting but failing to have an ecstatic experience, got postpartum psychosis, an ailment that appeared to some observers to have increased sharply in the 1950s [along with the emphasis on natural childbirth].

Focus on bonding conveys images of proper parental behavior. The measures of attachment — smiling, touching, gazing in the eyes — reflect conceptions of good parenting held by the major consumers of bonding research, the educated, middle to upper-middle-class couple. These behaviors are not an essential component of attachment, but as bonding programs become more common they become part of a general conception of good parenting applied (coercively) to all individuals.

Medicine changed in response to its changed clientele, but it is still a significant force in shaping proper notions of birth and parenting. Parents depend heavily on guides to parenting written by physicians. The classic work of this type is Dr. Benjamin Spock's *Baby*

and Child Care — a volume which sold 30 million copies in five
editions since it was first published in 1945. Spock's book, like
other physician-authored guides to raising children, describes common childhood ailments but also offers advice on discipline and
other non-medical aspects of childrearing. As experts on children,
doctors extend medicine's control of parenting through infancy,
childhood and adolescence.

Conception and Careers: Parenting and the Workplace

> My baby is a new individual in my life whom I love dearly,
> but at this point I am not personally fulfilled in simply being a
> mother. I am finding it difficult to cope with the boredom and
> lack of intellectual stimulation in my life. I gave up my career
> in teaching because I felt it would be unfair to take my baby to
> a daycare center or babysitter. I'm very undecided as to what I
> should do.
>
> Like many new mothers I am faced with the hard decisions
> about the future of my career since my baby was born. I am
> full of doubts, and I'm uncertain how to maintain my career
> and raise my child satisfactorily. (quoted in Miller & Sollie,
> 1985, p. 398)

New parents established in their careers find it difficult to add the
care of children to their list of responsibilities. Most social scientific
studies of the transition to parenthood see the effort to balance career and family as the greatest problem of new parents. Traditionally mothers would interrupt their careers to care for children, but
today's new mothers are attempting to mix parenting and work.
This effort adds stress to parenting and puts pressure on employers,
who are called on to support the transition to parenthood with day-
care programs and/or extended leaves for mothers and fathers.

The coordination of career and conception places greater strain
on women. Young women entering the workforce today who do not
agree with the traditional female role expectations that limit occupational aspirations of women (Merriam and Hyer, 1984), find the job
market has not yet caught up with these liberated attitudes. The
career woman must come to terms with motherhood and its potentially negative effect on her vocation. In an historical study of work-

ing women in America, Cookingham (1984) demonstrates that women who worked before having children were more likely to work after childbearing. Recent data suggest this trend is continuing. The postponement of childbearing for career results in an increase in the number of new mothers who are working: in 1979, 34% of women with children under the age of one were employed outside the home, by 1986 this number rose to 46.8% (Mehren, 1986).

It is not surprising that in American society the difficulties associated with juggling parenting and an occupation are typically regarded as individual problems (see Hewlett, 1986). These problems are to be solved by calling on the extended family, negotiation of roles within marriage, or by a career hiatus. Seldom is the strain between job and parent seen as a structural problem requiring reform of the workplace. It is surprising that the lack of attention to the structural sources of new parents' problems pervades the work of social scientists. Rossi's (1968) call for research on the transition to parenthood spawned several studies of patterns of adjustment and quality of life among dual career couples becoming parents. But almost invariably the focus of these studies is on the ability of *individuals* to accommodate the new demands placed on them. Ross, Mirowski, and Huber (1983) see marital depression as a function of lack of consistency between preferred and actual employment of the wife. Sekaran's (1983) study of quality of life in dual career families focuses on individualistic variables like career salience, self-esteem, and role stress. Elman and Gilbert's (1984) attempt to understand the conflict between parental and professional roles led them to look for a variety of individual "coping strategies." La Rossa and La Rossa (1981) self-consciously adopt a conflict model to study the transition to parenthood but, like the studies cited above, they fail to consider the way the structure of the workplace intervenes in the lives of new parents.

Employers are making a few halting steps to accommodate new parents. A survey of the parental leave policies of 384 corporations reveals the overwhelming majority offer some type of disability leave for new parents, although there is great variation in the length of leave, the amount of pay during leave, the availability of leave to fathers as well as mothers, and the type of job guaranteed upon return (see Mehren, 1986). Employers are gradually becoming interested in the provision of day care services, seeing these services as a way to reduce employee absenteeism, lateness, and turnover. In addition to on-site child care (see Reece, 1982), some businesses are coming together in consortiums to provide child care near the workplace. Others are creating programs to offer "sick-child care" for mildly ill children who cannot attend school (McMillan, 1986; Smith, 1986). Employers unable to support day care programs sometimes set up alternative and reduced work schedules for parents, but reducing time on the job often brings a reduction in pay and position (Kantrowitz, 1986).

The reluctance of employers to respond to the needs of new parents is at least partly based in the acceptance of medical definitions of pregnancy. The medical tendency to regard pregnancy as a disease requiring close monitoring and hospitalization spills over into the attitudes of employers who see pregnant workers as impaired workers. The lack of initiative on the part of employers is generating some legislative activity. The 1978 Pregnancy Discrimination Act requires employers with existing disability programs to treat pregnancy as they would any short term illness or injury. More recently, city governments are experimenting with proposals requiring developers of new commercial projects to either provide space for child care or to contribute to a city child care fund (McMillan, 1986).

Not all persons see day care as a panacea. Berger and Neuhaus (1977) believe that day care diminishes the ability of the family to act as a "mediating structure" and consequently reduces the healthy diversity of society. They are aware of the need for day care programs but feel such programs should be small and avoid professionalization in order to reflect the diversity of American families.

The relationship between parents and their children is greatly influenced by the workplace. Evidence indicates the timing of parenthood as well as the satisfaction with the parenting experience are affected by the programs employers make available.

Thinking About Children: Religious and Legal Institutions

The institutions of medicine and the workplace shape the way new parents act toward their children, but they provide little direction on how to think about children. The institutions of religion and law play an important part in guiding our thoughts of who children are—their meaning, their desirability, their rights. Like other institutions, religion and law have responded to the changing character of new parents.

Traditionally, religious institutions are pronatalist, viewing children as highly desirable, a blessing from God. This is certainly true in the Judeo-Christian tradition of America (Psalm 127: 3-5):

> Children are a gift of the Lord;
> The fruit of the womb is a reward.
> Like arrows in the hand of a warrior,
> So are the children of one's youth.
> Blessed is the man whose quiver is full of them.

Note the inconsistencies between this passage and the styles adopted by today's new parents: contrary to delayed childbearing and small families, the admonition is to have several children in your youth. The church is placed in the difficult position of having to reconcile their traditions with contemporary lifestyles.

Different strategies have been used to reconcile pronatalist views with modern life. For religious fundamentalists, the response is to fault new parents for being selfish and to encourage committed Christian parents to "be fruitful and multiply." A more moderate position involves accommodation, the "domestication of belief" (see Hunter, 1983), reinterpreting the passage to fit the modern temperament. One evangelical pastor suggests that "not everyone's quiver is the same size"—for some, one or two children will fill a quiver. Liberal churches support the choices of new parents by emphasizing the biblical command to stewardship, noting that wise use of the earth's resources calls for limiting family size.

Like physicians, religious leaders are quick to offer advice to new parents on everything from childbearing to childrearing. The natural childbirth movement has a strong religious component. Wessel (1963) provided a Christian framework for natural childbirth, casting it as the duty of Christian mothers. The Seventh Day Adventists, the Mormons, and the Jehovah's Witnesses are among several conservative religious groups that encourage natural childbirth and home birth, couching their encouragement in a pro-family and/or anti-medical-intervention ideology. There is no shortage of advice on parenting coming from clerics and religiously oriented psychologists, a popular example being Dr. James Dobson—a Christian psychologist, author of several books on childrearing (e.g., Dobson, 1970; 1974; 1978) and host of a daily radio show, "Focus on the Family."

Legal institutions formalize societal definitions of childhood. In the realm of law, there is growing tension between the rights of parents and the rights of their children. The social philosophy of John Stuart Mill and John Locke shaped our modern notions of individual rights, but neither man entertained the notion that rights should be extended to children. In his essay, *On Liberty,* Mill noted that rights insuring "liberty of action" should only be given to those "[mature] in their faculties." Locke, disputing the analogy between the rights of kings and the rights of parents, points out that it is just to deny full freedom to children because of their lack of "reason." These paternalistic notions were challenged by the rights movements of the sixties and seventies. The initial focus of these movements was on the rights of minorities and women, but eventually the logic was extended to children (Holt, 1974; Palmeri, 1980).

Viewing children as individuals with rights apart from their parents creates a new catalog of problems. The problem of child abuse is one example. Pfohl (1977) offers an analysis of child abuse which sees it as a social problem "discovered" by radiologists looking to enhance their professional position. However, a notion of child abuse is difficult, if not impossible, to sustain in an environment that gives children no rights apart from their parents. The tension between parental authority and children's rights is evident not only in the case of child abuse, but also in instances of religious deprogramming, medical transplantation procedures that require "cooperation" from young siblings, and recent cases of children pressing charges against or suing their parents.

The tendency to see children as people with the full protection of law is well suited to the needs of new parents. Regarding children as adults in miniature eliminates their special claims based in dependency and enhances the freedom of parents from their children. But this extension of individualism into the domain of the family is not welcomed by all. A growing segment of the population is decrying the loss of childhood, rallying behind Elkind's (1981) observations of the negative effects of being a "hurried child." Traub (1986) suggests that we are moving into a "brave new world of the better baby" where parents compete to get their children in the best preschools and struggle to teach their children reading and computer literacy at early ages. As the battle over the proper role of children wages on, it demonstrates the important role institutions play in defining childhood (see Aries, 1962).

The institutions of religion and law converge on the issue of abortion. The central issue in the abortion debate is a rather ironic disagreement over whether the rights of the mother should take precedence over the rights of the fetus. The irony is found in the positions held by those on either side of the issue. Conservatives, who support the supreme right of parents over children, argue that the fetus has rights separate from its parents. Liberals, who seek to extend rights to all, deny fetuses the right of self-determination. The well known *Roe vs. Wade* decision, which legalized access to abortion, *limited* abortion to the early stages of pregnancy by declaring that when the fetus reaches a certain level of maturity it has rights apart from its mother and is protected by the constitution.

The moral quandary posed by abortion raises questions about the meaning and value of children. Answers to those questions are sought in the institutions of religion and law, both of which draw on the institution of medicine, to clarify and support their claims (see Feinberg, 1973; Wennberg, 1985). This institutional dependency underscores the importance of institutions to notions of parenting and children, and hence to the transition to parenthood.

III. CONCLUSION: NORMAL PARENTS — WHO SHAPES PARENTHOOD?

The most striking feature of the transition in the transition to parenthood is the enhanced control of institutions over the experience. Because today's new parents are having fewer children and are waiting longer to have them, they can not look to their own parents for advice on parenting. Instead, new parents must rely on institutions and their representative "experts." Parents sought the advice of experts as early as the 1930s, but the nature of parental reliance on that advice has changed. In the 1930s scientific advice was put into an array of advice coming from a variety of sources. The advice of experts had privileged status but it had to compete with, and was checked against, prevailing folk wisdom. New parents have a more limited array of advice to compete with advice from the experts, making them more susceptible to expert opinion.

Several observers express concern over the loss of parental autonomy to institutions. Donzelot (1979, p. 227) chronicles the modern "policing of families" by the institutions of medicine, education, and in the end, by government: "with [the family's] saturation by hygienic, psychological, and pedagogical norms, it becomes harder to distinguish the family from the disciplinary continuum of the social apparatuses." Berger and Berger (1983, p. 213) are worried about the intrusion of professionals into the lives of families. They call for the restoration of parental rights: "we feel strongly that parental rights should normally take precedence – not over children's rights, which are usually not the real issue – but over the claims of various professionals to represent the best interests of children." In the realm of medicine, Ehrenreich and English (1978) document the reign of experts over the health care of women and explore the medical subjegation of mothers. In separate studies Oakley (1979) and Nelson (1983) examined the patterns of expert influence in the area of childbirth and infant care. They discovered that middle-class women relied less on family and more heavily on classes and books (and hence, experts) than did working-class women.

In order to understand the growth of institutional control over the transition to parenthood, it is necessary to explore the place of risk in modern life. Most discussions of risk focus on the ways technology poses new threats to our lives. The emphasis here is on things like the dangers of nuclear technology and toxic substances – essentially "externally generated risks." But risks can also be generated "internally"; knowledge of this dimension of the increased risk of modern life is important to understanding the ability of experts – the representatives of institutions – to extend their control. "Internally generated risk" refers to the capacity of technology to transform events once considered routine and a normal part of life to "risky" events that need to be supervised and managed by experts. Granted, these events might have had a certain amount of danger associated with them, but before the advent of sophisticated technology those dangers were hazards to be endured; now they are "risks" to be "managed."

Perhaps the best example of this is childbirth. Birth has always been seen as a dangerous event. One of our colonial forefathers, Cotton Mather, instructed pregnant women, "Preparation for death is that most reasonable and most seasonable thing, to which you must now apply yourself" (quoted in Wertz and Wertz, 1977:21). In that era, the hazards of birth were shared equally among all classes of women and there was little the experts of the day could do to control them. The twentieth century brought us fetal heart monitors, anesthesia, C-sections, and the like, all of which allow the risks of birth to be managed. As developers and purveyors of this new technology, medical experts exert their claim to control the birth experience. Hence technology generates risk *externally*— through development of substances and techniques that could backfire or be misapplied—and *internally*—by improving control over the once routine experiences of life.

If the professions gain their authority through being "oddsmakers" of sorts, they extend their authority through a claims making process that is based on internally generated risk. As new technologies—both hard and soft—transform routine life experiences into manageable risks, more of our lives come under the control of the experts who apply those technologies. This observation adds a new dimension to our understanding of Weber's comment about the "disenchantment of the world." As the world becomes more "disenchanted" we become more subject to expert, professional control. We need (scientific) experts not only to tell us how to raise our children, but how to have good sex, how to manage our diets.

The institutional scripting of parenthood accomplished by experts is consistent with a service economy. New occupational opportunities are afforded by the increased reliance of parents on experts (physicians, psychologists) and adjuncts (lactation consultants, day care specialists). But reliance on experts and adjuncts also diminishes the freedom and competence of parents. Parents are subtly and not so subtly encouraged to conform to institutional notions of normal parenthood, notions which typically require expert assistance.

Today's new parents are like earlier generations of new parents in at least one way: becoming a parent alters one's relationship to institutions. Sociologists have long observed the conservatizing influence of aging. Undoubtedly a strong component of this move toward conservatism is the responsibility of parenthood and the consequent heightened concern with the future of society. The childless have less interest in the maintenance of society, the quality of the schools, the safety of the streets, and the state of the children's program at the local church. For new parents these are urgent issues.

The transition to parenthood provides a strong incentive to shape the institutions of society. Understanding the ways institutions transform new parents into "normal parents" is the first step toward the freedom to shape the parenting role and, in turn, to control the institutions that structure our lives.

NOTES

1. Of course there are other recent trends in birth, perhaps the most notable being the rise in teen pregnancies, but the trend toward delayed childbearing is more significant for two reasons. First, many teen pregnancies are terminated by abortion and thus do not eventuate in birth. Second, cultural notions of birth and parenting are more closely associated with the class of people who have postponed parenthood.

2. The number of establishments providing child care services increased from 24,813 in 1977 to 30,762 in 1982, mirroring the rise in working women with preschool age children (Bureau of the Census, 1985c; see also McMillan, 1986).

3. Nearly 66% of women over 30 with children are in the work force (Bureau of the Census, 1985c).

4. In Nelson's (1982) study of childbirth preparation among working- and middle-class women, doctors were most consistently cited as a "very important" source of information about childbirth.

5. It is this trend that caused Drs. Klaus and Kennell (1976; 1981) to change the name of their book from *Maternal-infant bonding*, to *Parent-infant bonding* when it came out in a second edition.

REFERENCES

Adamson, G. & Gare, D. (1980). Home or hospital birth? *JAMA; 243*, 1747-1748.

American Medical Association (1977). Statement on parent and newborn interaction. Chicago.

Aries, P. (1962). *Centuries of Childhood*. New York: Vintage.

Arms, Suzanne (1977). *Immaculate Deception*. New York: Bantam.

Arney, W. R. & Bergen, B. J. (1984). *Medicine and the Management of Living*. Chicago: University of Chicago Press.

Bellah, R. N., Madsen, R., Swidler, A., Sullivan, W. M. & Tipton, S. (1985). *Habits of the Heart*. Berkeley: University of California Press.

Berger, B. & Berger, P. (1983). *The War over the Family*. Garden City, NY: Anchor Press.

Berger, P. and Neuhaus, R. (1977). *To Empower People*. Washington, DC: American Enterprise Institute.

Bram, S. (1984). Voluntarily childless women: Traditional or nontraditional? *Sex Roles, 10*, 195-206.

British Medical Journal (1977). Helping mothers to love their babies. *British Medical Journal*, September 3.

Bureau of the Census (1985a). Household, families, marital status, and living arrangements: March 1985 (Advance report). *Current Population Reports*, Series P-20 (No. 402).

Bureau of the Census (1985b). School enrollment—social and economic characteristics of students: October, 1983. *Current Population Reports*, Series P-20 (No. 394).

Bureau of the Census (1985c). Fertility of American women: June 1984. *Current Population Reports*, Series P-20 (No. 401).

Chalmers, I. (1986). Evaluation of perinatal practice: Public rights and public responsibilities. *Birth, 13*, 155-164.

Cookingham, M. E. (1984). Working after childbearing in America. *Journal of Interdisciplinary History, 14*, 773-792.

DeVries, R. (1979). Responding to consumer demand: A study of alternative birth centers. *Hospital Progress, 60* (10), 48-51, 68.

DeVries, R. (1980). The alternative birth center: Option or cooption? *Women and Health, 5*, 47-60.

DeVries, R. (1983). Image and reality: An evaluation of hospital alternative birth centers. *Journal of Nurse-Midwifery, 28* (3), 3-10.

DeVries, R. (1984). "Humanizing" childbirth: the discovery and implementation of bonding theory. *International Journal of Health Services, 14*, 89-104.

DeVries, R. (1985). *Regulating Birth: Midwives, Medicine, and the Law*. Philadelphia: Temple University Press.

Dobson, J. (1970). *Dare to Discipline*. Wheaton, IL: Tyndale.

Dobson, J. (1974). *Hide or Seek*. Old Tappan, NJ: Revell.

Dobson, J. (1978). *Preparing for Adolescence*. Santa Ana, CA: Vision House.

Donzelot, J. (1979). *The Policing of Families*. New York: Pantheon.

Dreifus, C., (Ed.). (1978). *Seizing Our Bodies: The Politics of Women's Health*. New York: Vintage.

Elkind, D. (1981). *The Hurried Child*. Reading, MA: Addison-Wesley.

Elman, M. R. & Gilbert, L. A. (1984). Coping strategies for role conflict in married professional women with children. *Family Relations, 33*, 317-327.

Ehrenreich, B. & English, D. (1978). *For Her Own Good: 150 Years of the Experts' Advice to Women*. Garden City, NY: Anchor Press.

Faux, M. (1984). *Childless by Choice*. Garden City, NY: Doubleday.

Feinberg, J., (Ed.). (1973). *The Problems of Abortion*. Belmont, CA: Wadsworth.

Fuller, D. A. (1985, August 15). Parent magazines ride baby boomlet. *Los Angeles Times*, Part IV, pp. 1,5.

Galanter, M. (1974). Why the "haves" come out ahead. *Law and Society Review, 9*, 96-153.

Greenberg, M. (1985). *The Birth of a Father*. New York: Continuum.

Haire, D. (1972). *The Cultural Warping of Childbirth*. Seattle: International Childbirth Education Association.

Happel, S. K., Hill, J. K. & Low, S. A. (1984). An economic analysis of the timing of childbirth. *Population Studies, 38*, 299-311.

Hewlett, S. A. (1986). *A lesser life: The myth of women's liberation in America*. New York: Morrow.

Holt, J. (1974). *Escape from Childhood*. New York: E.P. Dutton.

Houseknecht, S. K. (1982). Voluntary childlessness in the 1980s: A significant increase? *Marriage and Family Review, 5*, 51-67.

Hunter, J. D. (1983). *American Evangelicalism: Conservative Religion and the Quandary of Modernity*. New Brunswick, NJ: Rutgers.

Jenkins, R. L. & Westhus, N. K. (1981). The nurse role in parent-infant bonding. *Journal of Obstetric, Gynecologic, and Neonatal Nursing, 5* (6), 114-118.

Jones, T. (1982). The importance of the pregnant male. In C. Phillips and J. Anzalone, *Fathering: Participation in Labor and Birth*. St. Louis: Mosby.

Kantrowitz, B. (1986, March 31). A mother's choice. *Newsweek*, pp. 46-51.

Kennell, J. et al. (1975). Evidence for a sensitive period in the human mother. In Ciba Foundation, *Parent-Infant Interaction, Symposium 33*, Amsterdam: Elsevier.

Klaus, M., Jerauld, R., Kreger, N., McAlpine, W., Steffa, M. & Kennell, J. (1972). Maternal attachment: The importance of the first post-partum days. *New England Journal of medicine. 286*, 460-463.

Klaus, M. & Kennell, J. (1976). *Maternal-Infant Bonding*. St. Louis: Mosby.

Klaus, M. & Kennell, J. (1981). *Parent-Infant Bonding*. St. Louis: Mosby.

La Rossa, R. & La Rossa, M. M. (1981). *Transition to Parenthood*. Beverly Hills, CA: Sage.

Litoff, J. B. (1978). *American Midwives – 1860 to the Present*. Westport, CT: Greenwood Press.

McMillan, P. (1986, April 7). A shortage of hands to rock the cradle. *Los Angeles Times*, Part II pp. 1, 3.

Mehren, E. (1986, May 6). Employers and their pregnant employees. *Los Angeles Times*, Part V pp. 1, 6-7.

Merriam, S. B. & Hyer, P. (1984). Changing attitudes of women towards family related tasks in young adulthood. *Sex Roles, 10*, 825-835.

Miller, B. C. & Sollie, D. L. (1985). The transition to parenthood. In J. Henslin,

(Ed.). *Marriage and Family in a Changing Society, 2nd edition*. New York: Free Press.

National Center for Health Statistics (1985). Advance report of final natality statistics. *Monthly Vital Statistics Report*, 34 (No. 5, Supp).

Nelson, M. K. (1982). The effect of childbirth preparation on women of different social classes. *Journal of Health and Social Behavior, 23*, 339-352.

Nelson, M. K. (1983). Working-class women, middle-class women, and models of childbirth. *Social Problems, 30*, 284-297.

Oakley, A. (1979). *Becoming a Mother*. New York: Schocken.

Oakley, A. (1980). *Women Confined; Towards a Sociology of Childbirth*. New York: Schocken.

Palkovitz, R. (1985). Fathers' birth attendance, early contact, and extended contact with their newborns: A critical review. *Child Development, 56*, 392-406.

Palmeri, A. (1980). Childhood's end: Toward the liberation of children. In W. Aiken & H. La Follette, (Eds.), *Whose Child?* Totowa, NJ: Rowman and Littlefield.

Parachini, A. (1986, March 25). Over-35 pregnancy no longer termed "risky." *Los Angeles Times*. Part VI, pp. 1, 4.

Parfitt, R. (1977). *The Birth Primer*. Philadelphia: The Running Press.

Pfohl, S. (1977). The "discovery" of child abuse. *Social Problems, 24*, 310-323.

Phillips, C. & Anzalone, J. (1982). *Fathering: Participation in Labor and Birth*. St. Louis: Mosby.

Reece, C. (1982, July-August). Bringing children to work. *Children Today*, pp. 6-21.

Ringler, N. et al. (1975). Mother-to-child speech at two years—effects of early post-natal contact. *Journal of Pediatrics, 86*, 141-144.

Rising, S. (1974). The fourth stage of labor: Family integration. *American Journal of Nursing, 74*, 870-874.

Robinson, B. & Barret, R. (1986). *The Developing Father: Emerging Roles in Contemporary Society*. New York: Guilford.

Romalis, S. (Ed.). (1981). *Childbirth: Alternatives to Medical Control*. Austin: University of Texas Press.

Ross, C. E., Mirowski, J. & Huber, J. (1983). Dividing work, sharing work, and in-between. *American Sociological Review, 48*, 809-823.

Rossi, A. (1968). Transition to parenthood. *Journal of Marriage and the Family, 30*, 26-39.

Rothman, B. K. (1981). Awake and aware, or false consciousness: The cooption of childbirth reform in America. In S. Romalis, (Ed.), *Childbirth: Alternatives to Medical Control*. Austin: University of Texas Press.

Ruzek, S. (1978). *The Women's Health Movement: Feminist Alternatives to Medical Control*. New York: Praeger.

Seiden, A. (1978). A sense of mastery in the childbirth experience. In M. Notman & C. Nadelson, (Eds.), *The Woman Patient*. New York: Plenum.

Sekaran, U. (1983). Factors influencing the quality of life in dual career families. *Journal of Occupational Psychology, 56*, 161-174.

Smith, L. (1986, May 16). Day care now available for the mildly ill child. *Los Angeles Times*, Part V, pp. 1,4.

Stewart, D. & Stewart, L. (Eds.). (1976). *Safe Alternatives in Childbirth*. Chapel Hill, NC: NAPSAC.

Stewart, D. & Stewart, L. (Eds.). (1977). *21st Century Obstetrics Now*! Chapel Hill, NC: NAPSAC.

Traub, J. (1986, March). Goodbye, Dr. Spock: Vignettes from the brave new world of the better baby. *Harper's*, pp. 57-64.

Ventura, S. J. (1982). Trends in first births to older mothers, 1970-79. *Monthly Vital Statistics Report, 31* (No. 2, Supp.) National Center for Health Statistics.

Wennberg, R. N. (1985). *Life in the Balance: Exploring the Abortion Controversy*. Grand Rapids, MI: Eerdmans.

Wertz, R. & Wertz, D. (1977). *Lying-In: A History of Childbirth in America*. New York: Free Press.

Wessel, Helen (1963). *Natural Childbirth and the Christian Family*. New York: Harper and Row.

Woolery, L. & Barkley, N. (1981). Enhancing couple relationships during prenatal and postnatal classes. *Maternal-Child Nursing Journal, 6*, 184-188.

Yankelovich, D. (1981). *New Rules*. New York: Random House.

Parenthood
and Adult Development

Philip R. Newman
Barbara M. Newman

We began this paper with the assumption that there is new psychological growth during adulthood. This is not an altogether new or bold assumption, yet it is surprisingly undeveloped in the research literature. In casting around for an explanation for how cognitive and emotional growth might take a new course in adulthood, we were struck by our own role of adulthood. In some cultures, becoming a parent is a major indicator of adult status. If any new experiences of adulthood were to produce a period of openness to new learning and to stimulate new coping strategies, parenting must certainly be a prime candidate.

The purpose of this paper, then, is to explore the parent role as a vehicle for stimulating further cognitive and emotional development. The emphasis of the paper is on the impact of parenting on adults, rather than on children. We begin by arguing that the nature of the attachment that is formed between a parent and his or her children has unique characteristics that distinguish it from the attachment formed by a child for his or her parents. We then focus on the process of parenting as a stimulus for six areas of cognitive growth and seven areas of emotional growth.

We focus on what we believe is possible when adults approach parenting as a positive, desirable role. We are aware that many adults resist or reject their parenting role. In some cases, adults who

Philip R. Newman, PhD, is Adjunct Professor, Department of Home Economics Education, Ohio State University; Barbara M. Newman, PhD, is Associate Provost for faculty recruitment and development, Office of Academic Affairs, Ohio State University, Columbus, OH 43210.

313

become parents turn against their children or drop to new, low levels of functioning. However, it is our intention to identify the growth promoting possibilities of this important role. Given the critical importance of parenting for species survival, it is highly unlikely that the enactment of the parent role should prove detrimental for most adults. On the contrary, we suspect that parenting brings new levels of insight and social commitment that contribute in positive ways to the overall evolution of the culture.

Parenting is certainly not the only aspect of adult experience that might contribute to new growth. However, parenting is a very common experience of adulthood and one that is both intense and prolonged. Thus, if we are searching for the mechanisms that may underly development in adulthood, parenting appears to be a most fruitful arena to investigate.

PARENTAL ATTACHMENT

The process of forming attachments and reworking them is a natural part of the development of individuals (Bowlby, 1958). As a child, you are part of a family system. Your initial attachments are focused on those primary caregivers who nurture and protect you. As a parent, you create an extension of this system that carries you, your offspring, and their potential offspring forward in time. The attachment of an adult to a child and the efforts of the adult to promote the child's growth open channels for new directions in the psychological development of the adult.

An understanding of the concept of social attachment is fundamental to an understanding of human relationships. During life, people are usually involved with a specific group of others who fill their needs and provide them with love, affection, and support. These are the people who occupy your thoughts and become the targets of many of your actions.

Attachment can be viewed as a characteristic of an individual, as when you identify the number and quality of a person's attachments. Attachment can be viewed as a characteristic of a dyad, as when you assess the quality of the mother-infant or father-infant bond. Attachment can also be viewed as a characteristic of a social system such as a family. When you specify the quality of the relationships and the pattern of affective bonds among family members, you are investigating attachment at the level of the family system. (See Figure 1.)

Usually attachment is described as an interactive process in which each partner is reactive to the presence and the behaviors of the other. There appear to be different kinds of attachment bonds. Harlow (1974) described five forms of attachment: a child's love for the mother, peer love, heterosexual love, maternal love, and paternal love. In his conceptualization, these forms occur in the order listed and each form of attachment requires the experience of the earlier forms.

For every normal person, there is a specifiable set of individuals who constitute the objects of attachment at every point in the life span. A person's attachment structure usually changes during the course of life (Kahn & Antonucci, 1980). The attachment structure of a young child may consist of mother, father, and sibling(s). The attachment structure of the same person as an adult may consist of wife, children, mother, two good friends, a sibling and a cousin.

A person's attachment structure may change during the course of the adult years. The loss of a spouse is an example of a radical change in a person's attachment structure that is experienced by many older adults. Anderson (1984) found that after widowhood, for example, relationships with siblings and distant kin became closer. Relationships with sons and daughters were intimate, but not much different for widowed and married women. Thus, the parent-child attachment was not really affected by the death of the spouse, but the attachments to other family members were changed.

Developmental psychologists have done a great deal of research over the past twenty years to describe the attachments of infants to their caregivers. In general, it has been found that infants try to remain near the object(s) of their attachment (Ainsworth, 1973). They tend to show distress when the object(s) of attachment is (are) missing (Schaffer & Emerson, 1964). Infants tend to be more relaxed and comfortable with the object(s) of their attachment and more uncomfortable with other people (Bronson, 1973). Researchers have shown that infants may be attached to more than one person (Lamb, 1976).

A. Attachments that describe an individual

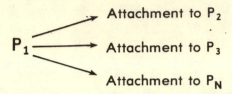

B. Attachments that describe a dyadic relationship

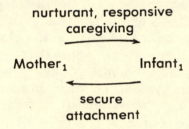

C. Attachments that describe a system

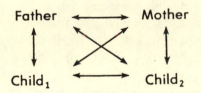

Figure 1. Three Levels of Attachment

We would argue that these signs of attachment apply for adults as well as for infants and young children. Adults try to remain near the objects of their attachment; they experience distress when the object(s) of attachment is (are) missing; and they are more relaxed and comfortable with the objects of their attachment, and more uncomfortable with other people. Evidence for the continuity of early parental attachment relationships can be inferred from surveys of adults and their parents. Evidence of continuing attachment relationships among parents and their adult children can be seen in the following characteristics: living in a neighboring community; frequently visiting and interacting over the phone; helping each other; experiencing the emotional intensity of the parent-child bond; sharing values, rituals, and norms; and expressing family solidarity (Troll, 1971; Hartup & Lempers, 1973).

In American society, there appears to be a strong norm for older parents to live in separate homes from their adult children. However, Shanas and her co-workers (Shanas et al., 1968) found that 84% of the people in their sample who were over 65 lived less than an hour's drive away from one of their children. About 30% of aging parents lived with their adult children. Shanas also found that a greater proportion of parents continue to provide help to their adult children than those who receive help from their children. In a more recent survey, Cicirelli (1981) found that 49% of the three hundred elderly adults he interviewed in Lafayette, Indiana had one or more children living in Lafayette as well.

The attachment of a parent for a child has many characteristics in common with the attachment of a child for a parent. However, we hypothesize that the attachment of a parent for a child is a new kind of bond that is in some ways distinct from the attachment of a child for his or her mother or father. One of the primary characteristics of this new bond is the strong sense of responsibility that parents feel for protecting and caring for the child. Emotional benefits of the attachment come not only from being with the child but from fulfilling the child's needs. Emotional stresses that come from the inability to meet the child's needs are powerful stimuli for the development of new coping strategies. The attachment to a child is also unusual in that it is a recurring bond. With the birth of each new child, there is a new well of emotional investment, one that does not replace or diminish the care and love that is felt for each previous child.

The attachment to one's parents as a child involves a situation in which the parents have primary responsibility for the safety, protection, and nurturance of the child. The young child may be strongly motivated to be near the parents and may feel emotionally secure in the situation. He or she does not, however, have to make major life decisions for the parent or perform the actions necessary to execute these decisions.

Attachments to one's mate, siblings, friends, and even sometimes to one's parents in adolescence are characterized by greater equality in relationship. The two parties to the attached relationship generally work out groundrules that allow the relationship to function in a mutually satisfying way. Sometimes, this means that one person provides nurturance, support, and affection for the other. At other times, the second person provides nurturance, support, and affection. Most often, the two partners in the attachment relationship have relatively equal positions in providing an emotionally satisfying relationship for each other.

Attachments to children require that adults take on responsibility for caregiving and protection. A child's chances for survival are literally in the parents' hands. Authority, resources, and responsibility are distributed unevenly. The parent has more or all while the child has little or none. A sense of emotional peace may be difficult to achieve when one carries total responsibility for the survival of a child. For most adults, this is not a situation that has been experienced before. Parents must learn to cope with this new type of stress resulting from attachment based on unequal responsibility.

Evidence for differences between the parents' attachment to children and the child's attachment to parents is found in research on the relationship of parents and their adult children. Parents appear to overestimate the affection and closeness that exists between themselves and their adult children. Parents think that they are more like their children in values and beliefs than the children's responses suggest. Parents tend to worry more about their children than their children worry about them. The adult children report a stronger feeling of kinship obligation than do the parents (Bengston & Troll, 1978; Cicirelli, 1981). Emotions tend to run strong in families, positive, negative, or both. The perception of family solidarity, however, remains strong among middle-aged and older family members despite conflicts over specific issues.

There is considerable evidence to suggest that parents perceive the outcome of their attachment for their children as deeply satisfying. Hoffman and Manis (1978) reported on the changes that husbands and wives described after having their first child. These are some of the statements of first-time parents.

1. The birth of a child changes one into an adult or represents the point of entry into the adult role.
2. The birth of a child brings new responsibilities.
3. The birth of a child means a new status in the community and among relatives and friends.
4. The birth of a child requires a readjustment of tasks.
5. The birth of a child leads to a transformation from "couple" to "family."
6. Couples see children as bringing them closer together because of interdependence of functions and the sharing of a common goal.
7. The child provides enormous satisfaction.

In the Hoffman and Manis research, 95% or more of men and women with little to high levels of education reported a great deal of satisfaction from parenthood of preschool and elementary school age children. For mothers with children at every age, parenthood was viewed as providing the greatest source of satisfaction among life activities. For fathers, parenthood was a strong source of satisfaction, but for fathers with children at certain ages being married was as or more important than parenting. However, parenting more often provided a great deal of satisfaction than the father's occupation.

The overwhelming positive feelings associated with parenting, particularly while children are at the preschool levels, indicates an harmonious chord between the parents' motives to insure the survival of their offspring and the child's need to be taken care of. These American parents experienced a strong sense of satisfaction as a result of the efforts they expended to take care of their young children.

Of course, the fact that parents feel a strong bond of affection for their children and a strong sense of commitment to the parenting role does not mean that there are no difficulties associated with parenting. It certainly does not mean that all adults are "good" parents. In Hoffman and Manis' survey, the following problems were identified:

1. Loss of freedom particularly for parents with young children.
2. Financial disadvantages.
3. Interference with mother's employment (this drops when children reach school age and mothers return to work).
4. Concerns about world conditions presenting dangers and uncertainties for children.
5. Concerns about the child's health and safety increase over the years as children move into adolescence.

As children get older they seem to interfere less with the parents' lives, but they become an increasing source of concern and worry for parents. Parents exchange high levels of caregiving and nurturing for high levels of vigilance. Parents worry more about girls than boys.

The emphasis of an adult's parental attachment shifts as children get older. In the Hoffman and Manis survey, parents of young children evaluated their success in terms of the love and affection they provided for their children. Parents of teenagers evaluated their success on the basis of whether or not there was communication with their children and an understanding of them. In a study of older mothers, Rossi (1980) saw changes in the parents' perceptions of the difficulties involved in parenting, but also changes in the difficulties involved in growing up. Mothers saw their children's teenage years as a period when it was more difficult for the child growing up than for the adults who were parenting.

Parents begin rather early to foster independence in their children. American families strongly value independence. This value is reflected in common childrearing techniques. Parents expect their babies to sleep in separate rooms. They place their babies down on the floor or in a playpen while they attend to other tasks. Babies are usually weaned at five or six months from the breast and toilet training begins in many families as soon as the baby can walk. Parents hire young adolescents to babysit for their infants while they leave the home. They urge their toddlers to feed themselves, to dress themselves, and to play by themselves. Almost 40% of three- and four-year-old children are enrolled in preschool or daycare. Many begin in all day programs as early as six months of age. These parenting strategies are viewed as appropriate preparation for establishing the level of independence necessary to cope with life away from parents.

At the same time, conflicts over independence are common. Parents complain about their child's willfulness. Although there are many things children do independently at their parents' urging, there are also many things children want to do independently which parents will not allow. In the best of situations, parents try to design the environment so that toddlers can function independently without risk to their safety. In the worst situations, toddlers are drastically restricted in their exploration of the environment and punished when they attempt to exercise their autonomy.

During the period of adolescence a dynamic conflict between attachment and independence appears to be played out in most families (Garbarino, Sebes, & Schellenbach, 1984). In adolescence the conflict over independence becomes intensified since a child's initiatives may have more clear and long-term consequences. The child's desire for independence is often expressed at a behavioral level. Adolescents may express their independence in the kinds of clothes they wear or the kinds of records they buy. Most adolescents do not achieve an independence of values. They do not have moral beliefs or life goals that are very discrepant from those of their parents. However, in studies of the differences in values between parents and adolescents, Lerner (1975) found that parents tend to minimize the extent of the differences while adolescents tend to maximize the extent of the differences.

Our sense is that the ambivalence that is expressed by adult children with regard to filial obligation toward their parents is based, to an important degree, on the way that the conflicts between attachment and independence are resolved during adolescence. For parents, the challenge is to adjust the attachment bond with the child toward a more mutual relationship. The issue of total responsibility and inequality of resources that characterized the early parent-infant attachment is not appropriate to the relationship with a child who is eighteen or twenty years old. This is a transition that is difficult for many parents to make. In some cases, parents abandon their sense of obligation so fully that an adolescent child feels rejected. In other cases parents may refuse to give up their authority so that an adolescent child has to fight for freedom or feel emotionally oppressed.

There is still a great deal left to explore about the nature of the attachment relationship between parents and their adult children. We know that parents do not stop being concerned about their children when the children reach adulthood. We know that parents and their adult children maintain contact and participate in mutual help giving. But the quality of the attachment from the parents' side has not been fully described. Anderson (1984) found that widows discuss different concerns with their adult children and with other attachment figures. They would discuss their emotional problems with their children, but not concerns about their health or finances. These concerns were more likely to be discussed with siblings. Do parents ever really think of their children in the same way that they think of friends or siblings? Do parents ever fully relinquish a view of themselves as the protector, the rescuer, or the one who knows best? How does the parental bond change when children have children of their own? These are questions that we will undoubtedly be able to investigate as the study of parenting takes on a more complete life span perspective.

Summary

The attachment process is central to human relationships. A person's attachment structure can change over the life course. Some characteristics of attachment are the same for the bond children form for their parents and the bond parents form for their children. But in some ways, the attachment of parents for their children is unique. It is normally characterized by a strong sense of responsibility and an uneven distribution of resources and authority.

Evidence suggests that most parents find their attachment for their child(ren) to be deeply satisfying. This is especially true for parents when children are in the preschool and elementary school years. Parents express more worries about their children as the children reach adolescence.

As children reach adolescence, there is a need to redefine the parent-child attachment toward a relationship of greater mutuality and equality. The quality of the parents' attachment for adult children has not been fully explored.

PARENTING AND COGNITIVE DEVELOPMENT IN ADULTHOOD

Cognitive growth in adulthood is prompted by discrepancies between the preparation, expectations and competence of the person and the demands of new roles and new situations. Parenthood might not be especially growth promoting for adults if everything they experienced as a parent were close to what they had expected and prepared for. However, from the time of the first pregnancy adults embark on a voyage of discrepancies and the unforeseen events of parenthood. This voyage begins as the adult makes an emotional and intellectual commitment to his or her unborn child. During pregnancy a relationship forms between the mother, the father, and the fetus. This relationship becomes more clearly articulated after fetal movement is felt. The strength of this relationship is illustrated in the following story.

Recently we visited with friends who had their second child about eighteen months ago. The mother suffered from preeclampsia during pregnancy. She was hospitalized for five weeks of her pregnancy as they waited for the fetus to develop to a stage that would permit it to survive before it was delivered. The waiting was like a game of Russian Roulette. How long could they keep the baby in utero without resulting in convulsions or death for the mother? The mother became increasingly ill as she waited for her baby to get big enough to survive. Eventually the physicians delivered the baby by Caesarian section at twenty-eight weeks gestation.

The baby was in the hospital seven more weeks until he was large enough to take home. A year and a half later, the baby is still chronically ill. He does not sleep through the night. He is tiny. He does not walk or talk. But he has a wonderful smile, and he is responsive to his environment. He is playful and enjoys the companionship of his older brother and friends. His parents are exhausted. They feel as though they are just emerging from a cocoon of total preoccupation with this strange childbirth experience. Nevertheless, they treasure their child and marvel at his capacity for survival.

In this situation, the parents were willing to risk severe illness for the mother in order to increase their unborn baby's chances of survival. The mother's life was temporarily confined to the hospital; she was separated from her older child, her husband, and her friends. She entered a period of progressive illness in order to provide a few more weeks of time in utero for her baby.

Entry into parenthood takes one down a new path that is jointly guided by the competencies, history, and vulnerabilities of the adult parents and by the competencies, history, and vulnerabilities of the children. There is no telling exactly what needs an infant will have. We all expect a healthy, bright, physically perfect child. But we may have a child who is born deaf, developmentally delayed, or low birth weight. We may expect a child whose temperament is a close match to our own, but we may have a child who is far more active, sensitive, or withdrawn than we are. We may expect a child to grow up and marry as we did, but we may have a child who chooses to remain single. We may expect a child who will bring honor to our family name, but we may have a child who becomes a criminal, a business failure, or who commits suicide.

Enactment of the parent role forces one to become more probabilistic in one's thinking. You simply cannot count on things turning out exactly as you had planned. Unpredictabilities can be serious, as in the example of the high risk pregnancy. Unpredictabilities can also be minor frustrations. Your baby spits up on the dress you were planning to wear to a party. Your son gets sick the night before you are to go away on a trip. Your babysitter cancels on Sunday when you and your husband are both to be at work on Monday. The degree of unpredictability in daily life increases dramatically from the moment you have your first bout of morning sickness and continues throughout the parenting years.

Encounters with unpredictabilities and discrepancies can produce a contingency based thinking. Adults learn to consider two or three possible outcomes for any given situation and to prepare for the alternatives. Encounters with diversity can also create a more highly differentiated view of reality. Parents recognize that their child is more complex than they had expected, and that they too as well as their spouse are more complex than they once had expected. All aspects of the family, but especially its capacity for flexible responding, become highlighted. Adults move from a rather stereotyped idea of what families are like and how they should function to a more individualistic view of their own family and its ability to cope with unpredictable and changing realities.

Involvement with limit setting and discipline bring another stimulus for cognitive growth. This is where some serious confusion about the parent role can begin. For example, when a child is an infant most parents would not get angry at the baby and scold him if he didn't fall asleep at a certain time. They would sing to the baby, rub his back, rock him in their arms, take him for a ride in the car, or try any number of other strategies to lull him off to sleep. But when the baby becomes a toddler, parents might assume that a refusal to go to bed is defiance. They may believe that the child is willfully opposing them. They may also believe that it is their responsibility as a parent to set firm limits and to show a child that there are consequences for breaking the rules.

The issue of adult authority is very strong for the parents of toddlers. An invisible audience watches as you enact your parental role. How were you treated when you disobeyed your parents? You were not allowed to get away with things. Are you going to let your child get away with them? You begin to hear the voices of your spouse, your parents, your in-laws, and your neighbors shaking their heads in disapproval. "You're too easy on the boy!" "You'll spoil him!" At the same time, you have just emerged from the experience of parenting an infant. This experience has left you feeling closer and more enmeshed in a person's life than you have ever felt before. How are you to switch from the nurturing protector to the force for law and order? How are you going to combine empathic caring and firm authoritativeness?

Parenting produces a philosophy of life. This philosophy is shaped and refined as your children change and grow. The degree to which you are open to the needs and messages your children send to you influences the development of your personal philosophy. The clarity of the values you carry with you from your earlier socialization, and the extent to which those values appear to apply to your adult life situation also influence this philosophy.

But the heart of the philosophy is forged in the process of meeting the needs of your own children. You may be surprised at the direction your philosophy takes. We certainly were. You may find yourself saying that your child's care and education are more important than your own career. You may find yourself saying that your children will have to learn that your needs and the needs of other adults come first. You may find yourself believing that you do not really have control over your child's destiny and that life in your family will be a process of mutual negotiation. You may find yourself believing that you really know what is best and that it is in the best interest of your children for them to do as you say.

The first expression of your philosophy is likely to be heavily influenced by what you remember from your own childhood. However, as your children become more articulate and competent, they become a more active force in challenging the logic or appropriateness of that philosophy. After all, you are not your parent, and your children are not you. The power of the situation frees you from your past. You are not required to do things as they were done but to do things in a way that makes sense for your children, your family, and your own needs.

This is the beginning of the truly proactive period of adult life. A deep sense of caring about the safety and survival of your children as well as your own analysis of the future fosters development during this period. The limits you set, the ways you enforce these limits, and the goals you articulate for your children have to make sense for the people in your family. Your children serve to connect you to the past, but they also free you from the past. You realize that your future and their future are not identical. You may be bound in to the agenda that was set for you as a child, but your children need not be bound by that same agenda.

One might expect that parenting would promote a greater appreciation for individual differences. It certainly has for us. There is no way we could have deliberately socialized our children to be different in the ways they are different. We do not possess many of their qualities and talents. We would not know what to do to try to make a child more willful or more fanciful or more energetic. We certainly would not be able to create the blend of qualities that have emerged in each of our children.

An appreciation of individual differences helps take some of the pressure off parents for being responsible for everything their children do. We could not get our son to eat green beans when he was an infant, and we still cannot get him to eat green beans. We have given it every effort, but we view it as something beyond our control. We now respect his right to have taste preferences of his own, and we expect him to respect our taste preferences when it comes to television viewing, music, and other differences in the way we like to spend leisure time.

Riegel (1976) identified the capacity to hold two or more opposing ideas in the mind at once as one of the characteristics of adult cognition. Parenting contributes to the development of this capacity. For example, parents say that as a result of having children they feel closer to one another. At the same time, they say that there is a greater division of labor and a more traditional definition of the male and female roles in family life (Hoffman & Manis, 1978). This is an apparent contradiction. Yet, a couple may feel closer to one another due to the shared bond they have with their child and the sense of mutual responsibility they feel for the child's well being. At the same time, the two partners may tend to emphasize different contributions to the parent role and identify distinct areas of childrearing responsibilities. The two opposing realities exist side by side, and they each exist in the mind of each parent.

The theme of attachment and separation provides another example in which adults hold two opposing ideas in the mind at once. Parents have both goals in mind as they parent. Most parents want to remain close to their children. They continue to have a strong bond of affection for their children, and they worry about their children's safety and welfare. At the same time, they take pride in signs of their children's independence and encourage their children to be self-sufficient. Both attachment and separateness are characteristics of the parent-child relationship and both make sense. Most parents work hard to develop bonds of mutual affection, and most parents work hard to make sure that their children are independent. In order to do this, parents must behave effectively while they hold two distinctly opposing concept systems in mind at the same time.

Another cognitive capacity that is strengthened through parenting is the ability to anticipate the future. Anticipation involves an assessment of probable outcomes and strategies for preparing for those outcomes. This is central to the parent function. Adults anticipate a child's need for food, and take supplies along when they leave the house. Parents anticipate a child's need for a safe environment and modify the home so that poisons, sharp objects, and electric outlets are inaccessible. As children get older, parents anticipate needs for social interactions, special educational opportunities, or skill development. Parents also anticipate dangers children may encounter and teach their children rules and strategies for avoiding those dangers.

The investment a person has in a child's survival and growth motivates careful thinking about the child's probable needs and vulnerabilities. Knowing about their children, parents anticipate areas where help is needed and where problems are likely to arise. Practice in anticipation is likely to improve this skill and to generalize to the use of anticipatory thinking in other domains of life, such as work and personal life planning.

A final cognitive capacity that is prompted by parenting is the expansion of consciousness. This expression refers to a broadening of awareness of self and others, a greater appreciation of past, present, and future, and the capacity to function at many levels of abstraction. The broadening of awareness of self and others occurs as parents try to fulfill a child's needs. Parents see the world from the perspective of their children as well as from their own perspective. They recognize that opposing needs may exist simultaneously and that both sets of needs have legitimacy. As parents struggle to create a family environment that is comfortable and flexible for people at different developmental levels, they become more and more aware that different points of view exist about the same objective reality.

An increased capacity to conceptualize past, present, and future occurs as parents anticipate their future and the future their children will encounter. Parents recognize that they and their children occupy overlapping but not identical futures. They also recognize the difference between their own past and the past as it appears to their children. When your children ask you if you had television when you were a child, you realize how distant your own past must appear to them. Yet for us, childhood seems only a moment ago. Although we all occupy the same present, the sense of time and its subjective meaning is extremely different for the infant, the toddler, the young adolescent, and the parent. These differences are highlighted in the parenting process as adults attempt to help their children delay gratification, plan for the future, or learn from the past.

The capacity to function at varied levels of abstraction is enhanced as parents interact with their children at every point of development. Parents have the opportunity to retrieve skills at the sensorimotor, preoperational, concrete operational, and formal operational levels of reasoning. The characteristics of each of these kinds of thinking is made more vivid as parents try to communicate with and influence their children. Parents are reminded of the kinds of thinking they used and relied on as children. They are also reintroduced to the subtleties of functioning at each of these levels. By renewing these cognitive skills, adults have the potential for approaching problem solving with a more flexible array of strategies. The ability to relieve tensions through the slow, relaxed breathing one observes in a resting baby is no less significant than the ability to conceptualize a new problem and begin to solve it.

Summary

Discrepancies between the competencies and expectations an adult has and the realities the adult encounters provide a stimulus for cognitive growth. Parenting is a role in which there is a great deal of discrepancy and usually a strong motivation to resolve discrepancy.

Parenting is viewed as having potential influence on six aspects of cognitive development during adulthood. First, parenting requires a more probabilistic view of the future and an accompanying contingency approach to planning. Second, parenting promotes the formulation of a philosophy of life in which the rules and limits parents impose on their children are related to central values and goals.

Third, parenting supports greater appreciation for individual differences and a more highly differentiated view of individual strengths, weaknesses, and potential. Fourth, parenting requires and promotes the capacity to hold two or more opposing ideas in the mind at the same time. Fifth, the need to protect and nurture children requires the development of greater skills in anticipating the future.

Finally, parenting has the potential consequence of expanding the realm of consciousness. This includes a greater awareness of self and others, an increased capacity to conceptualize past, present, and future, and the capacity to function at varied levels of abstraction.

PARENTING AND EMOTIONAL DEVELOPMENT IN ADULTHOOD

Robert White (1966) has suggested that one characteristic of change in adulthood is the expansion of caring. Parenting contributes to this process in several significant ways.

Parenthood brings a depth of commitment that is almost without analogy. Adults tie their lives to the future of their child in a blind act of faith. This speaks to the powerful instinct for survival that accompanies the commitment to reproduction and parenting. Parents struggle over how to express this commitment. Not all parents are required to put their lives on the line for the child's survival, yet some do. However, many parents say that they give up personal freedom, privacy, financial resources, sleep, and peace of mind. When problems are more severe, parents may give up economic security, mental health, or physical health in order to protect and nurture their children. This kind of commitment is not limited to the periods of infancy and childhood. For example, many parents of mentally retarded adults continue to support and nurture their children. Parents of a divorced daughter may take her and her children in to live with them until the daughter can find work. Adult children who become unemployed may turn to their parents for financial help.

The depth of parental attachment is fostered by the nature of the human infant's behavior. You watch with fascination as your baby is totally engrossed with eating. Her eyes close, her body relaxes, and she is focused on one thing—nursing. The comfort you give to infants by changing them out of cold diapers or wrapping them in warm blankets is deeply satisfying. One of the most relaxing activities of parenting we can recall was rocking our baby to sleep. As the tension flows out of the baby, it also flows out of your body. The baby teaches lessons about the total enjoyment of having one's physical needs met. Harlow (1976) has emphasized the role of contact comfort in an infant's attachment for mother. From a parent's point of view, contact with an infant can be equally powerful and comforting.

Infants explore in an immediate and physical way. They suck, grab, and gaze at their target, absorbing you in every way they can. The physical nature of these interactions opens up an intense channel of intimacy in the parent-infant relationship. There is no form of physical closeness quite like this. Hugging, rocking, tickling, tumbling, snuggling, and stroking a child open up avenues for the expression of affection that are often unused or under-used in adult relationships.

Parents of infants quickly find out they they are not in control. Their own patterns for sleeping, eating, and even bathing or eliminating become controlled by the baby's patterns. If one makes an effort to be a responsive parent, it soon becomes obvious that the power and control we thought were part of adulthood are simply illusory. Parenthood requires that a person learn ways to achieve a balance between meeting one's own needs and the needs of others. Fortunately most parents are invested enough in their children that they are willing to revise their views of control and authority in light of their children's needs.

As a parent of early-school-age and middle-school-age children, one has opportunities to introduce ideas, resources, and activities into a child's life. As your children gain in competence, they will bring ideas, resources, and activities from their own world into yours. This is a rich and stimulating time of parenthood. You try to model your values and beliefs in your behavior, and you enjoy the reinforcement that comes in the admiration your children have for you.

This is an important contribution to adult emotional development. Children can make you feel important. They tell you you are important. You can sense your importance to them in the way they react to you. You can sense your importance in the things other people say to you about your children.

This is a source of support and encouragement for parents. It continues to nurture the sense of responsibility that most people feel at the beginning of parenthood. It also strengthens the attachment that parents have for their children because children are such a powerful source of reinforcement for them. While at work, you may get the sense that someone else could do your job if you were not present. In a family, children send a message that you are really irreplaceable. No one has the meaning and value to your child that you do. The feeling that you matter and that your life has meaning because of your role as a parent makes an important contribution to your sense of psychological well-being.

Parents develop a strong sense of empathy for their children through the bond of attachment. The whole range of emotional reactions that may have been evoked in response to events effecting the spouse are now extended to events effecting the children. The first experience of this deepening of emotion is a parent's response to a newborn's cry. The first cries have an especially powerful effect. There is almost no way a mother can prevent herself from responding to these cries even when she knows that the cry is most likely only a signal for food, and not a signal of life-threatening danger. The reaction is immediate and intense. In another example of heightened emotional intensity, consider the way a parent feels when a nine-month-old child expresses separation anxiety. The baby clings, cries, and reaches out for you as you go out the door. The emotional response in the adult is powerful, even though the adult may know that the baby will stop crying shortly and that his needs will be adequately met by the substitute caregiver. As children grow up, the array of emotions they experience is often shared by their empathic parents.

Emotional development is also promoted by a parent's direct reactions to a child's behavior. Here we are not speaking about an empathic reaction to the child's emotional state, but a direct reaction to behaviors that parents view as desirable or undesirable. Children can provoke powerful emotional reactions in parents. They can make you feel warm, joyful, and proud. They can make you feel furious, guilty, and disgusted. Because of the deep commitment and love most parents feel for children, their emotional reactions to a child's behavior can be especially intense. It is one thing if someone else's child is rude or selfish. But, if your own child is rude or selfish intense feelings of anger, disgust, or embarrassment may be stimulated. Similarly, you may feel pleased by the success of a neighbor's child, but the success of your own child gives rise to the peculiar parental emotion called "gloating." This gloating involves a sense of pride in the accomplishments of someone who is an extension of you.

Adults may be surprised at the intensity of their reactions to a child's behavior. They may be unprepared to cope with those intense emotions or they may struggle to restrict the expression of those emotions as evidence of immaturity. However, we would suggest that the intensity of those reactions is an appropriate sign of the deep investment of the parent in the child and speaks to the potential for emotional intensity in human relationships that is usually unexpressed in daily social encounters.

A deepening of emotions and increased understanding of emotions is achieved as parents play a therapeutic role for their children. One of the primary parental functions is to help children maintain a sense of emotional well-being. Parents help their children understand, express, and cope with the emotions they are having. Children turn to their parents for comfort when they are frightened. They seek parental reassurance when they have been rejected or when they experience failure. They want their parents' approval when they succeed. In all these instances, many parents learn to listen, to reflect the child's feelings, and to try to help the child accept his or her emotional state.

Parents learn that if they want to be helpful to their children, they have to learn to remain emotionally objective. They try to listen carefully and offer support. As parents play out this role, they begin to think about the child's emotional reactions. The child's emotions are a stimulus for adult thoughts about the meaning of emotions and the value of these emotions for the child. Parents develop strategies for helping children manage their fears and doubts. These strategies may involve modifying behavior, as when a parent decides to limit television viewing before bedtime. The strategies may involve increasing a child's conceptual awareness as when explaining why a child might tease another child and how to handle teasing. The strategies may involve suggestions for emotional management as when one tells a child "Big boys don't cry." The advice and strategies parents communicate to their children contribute to their own adult analysis of emotional expression. We suspect that parents become more accepting of their own emotional expressiveness as they see the role of emotions in the daily lives of their children and as they experience the sense of closeness that comes from expressing and responding to emotions in the parent-child relationship.

Summary

Parenting contributes to the expansion of caring. Seven aspects of emotional development were discussed as potential consequences of parenting. First, parenting brings a depth of commitment that is tied to the responsibility one feels for the survival of a child. The depth of commitment is strengthened through the reinforcing nature of the infant's responses to attempts to meet his or her needs.

Second, parenting brings adults into contact with new channels for expressing affection. Third, parenting requires that adults achieve a balance between meeting their own needs and meeting the needs of others. Fourth, parenting enhances an adult's feeling of value and well-being through the significant role the adult plays in the child's life.

Fifth, parents achieve a degree of empathy for their child that widens the array of their emotional experiences. Sixth, parents may experience intense emotional reactions to their child's behavior. Seventh, many parents learn to assist their child in expressing and understanding emotions. By playing a therapeutic role for their children, parents may become more effective in accepting and expressing their own emotions.

CONCLUDING REMARKS

We want to emphasize that development is not complete as one enters the parent role. Through participation in parenting, new areas of growth can be stimulated and new competencies can be developed. New attachments are formed with each child in which the adult assumes the primary responsibility for the survival of a new person. This responsibility leads to many new questions about the meaning of one's own life as well as one's capacity to protect and provide for the life of another. The parent becomes the designer of the child's physical, social, and emotional environment.

Entry into parenthood is an irreversible transition. It involves one in lifelong relationships that must be continuously redefined. In this respect, parenting is one of the most difficult roles of adult life. Becoming a parent involves deeply intense emotional relationships that have to be managed. A parent quickly becomes aware of the centrality of his or her behavior for a child. As the child becomes involved in an expanding network of peers, heterosexual partners, a marriage partner, and children, the parent must adjust to being drawn into relationships that are not of his or her own making.

It seems obvious that a number of cognitive skills are potentially enhanced by being a parent, many of which relate to social cognition. Most of these have not been systematically investigated. While we know a fair amount about the skills that are developed up through the high school and college levels, we simply do not know much about the characteristics of these adult capacities. We assume that new methods of investigation will be necessary in order to examine these processes. It is not likely that most adults are aware of changes in these directions or that they could label these consequences of parenting.

The area of emotional growth is closely tied to the deep investment a parent has for a child. However, we expect that there is an optimal level of attachment for a child that allows a parent to benefit most from parenting experiences. If the parent is indifferent to the child, the level of empathy with the child will be less and the capacity to serve a therapeutic role for the child is unlikely to emerge. If the parent is overly identified with the child or unwilling to permit the child to differentiate, the degree of objectivity is lost that permits a greater understanding of the role of emotions in human relationships.

For the future, we urge a renewed commitment to the systematic investigation of psychological development during adulthood. Our paper proposes some basic, causal relations between parenting and continued growth in adulthood. These propositions can best be evaluated through longitudinal studies of adults as they experience the enactment of the parent role. Specific comparisons might also be made to assess the contribution of other life roles to some of the cognitive and affective gains proposed in this paper. Do people who have parented differ in important respects from people who have not parented? Given the increased control we have over our fertility, it is critical for us to understand the implications of alternative life paths for the further maturation of adults.

It is not surprising that we see parenting as contributing a deeply humanizing element to adult development. To the extent that adults are committed to their parenting role, they find it to be among the most satisfying achievements of a lifetime. Given the human being's propensity for adaptation and growth, we believe it is highly likely that this important adult role would provide a wealth of psychologically enhancing by-products. These by-products help sustain the parent during the nurturing period and invite future generations to look upon parenting with positive anticipation. To the extent that this does not happen in a society, the long-term survival of the culture is jeopardized.

REFERENCES

Ainsworth, M. D. S. (1973). The development of infant-mother attachment. In B. M. Caldwell and H. N. Ricciuti (Eds.) *Review of child development research, Vol. 3.* Chicago: University of Chicago Press.

Anderson, T. B. (1984). Widowhood as a life transition: Its impact on kinship ties. *Journal of Marriage and the Family, 46,* 105-114.

Bengston, V. L., and Troll, L. (1978). Feedback and intergenerational influence in socialization. In R. M. Lerner and G. B. Spanier (Eds.) *Child influences on marital and family interaction: A life-span perspective.* New York: Academic Press.

Bowlby, J. (1958). The nature of the child's tie to his mother. *International Journal of Psychoanalysis, 39,* 1-23.

Bronson, G. W. (1973). Infants' reactions to an unfamiliar person, In L. J. Stone, H. T. Smith, and L. B. Murphy (Eds.) *The competent infant.* New York: Basic Books.

Cicirelli, V. G. (1981). *Helping elderly parents: The role of adult children.* Boston: Auburn House.

Harlow, H. F. (1974). *Learning to love*. New York: Jason Aronson.

Hartup, W. W. and Lempers, J. (1974). A problem in life-span development: The interactional analysis of family attachments. In P. B. Baltes and K. W. Schaie (Eds.) *Life-span developmental psychology, Vol. 3*. New York: Academic Press.

Hoffman, L. W. and Manis, J. D. (1978). Influences of children on marital interaction and parental satisfactions and dissatisfactions. In R. M. Lerner and G. B. Spanier (Eds.) *Child influences on marital and family interaction: A life-span perspective*. New York: Academic Press, pp. 165-214.

Kahn, R. L. and Antonucci, T. C. (1980). Convoys over the life course: Attachment, roles, and social support. In P. B. Baltes (Ed.) *Life-span development and behavior*, Vol. 3. New York: Academic Press.

Lamb, M. E. (1976). Twelve-month-olds and their parents: Interaction in a laboratory playroom. *Developmental Psychology, 12*, 237-244.

Lerner, R. M. (1975). Showdown at generation gap: Attitudes of adolescents and their parents toward contemporary issues. In H. D. Thornburg (Ed.) *Contemporary adolescence: Readings*, 2nd ed., Monterey, California: Brooks/Cole.

Rheingold, H. L. (1969). The social and socializing infant. In D. A. Goslin (Ed.) *Handbook of socialization theory and research*. Chicago: Rand McNally.

Riegel, K. F. (1976). The dialectics of human development. *American Psychologist, 31*, 679-700.

Rossi, A. S. Aging and parenthood in the middle years. (1980). In P. B. Baltes (Ed.) *Life-span development and behavior, Vol. 3*. New York: Academic Press.

Schaffer, H. R. and Emerson, P. E. (1964). The development of social attachments in infancy. *Monographs of the Society for Research in Child Development, 29* (Whole No. 94).

Shanas, E., Townsend, P., Wedderburn, D., Friis, H., Milhhoj, P., and Stehouwer, J. (1968). *Older people in three industrial societies*. New York: Atherton Press.

Troll, L. E. (1971). The family of later life: A decade review. In C. Broderick (Ed.) *A decade of family research and action*. Minneapolis, Minnesota: National Council on Family Relations.

White, R. W. (1966). *Lives in progress*, 2nd ed. New York: Holt, Rinehart, and Winston.

Family Transition to Parenthood: Emerging Concepts for Sexual Health

Mary Steichen Calderone

INTRODUCTION

The material in this article is designed for health professionals to absorb on behalf of parents, particularly first-time ones. Health and education professionals, pediatricians and clinic nurses, have prime opportunities to act as teachers and interpreters to society on the health needs of new babies and of children at all stages of development. They will, of course, first have to cope with surprise and too often dismay that many feel about any discussion involving healthy sexuality in children. There will at first be deep-seated resistance to acknowledging what the growing fund of information about sexuality must, in the end, force us to recognize and honor from earliest infancy: human sexuality is one of the gene-programmed body-mind systems that function characteristically from very early in fetal life (Calderone 1983).

WHAT WAS, THEN

Margaret Mead in a 1968 speech provocatively titled "Is Sex Necessary?" noted how, as she grew up, most parents had little trouble in bringing up their children "as long as it prepared them for being the kinds of adults *their* parents were." She described parents in the post-World War I years as:

Mary Steichen Calderone, MD, MPH, is Adjunct Professor, Program in Human Sexuality in New York University's Department of Health Education, New York, NY 10003.

Trying to overcome the styles of communication between parents and children . . . styles appropriate to other groups and periods but that did not prepare children . . . for the world they were going to have to live in, [one] where these young people would, in their [own] turns, have to bring up *their* children in an unprecedented environment for which by then *they* would have no appropriate behavior guidelines.

WHAT IS, NOW

"Unprecedented" indeed, for that 1968 "now" has twenty years later turned into an extraordinarily different "now." Even Mead could not have foreseen the details of the dramatic environmental changes impacting worldwide on families today: chemical addictions, terrorism and forced migrations of individuals, families and whole populations, resulting in the increasing poverty, homelessness, one-parent families, and criminality at all social levels almost everywhere.

Except for Nature's clones that we know as monozygous siblings, every baby born is unique among humans. Yet across the world human beings deliberately achieve ad nauseam replication of negative human behaviors among the young by brutalization — whether via TV, example, planned experiencing, or deliberate display of imagery of negative human actions, values, beliefs and behaviors — that cannot fail to influence the natures and mindsets of the developing young who are our own descendants. We must face the inescapable: at this writing children are no longer treated as the world's most precious possessions, but, in a new and frightening switch, have become the world's most endangered species. Whether white, black or any other color, rich or poor, gifted or handicapped, growing numbers are becoming either future victims or future producers of victims.

Via satellites and media, world-wide happenings are reflected over and over in the bewildered, longing, frightened, emotionally starved faces of children of all but a relatively few nations among which the US is not numbered; *we* fall into the "mass child-abuse-by-neglect" category. Specifically endemic to the US are the constantly widening streams of unwanted, uneducated, unskilled abuse-destined offspring of teenage girls and single women. Some such mothers are instantaneously locked by the birth of their first child into continued child-bearing, most of them to remain single, poorly educated and welfare-dependent for life. Child sexual abuse itself continues to simmer, from time to time building up a head of steam that makes the news in one or another setting.

Because such impacts on young human life are so long and widely felt, parents in all fields, particularly the sciences, should be learning how to join their concerns to those of the health scientists, who themselves are no less troubled and baffled by the same conditions as are those in politics, religion, business, finance, education, the arts or other fields. Parents can be encouraged to support programs that create ways for enlisting ever more parents in trying to understand and improve local and world conditions for children. This paper is directed specifically toward positive efforts to identify, accept and support the realities and importance of a single broad, as yet only vaguely defined area, childhood sexuality.

TEENAGE SEXUAL ACTIVITY
AND PREGNANCY RATES COMPARED

Data confirm that the US has the highest teenage pregnancy rates of the Western world: in girls 15-17 the rate in the Netherlands is 8 per thousand, in England 20, in the US 60 per thousand! Our 18-19-year-old unmarried women produce 140 conceptions per thousand compared to 80 in France and 22 in The Netherlands for the same age groups. Yet the overall sexual *activity* rates per thousand differ little among adolescents in the US, Holland, Canada, England and France. (American Medical News 1985). Here the key question is why the great differences in pregnancy rates for the same age groups? One answer leaps out—the almost universally profound sexual ignorance deliberately inflicted on their children by most US parents throughout all social classes, not just about contraception, but about the most elementary and elemental sexual *facts*, even to the lack of correct names for various body parts and their specific functions. Most US adults (including those who would classify themselves as well educated), find it so difficult to understand and talk about sexual matters in any rational or serious way, that they fail their children about these are the very ages when most needed, consigning them to ignorance and confusion about sexual matters and feelings for the rest of their lives—at a moment that, properly used, might have helped avoid such sexual misadventure.

The question arises as to the reason(s) for such major disparities among Western nations. It is well known that England, Sweden, Holland and France have for many years included sex education in elementary curricula. In Sweden and Holland this has been so for enough time that the present generations of parents and grandparents are among those who, profiting from the pioneer course work in the childhoods, could pass on to their descendants their own sexual knowledge and attitudes even before these first entered school, thus reinforcing what the schools subsequently taught. Interpretation of all well designed and conducted studies shows that sexual knowledge from parents *and* schools serves not only to delay age at first intercourse but to reinforce high standards of sociosexual awareness and responsibility.

THE HUMAN PRODUCTION LINE

Post-medical public health training teaches that prevention in the long run proves to be more life-and-labor-saving than after-the-fact therapy. Child-raising today could benefit from a preventive model for sex-related problems. The challenge to professionals is to design and implement such an approach for today's recognized health field of sexuality (WHO 1975). In the US the extent of the need for abortion constitutes a national disgrace, contrasting with the far lower abortion rates in the countries listed above. Every abortion falls into the obvious barn-door-locking category. The question to answer is how, and by whom, can US parents be helped to teach and motivate their *pre*-teenagers to think ahead, reason, and come to well considered decisions about their own future sexual behavior, in ways that would logically lead to avoidance of pregnancy. Saying and acting on "NO" or "WAIT" to self and/or other is obviously a major first step.

Learning to respect intelligent living by teaching parents to emphasize the four Ts—time, trust, teaching, truth—can lead ultimately to broadened understanding that a nonpregnant sexually active teenager can become a citizen more useful and acceptable to herself, her family, her society and her own future family, than a pregnant one! The same philosophy would certainly also apply to the male who made her pregnant.

Where abortion is undesired or unavailable the pregnant teen must carry to term. Here the waiting months should be utilized for intensive learning about babies and their rearing, and continued after birth for the following ten years, especially as to a baby's nature and needs, and how to deal positively with a child's God- and Nature-given endowments. Health and education professionals are essential here to teach such a health-promoting preventive approach to childrearing. Every unwanted repeat pregnancy is a link in an endless chain of ignorance, an unconscionable waste of human material to be charged against adult inertia.

Also it is now rarely possible to bask in the old-fashioned anticipatory aura of parenthood with plenty of extended family around to give a hand. And, with today's increasing proportions of families so close to or below the poverty level, the earning power of two adults is too often an obligatory lifebelt for bare survival.

Growing socioeconomic burdens due to increasing numbers of unplanned births to single mothers already living at or below the poverty level inevitably cause growing social stresses. The meager support services for such families offer little chance for these to be aware of the importance of the pre-birth months of *first* pregnancies for intensive learning about the realities of babies—what they *are*, and especially what they are *not*: babies may take years to fulfill their potentialities as the givers of love dreamed of by immature parents, for babies are insatiably absorbed in their own absolute requirement of it! For babies are very far from being the mere blobs of human flesh that only eat, sleep, cry and eliminate, that most inexperienced parents initially consider them to be. For development adequate to fulfill each one's specific genic program, a newborn must have continuing opportunities to expand in anticipation of, and support for, successful negotiation of each growth stage, in a close relationship with at least one parent who communicates consistently about *all* daily and/or occasional happenings, or changes in previously consistent happenings. Such evolution is in order to prepare for successful negotiation of each growth-and-development stage. In short, we need to help parents perceive their newborn as a *human* being, a *person*, a *person*ality-in-the-making (Brazelton 1981).

The developing human being is richly endowed with its own idiosyncratic ways, subtle and not so subtle, for modifying, adapting to, blocking out, compensating for, or escaping from, stresses or lacks in its surroundings or in the norms its caregivers try to impose on it. Whether at various forks in the road the child goes one way or another will depend in great measure on its given set of genes, for a "good" or "bad" personality trait is rarely born full-blown into the child but is progressively "conditioned" by the way the child is treated in its first ten minutes, hours, days, weeks, months—and years. In these blocks of time, how the parents feel about and behave toward the baby and its sexuality, and toward each other's and their own sexualities, will result in accumulated impacts powerfully, decisively, and often unexpectedly, affecting the outcomes in the child's future.

One thing is certain: no infant can communicate directly to its parents what its needs are. But clearly, definitively, and often effortlessly it does communicate to those caring and skilled enough to observe and interpret its language, whether it is or is not receiving fulfillment of its absolutely essential need for love and consistent caring. What lack of these can do to a baby or child has long been known (Landreth 1967) and daily observed in various societies.

THREE MAJOR HUMAN ENDOWMENTS: BODY, MIND, SEXUALITY

Why *human*?

Because ours is the only species with the power to choose to ignore or nullify its own gene programming, humans can and do exactly that, sometimes to stressfully undesirable results. Consider the training of a ballerina—its stresses, strains, pains, distortions, cripplings, sacrifices, artificialities, forced on to living or to relationships on behalf of extraordinarily beautiful moments. The only parallels in animal species are those enforced or "trained" as animal performers, whether wild or domesticated. It has been generally recognized as dangerous to children to try to use similar animal "training" methods on human young, so parents today merit help from professionals knowledgeable in child behavior *before* they are aware they are in need of it. Group discussions of all the obvious considerations will enlighten many parents, and at the same time lighten their burden of ignorance about the realities of being born a baby today in contrast to other more caring, fostering times.

Of course society has learned how to meet many needs of body and mind with knowledge and success: the mind is taken to school for learning, the body to informed regimens of diet, living and sports. But sexuality, the third major human endowment, is different in that it partakes of and expresses itself through both the mind and the body in linkages that depend greatly for their ultimate expressions on when, with whom, and how, sexual awareness and expression become operative and have impacted on memory. The cumulative impressions of all these have, as accumulated, been woven into the two memories (conscious and unconscious) of the baby, to be remembered occasionally and woven in on the loom of the child's close human relationships and their constantly accumulating impressions. The results are sometimes remembered, but as often are laid aside in the unconscious as Freud postulated, to emerge sometimes opportunely, but too often inopportunely.

Because of the many complexities and conflicts that may become embedded in the final results, one important clarification is to learn to distinguish between the two separate human systems of *reproduction* and of *sexual response*. Until very recently these two have been confused and lumped together, adding to rather than resolving the confusion between sex and sexuality, as well as their non-joint and conjoint rules (Calderone 1983).

Even twenty-five years ago the word *sex* was used either to denote gender, or as a rubric for a series of planned or random genital acts. The word might still be used only for these purposes, except that in 1964 the formation of SIECUS (Sex Information and Education Council of the US) brought to public and professional consciousness and usage, a more inclusive and much needed term, *sexuality*, a word term that has come to include the complex of components of the individual human being's sexual endowment, learning, acts, experiences, remembrances, thoughts, behaviors, aspirations, dreams, fantasies and relationships—whether consciously remembered or buried so deep as not to be easily recalled.

Thus it is clear that human sexuality should be recognized as an entity that forms a key part of a human being's life in that it is subject to being enjoyed, feared, anticipated, taught, exploited, used wisely, or misused to the damage of one or more others as well as of the self. Its three major components are classified as follows.

Gender Identity

It has been established (Money and Ehrhardt 1973) that, within the sexual system, a child should by three years ordinarily have become correctly aware and convinced of by its own genitalia that "I am a girl/boy." Those children whose genitalia are so ambiguous that the gender has not been possible to identify with certainty should not, after age three at the latest, receive surgery designed to *change* their gender identity without prolonged careful study by experts. If that age has been passed the child will generally do best with a surgical adjustment *confirming* the gender identity they have accepted. Thus a male born with undescended testicles and an underdeveloped small penis might have been carelessly identified at birth as a female with a prominent clitoris. After the age of three surgery if indicated should be used to sustain her self-accepted identity as female, with excision of the abdominal testes and, at puberty, the beginning of life-long administration of estrogen to ensure feminine body build, breasts, distribution of hair and ultimate capacity for marriage (childless because lacking menstruation and ovulation) eventually, by surgical creation of a sexually functional vagina. All such complexities must certainly be handled with much time and skill given to supportive psychotherapy.

It is important to bear in mind that any confusion about gender identity bears no relationship to homosexuality. Regardless of their sex-object choices, the gender identity of both male and female homosexuals is clear, sure, and in agreement with their anatomy.

Gender Role

Every society, and each cultural or religious group within it, will inevitably have its own definitions for appropriate gender role behaviors to be taught to its young of both genders. As long as the society and its sub-groups are consistent that these definitions apply more or less equally to members of both genders, there may be little conflict. But when one gender sets itself subtly or overtly over or against the other, or proclaims or acts out its feelings of superiority over the other, or tries to control all major activities and decisions, such efforts can go counter to the deepest yearnings and potentials of the members of the gender being down-graded, regardless of their gender. In the US mothers of toddlers are often noted, after a child's tumble, to comfort their small girls to significantly higher levels of time and intensity than they accord their little boys, some of whom even get very early pushed away with the admonition to "Stop crying, real men never cry!"

Parental homophobia might also get a small boy scorned or vilified for playing tenderly with a doll, as a result of which years later, as a heterosexual father he might be unwilling, unable or unskilled to express the tender fatherly love his own tiny son craved. In spite of such persisting or recurring attitudes among US men, considerable revision of formerly rigid concepts of what constitutes acceptable gender role feelings and behavior has slowly evolved in this country.

But the roles of women in this society began to change some time ago, and were broadened by the women's movement as to what women wanted to, could, and might appropriately do and be — and did. This served to raise the consciousness of men, many of whom have themselves exulted over the changes in their own centuries-old stereotypes. Meanwhile, though sexual harassment and/or exploitation continue, women keep pace by expanding their repertoires and venues as they open up new fields of activity for themselves. Some developmental push-pulls can be expected to affect parent-child relationships in view of the great social changes in so many areas of the world. Expectably, the new flexibility in gender roles has generally been more welcome and easy to achieve by those in the upper levels of the socioeconomic and educational scales. The obvious and pressing need for women to work on behalf of family, whether single or two-parent, will perhaps serve to embed whatever changes in gender roles have come about.

Genitality

This is the aspect of sexuality most usually taken for granted as making up its whole or at least its paramount element. It therefore demands a meticulously scientific approach to lead to its deepened comprehension. In the US society, however, genitality has come to be looked upon on the one hand as a life component impossible to escape, and on the other hand as most frivolously and exploitatively to be treated. Thus our dichotomous attitudes lead to sexuality as being universally longed for and sought after, or as the most intriguing but nevertheless most frightening, distorted, obsessive and, simultaneously, the most denied aspect of life.

It is common to find parents and even some professionals rationalizing that genital pleasure and desire do not and/or should not begin until puberty. This is self-serving, for belief in it as fact lets everybody conveniently off the hook, except for the younger children, of course, about whom the theory goes that "children are not interested in learning about sex until puberty!" It is characteristic of puberty that it is, almost to the second, the exact moment when adolescents begin to be entirely disinclined to listen to and/or learn from, anyone who is not also adolescent. So the entire assumption manages to maintain in everyone's minds the single major *untruth* that keeps the tragedy-pot unmerrily boiling over: sexuality and reproduction are one and the same!

Sexuality and reproduction are in actuality two distinct and separate body systems that function interdependently for only a relatively tiny number of flashing instants over one's life span. Many are the fantasies about them: as to pleasure, only the male is supposed to be really capable of it, and as to that bellwether of puberty, menstruation, an unexpected though small toll of pregnancies has been chalked up to girls who have never yet menstruated. Each system with its own set of organs, functions, brain-and-body interconnections and demonstrable importance, fills specific needs in the life span of each person, male or female. It was dramatic to see the visibly firm confirmation of the existence of a human sexual response system, in the revelation by ultrasound photography that the male fetus has erections from as early as 17 weeks' gestation (see ultrasound photo, Figure 1, by Alley at 29 weeks). In her report Alley observed that the interval for the erections was 90 minutes — the same as recorded in laboratory studies of normal adult sleeping males (Fisher, Schiavi et al. 1975). In the absence of pa-

FETAL ERECTION AT 29 WEEKS, REVEALED BY ULTRASOUND EVERY 90 MINUTES.

Ultrsonogram first published by Dr. Mary Steichen Calderone at the 6th World Congress of Sexology, May 1983, Washington, D.C.

The mother lies on her side, showing the fetal thighs R and L. The tiny erect penis is between them, the scrotum showing black under it. From Norfolk General Hospital, Norfolk, Virginia, USA. The every-90-minute periodicity coincides with that seen in laboratory observations of normal adult sleeping males.

Credit: Deborah Alley, RDMS (Registered Diagnostic Medical Sonographer, now of the Department of Maternal-Fetal Medicine, Children's Hospital of the King's Daughters, Norfolk, VA. USA

Copyright SIECUS Report, 1983. For permission to reproduce, please werite M.S. Calderone MD, MPH, New York University, 639 Greene St., 6 FL. New York, NY 10003.

FIGURE 1

thology these can continue for the life span and are useful in the differential diagnosis between erectile problems due to difficulties of organic or of psychologic origin.

With present technology it is not yet possible to determine whether analogic sexual behavior is identifiable in the female fetus. Langfeldt (1980) however, reported cyclic vaginal lubrication occurring regularly in newborn girls. The Kinsey studies on females

(1953) revealed that infant girls could by self-stimulation (pressing the thighs together) induce reactions that clearly resembled orgasm, with spasmodic body tension, flushing, grimacing, quivering and sudden relaxation followed by sleep. If girls are thus sexually potent from birth, then analogically it could be posited that they join males in being sexually functional from early fetal life. Such findings serve to antecede and explain what parents and other caregivers the world over have noted over the ages — the universal drive of toddlers and young children for simple genital self-pleasuring by a considerable variety of ways and means (Landreth 1967).

"Playing doctor" is a favorite name-for-a-game passed down from generation to generation by the "spontaneous generation" of direct peer imitation. Today it is likely to be looked upon by most child psychiatrists as a natural developmental aspect of growth, exploration, and learning among young peers (Langfeldt 1980, Oremland 1977), just as is simple body touching among young children (Blackman 1980). Such looking and touching among very young pre-schoolers is recognized as having a useful role in confirming and reconfirming the anatomies of both sexes as normal in each case, so that same-sex young children are secure in identifying their same- and opposite-sex peers.

At these ages also, explication of the usefulness of the genitals in the creation of a baby can be in straightforward terms of "When you are grown-up and married —" and sets the stage for later discussions of responsibility in sexual decision-making.

Affirmation and validation of the genitals as being OK to touch because one of their three gene-programmed purposes *is* to give pleasure *by* being touched, is a difficult but vital step for parents *and* professionals to take. It is difficult because of the almost universally held superstition that such touching is not only bad and evil but is in some way unnatural — and also because even open-minded professionals shrink from the thought that they might be quoted as *recommending what others hold as sinful*. The answer is simple: no one need recommend something that will inevitably happen over and over in any case. And nothing that is gene-programmed into every human child born should, in conscience ever be condemned as scientifically evil, much less as "unnatural." In this parents can accept professional assurance that early orientation toward positive attitudes and responsibility for privacy and noninvolvement of others — that is, *socialization* — can serve to create feelings of safety and comfort in how humans were and still are created to be:

> This is the way God and Nature made us, so it has to be OK. But it certainly also means that we must learn that everybody believes that sex should be very private between husband and wife who love each other. So when you feel like pleasuring yourself it is important to go into your room and be private with the door closed. Ask us all the questions you like about these private things, but never forget that other people like to decide what is best for their own children, not for other people's children. You can ask us and we promise always to tell you the truth. But we must never try to answer your friends' questions, and their parents should not try to answer yours. Everybody likes all these important things to be very private for each family. (Calderone & Ramey 1982)

Parents need professional help in accepting and learning such new language for their children, and should be offered such help well before they think they will be in need of it. In this way problems can be anticipated and/or provided for. Such guidance provides appropriate lore and background for recognizing, accepting, and helping to develop undistorted, this important and least understood third of the three specific endowments that delineate humans from all other species. The first two, the mind and the body, have been carefully served — the mind by education and the body by standards of good living habits and by sports. The third, human sexuality, from before birth expresses itself spontaneously and regularly through both mind and body. This is why, in a world still ridden by superstition, sexuality inspires such fear and embarrassment that communicating about sex and/or reproduction with children who are aware of the ways by which their own sexuality functions, can become a nightmare wall of silence for most parents. Constantly assuring each other that "later will be better/safer/less embarrassing/less inciteful to our precious child to try new (bad) things," "later" inevitably emerges as much *too* late, from the point of view of the child's now and future welfare.

Human sexuality over time expresses itself and is enjoyed through an interweaving of body/mind linkages, in which memories both forgotten or recalled continue to weave a dense tapestry of human images. The most often-asked question by parents is what to do *if* (never *when!*) "my child comes into the room when we are having intercourse?" My own standard answer begins with a single word, "Smile!" When the laughter indicating surprise and relief subsides, one can continue the answer with a short suggestion: "(Daddy) (Mommy) and I are having our private time when we like to play love games before going to sleep. You forget about the closed door. Next time be sure to knock and wait to be invited in, and we'll always do the same for you when we see *your* door is closed."

It is timely that the need to understand human sexuality now forces us to differentiate intelligently between the two sex-related body-mind systems. *Reproduction* is primarily a single-purpose body-oriented and governed system. Human *sexuality*, on the other hand, is a multi-purposed mix of quite different significance and proportions by which the physical aspects of sexuality are all too often influenced by and/or experienced as, long-buried infancy/ childhood memories or traumata. We are still struggling to identify and place in perspective its many true functions and purposes.

SUMMARY

Many are the scientists who have recognized an almost mystical side of their natures leading them to a profound sense of divine planning, when they meet with phenomena that are beyond hard explanation. Such feelings have been expressed by eminent physicists, astronomers, and philosophers, particularly when dealing with the complexities of outer space. To hear two such men muse toward the end of a finely produced television series, the Creation of the Universe, "What was *there* one second before the Big Bang began our universe?" was an eye opener. So was the similar sense of awe expressed by William Blake in his late eighteenth century poem "The Tiger,"

Tiger, tiger, burning bright
    In the forests of the night,
What immortal hand or eye
    Could frame that fearful symmetry?

One's own awe can pervade the contemplation of such elementary facts as that Nature has made it not impossible but certainly improbable, for an apparently *pre*pubertal girl to be involved in the creation of a new human life. The first twelve years actually serve as a period of grace, a kind of safe interval for loading the developing child's computer-like mind with sound and therefore protective information and attitudes. Coupled with teaching in self-responsibility and parental values, and with a growing sense of mastery over his or her own body and its activities, the average child can arrive at puberty ready to recognize and adjust to all that this landmark event implies.

The twelve critical prepubertal years provide professionals and parents with time for laying a foundation of information and attitudes for understanding and acceptance of the normal sexuality of childhood and its needs. This can help release parents from whatever false attitudes of ignorance, shame and repulsion their own upbringing may have left them with, from which their own relationship may be suffering. Careful studies of children 5 to 15 in the English-speaking countries of Australia, US/Canada and Great Britain (Goldman & Goldman 1982) provided ample grounds for anger over the sexual lies and idiocies with which the children's minds had been filled and undoubtedly warped. Certainly these will require far more efforts eventually to revise toward normal meanings in sexuality than would have resulted from transmission of the truth in the first place. In this regard US children were found to be about 2 years retarded as compared to the other English-speaking children. It was timely that ultrasound technology in 1983 at last provided us with the living proof of fetal sexual functioning along with that of the other fetal body systems. Only the reproductive system remains on "hold" until puberty.

Q.E.D.

"Telling" children about difficult sexual topics such as genital pleasure should be done with a comfortable sense of *sharing* with them some wonderful God- and Nature-given truths, and never with a vague, embarrassed or joking manner. This is hard for most parents, but looking upon it as family *conversation* will ease matters. Verbalizing frequently in simple language about many subjects including sexual ones, can begin as early as does language, making it easy to continue and enlarge such talks between parents and children during the period into and through adolescence: "So what crazy things about sex did the kids in school say *this* week?" (Calderone & Ramey 1982).

At the supermarket I once heard a woman's voice behind me say cheerfully, "Remember, Johnny, that's for in the car or for when we get home." I felt sure of what I would see when I turned. Yes, Johnny age 2-3, looking bored in the shopping cart, was just pulling his hands out of his pockets. His mother smiled down at him and reinforced this with M&Ms. By not scolding him and by taking his masturbation for granted, she was emphasizing that *he* was in charge of his body, but that his behavior was OK only in privacy appropriate to time and place.

Shortly before Diana's third birthday her Daddy took her to the American Museum of Natural History. Fascinated, she ran from exhibit to exhibit with a constant stream of questions and observations, to which her father responded accurately and simply. Struck by the life-size whale model hanging from the ceiling she exclaimed. "But it doesn't have any water to swim in!" In the days following she mentioned this concern several times, showing development of logical thinking.

Diana had, since before two years old, come to know the correct names for all of her visible and/or touchable body parts. Whether working up from her toes or down from her head, her voice never changed when, between knee and tummy button, she would correctly name "vulva." One day as her Daddy was changing her diaper, Diana remarked casually, "You keep your penis in your pants." Her father responded just as casually with "Yes, and you keep your vulva in your diaper the way everybody prefers it. But some day when you don't need the diaper any more, you can keep your vulva in some pretty panties Mommy and I have all ready for you." Some time later in talking about going to preschool with her best friend Rachel, Diana's parents discussed with her the kinds of things it's OK to discuss at school, and things better to discuss at home.

Rachel, almost three, and her mother were watching one of Public TV's Nature films the children both adore. This one was about mountain lions, and one female was giving birth. Suddenly Rachel turned to her mother, exclaiming, "Did that baby come out of her *anus*?" "No," her mother explained. "Only bowel movements ever come out of anuses. That baby came out of her vagina, just as you came out of mine!" Rachel absorbed this, and turning back to the program she exclaimed, "What a *wonderful* idea!"

Quite young children can learn not only the wonderful truths about how a baby exits from its mother, but the equally full-of-wonder truth about how it gets started there in the first place, is nourished, grows, has a beating heart, sleeps with REM eye movements, urinates a tiny little bit every 30 minutes into the fluid in which it floats, moves and kicks etc., until it is ready to be born. Eventually she will also learn about the relationship of ovulation to menstruation, and how important it is for an ovum not to meet with a sperm to make a baby unless there are two parents ready to take care of it, and all that it means to be "ready" to take care of a baby. Boys and girls who grow up unable to remember a time when they did not have access to truthful sexual information will be those who were in close-trusting relationships with their parents, and the toll of teenage pregnancies will drop sharply—all in a wonderful sequel to Rachel's "wonderful idea!"

Finally, parents and professionals must come to recognize that even though "good" school sex education programs can play constructive roles by providing accurate information, when it comes to forming early attitudes of honor, belief, self-esteem, and trust in children about sexual and other intimate matters, no school can ever be expected to replace what the parents themselves failed to do for their children in those first, most critical five years before ever school began.

NOTE

1. The sixties and seventies were outstanding decades of new and highly revealing studies on children's sexual development, appearing in several special collections. One such is the Oremlands' *The Sexual and Gender Development of Young Children* (Cambridge, MA, Ballinger Publishing Company, 1977). The Montreal Conference listed above was another groundbreaker, as was the Goldman study. I feel that during the foreseeable future, it will be of greatest importance to stop expecting any groundbreaking or earthshaking studies. The information now available should be studied and evaluated by all, and a workable, sensibly applicable sexual learning theory should be developed.

REFERENCES

Blackman, N. (1980). Pleasure and touching: Their significance in the sexual development of the preschool child. In Samson J.M. (ed.): *Proceedings of the International Symposium on Childhood and Sexuality*. Montreal: Editions Etudes Vivantes.

Brazelton, B. (1981). *On Becoming a Family: The Growth of Attachment.* New York: Dell.

Calderone, M. (1983). Fetal erection and its message to us. *SIECUS Report, II* (5/6).

Calderone, M. and Ramey, J. (1982). *Talking with Your Child about Sex.* New York: Random House.

Cancila, C. Teen pregnancy, abortion rates, highest in U.S. (Alan Guttmacher Institute study), reported in *American Medical News*, March 29, 1985).

Fisher, C., Schiavi, R., & Edward, A. (1976). Assessment of nocturnal REM erection in differential diagnosis of male impotence. *Sleep Research Brein Information,* 5:42.

Goldman, R. & Goldman, J. (1982). *Children's Sexual Thinking.* Boston: Routledge and Kegan Paul.

Kinsey, A., Pomeroy, W., & Martin, C. (1953). *Sexual Behavior in the Human Female.* Philadelphia: W.B. Saunders Co.

Landreth, C. (1967). *Early Childhood: Behavior and Learning.* New York, Alfred Knopf.

Langfeldt, T. (1980). Aspects of sexual development, problems and therapy in children. In Samson, J.M. (ed.): *Proceedings of the International Symposium on Childhood and Sexuality*. Montreal: Editions Etudes Vivantes.

Mead, M. (1969). Is sex necessary? *SIECUS Newsletter, 4*(3).

Money, J. and Ehrhardt, A. (1975). *Man & Woman, Boy & Girl.* Baltimore: Johns Hopkins University Press.

WHO (World Health Organization) (1975). *Education and Treatment in Human Sexuality: The Training of Health Professionals.* Geneva, Technical Report No. 572.

The Challenge of Working with New Fathers: Implications for Support Providers

Glen F. Palm
Rob Palkovitz

SUMMARY. The interest in fathering and parent education services for fathers leads to some important questions for professionals who work with parents of young children. This paper explores contemporary patterns of paternal involvement and reports on a study of fathers' perceptions of education for parenting. Differences between males and females are presented as important considerations for designing parent education programs. Practical suggestions are offered for attracting and serving a broad range of men with parent support and education services.

The changing role of fathers and the renewed interest in parent education during the last decade has led to the development of parenting classes and support groups for fathers (see Kliman, 1984). As fathers become more involved in parent education programs an important set of questions emerges. What are new fathers' needs, expectations, and perceptions of education for parenting? What types of programs are most effective at transforming fathers' motivation and interest into parenting skills and knowledge? Do fathers have different educational needs and learning styles than mothers? This paper will explore fathers' perceptions of the parenting role, some probable differences between fathers and mothers as they

Glen F. Palm, PhD, is Professor, Center for Child and Family Studies, St. Cloud State University, St. Cloud, MN 65301; Rob Palkovitz, PhD, is Assistant Professor, Department of Individual and Family Studies, College of Human Resources, University of Delaware, Newark, DE 19716.

357

come into parent education programs and some practical suggestions for attracting and integrating a broader range of men into parent support programs.

BASIC ASSUMPTIONS

There are four basic assumptions about fathering in contemporary America that form a foundation for the following analysis of
parent education for new fathers.

1. The Role of Fatherhood Is Presently in a State of Flux

The role of the father is changing (Palkovitz, 1986, 1987a), but
the direction of change is unclear and is likely to be different for
individual men. The increase of father involvement in children's
lives has been emphasized in recent empirical and popular literature. However, this increase is counter-balanced by two other important trends. First there is some indication of a decrease in the
accumulated length of time that men spend with young children.
Smaller families mean that opportunities for learning parenting
skills through experience with children have decreased (Eggebeen
& Uhlenberg, 1985). There are also more single parent families
headed by women than at any other time in our history (Rotundo,
1985). At the other end of the involvement spectrum are househus-
bands, fathers with sole custody of their children, and dual career
families where both parents share caretaking responsibilities (Hanson & Bozett, 1985). The parenting roles assumed by men appear to
be broader than in the past. The different models of paternal involvement, while holding the potential to be liberating can also lead
to confusion.

2. There Are Important Differences Between the Ways
that Males and Females Approach and Think About
the Parenting Role

These differences are important to consider when designing and
conducting parent support and education sessions. Androgyny provides one model of the ideal parent. It is attractive to many involved
fathers, because it gives them the permission to be warm and nur-

turant without giving up their masculinity (Russell, 1978). Some studies have indicated that androgynous fathers are more involved with their children than fathers of traditional or undifferentiated sex role orientations (see, e.g., Palkovitz, 1980, 1984). It is unclear, however, whether fathers can be positively encouraged to be more androgynous, and if an increase in androgyny would correspond to greater father involvement in childrearing.

The model of androgyny attenuates any differences between men and women as parents in an attempt to abolish sex-role stereotypes. The adoption of an androgynous model has been positive for many parents, but as fathers attempt to carve out and define the parent role for themselves, some attention to male and female differences is necessary (Sayers, 1983). These differences do not have to connote inequality or inferiority for either sex. An understanding and awareness of the biological basis of differences can provide more control and flexibility (Rossi, 1983). Differences do not have to trap either men or women into stereotypical roles. In fact, the positive qualities of androgyny may rest more in the fact that androgynous persons are flexible and well rounded in their behaviors than in the fact that they are androgynous per se.

Lamb (1978) has convincingly argued that sex roles become redefined after the birth of a child. Accordingly, short-term longitudinal data reported by Feldman and Aschenbrenner (1983) have demonstrated that the assumption of the parental role brings significant changes in parents' masculinity and femininity. Specifically, both men and women increase in feminine role behavior, feminine identity, and instrumental personality traits, and women decrease their levels of masculine role behavior.

It also appears that, with time, fathers garner more childcare experience and begin to feel more confident and competent in their ability to care for the needs of their infants. Correlational data show that higher levels of confidence and comfort in providing childcare are related to greater paternal involvement (Palkovitz, 1980).

McHale and Huston (1984) have reported differential influences on mother and father involvement. Specifically, fathers' involvement appears to be largely determined by their own attitudes and their wives; attitudes (Palkovitz, 1984) while mother involvement is most closely related to work involvement (McHale & Huston,

1984). Parent involvement appears to be highly influenced by sex role orientation, although to different extents and through divergent mechanisms for each sex. Specifically, nontraditional attitudes, skills, and preferences decrease overall levels of maternal involvement and increase paternal involvement with infants. Nonetheless, based on their cross-cultural work with nontraditional families, Frodi, Lamb, Hwang and Frodi (1982) have concluded that ideals, beliefs, and attitudes do not translate directly into behavior patterns in naturalistic settings.

Similarly, Palkovitz (1984) argued that although attitudes are important determinants of behavior, maximum adaptability requires that people respond to situational cues. Parents cannot allow their attitudes to obscure what specific action is necessary at the moment. As such, parents should be responsive to the needs of their infants and the situational demands as interpreted through the filter of their attitudes and belief system. The general picture emerging is that specific patterns of parent involvement are more largely dependent on the social context than they are on general parental attitudes. While relatively stable attitudes, personality variables, styles of relating and deeply held belief systems may dictate the bounds of global interaction patterns, situational determinants control the precise topography, expression, timing and intensity of behaviors within those widely prescribed bounds.

3. There Are Many Different Paths to Becoming and Being a "Good Father"

This statement should not be taken to mean that all men are on good paths. Many are lost and uncertain, while others stumble along in the ruts created by their own fathers. The only way that the fathering role can be evaluated is in the context of the family. In this context husbands and wives are constantly negotiating and adjusting their roles to meet both their family and personal needs. Recent interview data (Palkovitz, 1986) indicate that this negotiatory process may be more implicit than overt. Each father must evaluate his path according to his family situation. Fathers need guidance and support as they take on this task.

4. Being an "Involved Father" Today Takes Time, Motivation, Knowledge, and Skill

The development of a close relationship between father and child involves a combination of factors (Pleck, Lamb, & Levine, 1986). Being an involved father is not an easy task for men to integrate into their lives. Many men would like to see the "executive summary" to effective child-rearing and one-minute shortcuts to intimacy with their children because they have limited time and energy. While it is comforting for parents suffering from role strain to hear that the quality of time spent with children is more important than the quantity of time, it is probably oversimplifying the matter. In reality, there is a relationship between quantity and quality of time spent with children. Simply stated, an unspecific minimum amount of time is required before children are "ready" for quality time. They may be sleepy, hungry or ill during the brief encounter scheduled, and ready for quality time later. As such, parents who can afford to invest great quantities of time with their children are more likely to *share* quality time with them when it is appropriate. Parenting is a process, an ongoing experience that takes time, energy, and openness to learning (Brooks, 1981).

There is, in reality, a continual struggle between role efficiency and fulfillment. At a certain level, efficiency of operation comes from matching skill levels to tasks and assuming mutually exclusive role assignment and function fulfillment. We live in a world of specialists for precisely that reason. However, fulfillment is related to diversification of interests and experiencing a variety of roles. Families should be encouraged to creatively work out the unique balance that they need in order to experience efficiency, and fulfillment in both parenting and marital roles. This may be easier said than done. For example, if a couple is for some reason opposed to arranging alternative care for their children, they have some major obstacles to overcome in finding that balance of efficiency and fulfillment. If they find strict adherence to traditional sex roles too limiting, both may decide to work part-time and to provide child-care part-time. However, they would each need to work more than half-time in order to maintain their standard of living, because benefits are typically reduced for part-time employees. Further, the typical American female earns fifty-nine cents on the dollar for performing the same job at the same proficiency level as a male. As such, if the couple wished to maximize their earning for time invested in work, the male should work proportionately longer hours than the female. Finally, to avoid the need to arrange for alternative care, the couple would need to find jobs with staggered work schedules. This solution, however, detracts from the amount of time left to invest in the marital relationship.

In summary, a shift in the fathering role seems to be in the direction of greater direct involvement for many men. As more women enter the workforce and share the role of provider, men are likely to face greater pressure to share the role of caretaker and nurturer (Lewis, 1986). Parent support and education will become more relevant for men as they take on these new responsibilities and roles. It is important that parent and early childhood educators begin to recognize the unique needs of fathers during this time of transition and that they guide and support men in their search for a meaningful and fulfilling role as a parent.

MODELS OF PATERNAL INVOLVEMENT

Fathers are involved in their children's lives in a variety of ways. A father's perception of his role will determine to some extent the amount and type of involvement that he will have with his child (Palkovitz, 1980, 1984). Russell (1983) conceptualizes a continuum of involvement that includes four distinct types of fathers. The model presented here is an adaptation of Russell's model and proposes five different levels of paternal involvement. The model describes a wide range of paternal involvement based on the father's perception of his role in the direct care and nurturance of his children.

1. The uninterested and unavailable father. This is the father who has little interest or time for his children and tends to be absent both physically and psychologically.

2. The traditional father. The traditional father has a strong commitment to family in his primary role as breadwinner. He also defines his role in terms of some participation with and responsibility towards his children.

3. The assistant parent father. This father is like the traditional father but does not limit participation to traditional domains. The assistant parent is a mother's helper, a father who is seen as capable of taking over sometimes but does not share equally in the tasks and responsibilities of childrearing.

4. The co-parent father. The co-parent model is one that is held up as the ideal in many dual career families because it reflects an egalitarian spirit. This father lives in a shared-caregiving family and has taken participation another step in publicly rejecting the traditional notion of fatherhood by sharing in some equitable manner the responsibility of day-to-day care for his children.

5. Primary parent father. The primary parent father is the house-husband or the single custodial father. This father has the primary responsibility for the day-to-day care of his children.

Men's perceptions of these different levels of involvement influence their motivation for seeking parent support and education. The father who perceives himself as a primary parent or a co-parent is more likely to be motivated to seek our parent support opportunities. Fathers may move back and forth on this continuum of involvement. Regardless of their current levels of involvement, all fathers deserve and can benefit from support and guidance in selecting and carrying out their parenting roles.

LEVELS OF PATERNAL INVOLVEMENT

The research on actual levels of paternal involvement is sparse and in some cases contradictory. Studies on the quality and quantity of time fathers spend with their children vary (e.g., Rebelsky & Hanks, 1971; Kotelchuck, 1977; Palkovitz, 1980; Pederson & Robson, 1969). Most studies do not differentiate between weekdays and weekend days when fathers have more time to spend with their children (Palm, 1985a). As the continuum of father involvement points out, any attempts to generalize the quantity of time that a father spends will be misleading because of the wide range of paternal behaviors, styles and perceptions of what works and what levels of involvement are appropriate.

The one area where dramatic changes in paternal involvement have been documented is in the labor and delivery process. A recent

Gallup Poll (cited in Kliman, 1984) indicates that approximately 80% of fathers attend the birth of their child today in comparison with 27% a decade ago. This is a hopeful sign that paternal involvement is on the rise. Although paternal birth attendance represents a minimal investment, there is hope that this change will be associated with further changes in paternal behavior and involvement. However, the actual influence of father's birth attendance on later behavior by fathers is unclear. Palkovitz (1985) reports in his review of the literature on fathers' birth attendance, that positive effects on father-child relations depend upon more than the father's presence at birth. While father's presence at birth may be beneficial to the mother to the developing family, and a "peak" experience for some men, it will not by itself create a permanent sense of intimacy between father and child. In reality, we do not know what, if any, are the effects of paternal birth attendance on subsequent father involvement.

In a recent survey of father involvement in programs for young handicapped children (Palm, 1985b) the reported levels of involvement were low. Only 40.5% of the fathers attended parent conferences, 18.9% came to the program to observe and 15.4% attended parent education sessions. These low figures may be explained by fathers' unavailability due to work schedules, but also probably reflect fathers' differing perceptions of the male parenting role. One encouraging sign was that two-thirds of the programs reported that father involvement had increased over the last three years.

The levels of the father involvement in Early Childhood and Family Education (ECFE) programs in Minnesota are also informally reported to be on the rise. These programs are funded as part of community education in over 300 school districts. The programs are designed for parents and their young children age birth to five years. Approximately 27% of the fathers in one of the ECFE programs participated in a group interview process as part of a study of fathers' perceptions of parent education (Palm, 1986). These fathers were part of 14 different parent groups that meet weekly in the evenings for a period of 25 weeks during the school year.

The profile of the 38 fathers who participated in this study and attend evening parent education classes is revealing. Most of the fathers (75%) are at least 30 years old. The education level of the fathers is high, 65% are college graduates and 40% have done post-graduate work. The household income was also high with over 50% of the incomes reported at $35,000 or above compared to the local median income of $21,000. Approximately 75% of the men in the sample had wives that worked at least part-time. All were fathers of at least one child who was 0-3 years old. This profile seems consistent with other groups of fathers participating in support programs facilitated by Palm over the last seven years. There are men who do not fit the profile exactly, but the majority are well-educated, in their 30s, have above average household income, and working wives.

DIFFERENCES BETWEEN MOTHERS AND FATHERS

A majority of investigations has indicated that mothers spend greater time in routine caregiving than fathers do and that mothers display greater positive affection toward their infants than fathers (Belsky, et al., 1984, Parke & Sawin, 1980). Fathers are more animated in mimicking infant facial expressions (Parke & Sawin, 1980) and tend to spend more time in noninteractive behavior (e.g., reading the paper, watching television) than mothers (Belsky, et al., 1984). Overall, the fathers have less contact with their infants than mothers do, and tend to spend more of their contact time in play rather than in caregiving activities (Belsky, 1979; Kotelchuck, 1976; McHale & Huston, 1984; Russell, 1978). Thus, despite the renewed emphasis on role flexibility, differential amounts of time spent in routine caregiving is reflective of more traditional child care activity (Kotelchuck, 1976; Rendinea & Dickerscheid, 1976; Parke & Sawin, 1980). In the typical family, fathers tend to engage in more plan than caregiving, to give preferential attention to boys, and to reinforce sex stereotyped behavior in both sexes (Jones, 1985).

Once again, however, situational influences can alter traditional patterns of role division significantly. When the delivery of the child is characterized by atypicality (e.g., prematurity or caesarean birth) fathers increase their involvement relative to mothers and relative to fathers in families where the deliveries have gone smoothly. The precise duration of increased paternal involvement is unknown under these circumstances.

Parke and Sawin (1980) have reported that with the passage of time, mothers and fathers tend to converge in their behavior in the immediate postpartum period to more homogeneous roles by three months of age. As a child is weaned, a father has greater opportunity to participate in a wider range of caregiving behaviors, as well as to experience one of the more pleasant and gratifying caregiving tasks. At the same time, the mother is given freedom to decrease her caregiving involvement. Thus, with increasing child age, one would expect to find greater consistency in parental behaviors. That, in fact, is what is observed. Belsky et al. (1984) reported a decrease in the magnitude of mother-father differences over the time span from 1-9 months, although mothers were significantly more involved with their infants at each measurement than their husbands.

One of the major questions posed in the Palm (1986) study was whether fathers perceive major differences between themselves and their wives. The fathers who are involved in parent education programs seem to feel that there are no differences and that mothers and fathers are both competent caretakers. This belief seems to be based on two notions. First, the fathers involved see themselves as co-parents, as opposed to assistant, traditional or uninterested fathers. It is also based on the notion that any sex differences between mothers and fathers are related to sex-role stereotypes that these men and their wives are trying to break away from. It appears that fathers generally perceived that they may bring some differences into parenting, but many are attempting to share parenting because of working wives, and differences between mothering and fathering become blurred in these family systems.

Fathers' Base of Knowledge Is Probably Very Different from Mothers'

In the Palm (1986) study fathers consistently identified their wives as avid readers of child development and parenting literature. The fathers reported that they depended upon their wives to sift through this literature because they didn't have time to read. One father referred to his wife as "a walking encyclopedia." Data indicate that men are also less likely to attend parenting, infant development or child development classes at the college level (Palkovitz, 1987b). There are typically ten women for every man in a variety of classes related to the child development or the parenting role, including courses focused on fathers. This is an important area of difference between men and women before they become parents, and it doesn't appear to change after becoming parents. Men seem to depend upon their wives to seek and find answers about child development and effective parenting, suggesting that women are viewed as the childcare specialist, particularly with young children. Women also attend parent education classes more frequently after the birth of their children so that differences in this area continue to exist (Palm, 1985b).

Fathers' Experience Base Is Different from Mothers'

Men are not as likely as women to have experience taking care of young children before becoming parents. Girls are more likely to babysit for siblings or neighbors. In addition, once a child is born the mother is the most likely to stay home with the child (Palkovitz, 1986) and her experience base continues to expand.

Some of the research on fathers and their sensitivity (e.g., Parke & Sawin, 1975) suggests that fathers are as sensitive as mothers to their baby's auditory cues. However, these measures are relatively gross and don't focus on the more subtle cues that an "experienced caretaker" picks up. As mothers spend more time with their children than fathers do, differences in experiential knowledge increase. Power (1985) found that mothers of toddlers are more sensitive to children's communication cues and better at engaging children in toy play. The implications of this difference are difficult to project, but they suggest that fathers who are attempting to be co-parents may have to invest additional time and energy to "catch up." They will find it difficult to match mothers' skills whether developed through experience or based on "precultural" differences.

Interactional Styles of Fathers and Mothers Are Different

This is one area that has been researched with all ages of children, and the results of these studies have consistently shown differences between mothers and fathers (Lamb, 1981). Fathers are described as being more physical, tactile, and arousing. Mothers are more verbal and calming. These differences are likely to have an impact upon the parent-child relationship or at least the child's perception of this relationship. It will be interesting to see if this pattern of differences changes as men take more responsibility for caretaking. Will the androgynous father's interaction patterns more closely resemble typical maternal interaction patterns? At this point the evidence is unclear. Radin (1982) found that "equalitarian" fathers continued to be similar to traditional fathers in terms of their sex-role orientation and strictness. In his review of literature on male early childhood educators, Robinson (1986) notes that there are more similarities than differences between male and female teachers. It would be instructive to study caregivers and teachers in the context of fathering. Palkovitz (1984) reported that androgynous fathers engaged in high frequencies of both traditionally masculine behaviors (e.g., rough and tumble play) and traditionally feminine behaviors (e.g., caregiving, expressing affection).

Fathers Have Fewer Support Systems Available to Them

One research study (Riley & Cochran, 1985) suggests that fathers are not as likely as mothers to talk with relatives about childrearing issues. The literature on parenting is also primarily directed towards women, with articles most commonly appearing in women's magazines or in the "home section" of the newspaper. Even those men who do decide to assume primary responsibility in the househusband role have a harder time breaking into the neighborhood support system for parents (see, e.g., Steinberg, 1977). As fathers take on more childrearing responsibilities they will need both formal and informal support systems to assist them in becoming and feeling like competent caregivers.

Fathers' Perceptions of and Value of the Parenting Role Are Generally Different from Mothers'

In general the parent role appears to be less central to men's lives. One of the themes that appeared in group discussions with fathers (Palm, 1986) was that it does not take a great deal of skill or knowledge to be an effective parent. Fathers who do not take on the major responsibility for meeting their child's needs may be deceiving themselves into thinking that competence in parenting can be easily attained. Similarly, Grossman (in press) found that fathers most satisfied with their careers were the least involved with their children. Lamb (1981) describes the salience of fathers as related to their novelty and differences from mothers. This sense of importance to the young child may tend to give a father a sense of intimacy and competence which may not generalize to a more representative and long-term caregiving role.

The above differences are described not to create a stereotype, but an awareness that fathers come to parent support and education programs with different knowledge, experiences, and perceptions about parenting. They may need to work on different skills than mothers. Because of the differences described above, it may be necessary for parent educators to use different methods for fathers and mothers, even if they perceive themselves as co-parents and are sharing the caretaking role. There are also important individual differences that are relevant to the parent educator, but often these differences are not considered in providing parent education to both men and women. Fathers often face the model of the "good parent" as the mother and are expected to emulate the "mothering" role. Parent educators tend to implicitly express a bias that mothers are primary caregivers and fathers assistant parents by stressing the (as yet unsubstantiated) assertion that mothers "allow" fathers to participate in caregiving, and that fathers learn parenting skills by observing mothers.

EDUCATIONAL STRATEGIES FOR INCREASING FATHER INVOLVEMENT

The differences between men and women that have been described form a basis for formulating strategies to involve fathers. In general, we would advocate providing at least some separate sessions for fathers. There are six different areas where suggestions can be made for increasing father involvement and satisfaction in parent education programs.

Time as an Important Factor

There is no universal "good time" for fathers. However, fathers are more likely to attend if they do not have to take off from work. Most men (and women) do not have flexible work hours. Evening times are better for most fathers, but fathers will have to deal with the "fatigue factor" if they attend evening sessions. Saturday classes for parents and children may also work for some fathers especially if they are already responsible for their children at this time. Saturday sessions can provide both a time and structure for fathers to be with their children.

Location and Sponsoring Organization

Typically parenting programs are run by female staff members in education or health care settings. These settings are not comfortable for many men. For example, sitting in desks in the local school building may bring back negative feelings associated with school as well as being physically uncomfortable. Female staff and a predominance of female parents may also pose a problem or accentuate inhibitions for some men. Not only does the topic appear to be female territory, but so does the space and social climate. Some men enjoy being singled out as the exceptional male parent who cares about his children, while other men quickly decide that this "parenting group" is really a mother's group. Female facilitators and groups are also likely to be more sympathetic and supportive of the perspective of mothers than fathers. While these barriers are subtle, they can be very powerful. Parent educators need to be sensitive to creating an environment where men will feel both welcome and comfortable.

Recruitment of Male Parents

Most advertising for parent education is directed towards female users and appears in traditionally female environments. The most effective way to recruit fathers is through the mother (Palm, 1986). Occasionally, a father will bring a male friend to a class. Realistic efforts to recruit men in their own environments and in a personal manner should be made. Some suggestions for recruiting fathers follow.

1. Special invitations may be mailed directly to fathers. Names of new parents can often be gathered from the newspaper, and addresses found through telephone directories.
2. Encourage men already in the group to invite men friends.
3. Plan special introductory sessions for fathers. Activities of interest to men, not directly focused on parenting could encourage initial attendance.
4. Advertise in more traditional male settings (e.g., Sports Page).
5. Use photographs of male participants as part of brochures or advertisements.
6. Use the workplace as an environment for contacting fathers.
7. Recruit fathers through childbirth classes. This may be a successful strategy because fathers attending such classes are already demonstrating interest and involvement in one aspect of their role. Providing a structure (and an invitation in a supportive environment) for them to continue participation would be expected to yield good expectations.

Diversity of Formats

The traditional approach of a parent discussion group does not appear to appeal to fathers. Our experience suggests that fathers are less likely to make a commitment to this type of group and may not feel as comfortable discussing parent issues and problems. Fathers may not feel that they are important to the functioning of a parent discussion group. It is important to appeal to a variety of fathers. Some ways to reach out to more fathers are:

1. Create a special page in a newsletter that is specifically directed towards fathers, or, devote a separate newsletter to fathers and men's issues.
2. Plan occasional one time lectures on a topic that fathers may

find interesting. Monitoring fathers' comments and questions for thematic interests during regular meetings can give clear indications of shared interests.

3. Provide an activity group for fathers so that they will spend time doing specific activities with their children. Fathers feel more comfortable involved in specific activities and value spending time with their children.

4. Start a support group specifically for fathers. There are some fathers who want support and positive role models provided by other men.

5. Occasionally break into fathers and mothers discussion groups as part of a regular parent education class. This should be done in a manner which addresses special needs and interests without emphasizing differences between maternal and paternal roles.

6. Plan special field trip activities for fathers and children such as camping.

7. Create special parent support groups or recruit fathers from existing structures/groups (e.g., some churches have different types of support groups in place. Starting a father's or parent support group within the church would have the advantage of the preexisting relationships/groups to draw on. Another example would be a computer user's group).

Experimental studies have demonstrated that fathers are more involved with their children as a function of having been given experience or training in childcare. As such, it appears to be fruitful to expand fathers' experience with infant care, competence and comfort (Kotelchuck, 1976; McHale & Huston, 1984; Palkovitz, 1980; Parke et al., 1980). It has also been argued that parental expectations and perceptions may be more important than the actual course of the events of parenting themselves (Palkovitz, 1985). As such, one important avenue for designing parent support groups is to provide information concerning the normal course and range of child development and parent-child interaction. Preparing parents to experience a range of events is preferable to having them formulate tightly bound expectations for specific interactions and events. Childbirth preparation classes represent a viable context for the implementation of these ideas. Alternatively, Belsky (1985), based on his series of family research projects, has concluded that the most effective means of influencing parent-infant relations is to focus more attention on the marital relationship.

Recruiting Male Staff Members

To our knowledge, accurate statistics on proportions of men in early childhood education and parent education are not readily available. In a study of DAC programs in Minnesota that worked with young handicapped children (Palm, 1985b) only 2% of the staff that worked directly with the children were males. Similarly, the Men in Child Care Project estimates that only 1-2% of the teachers working with young children are males. These numbers are discouraging, but male early childhood teachers are only one source of potential parent educators. There are male social workers, psychologists and educators who may be willing to organize or at least facilitate parent groups for fathers. Finally, experienced fathers with strong interpersonal and organizational skills represent an underutilized source of support providers.

Focus on Male Strengths

A final way of appealing to fathers is to identify some of the traditional male strengths that may be related to parenting. This is difficult because there is a tendency to think of parent characteristics such as sensitivity, communication, and nurturance as areas where men have deficits (Betterman, 1984). It is important to begin to identify some strengths that have been attributed to males such as playfulness, leadership, adventure, and independence. These strengths, coupled with male interests, can be used to design attractive parent programs for fathers. For example, the parent-child activity groups for fathers which are most popular are wood projects and gym activities. These activities involve "male" interests and areas where men may feel they have some skills to share with their children. A focus on "male" strengths provides a familiar and comfortable starting place.

CONCLUSION

Fathers are in the midst of a transition to a broader range of parental roles. During this transition men have a right to parenting education classes and support services that recognize their unique needs, affirm their "natural strengths," and provide them with skills that are related to their perceptions of the fathering role. Parent educators have the responsibility to recruit fathers in an active manner, to assist fathers in determining their goals and needs, and to provide support and affirmation.

Parent support and education providers must be aware of their own biases, values and styles. While they may be excellent parents themselves, there are numerous ethical issues for consideration. Educators should have as a goal, exposing others to a range of parental role possibilities, communication skills and styles. Our goal should *not* be to make each parent an androgynous co-parent. Rather, we must devise creative ways to help others chose from a range of family support patterns optimally matching their own unique blend of skills, strengths, desires and lifestyles. Supporting both mothers and fathers in flexible cooperation should maximize personal, interpersonal and family strengths, to the benefit of all.

REFERENCES

Belsky, J., Gilstrap, B., and Rovine, M. (1984). The Pennsylvania infant and family development project, I: Stability and change in mother-infant and father-infant interaction in a family setting at one, three and nine months. *Child Development, 55,* 692-705.

Betterman, G. (1984). *Fathering.* White Bear Lake, MN: Minnesota Curriculum Services Center.

Brooks, J. B. (1981). *The process of parenting.* Palo Alto, CA: Mayfield Press.

Eggebeen, D. and Whlenberg, P. (1985). Changes in the Organization of Men's Lives: 1960-1980. *Family Relations, 34,* 211-220.

Feldman, S. S. and Aschenbrenner, B. (1983). Impact of parenthood on various aspects of masculinity and femininity: A short-term longitudinal study. *Developmental Psychology, 19,* 278-289.

Frodi, A., Lamb, M. E., Hwang, C. P., and Frodi, M. (1982). Father-mother-infant interaction in traditional and non-interactional Swedish families: A longitudinal study. *Alternative Lifestyles, 4,* 6-13.

Grossman, F. K. (in press). Fathers and children: Predicting the quality and quantity of fathering. *Developmental Psychology.*

Hanson, S. and Bozett, F. H. (1985). *Dimensions of Fatherhood*. Beverly Hills, CA: Sage.

Kliman, D. G. and Kohl, R. (1984). *Fatherhood USA*. New York: Garland Press.

Kotelchuck, M. (1975). Father Caretaking Characteristics and Their Influences on Infant Father Interaction. Paper presented to the American Psychological Association, Chicago.

Lamb, M. E. (1981). The development of father-infant relationships. In M. E. Lamb (Ed.), *The Role of the Father in Child Development*, pp. 459-488. New York: Wiley.

Lamb, M. E. (1978). Influence of the child on marital quality and family interaction during the prenatal, perinatal, and infancy periods. In R. M. Lerner and G. B. Spanier (Eds.), *Child influences on marital and family interaction: A lifespan perspective*. New York: Academic Press.

Lewis, R. A. (1986). Men's changing roles in marriage and the family. *Marriage and Family Review, 9*, 1-10.

McHale, S. M., and Huston, T. L. (1984). Men and women as parents: Sex role orientations, employment, and parental roles with infants. *Child Development, 55*, 1349-1361.

Palkovitz, R. (1987a). Consistency and stability in the family microsystem environment. In D. L. Peters and S. Kontos (Eds.), *Annual advances in applied developmental psychology, Volume II*, pp. 40-67. New York: Ablex Publishing Company.

Palkovitz, R. (1987b). Enrollment data for child development, parenting and infancy classes. Unpublished course registration data, University of Delaware.

Palkovitz, R. (1980). Determinants of involvement in first time fathers. *Dissertation Abstracts International, 40*, 3603b-3604b. (University Microfilms no. 8105035).

Palkovitz, R. (1984). Parental attitudes and father's interactions with their five-month-old infants. *Developmental Psychology, 20*, 1054-1060.

Palkovitz, R. (1985). Fathers' attendance, early contact, and extended care with their newborns: A critical review. *Child Development, 56*, 392-406.

Palkovitz, R. (1986). Projected and actual discussion of child-care tasks by first-time parents. The second annual international parenting symposium: The challenge of parenting in the 80's. Philadelphia, 3/86.

Palm, G. (1985a). Quality Time: The Search for Intimacy. Paper presented to the First Symposium on Parenting, The International Society for Parenting Research, Chicago.

Palm, G. (1985b). Creating opportunities for father involvement. *Nurturing News, VII*, 4, 12-13.

Palm, G. (1986). *The Challenge of Educating Fathers*. Paper presented to the Second Symposium on Parenting, The International Society for Parenting Research, Philadelphia.

Parke, R. D. and O'Leary, S. (1976). Father-mother-infant interaction in the newborn period: Some findings, some observations, and some unresolved issues. In M. K. Riegel and J. Meacham (Eds.) *The developing individual in a changing world: Vol. II. Social and environmental issues*. The Hague: Mouton.

Parke, R. D. and Sawin, D. B. (1975). *Infant characteristics and behavior as elicitors of maternal and paternal responsibility*. Paper presented at the biennial meeting of the Society for Research in Child Development, Denver.

Pedersen, F. A. and Robson, K. S. (1969). Father participation in infancy. *American Journal of Ortho Psychiatry, 39*, 466-472.

Pleck, J. H., Lamb, M. E., and Levine, J. A. (1986). Epilog: Facilitating future changes in men's family roles. *Marriage and Family Review, 9*, 11-16.

Power, T. G. (1985). Mother and father infant play: A developmental analysis. *Child Development, 56*, 1514-1524.

Radin, N. (1982). Primary caregiving and role-sharing fathers. In M. E. Lamb (Ed.), *Non-traditional Families: Parenting and Child Development*. Hillsdale, NJ: Lawrence Erlbaum Associates.

Rebelsky, F. and Hanks, C. (1971). Father's verbal interaction with infants in the first three months of life. *Child Development, 43*, 63-68.

Riley, D. and Cochran, M. (1985). Naturally occurring childrearing advice for fathers: utilization of the personal social network. *Journal of Marriage and the Family, 47*, 275-286.

Robinson, B. E. (1986). Men caring for the young: a profile. *Marriage and Family Review, 9*, 151-162.

Rossi, A. S. (1984). Gender and parenthood. *American Sociological Review, 49*, 1-19.

Rotundo, A. E. (1985). American fatherhood. *American Behavioral Scientist, 19*, 7-21.

Russell, G. (1978). The father role and its relation to masculinity, femininity, and androgyny. *Child Development, 49*, 1174-1181.

Russell, G. (1983). *The changing role of fathers?* St. Lucia, Australia: University of Queensland Press.

Sayers, R. (1983). Male-parenting: Beyond the female agreement. In Robert Sayers (ed.), *Fathering: It's Not the Same*.

Steinberg, D. (1977). *Fatherjournal: Five years of awakening to fatherhood*. Albion, CA: Times Change Press.

"And Baby Makes Three": An Examination and Application of Georg Simmel's "Socialization of the Spirit" Theory

Kris Jeter

Molly and me and baby makes three.
We are happy to be in my blue heaven.

— George Whiting
My Blue Heaven

The 1927 song "My Blue Heaven," popularized by Gene Austin, presents an idyllic, romantic view of life when a couple — by plan or by chance — expands its family to include a baby. In actuality, the balance of family life is skewed and life is never the same again. In this analytic essay, I will:

1. write a brief biography of philosopher, sociologist George Simmel and describe his theory of the "Socialization of the Spirit";
2. differentiate the dynamics of dyadic and triadic family forms utilizing the work of Georg Simmel;
3. hypothesize the utilization of larger group support — actual kin and archetypal deity — by a couple in transition;
4. present one anthropological story of the birth of a first child supported by actual kin; and
5. present two mythological heritages of archetypal deities who support a couple with child.

The presence of the third person provokes change, differentiation, and movement. Larger group support of actual kin and archetypal deities can assist the dyad to retain its balance as it welcomes a baby and enlarges into a triad.

GEORG SIMMEL
AND THE
"SOCIALIZATION OF THE SPIRIT"

one has the feeling that Simmel . . . insistently prefers Cinderellas among experiences (so to speak), either to reveal, precisely in them, his virtuosity of philosophizing . . . or to show how, even from them, paths lead into ultimate depths.

—Emil Utiz
Simmel und die Philosophie der Kunst

Georg Simmel was born in Berlin on 1 March 1858, the youngest of seven children. His father, a manufacturer of chocolate, died when Simmel was young. He then came under the care of a guardian, a family friend who had founded and administered an international publishing house for music. Simmel inherited from his guardian sufficient monies to live as a scholar.

Simmel spent his adult life at The University of Berlin. First, he studied history. He then changed his major to philosophy with a minor in medieval Italian and emphasis on Petrarch. In 1881, Simmel was awarded a doctorate; his dissertation was entitled, "The Nature of Matter according to Kant's Physical Monadology." He was an honorary professor of philosophy without faculty status and paid fees directly by his "hearers" (students) rather than receiving a salary from the University. Although Simmel was respected by his professional colleagues and students, he did not fit the mold of nineteenth century German academia. His interests were too broad, his classes too popular, and his style too jocular.

Simmel taught classes on art, Darwin, ethics, history of philosophy, Kant, logic, Lotze, modern philosophy, pessimism, philosophy of art, philosophy of religion, political psychology, psychology, Schopenhauer, social psychology, and sociology. He guided his learners "down an oblique pit into the mine" (page xvii). He did not simply lecture: he excited, incited, and ignited his students. One hearer wrote, "'Just about the time when . . . one felt he had reached a conclusion, he had a way of raising his right arm and, with three fingers of his hand, turning the imaginary object so as to exhibit still another facet'''' (page xvii).

Simmel's publications were extensive and addressed aesthetics, epistemology, ethics, metaphysics, and the philosophy of art, contemporary civilization, history, and sociology. In particular, some of his subjects were Michelangelo, Rembrandt, and Rodin; the Alps, Florence, and Venice; adventure, love, and shame; and landscapes, money, and ruins. His style of writing was to note a multitude of ideas and thoughts, and then later to develop and perhaps connect them through digression into an essay. A few of Simmel's unique concepts which lie concealed in his texts are presented below:

> Objectivity toward people often hides the most boundless solipsism.

> In comedy, a highly individual fate is fulfilled by typical characters; in tragedy, a general human fate by individual characters.

> All that can be proved can also be disputed; only the unprovable is indisputable. (page xx)

> We think we actually understand things only when we have traced them back to what we do not understand and cannot understand — to causality, to axioms, to God, to character. (page xxi)

Simmel did not write an autobiography and there is little existing correspondence, only professional writings. It is curious that an academic whose life was spent only in the ivory tower had empathy for the human condition and could articulate his compassion in luminous lecture and essay. It is assumed that his rich inner life, passionate yearning, quick intellect, unbridled imagination, and wide reading married within and blossomed forth.

Simmel believed that the discipline of sociology should promote the "socialization of the spirit." The spirit is to be taught to be autonomous, independent, self-contained, and self-governing. With such education and support, the spirit can truly be the animating force and vital principle within each living being. Simmel synthesized his philosophy on life in social systems of any size into one sentence. "To treat not only every person, but every thing as if it were its own end: this would be a cosmic ethics" (page xx). As a Kantian scholar, Simmel expanded upon the Kantian imperative, to act that one's behavior might be practiced by every other person with no deleterious affect to the common good. The individual must experience the multiple forms of culture which ultimately may or may not have anything to do with personal interests. The paradox is that a person achieving personal selfhood must be exposed to the collective culture. The harmonization of an individual with culture is a struggle of the self.

Simmel extended Kant's philosophical principles; both reconciled emerging scientific discoveries with the nature of human knowledge. Simmel viewed "form" as a stable element among the variable of content. Life is a process by which individuals become. Simmel, as a philosopher of sociology, applied the concept of "form" to his work on processes, social process, social relations, social structure, social system, and types of interaction. As an historian, he provided examples from the chronicles of time to support his theory on social forms. Simmel was especially fascinated by the effects of varied numbers of individuals on social structures. His theory of dyadic and triadic family forms is presented in this analytic essay.

When Simmel learned that he had cancer of the liver, he moved to the Black Forest to complete a book on metaphysics, *Lebensanschauung (View of Life)*, and to die. Friends and family indicated that he attained perfection in this time and "what he once said of a beloved person, applied to him: he was 'a flower on the tree of [hu]mankind'" (page xxiii). Georg Simmel died 26 September 1918.

DYADIC AND TRIADIC FAMILY FORMS

Once upon a time, there was a man with two wives. One wife named Hannah was old and one wife named Bannah was young. Each wife loved her husband very much. The husband would rest his head upon the elder's lap for sweet sleep; Hannah would carefully pick the black hairs from his head so he should appear wise as she. And, the husband would rest his head upon the younger's lap for sweet sleep; Bannah would carefully pick the white hairs from his head so he should appear vernal as she. In short time, the man's head was completely bald. The moral of the story is, "Between Hannah and Bannah, vanished are our beards."

— Syrian folk tale
When One Man has Two Wives

(S)he who has one child is a slave:
(S)he who has more is their master.
— Proverb

The Syrian folk tale and the proverb tell of the ancient's knowledge of triadic families. Whether a triad was composed of one husband and two wives or one couple and one child, it was considered unbalanced. Below is a discussion of Georg Simmel's theory of social structures of one, two, three, and more individuals and the process inherent to each body. This theory is then applied to the marital dyad, the family in transition, and the extended family.

The Isolated Individual

"The isolated individual" infers that there is a society who can influence and pressure a person to be apart, physically and emotionally. "The feeling of isolation is rarely as decisive and intense when one actually finds oneself physically alone, as when one is a stranger without relations" (page 119).

The Dyad

The dyad is a pair of two associated persons. The dyad as the basic social group "contains the scheme, germ, and material of innumerable more complex forms" (page 122). The two members of a dyad choose a common goal and conceal details of this goal from the public. A dyad regularly engages in "triviality" (page 125), activities unique to them. It also shares "intimacy" (page 127), the positives and negatives of daily life, often to the detriment of cognitive, rational information. Members of a dyad fee free to express personal values. Individuality of the two members is honored and celebrated.

A dyad, more than any other group, is cognizant of the effect of death on its viability. "It makes the dyad into a group that feels itself both endangered and irreplaceable, and thus into the real locus not only of authentic sociological tragedy, but also of sentimentalism and elegiac problems" (page 124). "The dyad represents both the first social synthesis and unification, and the first separation and antithesis" (page 145).

The Triad

The triad is a group of three associated persons. The triad changes internally according to issues. Within a triad, a member may be within a dyad or be the isolated individual. Expectations of behavior are modified in consideration to the new member. Adaptive behaviors occur in view of these new expectations. One person in a triad may act as a mediator and the triad assumes a state of tranquility and becomes a group; or there are the possibilities of the majority ruling the minority, or one person rule.

The Larger Group

A larger group is a group of four or more associated persons. The dynamics of this group are similar to the dynamics of a triad except there are more possible interactions and increased number of expectations of appropriate behaviors. A larger group requires individuals to conduct work and to provide leadership. Members assume a hierarchical order of status and roles which may be prescribed by social custom and cultural values or occur from interaction. Where prescription is the process, hierarchy occurs when individuals who best meet group needs are elected to higher group status.

Marriage

Marriage is a process to create a unique dyad. First, it is a formal institution. During courtship, parents, guardians, matchmakers, spiritual advisors, relatives and other members of the community note, support, or reject its formation. The dyad is transformed in marriage from a simple social unit into a "super-personal, histori-cal-social" (page 130) entity. Consummation of the marriage is given the communal blessing with expected procreation and subse-quent nurturing and parenting of the newborn — all within the pro-tection of the marriage covenant.

Second, marriage is a merging of the opposites. Feminine and masculine represent two dualities; it is precisely because of their contrasts that they can strive toward union. Two people elect to hold their egos in abeyance to uphold the honor of their family unit. This results in a social group, unsurpassed in its expression of per-sonal familiarity.

Birth of the First Child

The birth of the first child transforms the dyad into a family. The yearning for union becomes a rationale for life itself and individual egos merge and fuse with each other in procreation. The dyad opens up to accept an absolutely dependent baby into its group.

The child is a secondary link between the parents. The child en-hances the dyad. In some cultures, the husband respects his wife for the first time in their marriage with the appearance of the earliest child, especially a son. Destiny is being fulfilled and generational continuity of family name and tradition is enhanced. Also, the child, as a product of a dyad, may detract from the couple's inti-macy, separating the generators of her or his life.

The manner in which the first child is accepted into the family tends to be repeated as each new child is born. Furthermore, the management style utilized with the birth of the first child indicates ways the family handles new challenges.

Extended Family

Georg Simmel described the extended family as a group number-ing 20 to 30 individuals. In the *pater familias*, the father presides over the lives of each member to promote the good of the family as well as himself. The exertion of power and control is feasible with a group under 30 in number. The kin network can be self-maintaining if members are confident in each other, live a spiritual life, and engage in rituals.

PARTICIPATION MYSTIQUE

In 1926, Lucien Levy-Bruhl studied the thought processes of aboriginal societies. He believed that during Paleolithic and Neolithic times, 400,000 to 10,000 B.C.E., the food-gatherer, and primitive hunter and agricultural peoples were members of a corporate body. Life was lived in "participation mystique"; the kin network acted as one person, one communal and collective entity, which spanned the historic continuum of the larger group, respecting and replicating its centuries-earned knowledge of life on earth within the boundaries of nature, geography, and weather.

Mircea Eliade also examined archaic groups of people. Each action — food gathering and preparation, washing, play, sexuality — was regarded as a sacred activity.

Food acquisition was the primary activity. With spring, vegetation grew, humans thrived. Food was the nexus between life and death, the elixir of rejuvenation, the fountain of pulse and impulse. Eating was communion.

Likewise, water quenched the dry earth, animals, and humans. As a drink and a douche, this soma cleaned, cooled, healed, and soothed. Water rising up through the earth from unseen springs carried the mystery of the unknown, the unseen.

Sexual and athletic play were pleasurable, invigorating, and sedating to the participants and the earth on which it occurred. The moon, not the penis, impregnated the woman. The moon, a body who waxed and waned each 28 days, was sister to the woman, who bleeds each 28 days. Thus, the woman's blood, in rhythm with the moon, coagulated into a fetus. The moon protected and guarded the woman and her offspring.

The spiritual life and reenactment of rituals connected the kin to original deity, ancestors, each other, and the future. The lives of deities were told in stories and repeated in dance and theatre. Being married and bearing the first child was simply embodying the universal story. Living and archetypal kin folk were called forth to assist individuals through to the next stage of development.

Today, in contemporary Western society, few individuals live in extended patriarchal families. Larger group support may come from family in proximity, friends, support groups, and professionals.

The utilization of a larger group support — actual kin and archetypal deity — by a couple in transition can assist the triad to assume a state of tranquility and become a group. Conscious creation and interaction with a kinship system can be a step toward living once again in "participation mystique." Below are examples of how cross-cultural actual kin and historical archetypal deities have assisted the family in transition.

ACTUAL KIN

The family is a human institution, not found in its totality in any prehuman species. It required language, planning, cooperation, self-control, foresight, and cultural nearing, and probably developed along with these. . . . The family was essential to the dawn of civilization, allowing a vast quantitative leap forward in cooperation, purposive knowledge, love, and creativeness.

—Kathleen Gough
The Origin of the Family

Nobody has ever before asked the nuclear family to live all by itself in a box the way we do. With no relatives, no support, we've put it in an impossible situation.

—Margaret Mead
Pioneer Explorer of Humankind

The aboriginal nuclear family and its kinship system developed rites of passage and taboos about life transitions. The birth of a child in times of plenty could be welcomed as a joyful addition. In times of scarcity, the child was considered a threat to the reduced supply of foodstuffs. Below are definitions of the nuclear family and the kinship system. The aboriginal kinship systems, ritual, taboos, and childbirth taboos are discussed. The Kado custom regarding birthing the first child of the nuclear family is told as one example of how one kinship system even today, as in times past, assists the dyad to expand through the recreation of its ancient custom of welcoming the first child.

The Family and Kinship System

The nuclear family is a marital dyad of other adult kin who together live in a home, share assets and liabilities, and rear children. A kinship system is a social and cultural organization of nuclear families connected by birth and marriage. Each kinship system weaves families together into an exceptional fabric through the telling of its ancestry and fortune and the assigning status and expectations. Implicit to the kinship are norms of behavior regarding division of labor, existence of status regarding property ownership and leadership, recognition of social fatherhood, and taboos on incest.

Aboriginal Kinship Systems

G. P. Murdock has identified and classified 175 hunting and gathering societies surviving today; study of these societies has provided us with information on how our ancestors, the food-gatherer, and primitive hunter and agricultural peoples during Paleolithic and Neolithic times might have lived and living examples of the "participation mystique." The hunters live in kin groups of 50 people or less, although the group may number from 20 to 200. The kin group contains families. Each person works and division of labor is according to age and sex. Leadership roles are accorded to the wise ones. The Shaman provides spiritual guidance. The Story Teller hears and tells the customs, genealogies, history, laws, and news. The hunters reside in temporary dwellings and may move within a large territory according to the season. The community owns resources and these and personal belongings are shared. Moreover, the community, as a collectivity of individuals, is an aggregate of knowledge and skills. As members of the kin group face new stages of growth and development, they call upon their family as well as their kin group for support. The birth of the first child to a dyad is one occasion for requesting and receiving advice, counsel, and assistance from the community.

Ritual

French Sociologist Emile Durkheim studied South Sea island natives to discover the original purpose of religion before it was bureaucratized, formalized, and professionalized. He found that aboriginal beliefs and rituals foster relationships between people themselves. Through religion, people can share joyous moments of birth, harvesting, marriage, planting, winter solstice, and the vernal equinox. Frightening periods of time, such as bereavement, and not faced alone. Myths on the lives of deities inspire people to assist other people. Reenactment of rituals lets people know that they are not alone and that they have courage, hope, patience, purpose, and strength to renew themselves and live. The rites remind individuals that they have kin and friends to lessen burdens, to fill voids, to respond through active presence, compassion, empathy, listening, love and physical comforting.

Taboo

Taboo isolates and names a behavior, location, name, person, or thing as undoable, unspeakable, and untouchable. The rationale for the taboo may be due to perceived enigmatic energy, impurity, or sacred quality. A taboo may promote predictable outcomes. The breaking of a taboo leads to a taboo vindicating itself and the violator suffering injury and death. Myths tell of deities' and ancestors' lives made fortunate and prosperous or failing and painful due to the attending to or breaking of a taboo.

Childbirth Taboos

The birth of a child is associated with three separate and interrelated taboos. The source of the taboos is the fear of the unknown — the cessation of menstrual blood; the appearance of a baby with its bloodied umbilical cord who emerges from incomprehensible spirits in an uncharted universe; and the immediate and prospective life for the newborn.

Because the baby comes forth from the womb of the women, taboos are gender-related. Generally, women separate themselves from men for birthing and seek community with kin women. This custom, thought to be an inheritance of the matrilineal era, provides privacy for the mother and protects men from the unknown blood and life force peculiar to childbirth. In Africa and India, women retreat to their mother's home for the birth of their first child. Often, this child is assumed to be a member of the maternal grandparent's family.

Some cultures require the woman to give birth alone. According to kinship group norms and territory, this may be in a British Columbia forest, Japanese wooden shelter, La Plata river bank, Indian house, Russian Smolensk barn, or the South African grandmother's home. During inclement weather conditions, the seclusion may be provided in the home with only a curtain or screen.

The man may enact the *couvade*, be apart from the women and behave as if he himself is birthing the child. This custom is common in Albania, Africa, China, Corsica, India, and South America. The couvade may be an outgrowth of the change of a society from matrilineal to patrilineal; the father expresses his just claim to the child. Also, the father, separated from his child, may feel ill and need attention.

Contrary to this practice is the rarer custom of men attending and perhaps assisting the birth. For instance, the husband of the Marquesas Island even joins his wife in the after-birth bath, to be close to her and their child's blood.

The fears of the unknown tends to disappear after appropriate rituals. These rites of passage may be ceremonial cleansing or naming.

The Kado

Baba of Karo has described the significance of the birth of the first-born of the Kado, originally of Borneo, and now of Nigeria. Upon learning of the impending pregnancy, the couple moves from the wife's parent's compound to the husband's parent's compound. The wife sleeps apart from her husband. Each morning, the mother-in-law checks in on the mother-to-be. When the young wife starts to have contractions, the mother-in-law contacts her daughter-in-law's female relatives.

The new mother feels embarrassed to have borne a child and rejects the newborn. Her mother, father's sisters, and midwife nurture the baby and urge the new mother to assume her rightful role. The young mother dismisses her role and conceals her face in her hands, not looking upon or touching the child. Likewise, the new father avoids his new role and hides in the compound of a man friend. It is not until after the naming day that the relatives take the new family to the compound of the mother's father and to her mother's hut. This will be the first time that the parents will feel more at ease about the expansion of their family and hold their child.

ARCHETYPAL DEITIES

They walked with Truth (Apollo) and Beauty (Aphrodite) at their sides. They raced with daemons of excellence, the spirits of past athletes running beside them, urging them on. They traveled with Hermes, danced and ran with Dionysius, and sailed the seas under the guardianship of Poseidon. They fought for the rights of married women, children and the home with the tenacity of Hera and harvested the crops with Demeter beside them . . . the concept of Psyche gave the Greeks their infinite love and delight in nature and an extraordinary courage in exploring it. Into every nook and cranny of the world the spirits of gods and heroes had already ventures . . . [They] crossed the seas in the path of Odysseus, entered labyrinths of mind or nature wherein Theseus had already slain the minotaur.

— Charles Hampden-Turner
Maps of the Mind

Charles Hampden-Turner eloquently related the life-style of ancients. Both divine and human relationships were valid and vital. Individuals had ever-living deities as ancestors, and also lived in actual kinship networks. Throughout the centuries, the deities have survived and resurfaced as archetypes to assist family members through their developmental stages. The concept of archetype is defined below. The archetypes of the family triad — father, mother, and child — are discussed. Examples of Chinese and Roman deities integral to the childbirth and rearing aspects of family life are presented. Contemporary individuals, as did their ancestors, may find that they themselves are living out archetypal stories, and may feel secure that they are not alone in their life experiences.

Definition of the Archetype

The folklore and mythology expressed in various art forms about childbirth are rich, providing us with varied friendly deities, role-models, and prototypical options for child care and protection. Immersed in the depths of the human psyche is the universal, primordial, collective unconscious inhabited by archetypes, internal forces of energy which seek to organize the psyche's varied interactions and sustain the endurance of the ego consciousness. These archetypes are spontaneously expressed cross-culturally as vital life forces and image in art, fantasies, dreams, fairy tales, and myths. It is through the archetypal images that the human being reveals profound unconscious longings and yearnings (Jung).

Thus it is in the ancient stories, "the depersonalized dream," that we search for the goddesses and gods of childbirth, nurturance, and protection, "the personalized myth" (Campbell). Tradition links one individual to another. The dyad, in process of becoming a triad through the incorporation of a child, can maintain balance and harmony through the acknowledgement of a larger group of traditional archetypes.

Archetypes of the Family Triad

Biologist Adolf Portmann compared the developmental stages at which varied mammals emerge from their mothers. Of all mammals, human infants are born with the fewest skills and most dependency needs. While other mammals mature as a fetus within their mother to move and communicate upon birth, the human's first year of life outside of the womb is spent preparing to walk and talk. Mario A. Jacoby contends that life in the womb is remembered by many as paradise — warm, secure, content; all needs are satisfied. Upon being thrust into the world, life is a struggle and each need is met or not met by female and male parents and guardians. Paradise is lost and the balance of life is spent remembering and yearning for its splendor.

Jungians believe that each person has within a feminine *anima* and a masculine *animus* core grouping of archetypes. Both the anima and the animus present themselves as an artichoke to be peeled. As an individual peels the anima, the birth mother and other women of the lifetime are met. Likewise, as an individual peels the animus, the birth or social father and other men of the lifetime are met. Underneath the feminine and masculine life experiences are layers of archetypal images which speak at the appropriate time as a guide to the life mission. The center of each core grouping, as the artichoke, is the heart, the universal symbol of the connection between all life.

The Father Archetype

The Latin word, *animus*, and the Greek word, *anemos*, mean breath, wind, spirit. It is difficult to see the wind itself, only the effects of its action. The father archetype may be positive, as the *Logos spermatikos*, seed-bearing spirit, presenting the world with options and demanding consciousness. Or, the father archetype may be negative, as Uranos, who submerges his children within the bowels of Mother Earth.

The Mother Archetype

The anima is the soul, the immaterial essence, animating principle, actuating cause of life. The Eros of the anima relates us to our inner selves, each other, and the world. The Latin word, *mater*, is the word from which the English words, mother and matter, are derived. The mother archetype may be positive, creative and protective, such as Madonna presenting the human milk of nurturance and kindness required to sustain life; or negative, destructive and cruel, such as the goddess Kali of India who eats children.

The Child Archetype

The child archetype represents remembrance of, yearning for, and movement toward paradise lost. The child tumbles helpless from Mother Nature into a world of strife and unfathomable enemies. Yet, she or he is armed with unimaginable, all-encompassing energies with which to conquer the unknown future and realize the true self.

Chinese Deity

In 1940, Clarence B. Day wrote "Childbirth Lore Among the Chinese." Children, especially male, are considered the special gift of the deity to families. Children are the source of great happiness. Couples appeal to Sung Tzu Niang Niang, a form of Kuan-yin, the Goddess of Mercy. When couples have experienced a long time without child, or experienced stillbirth, they pray to Kuan-yin herself and T'ien Hou. If a couple suspects danger, they contact T'ai Chun Hsien Niang or Yang T'ai Chun, a goddess of easy childbirths; or Hsieh Jen Hsing Chun, a star-goddess of Childbirth; or Hsieh Kuang Hsing Chun; or Ti'en Sheng or Ts'ui Sheng.

Three to seven days after the child is born, sweet confectioneries, rice, and wine are presented to the god and goddess of the bed, Ch'uang Kung and Ch'uang P'o. The child is then bathed, dressed, and presented to deity of the home and especially the bed. Pictures of Ch'uang Kung and Ch'uang P'o are placed on the wedding bed and other beds to insure pleasant sleep and dreams, vigorous health and vitality, harmonious temperament of newborns and children.

Pao Tung Chiang Chun, the warrior general, welcomes all children to life. The guardian of children is Chang Hsien the Immortal. He projects his peachwood arrow at the canine in the sky which defiles and eats children. A manifestation of Chang Hsien is Chang-Hsien Sung Tzu who specializes in protecting male children. Wang Mu protects female children. She is the most powerful in the use of magic of the Pa Hsien, the Eight Immortals.

In North China, there are the nine Niang-Niang: T'ien Hsien—Heavenly Goddess; Sung Tzu—goddess of child's grace and blessings; Tse-Sun—goddess of prosperity; Ts'ui Sheng—goddess of easy childbirth; Nai Mu—goddess of wet nurses; P'ei Yang—goddess of nourishment; Yen-Kuang—goddess of babies' eyesight; Tou-Chen—goddess of smallpox; and Pan-Chen—goddess of scarlet fever.

K'ai Kuan Hsing, the "Open-Shut Star," is witness to the difficult stages of a child's growth and development, such as infancy and adolescence. This deity is acknowledged one hundred days after the child's birth, and on the third, sixth, and ninth birthdays.

Tzu I is the deity of the child's first schooling. Wang Mu and Pen Ming receive praise on the sixteenth birthday.

On each birthday, the family acknowledges Pen Ming Hsin Chun, the Individual Fate Star. Pen Ming Hsin Chun, in some areas, is the patron star for males, and Hsi Ch'ih Wang Mu, Royal Mother of the Western Pool, is the patron goddess for females. Hsi Ch'ih Wang Mu is the ancient manifestation of the ultimate Yin, the Earth, and lives in the K'un-lun Mountains of West China. She is portrayed holding the peach, symbol of long life, and protects the woman over her life course.

Roman Deity

In 1896, Alexander Francis Chamberlin wrote *The Child and Childhood in Folk-Thought*. Each culture has deity to protect the young and insure the continuation of the tribe. In ancient Rome, numerous deities were praised.

Opis retrieves and extracts the baby from mother earth's breast. Diespiter introduces the newborn to daylight. Parca or Partula preside over the childbirth.

Cunina guards the still and rocking cradle. When the baby cries, Vaticanus opens the mouth so all hear. Rumina insures that breast is full and giving. Diva Potina provides proper liquid, and Diva Edusa, nutritious food for the child. Cuba presides over the sleeping child. Ossipaga creates hearty bones and Carna puts healthy flesh on the bones.

When the toddler falls, Levana picks the child up. Statinus and Dea Statina witness the child's standing position and Peragenor or Agenona, the child's activities. Abeona and Adiona watch over journeys.

Deus Catus Pater teaches keen insight; Dea Mens, cognitive skill; and Numeria, arithmetic. Minerva provides the child with a memory. Fabulinus instructs the child in speech and Camoena in song.

Deus Onus gives advice and counsel. Voleta and Volumnus presides over right intention. Venilia provides hope for the future.

CONCLUSION

Sweet bird of promise, fresh and fair,
Just moving in the morning air.
The morn of life but just begun,
The sands of time just set to run!

Ah, baby! little dost thou know
How many yearning bosoms glow,
How many lips in blessing move,
How many eyes beam looks of love
At sight of thee!

—Joanna Baillie
To Sophia J. Baillie, An Infant

Parenthood is a transition with potential multiple stresses as a consequence of disruption of routines and rituals in place and already working for the dyadic pair. With the absence of the transactional matriarchal and patriarchal family forms in modern complex societies, there are few support groups to assist new parents in effecting a transition to parenthood. Learning the parenting role and making adjustments to maintain the marital relationship is done largely by self instruction. Experience is the prime teacher with limited anticipatory socialization to these important new roles as parents and to changes in the marital relationship. Yet there is a lengthy history of support derived from actual kin and archetypal deities exemplified in tribal societies and Greek, Roman, and Chinese legends. The task for the modern couple experiencing the transition is to examine this history of the ancient and tribal societies, cultures of the "participation mystique," to obtain knowledge, social and emotional support for the consequences of childbearing and nurturing. Another step is to learn from this history that one needs a support group to maintain a triad and larger family units. If such an extended family network is unavailable because of geographical dispersion, then the task is to create one; an everyday family unrelated by blood or marriage, but one based on intimacy, caring, and affection, able to create family rituals and behaviors conducive to a nurturing environment for the newborn and their parents.

REFERENCES

Baba of Karo. "The Ritual of Childbirth." *Birth: An Anthology of Ancient Texts, Songs, Prayers, and Stories*. Editor, David Meltzer. San Francisco, CA: North Point Press, 1981.

Bachofen, J. J. *Myth, Religion, and Mother Right*. Ralph Manheim, Translator. Princeton, NJ: Princeton University Press, 1967.

Briffault, R. *The Mothers*. Three Volumes. New York, NY: Macmillan, 1927.

Campbell, J. *The Hero with a Thousand Faces*. Second Edition. Princeton, NJ: Princeton University Press, 1968.

Chamberlin, A. F. *The Child and Childhood in Folk-Thought*. New York, NY: Macmillan, 1986.

Chamberlin, A. F. "Gods and Goddesses of Motherhood." *Birth: An Anthology of Ancient Texts, Songs, Prayers, and Stories*. Editor, David Meltzer. San Francisco, CA: North Point Press, 1981.

Day, C. B. "Childbirth Lore Among the Chinese." *Birth: An Anthology of Ancient Texts, Songs, Prayers, and Stories*. Editor, David Meltzer, San Francisco, CA: North Point Press, 1981.

Day, C. B. *Chinese Peasant Cults: Being a Study of Chinese Paper Gods*. Shanghai, China: Kelly and Walsh, Ltd., 1940.

Downing, C. *The Goddess: Mythological Images of the Feminine*. New York, NY: Crossroad, 1984.

Durkheim, E. *Les Formes elementaires de la vie religieuse*. Paris, France: F. Alcan, 1912.

Eliade, M. *The Myth of the Eternal Return or Cosmos and History*. Translator, Willard R. Trask, Princeton, NJ: Princeton University Press, 1965.

Entwisle, D. R. and S. G. Doering. *The First Birth: A Family Turning Point*. Baltimore, MD: The Johns Hopkins University Press, 1981.

Farber, B. *Kinship and Class: A Midwestern Study*. New York, NY: Basic Books, 1971.

Gough, K. "The Origin of the Family." *Marriage and the Family: A Critical Analysis and Proposals for Change*. Carolyn C. Perrucci and Dena B. Targ, Editors. New York, NY: David McKay, 1974.

Grahn, J. *Another Mother Tongue*. Boston, MA: Beacon Press, 1984.

Hallman, R. J. *Psychology of Literature: A Study of Alienation and Tragedy*. New York, NY: Philosophical Library, 1961.

Hampden-Turner, C. *Maps of the Mind*. New York, NY: Macmillan, 1981.

Harding, M. E. *Woman's Mysteries: Ancient and Modern: A Psychological Interpretation of the Feminine Principle as Portrayed in Myth, Story and Dreams*. New York, NY: Harper Colophon Books, 1976.

Houston, J. *Life Force: The Psycho-Historical Recovery of the Self*. New York, NY: Dell, 1980.

Jacoby, M. A. *Longing for Paradise: Psychological Perspectives on an Archetype*. Myron B. Gubitz, Translator. Boston, MA: Sego Press, 1985.

Jeter, K. "The Role of the Senses and Memory as Agents of Change in Creating The Possible Society: An Analytic Essay with Learning Experiences." *Connections and Continuity*. Kris Jeter, Editor. Newark, DE: The Possible Society, 1985.

Jung, C. G. *The Archetypes and the Collective Unconscious*. R. F. C. Hull, Translator. Second Edition. Princeton, NJ: Princeton University Press, 1968.

Leach, M., Editor. *Funk and Wagnalls Standard Dictionary of Folklore, Mythology, and Legend*. San Francisco, CA: Harper and Row, 1984.

Levi-Bruhl, L. *How Natives Think*. New York, NY: George Allen and Unwin, 1926.

Murdock, G. P. *Ethnographic Atlas*. Pittsburgh: University of Pittsburgh, 1967.

Neubert, R. "Pioneer Explorer of Humankind." *New Realities*, Volume 2: Number 2, June 1978.

Portmann, A. *Zoologie und das neue Bild des Menschen (Zoology and the New Image of Man)*. Hamburg, Germany: Rowohlt, 1958.

Rabuzzi, K. A. *The Sacred and the Feminine: Toward a Theology of Housework*. New York, NY: Seabury Press, 1982.

Simmel, G. *The Sociology of George Simmel*. K. Wolff, Editor. Glencoe, IL: Free Press, 1950.

Smith, M. *Baba of Karo: A Woman of the Moslem Hausa*. New York, NY: Frederick A. Praeger, 1964.

Stevens, A. *Archetypes: A Natural History of the Self*. New York, NY: Quill, 1983.

Utiz, E. "Simmel und die Philosophie der Kunst." *Zeitschrift fur Aesthetik und allgemeine Kunstwissenschaft. XIV:__*, 1920, 1-41 (12, 8).

Wieingartner, R. H. "Georg Simmel." *The Encyclopedia of Philosophy*. Paul Edwards, Editor. Volume Seven. New York, NY: Macmillan, 1967.

Whiting, G., Song Writer. W. Donaldson, Lyric Writer. "My Blue Heaven." 1927.

Yolen, J., Editor. *Favorite Folktales from Around the World*. New York, NY: Pantheon, 1986.